HOW TO SAVE YOUR BUSINE$$ FROM YOURSELF

§

An A to Z Common Sense Guide
To Managing Your Business

Lynn C. Miller

With

Bambi L. Miller

To my Father, Vincent Chandler Miller,

who did not know the meaning of the word, quit.

How To Save Your Business From Yourself

Second Edition

Published by
Lynn Miller Studio, LLC
P.O. Box 505
Green, Ohio 44232

Printed by Create Space4 Independent Publishing

Printed in the United States of America

Distributed by Amazon.com

Cartoon Art by Dennis McCabe Sketch Art, Akron, Ohio
Design Art by HR Designs, Akron, Ohio

ISBN-13: 978-1490448787
ISBN-10: 1490448780

CreateSpace Independent Publishing Platform, North Charleston, SC
Library of Congress Control Number: 2013919914

Doctorbizsaver is a registered trademark of Lynn Miller Studio, LLC

www.doctorbizsaver.com

Acknowledgements

Over the years, I have read, pondered and dissected countless volumes of business lore. But, something was always missing. I was still searching for that special work that is not written from a thirty-thousand foot view and is directed to normal folks who labor in small businesses, day after day. I was in need of a book that tells it like it is. In short, I wanted something that would put the entrepreneur face to face with the reality of starting early, working late, and making something out of nothing.

I am enormously thankful for the generosity and knowledge of friends, both business and personal, who gave me their support and agreed that the small business owner needs a path to follow, a book that can serve as a daily guide to becoming successful in business.

Regis Dauk is a SCORE counselor, and retired VP of Human Resources for MTD Products Inc. Regis provided invaluable assistance with all Human Resources discussions in this book. Human Resources is a difficult and constantly changing area of business. I greatly appreciate his time and contribution.

Randal Longacher, CPA, LUTCF, co-owner of Tuscarawas Tax & Insurance Service is one of those rare CPAs who has a flare for business. As we say in business parlance, *"he gets it."* Randy understands the day-to-day operation of a wide variety of small businesses and is a human encyclopedia of valuable business information. His assistance is priceless.

Heidi Hopkins, co-owner of Corporate Ladder Search Partners is extremely knowledgeable about recruiting, both generally and specifically. She has a business savvy that is tough to match when it comes to finding the right person for the right job. And, thanks to Heidi, I will never again refer to search firms as head hunters.

I would also like to thank the members of SCORE, a national group of tireless men and women in businesses who give of their time, knowledge and guidance to all who ask for help, for no recompense whatsoever. I am proud to be an active member of our local SCORE, Chapter 81 in Akron, Ohio. They are always there to offer their assistance, whenever and wherever necessary.

Chad Archbold, CPA is also a good friend who has been more than willing to fill me in on some of the finer intricacies of finance. Chad is involved in a government setting and occasionally has a slightly different approach to situations involving government business. His help has been invaluable.

I want to thank Jim Smith. I worked for Jim in a branch operation for a national company in the early eighties. When Jim promoted me to Branch Manager, the business was headed in the wrong direction. With Jim's guidance, we became an award winning operation and the number one customer satisfaction branch in the company. But, most of all, Jim proved to me that empowerment of others is the only way to lead. I truly believe that you will never reach your peak of success until you learn to delegate, empower and trust others.

Jack Welch said it best....

"Good business leaders create a vision, articulate the vision, passionately own the vision, and relentlessly drive it to completion." [1]

Table of Contents

Introduction 11

Chapter A 16

   ACCOUNTANTS 16

   ACCOUNTING 17

   ADVERTISING 38

   AGE DISCRIMINATION 41

   AMERICANS WITH DISABILITIES ACT (ADA) 41

   AMORTIZATION 42

   ANGEL INVESTORS 42

   ARBITRATION (See also MEDIATION) 42

   ASSET-BASED LOANS 43

   ATTORNEYS 43

   AT-WILL EMPLOYMENT (See also TERMINATION / FIRING) 43

   AUDITS 44

   AWARDS (See also INCENTIVES) 46

Chapter B 48

   BACKGROUND CHECKS 48

   BANKS 48

   BARCODES/UPC's 49

   BENEFITS 50

   BETTER BUSINESS BUREAU (BBB) 53

   BILLS 53

   BOARD OF DIRECTORS 54

   BONDING 56

   BREAKEVEN POINT 57

   BURNOUT 58

   BUSINESS FORMATIONS / STRUCTURES 59

   BUSINESS PLAN 60

   BUY-SELL AGREEMENT 62

Chapter C 64

   CAPITAL (RAISING MONEY FOR YOUR BUSINESS) 64

   CASH DRAWER/CASH REGISTER 66

   CASH RESERVE 68

   CELLULAR PHONES 68

   CHARITIES 70

   CHECKING ACCOUNTS 71

   COLLECTIONS 76

   COLLEGE TUITION REIMBURSEMENT 81

   COMPENSATION 82

   COMPETITION 87

   COMPUTERS 88

   CONFIDENTIALITY AGREEMENT / NONDISCLOSURE AGREEMENT (NDA) 91

CONSULTANTS 91

CONTRACTS 92

CREDIT 93

CUSTOMER RELATIONS 98

CUSTOMER SITE BEHAVIOR.. 99

CUSTOMER SITE PREPARATION 99

Chapter D... 101

DAY ONE... 101

DECISIONS 103

DELEGATION... 103

DEMOTIONS 103

DEPRECIATION (See also SECTION 179 OF THE IRS TAX CODE)................................ 105

DISCIPLINING EMPLOYEES (See also TERMINATION/ FIRING)................................... 105

DISCOUNTS 108

DISTRIBUTORS 110

DRESS CODES... 111

DUE DILIGENCE.. 113

Chapter E 114

EMPLOYEE DEDUCTIONS / GARNISHMENTS (OTHER THAN THE STANDARD DEDUCTIONS) 114

ENTREPRENEUR 115

EMPLOYEE HANDBOOK 115

ENVIRONMENTAL PROTECTION AGENCY (EPA)... 117

EQUAL PAY ACT 118

EQUITY-BASED LOANS (See also ASSET-BASED LOANS)... 118

EXCLUSIVITY (See also FRANCHISING) 118

EXEMPT VS. NONEXEMPT EMPLOYEES 119

EXIT INTERVIEW 120

EXIT STRATEGY 120

EXPENSE ACCOUNTS 121

Chapter F... 126

FACILITY 126

FAMILY 128

FAMILY MEDICAL LEAVE ACT (FMLA) 130

FICTITIOUS BUSINESS NAMES (DBA's).. 130

FINANCIAL STATEMENTS (See ACCOUNTING: Key financial statements) 131

FIRING EMPLOYEES (See TERMINATION/FIRING).. 131

FLEX TIME 131

FORECASTING... 131

FOREIGN ACCOUNTS 145

FORMS 145

FRANCHISING (See also EXCLUSIVITY) 146

FREIGHT/SHIPPING... 147

Chapter G... 150

GARNISHMENTS 150

GOALS	150
GRANTS	151
GROSS MARGIN / GROSS PROFIT	152
Chapter H	155
HIRING	155
HOLIDAYS (See BENEFITS)	158
HOME EQUITY LOAN / HOME EQUITY LINE OF CREDIT	158
HOURLY EMPLOYEES	159
HOURS OF BUSINESS OPERATION	162
HOURS OF WORK (See also BURNOUT)	163
HUMAN RESOURCES (HR)	163
Chapter I	167
IMMIGRATION & NATURALIZATION SERVICE (INS)	167
INCENTIVES (See also AWARDS)	168
INDEPENDENT CONTRACTORS	169
INFORMATION DISSEMINATION	171
INSURANCE	172
INTEGRITY AGREEMENT	174
INTERNAL REVENUE SERVICE (IRS)	174
INTERNET	174
INVENTORY	176
Chapter J	183
JOINT VENTURES	183
Chapter K	184
KEY MAN INSURANCE (See INSURANCE: Key Man Insurance)	184
KEYS	184
Chapter L	186
LAYOFFS (See also REDUCTION IN FORCE)	186
LEADERSHIP	186
LEASING YOUR PRODUCTS TO YOUR CUSTOMERS (See also FACILITY: for leasing a building)	187
LETTERS OF INTENT	189
LICENSES, PERMITS, ZONING	189
LOANS	190
LONG-DISTANCE CALLING	192
Chapter M	194
MANAGING YOUR COMPANY	194
MANUFACTURING	198
MARKETING	198
MATRIX MANAGEMENT	199
MEDIATION (See also ARBITRATION)	200
MEZZANINE CAPITAL	200
MISSION STATEMENTS	201
MONEY	201
Chapter N	203

NON-COMPETE AGREEMENTS 203

Chapter O 205

OCCUPATIONAL SAFETY & HEALTH ADMINISTRATION (OSHA) 205

OFFICE SUPPLIES 205

OUTPLACEMENT ASSISTANCE 206

OVERTIME 207

Chapter P 209

PAGERS 209

PARKING 210

PARTNERS 211

PAYDAY LOANS 212

PAYROLL 212

PERFORMANCE EVALUATIONS – REVIEWS 213

PERKS (PERQUISITES) 215

PERMITS, CERTIFICATIONS AND LICENSES 217

PETTY CASH 218

PHONES (See also CELLULAR PHONES) 218

PLANNING (see also BUSINESS PLAN and FORECASTING) 219

PRIME RATE 220

PRODUCTION 220

PROFIT 222

PROMISSORY NOTE (see also PAYDAY LOANS) 222

PUBLIC RELATIONS 223

PURCHASE ORDER FINANCING 223

Chapter Q 225

QUALITY ASSURANCE 225

Chapter R 226

RATIOS 226

RECRUITING 228

REDUCTION IN FORCE (RIF) (See also OUTPLACEMENT ASSISTANCE) 228

RELOCATION OF AN EMPLOYEE 230

RETIREMENT FOR EMPLOYEES 231

RETIREMENT FUND 232

RUMORS 232

Chapter S 233

SAFETY 233

SALES 233

SCORE 237

SEARCH/STAFFING FIRMS 237

SECTION 179 OF IRS TAX CODE (See also DEPRECIATION) 240

SECURITY/SURVEILLANCE 240

SEMINARS (See TRAINING) 242

SEXUAL HARASSMENT 242

SHIPPING (See FREIGHT/SHIPPING) 243

SHRINKAGE 244

SICK DAYS / SICK LEAVE (See also FAMIILY MEDICAL LEAVE ACT [FMLA]) 244

SIGN-ON BONUS 244

SIX SIGMA 245

SMALL BUSINESS ADMINISTRATION (SBA) 246

SMOKING POLICIES 247

SOCIAL MEDIA MARKETING 249

SUPPLIERS (See VENDORS) 249

SWOT 250

Chapter T 251

TARGET MARKET 251

TAXES 251

TELECOMMUTING 252

TERMINATION / FIRING 252

THIEF IN THE HOUSE 258

TOLL - FREE NUMBERS (See LONG-DISTANCE CALLING) 259

TOOLS 259

TRAINING 260

TRIBAL ACCOUNTS / RESERVATION BUSINESS 265

TURNKEY PRICE 265

Chapter U 266

UNIFORMS 266

UNIONS 267

Chapter V 268

VEHICLES 268

VENDORS 272

VENTURE CAPITALISTS 275

Chapter W 276

WEBSITE (See also INTERNET) 276

WOMEN OWNED SMALL BUSINESS PROGRAM (WOSB) 278

WORKFORCE GUIDELINES 279

Chapter XYZ 281

YEAR-TO-DATE (Y-T-D) 281

ZERO-BASED BUDGETING 281

REFERENCES 282

Introduction

So, you are a business owner . . . or at least thinking about it. Maybe you are starting your business from scratch. Maybe you are buying an existing business. Or maybe you are simply tired of sitting around after an early retirement and have decided to risk some, or all, of that hard-earned savings you have been stashing away for the last 30 or 40 years. Regardless, you want to get *out* of the business of making money for others and *into* the business of keeping what is rightfully yours — your share of the profits.

Will you become a proud business owner who is still thriving after the next 5 or 10 years? Or will you succumb to the odds and fail, with nothing to show for your work but the loss of your hard-earned retirement and savings? And, don't forget all the legal and family headaches that go along with those financial burdens that may follow you around in the years ahead.

If you own a one-chair beauty salon, this book is for you. If you are the owner of a $100 million, 350-employee manufacturing business, this book is for you. If you are considering owning your own business in the future, this book is for you. Whether your business is small or large, you will learn many things within these pages that will make your life easier and result in increased profits for you and your employees.

Take the time to read and unearth the gems that can convert your business into a well-oiled machine. Discover the difference in working in a vigorous, organized environment or pounding your head against the wall, day in and day out, scraping for every dollar of profit.

Ray Kroc waited until he was 52 to pursue his dream.[2] It took guts to do it. Henry Ford went broke five times before he founded The Ford Motor Company.[3] He did pretty well once he got his act together. And, of course, we all know that Thomas Edison failed 1,000 times before inventing a sustainable light bulb that would burn for more than a few seconds.[4]

With proper planning and execution, there is no reason why you cannot go into business for yourself and become a success. Every day, common, ordinary, hardworking people just like you cross the line to entrepreneurship. There are winners who never graduated from high school. There are losers who have multiple college degrees.

Thomas Jefferson once said, "I'm a great believer in luck, and I find the harder I work, the more I have of it."[5] This book is an effort to prove to you that managing and operating a business is 10 percent luck and 90 percent common sense. You can manage your business successfully by following the common-sense guidelines you are holding in your hands.

It often seems that common sense is the least common of all human values. Please forgive and overused cliché, but managing a business is not rocket science. It is simply a matter of learning to "Plan your work and work your plan."[6]

Why delay any longer? This book is designed to provide the knowledge that will help you make day-to-day decisions about most of the things that drive business owners batty. Whether you are new to business or an old hand at business, there is always something to learn. Business management is a learned profession. Great business leaders are not born with the knowledge that makes them extraordinary. They have simply taken the time to learn the ropes and apply their skills. Now it is your turn.

LYNN MILLER'S

DAILY DOZEN

Over the years I have accumulated a number of gems from mentors, bosses, and associates. I call them my Daily Dozen. Follow these simple rules to simplify your life. Violate one rule and it will lead to problems with the others.

1. Never do anything illegal or get involved with anyone who does anything illegal.

2. Always retain majority control of your business.

3. Always be proactive.

4. If it sounds too good to be true, it probably is.

5. Find a mentor who challenges you.

6. Do not burn yourself out.

7. Get a second opinion. You are not expected to know everything.

8. Keep it simple. Managing a business requires common sense.

9. Hire people who are not afraid to tell you when you are wrong.

10. Your business is either growing or dying. Sell! Sell! Sell!

11. Do something you love.

12. You, and you alone, are responsible for your success or failure.

14 WAYS TO KILL YOUR BUSINESS

We affect our businesses daily with positive and negative decisions that enhance or detract from our abilities to make the profit we, our stakeholders and employees deserve. No one is perfect. Learn from your poor decisions and do it differently next time. The following is a list of 14 Ways to Kill Your Business. Some are sure death, while others allow your company to die slowly.

1. No business plan

2. Absentee leadership

3. Undercapitalization

4. Ignore your cash flow

5. Expand too quickly

6. Fail to forecast

7. Fail to utilize a mentor(s) who complements your style

8. Try to be too many things to too many people

9. Do all your business with too few key customers

10. Fail to recognize a downturn in the economy

11. Underprice your competition rather than selling quality

12. Fail to improve as your competition improves

13. No succession plan

14. Fail to maintain a healthy lifestyle

Before You Get Started

Start by sitting down with this book and reading it through, cover to cover, before going any further. Your time will be well spent and will give you an overview of your strengths and weaknesses. When you are finished, you will find that —even if you are already a business owner—you have read about things that are unfamiliar. In short, you have discovered the *things you do not know* that can dramatically affect your business, positively or negatively.

Topics and subject matter are arranged alphabetically so you can quickly and easily find the information you seek. You will also notice many cross references. Where topics closely overlap, the subject matter is tied to similar topics to create a more complete learning experience.

Why wait? There's no time like the present—start reading!

Start Your Business for the Right Reasons

Reasons for starting your own business are plentiful - especially when you have had a rough day at the office. Some of those reasons are real, others are half-truths, and still others are absolute myths. Make sure you know the truth when you make your decision. Here are a few things to consider if you are really serious about becoming an entrepreneur:

I am my own boss. In fact, you have many bosses. They include your stakeholders, your family, your employees, your bank, your customers, your vendors, your financial sources, and Uncle Sam. You are your own boss when, and only when, you have satisfied everyone else involved with your business.

I am in charge of my income; I get paid first. The reality is that you get paid last—if your business is profitable enough to provide you with a paycheck.

I have numerous tax advantages. Be careful. Your friends and business acquaintances are going to tell you that a small business is the best tax shelter available. Remember that the IRS follows a very strict set of standards. So must you.

I set my own schedule. When you are working for someone else, you can simply say "No" to overtime and weekends. Another employee will take up the slack. This doesn't apply when you are a business owner. You take up the slack when no one else is available or when you cannot afford to pay someone else to do the job.

I have no set vacations. This is both a blessing and a curse. Until you are comfortable turning the keys to the cash register over to a trusted employee, you get no vacations or days off.

There is less pressure. When you are working for someone else, you feel an obligation to put in a hard day's work. That pressure comes from your own sense of integrity, as well as your boss's expectations. You have only invested your time. If the company fails, you can always find another job. In your own business, pressure comes from a variety of sources, including your family. But when you succeed, the rewards are numerous and unparalleled.

If those dummies I work for can run a business, anyone can. Odds are that you will have a greater appreciation for those "dummies" after you have had the opportunity to market your own product or service. Cultivating a profitable business is a lot like raising a child. The surprises are often more numerous than the planned events. Things are not always as they appear. Nonetheless, I am fond of saying that business management is largely common sense. You must make the right decisions at the right time, plan your work and work your plan. Step back and take a look at those "dummies" after you have had the chance to *do it the right way*. You may gain a perspective that escaped you prior to going into business for yourself. Managing your own business is hard work, but if you are up to the challenge, you will reap life-altering rewards.

Chapter A

ACCOUNTANTS

Do I need an accountant? Absolutely! And not just any accountant, but a CPA (Certified Public Accountant). You may also choose to hire a bookkeeper or controller or perform the in-house bookkeeping functions yourself. But when tax season arrives, pay a CPA to get the job done correctly – and in a timely manner. If you do employ a bookkeeper, be sure your accountant and bookkeeper are on the same page from day one.

What is a CPA? CPA stands for Certified Public Accountant. This designation tells you that your accountant has taken the time to gain the necessary education and experience to pass state boards so that she can utilize the CPA certification. CPA designations are awarded by each state for accountants practicing in that state. If an accountant is a CPA in one state and moves or practices across state lines, she may be required to meet new requirements to practice in another state or practice via state-to-state reciprocity, where available.

CPA's generally are careful to remain within the boundaries of the law to protect their certifications. That said, do not be fooled by the designation alone. CPA's are not created equally. Many specialize in areas that may have nothing to do with your particular business. Many have not touched a business tax return in years. When hiring a CPA, be sure that you are comfortable with the individual's background and experience to handle your account.

In addition, a CPA must regularly participate in continuing education requirements to maintain her certification. Public accountants are under no constraints to take continuing education courses. Nor are they under any constraints to do anything to earn the title "accountant."

This does not mean that non-CPAs do not participate in ongoing education. It does mean that ongoing education is a choice for a non-CPA accountant. Most attend annual courses or seminars essential to staying current with IRS rules. It is probable that most are conscientious in their areas of expertise. However, you are still encouraged to choose a CPA for work that extends beyond day-to-day accounting and bookkeeping.

WHAT SHOULD I DO? Before you open your doors, you will need a CPA to assist you in setting up your business accounts in a manner that she specifies. She will put you on a cash or accrual basis and will suggest accounting software that meets your business needs *(see also ACCOUNTING: Cash accounting method and Accrual accounting method)*.

If you are new to business, start with QuickBooks, Quicken, or a similar program that encompasses all facets of small business accounting. Let your accountant know that you want something that you will understand. Take a class or two and learn the system. Ask your CPA for assistance if you need help setting up your books. When the task becomes too difficult or time consuming, you may want to consider a staff bookkeeper or staff accountant. Or, you may opt for a contract accountant – one who serves your needs for a fee. In any case, you need someone on the inside to conduct day-to-day accounting.

When hiring an accountant, ask for three references and check them out thoroughly before making a decision. You want to employ an accounting firm or individual CPA who will take an active role in setting up your General Ledger, Chart of Accounts, Payables, Receivables, daily transaction forms and Payroll. She should also handle your Income Statement, Balance Sheet and Cash Flow Statement. Your CPAs list of concerns is considerably longer. But if she is capable of handling the foregoing items, she will provide a reliable framework for carrying out your day-to-day business transactions and will be able to provide the statements and information that are necessary for you to manage your business.

ACCOUNTING

Cash accounting method. The cash accounting method is normally utilized by small businesses due to its simplicity. It works like this: On the date cash is received or paid out, regardless of product or service delivery date(s), the cash is booked as income or expense. If you sell a product or service in January and are not paid until March, the income is booked in March when payment is received, not January when the customer received the product or service. Expenses are treated similarly. When the vendor or service provider is paid, regardless of when the product is received, the expense is recorded.

There are weaknesses in utilizing the cash method. You may lose clarity regarding dates of purchases and sales since a cash basis system is strictly tied to the date of payment or pay-out. In the months that cash influx is abundant, you may assume great profitability. In actuality, you may have collected a large number of credit sales from prior months, while your current month's sales are poor. On the other hand, you may have large sales or expenditures that do not hit your books until months after the transactions when cash is actually paid or received.

Accrual accounting method. When the product or service is delivered, the income is recorded on your books, whether or not payment has been received. Expenses are treated similarly. If you are engaged in a business that involves storage and movement of inventory, such as manufacturing, you may want to consider the accrual method.

There are weaknesses in utilizing the accrual method. You may lose clarity regarding your cash flow. Even though an accrual based accounting system gives you an accurate picture of the actual timing of sales and purchases, you must investigate further to stay on top of actual dates and amounts of cash collections and payments.

Also, IRS regulations may force you into accrual basis accounting if "your business has sales of more than $5 million per year, or your business stocks an inventory of items that you will sell to the public and your gross receipts are over $1 million per year. Inventory includes any merchandise you sell, as well as supplies that will physically become part of an item intended for sale.[1]

WHAT SHOULD I DO? Once you and your accountant decide on your accounting method, you must have IRS approval to convert to another method. Confer with your accountant or the IRS for up-to-date regulations before you choose an accounting method. Agree on the accounting method you intend to use, prior to setting up your books.

Key financial statements. The most commonly utilized financial statements are the Income Statement, the Balance Sheet and the Cash Flow Statement. Many entrepreneurs feel that formal accounting classes are necessary to understand these valuable accounting tools. Consequently, they either leave that function to an accountant or bookkeeper, or forego utilization of these statements altogether. In either case, the entrepreneur is missing out on information that will allow her to take management of her company to the next level. I strongly believe that mastery of these three accounting statements will allow a business owner or manager to convert financial logic to positive action that will carry the company to a higher level of success. So, let's read ahead and take the mystery out of understanding financial statements.

First key statement - Income Statement (Figure A-1). We will start with the Income Statement. Depending on the industry or company, an Income Statement may also be referred to as a Profit and Loss (P&L) or an Operating Income Statement. The Income Statement is your day-to-day guide to the health of your company. It provides an accurate picture of your profits or losses over a period of time, usually a month, a quarter, or a year. It displays all your revenues (products and/or services sold), the cost of those products and/or services, and the expenses associated with your business.

Subtract cost of goods sold from revenue and the result is gross profit. Subtract expenses from gross profit and the result is Net Profit.

The Income Statement of ABC Company (Figure A-1) is typical of a business that produces or purchases a product that is sold, business to business (B2B) or business to consumer (B2C). Accountants stylize Income Statements, utilizing terms familiar to a particular business or industry, and may categorize revenues and expenses differently, depending on the accountant's preferences.

Figure A-1

INCOME STATEMENT
ABC Company
December 31, 2015

	Jan	Feb	Mar	Apr	May	Jun	Jul	Aug	Sep	Oct	Nov	Dec	Totals	Rev. %
Sales	44,000	38,000	40,000	42,500	47,500	49,500	57,500	65,000	62,500	81,000	82,500	92,500	702,500	100.00%
Cost of Goods Sold	24,200	20,900	22,000	23,375	26,125	27,225	31,625	35,750	34,375	44,550	45,375	50,875	386,375	55.00%
Gross Profit	19,800	17,100	18,000	19,125	21,375	22,275	25,875	29,250	28,125	36,450	37,125	41,625	316,125	45.00%
Expenses														
Advertising	2,420	2,090	2,200	2,338	2,613	2,723	3,163	3,575	3,438	4,455	4,538	5,088	38,638	5.50%
Bank Expense														
Checking	100	50	50	50	50	50	50	50	50	50	50	50	650	0.09%
Credit Card Costs	616	532	560	595	665	693	805	910	875	1,134	1,155	1,295	9,835	1.40%
Commissions - Sales	2,200	1,900	2,000	2,125	2,375	2,475	2,875	3,250	3,125	4,050	4,125	4,625	35,125	5.00%
Dues & Subscriptions											450		450	0.06%
Insurance	735	0	0	735	0	0	735	0	0	735	0	0	2,940	0.42%
Legal & Accounting	250	250	250	250	250	250	250	250	250	250	250	250	3,000	0.43%
Office Supplies	50	50	50	50	50	50	50	50	50	50	50	50	600	0.09%
Rent - Building	4,500	1,500	1,500	1,500	1,500	1,500	1,500	1,500	1,500	1,500	1,500	1,500	21,000	2.99%
Rent - Inventory Storage	100	100	100	100	100	100	100	100	100	100	100	100	1,200	0.17%
Salary - Administrative	2,500	2,500	2,500	2,500	2,500	2,500	2,500	2,500	2,500	2,500	2,500	2,500	30,000	4.27%
Salary - Owner	4,000	4,000	4,000	4,000	4,000	4,000	4,000	4,000	4,000	4,000	4,000	4,000	48,000	6.83%
Salary - Sales	4,000	4,000	4,000	4,000	4,000	4,000	4,000	4,000	4,000	4,000	4,000	4,000	48,000	6.83%
Taxes & Benefits	1,905	1,860	1,875	1,894	1,931	1,946	2,006	2,063	2,044	2,183	2,194	2,269	24,169	3.44%
Telephone	550	550	550	550	550	550	550	550	550	550	550	550	6,600	0.94%
Trade Shows & Exhibits			5,000							5,000			10,000	1.42%
Travel	660	570	600	638	713	743	863	975	938	1,215	1,238	1,388	10,538	1.50%
Utilities	554	563	573	562	558	613	652	701	601	550	576	785	7,288	1.04%
Vehicle Allowance	800	800	800	800	800	800	800	800	800	800	800	800	9,600	1.37%
Warehouse Supplies	132	114	120	128	143	149	173	195	188	243	248	278	2,108	0.30%
Website	4,000	250	250	250	250	250	250	250	250	250	250	250	6,750	0.96%
Total Expenses	30,072	21,679	26,978	23,063	23,047	23,391	25,321	25,719	25,257	33,615	28,122	30,226	316,489	45.05%
Net Profit	-10,272	-4,579	-8,978	-3,938	-1,672	-1,116	554	3,532	2,868	2,836	9,003	11,399	-364	-0.05%

Your Income Statement is an intense and realistic financial portrait of your business for the past month, year, or even years. Spot your opportunities and weaknesses and convert them to positive action.

ABC Company's Income Statement Assumptions. Before diving into any Income Statement, there are a few things you should know about the business operation. These are called assumptions. The assumptions for ABC Company will give you a better understanding of ABC Company's Income Statement.

First year in business, beginning January 1, 2015.

The owner has a personal credit line of $175,000, collateralized by his residence, from which he can borrow at any time, and loan necessary cash to ABC Company.

Product – Special tool to be utilized by aircraft manufacturing, maintenance, repair and rental companies. Similar tools exist, but are not as efficient and durable as ABC's tool.

Product sells for $500 per unit.

Material cost = $175 per unit.

Material is manufactured by and purchased from outside sources and assembled by a subcontractor.

Subcontractor charges $100 to assemble & package 1 product unit.

Materials include packaging, pallets, inbound shipping and banding.

Advertising = 5.5% of Sales.

50% of sales are sold via credit card, at 2.8% fee per transaction, including all incidental costs.

Sales Commissions = 5% of Sales Revenue (2 Salespeople).

Rent is $100 monthly for raw material & finished goods storage at the subcontractor site.

Finished goods are shipped from subcontractor to ABC Company, on demand.

ABC Company wants to turn their inventory 12 times per year.

Administrative Salary = 1 admin/bookkeeper @ 30,000 per year

Sales Salaries = $24,000 X 2 salespeople

Warehouse Supplies = 3 tenths % of Sales Revenue

Vehicle Allowance = $400 per month X 2 salespeople

Now, let me share my approach to examining ABC Company's Income Statement (Figure A-1). Your company's account names and placements may differ from this example, but the manner in which an Income Statement is examined is pretty much the same for any company. ABC Company sells its products at a 45% gross margin. ABC Company owns the patent and all rights to the product. They just wrapped up their first year in business and broke even in their seventh month, while finishing with a Net Loss of -364 for the year. Not bad for a startup business. Most businesses break even between six and eighteen months, with the majority breaking even in the thirteenth month. An Operating Loss is common for a first year business.

Figure A-2

INCOME STATEMENT
REVENUE SECTION
ABC Company
December 31, 2015

	Jan	Feb	Mar	Apr	May	Jun	Jul	Aug	Sep	Oct	Nov	Dec	Totals	Rev. %
Sales	44,000	38,000	40,000	42,500	47,500	49,500	57,500	65,000	62,500	81,000	82,500	92,500	702,500	100.00%
Cost of Goods Sold	24,200	20,900	22,000	23,375	26,125	27,225	31,625	35,750	34,375	44,550	45,375	50,875	386,375	55.00%
Gross Profit	19,800	17,100	18,000	19,125	21,375	22,275	25,875	29,250	28,125	36,450	37,125	41,625	316,125	45.00%

Sales (Figure A-2). Sales of $702,500 represent all the revenue that came into ABC Company during its first year in business. The last column, to the right, represents the percentage of each category, in relation to Sales. Since $702,500 is Sales, the figure in the last column is 100%.

Cost of Goods Sold (Figure A-2). Cost of Goods Sold represents the total cost of materials, labor, packaging, labeling, packing materials, freight and other costs associated with the goods that are sold. The product is ready for shipment when it arrives at ABC Company. The total Cost of Goods Sold for ABC for 2015 is $386,375, or 55% of Sales. Cost of Goods sold is of significant importance since it has a major influence on your profit. Everything you save in this category – without cheapening your product's appearance or performance – drops straight to your bottom line.

Gross Profit (Figure A-2). Gross profit, in the amount of $316,125 is left over after we subtract the Cost of Goods Sold from Sales. Gross Profit is 45% of Sales. This percentage is called the Gross Margin. The Gross Margin is obtained by dividing Gross Profit by Sales. The calculation is $316,125 ÷ $702,500 = 45%.

Gross Margin is critically important to your business because it directly impacts the percentage of every dollar of Sales that is left over to cover all other Expenses and leave a reasonable Net Profit (*See also GROSS MARGIN / GROSS PROFIT*). ABC Company's gross margin is comparable to that of their competitors who sell similar products. ABC Company's product is new to the market and should enjoy its present gross margin until competitors catch on and eventually bring the price down, thus lowering gross margins.

INCOME STATEMENT
EXPENSE SECTION
ABC Company
December 31, 2015

Figure A-3

	Jan	Feb	Mar	Apr	May	Jun	Jul	Aug	Sep	Oct	Nov	Dec	Totals	Rev. %
Expenses														
Advertising	2,420	2,090	2,200	2,338	2,613	2,723	3,163	3,575	3,438	4,455	4,538	5,088	38,638	5.50%
Bank Expense														
Checking	100	50	50	50	50	50	50	50	50	50	50	50	650	0.09%
Credit Card Costs	616	532	560	595	665	693	805	910	875	1,134	1,155	1,295	9,835	1.40%
Commissions - Sales	2,200	1,900	2,000	2,125	2,375	2,475	2,875	3,250	3,125	4,050	4,125	4,625	35,125	5.00%
Dues & Subscriptions	0	0	0	0	0	0	0	0	0	0	0	450	450	0.06%
Insurance	735	0	0	735	0	0	735	0	0	735	0	0	2,940	0.42%
Legal & Accounting	250	250	250	250	250	250	250	250	250	250	250	250	3,000	0.43%
Office Supplies	50	50	50	50	50	50	50	50	50	50	50	50	600	0.09%
Rent - Building	4,500	1,500	1,500	1,500	1,500	1,500	1,500	1,500	1,500	1,500	1,500	1,500	21,000	2.99%
Rent - Inventory Storage	100	100	100	100	100	100	100	100	100	100	100	100	1,200	0.17%
Salary - Administrative	2,500	2,500	2,500	2,500	2,500	2,500	2,500	2,500	2,500	2,500	2,500	2,500	30,000	4.27%
Salary - Owner	4,000	4,000	4,000	4,000	4,000	4,000	4,000	4,000	4,000	4,000	4,000	4,000	48,000	6.83%
Salary - Sales	4,000	4,000	4,000	4,000	4,000	4,000	4,000	4,000	4,000	4,000	4,000	4,000	48,000	6.83%
Taxes & Benefits	1,905	1,860	1,875	1,894	1,931	1,946	2,006	2,063	2,044	2,183	2,194	2,269	24,169	3.44%
Telephone	550	550	550	550	550	550	550	550	550	550	550	550	6,600	0.94%
Trade Shows & Exhibits	0	0	5,000	0	0	0	0	0	0	5,000	0	0	10,000	1.42%
Travel	660	570	600	638	713	743	863	975	938	1,215	1,238	1,388	10,538	1.50%
Utilities	554	563	573	562	558	613	652	701	601	550	576	785	7,288	1.04%
Vehicle Allowance	800	800	800	800	800	800	800	800	800	800	800	800	9,600	1.37%
Warehouse Supplies	132	114	120	128	143	149	173	195	188	243	248	278	2,108	0.30%
Website	250	250	250	250	250	250	250	250	250	250	250	250	6,750	0.96%
Total Expenses	30,072	21,679	26,978	23,063	23,047	23,391	25,321	25,719	25,257	33,615	28,122	30,226	316,489	45.05%

Expenses (Figure A-3). Expenses are all the costs to your company, over and above, Cost of Goods Sold.

Let's examine each line, looking for trends that appear abnormal. For example, you may notice that Rent-Building is $4,500 in January, but drops to $1,500 in subsequent months. January was ABC Company's first month in business. The January Rent entry reflects an extra $3,000 for 2-months rental deposit. ABC Company chose to treat their 2-months rental deposit as an expense, since there is a chance that the deposit will never be returned.

You may also notice that the Website entry is $4,000 for January and $250 for each subsequent month. The January entry reflects the price to build the website – a one-time fee - and $250 represents the monthly hosting and maintenance fees for the site.

Advertising is a moving target, as are Credit Card Costs, Commissions-Sales, Office Supplies, Travel and Warehouse Supplies. Each of these items is tied directly to Sales, as a percentage. ABC spends 5.5% of Sales on Advertising, 1.4% on Credit Card costs, and so on. These expenses are referred to as Variable Costs because they fluctuate, month-to-month, with the rise and fall of Sales.

The remaining expenses are Fixed Costs. Checking, Dues and Subscriptions, Insurance, Legal & Accounting, Rent, Salaries, Taxes & Benefits, Telephone, Trade Shows & Exhibits, Utilities, Vehicle Allowance and Website do not normally vary, month-to-month. These expenses may increase or decrease at some point, but are predictable and change infrequently.

Scan each expense item, line by line, month by month? Does the expense parallel the company forecast? Does the expense show any unusual entries? Should the expense be increased? Should the expense be reduced? Should the expense be done away with, completely? Investigate abnormalities and correct if necessary. Convert your findings to positive actions, as needed. Always look for ways to cut unnecessary expenses.

Net Profit (Figure A-1). Net Profit is the culmination of all your hard work. Your wins and defeats come to rest here. Did you make your forecasted income or did you fall short of your projections? For the answer, let's go back to Figure A-1, the Income Statement.

ABC Company shows an Operating Loss of -$364 for the year. By comparison, their competitors are yielding Net Profits equal to 15 to 18 percent of Sales. Let's take a closer look at the Income Statement and find some of the possible answers to increasing Net Profit.

ABC Company's goal is to reach a Net Profit of 15% by December 31, 2016, and 18% by December 31, 2017. To do so, they must produce Sales of at least $1,444,000 in 2016, assuming that Fixed Expenses remain static. That requires an increase in Sales of $741,500 in 2016, more than double their sales in 2015. The question is, can they reach a sales goal of this magnitude with their current sales staff or is it necessary to add salespeople, which increases expenses and reduces the profit that each sale sends to the bottom line. You will find all figures pertaining to ABC Company's 2016 forecast in the section entitled, *FORECASTING*.

This is how you approach the various areas of your Income Statement. Look into the details and trends, as well as each line item's effect on other line items, if changes appear necessary. Convert your findings to positive action and redefine your forecasts, based on actual historical numbers and future goals.

What other key statements affect, or are affected by, the Income Statement? Although your Income Statement probably packs the most information, of all the key statements, it does not tell the whole story. Your Income Statement does not reflect the company's Cash position, Accounts Receivable, Inventory or other Current Assets. Your Income Statement tells you nothing about Fixed Assets, Current Liabilities, Long-

Term Liabilities or Retained Earnings. All these items are found on the *second key statement*, the Balance Sheet.

Your Income Statement also lacks the information pertaining to the usage of Cash. How much Cash is on hand? How much new Cash will flow into your business in the coming weeks or months? How much Cash will flow out? Cash Flow is a major concern to your day-to-day operation, particularly in the early days when cash is not readily abundant. Your Cash Flow Statement is the *third key statement* that interacts with your Income Statement. Remember! Out of Cash means you are Out of Business.

WHAT SHOULD I DO? Spend time with your accountant until you have a complete and intimate understanding of your business Income Statement. Share this information with your managers and staff so they have an up-to-date picture of the state of your business and can take responsibility for the portion of the Income Statement that is relevant to their individual departments and the company as a whole.

No prior accounting knowledge is necessary to understand your Income Statement. With a little practice, you will become adept at converting your Income Statement to useful information. Income Statements are always used by lenders to evaluate loan applications.

Additional Resources: Accountant, bookkeeper, SBA.

Second key statement - Balance Sheet (Figure A-4). The Balance Sheet is the only document that gives you a snapshot of the state of your business at a specific point in time. It is an integral part of understanding and managing your company. Regrettably, Balance Sheets are among the most misunderstood of all financial statements. Many seasoned business people have a good-to-excellent understanding of the power of the Income Statement and the Cash Flow Statement. They are generally able to convert the numbers and trends on these reports to positive action in their business operations. Income statements and Cash Flow Statements are straightforward. Balance sheets must be balanced by their very nature, thus giving the impression that you must be an accountant to understand the numbers. Hence, Income Statements and Cash Flow Statements steal the show and appear to have all the information necessary to manage your business. Unfortunately, this is not true.

Much of the power of Income Statements and Cash Flow Statements is lost without input from the Balance Sheet. The Balance Sheet tells you where you stand with accounts receivable collections, inventory turnover, the state of your assets, liabilities, and net worth. Many of the valuable business ratios discussed in this book are derived from calculations that involve the Balance Sheet. While the Income Statement and Cash Flow Statement are two legs of the business stool, the Balance Sheet is the equally important third leg.

Now let me share my approach to examining the Balance Sheet (Figure A-4). Once again, your company's account names and placements may differ from this example, but the manner in which a Balance Sheet is examined is pretty much the same for any company. The Balance Sheet is organized in order of liquidity. The faster an item can be converted to cash, the earlier it appears on a Balance Sheet. Hence, Cash is followed by Accounts Receivable, and then Prepaid Expenses on ABC Company's Balance Sheet. Current Assets are more liquid that Fixed Assets, and so on. Nothing is more liquid than Cash. Examine your Balance Sheet on a monthly basis, or more often if necessary.

BALANCE SHEET				
ABC Company				
December 31, 2015				
Figure A-4				
ASSETS		**LIABILITIES**		
Current Assets		Current Liabilities		
Cash	$35,422	Accounts Payable	$25,575	
A/R	6,000	Current Loans	3,000	
Inventory	25,575	Total Current Liabilities	28,575	
Prepaid Expenses	450			
Total Current Assets	67,447	Long-Term Liabilities		
		Bank Loans	19,000	
		Total L-T Liabilities	19,000	
		Total Liabilities	47,575	
Fixed Assets		Owners' Equity		
Fixtures & Equip.	10,000	Owners' Investment	73,872	
Vehicles	44,000	Retained Earnings	0	
Total Fixed Assets	54,000	Total Owner's Equity	73,872	
Total Assets	$121,447	Total Liabilities & Equity	$121,447	

ABC Company Balance Sheet Assumptions:

Accounts Receivable, in the amount of $6,000, represents credit afforded a customer for a December, 2015 sale, but is not yet collected.

Prepaid Expenses represents prepayments for Dues & Subscriptions.

Equipment represents 2 vehicles and miscellaneous machinery.

ABC Company owes $3,000 for a computer and $19,000 for vehicles.

On the Balance Sheet, Retained Earnings is shown to acquaint the reader with its concept and placement. ABC Company has no Retained Earnings.

First, let's have a look at **Current Assets**, also referred to as liquid assets, those that can be converted to cash in less than a year. Obviously, cash needs no conversion.

Cash (Figure A-4). You may have heard the old saying, *Cash is king. If you are out of cash, you are out of business.* ABC Company has $35,422 in cash, in the bank, as of December 31, 2015. It's cold, hard dollars – ready to spend. But, ABC's Income Statement (Figure A-1) shows an Operating Loss at the end of the year of -$364. ABC Company still has $35,422 in Cash. How can this be?

Net Profit on the Income Statement does not convert to cash on the Balance Sheet. Cash is constantly flowing in and out of the company, as needed. So, you can see that ABC Company can have $35,422 in the bank, even though the company is showing a loss of -$364.

When ABC Company becomes profitable, cash will still fluctuate up and down, depending on how fast customers pay, how much credit is offered, how much is outstanding in Accounts Receivable, and how much cash is needed to fund long-range projects. If an owner can afford to pump cash into a failing company, he can fill the checkbook at will, while the company continues to fail and show a Net Loss. Cash is only a single element of the equation. Consequently, the Balance Sheet can be heavy in cash while the company is floundering and unprofitable.

At the moment, ABC Company is in fine shape. Their Income Statement shows that Total Expenses are running around $30,000 a month in the last quarter of 2015. As we mentioned earlier, the owner can tap his personal $175,000 credit line if it becomes necessary to loan cash to his company.

Let's be clear that it is absolutely necessary to understand the role that cash plays on your company's Balance Sheet. Also remember that running out of cash means that you are out of business. Always have a cash alternative available at a moment's notice. The best alternative is a credit line because you can borrow only the amount needed and you can pay it back as soon as the need is covered by cash that flows in from new sales.

A company that has a sizable cash reserve or the ability to generate substantial cash is also a company that creates greater opportunity with less risk than a company without substantial cash. Many investors consider cash the number one indicator of a company's capability to grow, survive risk and repay debt. Never forget. Cash is king.

Accounts Receivable (Figure A-4). Accounts Receivable is money that is owed to your company by customers who have received products/services from you, but have not paid in full. Accounts Receivable is an asset because the money that is owed rightfully belongs to ABC Company. ABC Company's customers owe them $6,000. The $6,000 worth of product that was sold is in the hands of ABC's customers.

This piece of information does not show up on ABC Company's Income Statement. The Income Statement recognizes all revenues, but not the payment of revenues. It does, however, show up on the Balance Sheet as Accounts Receivable. Without a Balance Sheet, the owner would not be aware that the company is owed $6,000 and could mistakenly think that he was paid in full and that $6,000 is missing.

Inventory (Figure A-4). Inventory is entered on your Balance Sheet at cost – that is, the amount you paid for the inventory. There are essentially three types of inventory. They are: 1) Raw materials – the component parts that make up your finished goods; 2) Work-in-process – partially assembled goods, not ready for sale; 3) Finished goods – the portion of your inventory that is ready for sale and shows up on your Balance Sheet.

ABC's Balance Sheet shows that they have $25,575 of finished goods that are ready to be sold and shipped to customers. Once again, $25,575 is the cost of the finished goods that are ready to be sold. In the section that deals with ABC Company's Income Statement Assumptions, we learned that the cost of each unit of finished goods is $275 ($175 in materials and $100 in labor). Divide $275 into $25,575, ABC's current inventory, and you learn that ABC has enough inventory on-hand to satisfy sales of 93 units in January, 2016. ABC's Income Statement tells us that in December of 2015, ABC sold $92,500 of product at $500 per unit. Divide $92,500 (Sales) by $500 (Unit Sale Price), and you realize that ABC sold 185 units in December. If we assume that January will produce sales of 185 units, and maybe more, we are at least 92 units short in our current inventory. At a minimum, we need 92 more units on-hand to satisfy January 2016 sales, at a cost of $25,300 (92 units X $275 per unit cost). So, you can see where ABC Company's Balance Sheet gives us absolutely priceless information that is not available on the Income Statement.

Carry this one step further and notice once again that ABC has $35,422 cash on hand, going into January of 2016. In spite of the necessity to purchase $25,300 in additional finished goods inventory, ABC Company should not require additional cash to make it through January if December's receipts are a valid indication of January 2016 revenues. In the event that revenues do fall short in January, ABC Company's owner can reach into his $175,000 personal credit line and loan the necessary cash to his company.

Most companies in ABC's industry turn over their inventories about 12 times a year. This means that ABC Company should strive to have enough finished goods on the shelf at the beginning of the month to satisfy that month's sales. When that month is over, they should purchase enough finished goods for the following month to satisfy forecasted sales, and so on.

Very few companies are able to accurately forecast sales to a point where they can order the exact amount of inventory that is necessary to satisfy the coming month's sales. There are just too many factors to overcome for 100% accuracy. Managers try to be as efficient as possible for a number of reasons. Inventory takes up space and space costs money. If you purchase too much inventory to satisfy your needs, your money is invested in excess inventory until it is sold to customers. If you purchase too little inventory, you may be forced to overpay for goods, or miss out on valuable discounts. You may also experience inventory shortages due to shipping or production delays. Pay close attention to inventory in reference to sales and always have at least 3 sources when emergencies occur.

Prepaid Expenses (Figure A-4). Prepaid expenses are those that are paid in advance of consuming a product or service you have purchased. Dues & Subscriptions are a good example. ABC Company paid $450 in December 2015, in advance, for 2016 dues and subscriptions. The unused portion of the payment is referred to as *prepaid*, because ABC Company purchased an asset in advance that has not yet been delivered. Hence, the dues and subscriptions are paid for in 2015 and used in 2016. Other categories that may show up on a Balance Sheet as Prepaid are insurance, retainers for legal or other professionals and rent, if paid more than a month in advance. Prepay expenses only when absolutely necessary or when the transaction is too profitable to pass up. Money is a commodity and has a cost. When you prepay an expense, the other company is using your money for free.

In terms of ratios, there are two key ratios that go hand-in-hand with Current Assets. They are the Current Ratio and the Quick Ratio. The Current Ratio is Current Assets divided by Current Liabilities. In the case of ABC Company, the calculation would be $67,447 ÷ $28,575 = 2.36 to 1. In other words ABC Company has $2.36 of Current Assets to every dollar of Current Liabilities. This is just about the minimum to attract investors. Three to one is more desirable.

The Quick Ratio, also known as the Acid Test Ratio, is essentially the same calculation, but excludes Inventory from the equation. If we exclude Inventory from Current Assets ($67,447 - $25,575 = $41,872), ABC's Quick Ratio is $41,872 ÷ $28,575 = 1.47 to 1. Without inventory, ABC Company has $1.47 of Current Assets to every dollar of Current Liabilities. Inventory is often excluded from the calculation because investors want to know what will transpire if ABC Company has difficulty turning their finished goods inventory into quick cash in the event of default (*See also **Ratios**).

Now, let's examine **Fixed Assets (Figure A-4)**, those that will take more than a year to be converted to cash. ABC Company has $54,000 in Fixed Assets. Examples of Fixed Assets are plant, land, machinery, office equipment, tools and vehicles. When a potential stakeholder or lender examines your financials, she sees fixed assets as possible collateral, in the event you default on a loan. The depreciable value of a fixed asset is also important because it indicates the probable life of that asset as collateral. In the case of ABC Company, depreciation will be added to the first Balance Sheet of 2016. *(See also **DEPRECIATION**).*

Fixtures & Equipment (Figure A-4). ABC Company has $10,000 in Fixtures and Equipment. Fixtures are those items that are attached to and considered part of real property or vehicles. Real property is anything that is attached to the land, such as buildings, silos or water towers. Fixtures are items such as lighting, HVAC and pumps. Equipment is anything that provides something for a specific purpose, such as presses, welders, copiers, computers, furniture, ovens, robots, or lathes.

Vehicles (Figure A-4). Vehicles refer to those that are utilized for business purposes. Typical vehicles are trucks, vans, cars, buses, planes, trains, helicopters, boats, or numerous other types of vehicles that are necessary to carry out business. Most business owners use a personal car to drive during working hours, travel to and from work and, to and from appointments. Business vehicles do not include those that are driven by spouses and other family members who do not work in your business. ABC Company has $44,000 in vehicles.

Total Assets (Figure A-4). This is simply the sum and total of all the assets of the company, current and fixed. Notice that Total Assets ($121,447) are equal to Total Liabilities and Equity ($121,447). Every cent that comes into your company (Assets) must be accounted for in some way on the opposite side of the Balance Sheet (Liabilities and Equity).

The next section on the Balance Sheet (**Figure A-4**) is **Current Liabilities,** those debts that a company is due to pay within one year. ABC Company had Current Liabilities of $28,575 as of December 31, 2015. Your banker, lenders and stakeholders closely watch the relationship of Current Liabilities to Current Assets. At a minimum, try to maintain Current Liabilities at a level that does not exceed half of Current Assets. If possible keep Current Liabilities at one-third of Current Assets, or less.

Accounts Payable (Figure A-4). These are short-term debts that a company is required to pay off within one year. The company may have procured inventory, purchased a piece of equipment on a payment plan, or borrowed from a lender on a short-term basis. Look under the Current Liabilities category on ABC's Balance Sheet and you will see Accounts Payable, in the amount of $25,575. This particular payable offsets the $25,575 that appears in the Inventory classification under Current Assets. Also see Current Loans under Current Liabilities. This $3,000 is for a computer that was purchased on credit, with the understanding that it will be paid off within one year of the purchase date.

You will not find Accounts Payable on your Income Statement and you will never know exactly what you are spending unless you pay attention to Accounts Payable on your Balance Sheet. Your Income Statement gives you overall categories such as Advertising, Sales Commissions, Dues & Subscriptions, Insurance, Vehicle Allowance, Salaries and Supplies. But, it does not allow you to drill down into your expenses to determine exactly how and when you are spending your money.

Long-Term Liabilities (Figure A-4). These are debts that will be paid off more than a year after purchase. Examples of long-term liabilities are bonds, bank loans, real-estate mortgages, vehicle loans, and debentures, which are loans that are not backed by collateral. Long-term Liability indicates that the item in question has a substantially longer life than those that are itemized under Current Liabilities. ABC Company's sole long-term liability is a 5-year bank loan for vehicles, in the amount of $19,000.

Total Liabilities (Figure A-4). This is simply the sum and total of all the liabilities of the company, current and long-term. ABC Company's Total Liabilities are $47,575. You may recall the Current Ratio, mentioned earlier. Total Assets should be at least twice a company's Total Liabilities, at a minimum. Three times is better. Keep your eye on this key ratio as you grow and add assets and liabilities.

Owner's Equity Figure A-4). Owner's Equity is the owners' net worth in the company. Equity is everything that is left over when we subtract Total Liabilities (everything we owe) from Total Assets (everything we own). ABC's Total Assets are $121,447. The company's Total Liabilities are $47,575. Subtract $47,575 from $121,447, which leaves us with Owner's Equity, in the amount of $73,872. Owners can increase Owner's Equity in a company only by increasing profits, increasing assets or reducing expenses.

Owner's Investment (Figure A-4). Owner's Investment ($73,872) is that portion of Owner's Equity that the owner(s) puts into the company. An owner's investment could be cash, or it could be any number of things, such as real property, equipment, vehicles or stock. In the case of ABC Company, Owner's Equity is comprised solely of the Owner's Investment since there are no Retained Earnings.

Retained Earnings (Figure A-4). When your company turns a profit, you essentially have two choices. You can distribute the profit to yourself and your shareholders, or you can keep a portion of the profit and reinvest it in your company? Retained Earnings are cumulative, from the very first day the company went into business. Retained Earnings are that portion of company profits that are plowed back into the company for research & development, to replace worn machinery, buy a new building, upgrade your fleet or simply pay off debt. The stipulation is that these earnings must be invested in your company.

Before you make a decision to distribute profits, have a look at the overall well-being of your company and determine if your needs will require an infusion of cash that can come from Retained Earnings rather than other, more expensive options.

As you can see, ABC Company has no Retained Earnings. The category has been added for explanation only.

Total Owner's Equity (Figure A-4). This is the amount that is leftover ($73,872) after we subtract Total Liabilities ($47,575 from Total Assets ($121,447), otherwise known as the owner's Net Worth. It includes the Owners' Investment and Retained Earnings.

Total Liabilities and Equity (Figure A-4). This ($121,447) is the final figure on the right side of the Balance Sheet and is equal to Total Assets ($121,447), the final figure on the left side of the Balance Sheet. The left side (Assets) must be equal to the right side (the total of Liabilities and Owners Equity). Otherwise, the Balance Sheet is incorrect.

WHAT SHOULD I DO? Examine your Balance Sheet, side-by-side, with your Income Statement and Cash Flow Statement. By doing so, you will get a better feel for the relationship among all three statements. As your business grows, you will learn what you can expect from each statement and how to convert each statement to positive action. No prior accounting knowledge is necessary to understand your Balance Sheet. Balance Sheets are usually used by lenders to evaluate loan applications.

Additional Resources: Accountant, bookkeeper, SBA. *See also Ratios.*

Third key statement - Cash Flow (aka Free Cash Flow) Statement (Figure A-5). Your Income Statement may show a profit, but you may not have enough cash on hand to purchase product you promised to deliver to your largest customer by the end of the month. Your Cash Flow Statement goes a step beyond the Income Statement and shows you exactly how much cash you have on hand to operate your business.

A Cash Flow Statement, or Statement of Cash Flows, has two primary functions. The first is to show a history of cash generation and cash usage over a specific period of time. ABC Company's Cash Flow Statement (Figure A-5) is a history of cash flow for October, November and December of 2015. The second function is to forecast cash flow generation and usage into the future to determine the amount of cash that is necessary for ABC Company to successfully carry out business.

CASH FLOW STATEMENT
ABC Company
December 31, 2015

Figure A-5

	October	November	December
Beginning Cash Balance	14,000	16,143	31,716
Cash Inflows			
Cash Receipts	76,000	82,500	86500
Owner Contributions	0	0	0
A/R Collections	0	5,000	0
Total Cash Inflows	90,000	103,643	118,216
Cash Outflows			
Inventory Purchases	(41,800)	(45,375)	(47,575)
Advertising	(4,446)	(4,528)	(5,077)
Checking	(50)	(50)	(50)
Credit Card Costs	(1,132)	(1,153)	(1,292)
Commissions - Sales	(4,042)	(4,117)	(4,616)
Dues & Subscriptions	0	0	(450)
Insurance	(735)	0	0
Legal & Accounting	(250)	(250)	(250)
Loan Payments	(646)	(646)	(646)
Office Supplies	(50)	(50)	(50)
Rent - Building	(1,500)	(1,500)	(1,500)
Rent - Inventory Storage	(100)	(100)	(100)
Salary - Administrative	(2,500)	(2,500)	(2,500)
Salary - Owner	(4,000)	(4,000)	(4,000)
Salary - Sales	(4,000)	(4,000)	(4,000)
Supplies - Warehouse	(243)	(247)	(277)
Taxes & Benefits	0	0	(6,641)
Telephone	(550)	(550)	(550)
Trade Shows & Exhibits	(5,000)	0	0
Travel	(1,213)	(1,235)	(1,385)
Utilities	(550)	(576)	(785)
Vehicle Allowance	(800)	(800)	(800)
Website	(250)	(250)	(250)
Total Cash Outflows	(73,857)	(71,927)	(82,794)
Ending Cash Balance	16,143	31,716	35,422

Notice that ABC's Cash Flow Statement includes only those categories that generate cash or require cash for payment. For example, if ABC purchases and item on credit, that transaction will not be included in the Cash Flow Statement until it is necessary to expend cash to pay the bill. Conversely, if ABC extends credit to a customer, the credit portion of the transaction will show up on the Balance Sheet as Accounts Receivable, but will not show up on the Cash Flow Statement until cash is collected to satisfy all, or a portion of the debt.

So, how do we approach a Cash Flow Statement? Let's look at October. The first category is Beginning Cash Balance. ABC Company has $14,000 of cold, hard cash in their checkbook, just waiting to pay bills. The next category – Cash inflows – shows Cash Receipts during October, in the amount of $76,000. Owner contributions refers to cash that the owner has added to the checkbook to shore up the company's cash position. You can see that no new cash has been added by the owner. A/R collections refer to Accounts Receivable. ABC has not collected any outstanding Accounts Receivable in the month of October. So far, we have $14,000 in the checkbook and Cash Receipts added to the checkbook, in the amount of $76,000, for Total Cash Inflows of $90,000 for the month. Sounds pretty good, so far?

The next category is Cash Outflows, which includes all the items that required ABC Company to pay cold, hard cash from their checkbook in the month of October. The largest item is Inventory Purchases, in the amount of $41,800, that we would not recognize if we did not look at ABC Company's Cash Flow Statement. Inventory purchases do not show up on the Income Statement. All the listed items require cash payments from ABC during the month of October. Total Cash Outflows amount to $73,857.

So, what's the bottom line? We started October with $14,000 in cash. We added $76,000 in cash. But, we paid out $73,857. Add the Beginning Cash Balance ($14,000) to Cash Receipts ($76,000) and we have $90,000 in cash in the checkbook. Now, subtract Total Cash Outflows ($73,857) from $90,000 and we are left with $16,143 in ABC's checkbook at the end of October.

Looking at November, we see that ABC Company improved their cash position. They began the month with $16,143 in their checkbook and finished with $31,716. And, December's cash improved from a beginning cash flow of $31,716 and finished with $35,422 in the checkbook. Cash Flow looks healthy and shows no need for a cash infusion from the owner's credit line.

WHAT SHOULD I DO? Treat your Cash Flow Statement as you would treat your checkbook. Initially, examine your Cash Flow Statement daily. Forecast sales, revenues, and expenses at least three months into the future and determine the amount of cash you will need to make it through the forecasted period. In the early days of your business, check your Cash Flow daily. Failure to forecast cash flow can ruin your credit and even your business. If you do not understand your Cash Flow Statement, talk to your accountant.

Cash flow is remarkably simple once you get the hang of it. This may be the most valuable tool you have in the early years of your business. No prior accounting knowledge is necessary to understand your Cash Flow Statement. Cash Flow Statements are routinely used by lenders to evaluate loan applications.

Additional Resources: Accountant, bookkeeper, SBA

Accounts Receivable *(See also COLLECTIONS)*. Accounts Receivable, by definition, are monies invoiced to your customers but not yet collected from your customer(s), whether current or past due. The Accounts Receivable Department involves a wide array of duties, including billing, bank deposits, account adjustments, collections, payment negotiations, handling customer problems and questions, handling received payments (cash, checks, and credit card), account reconciliations, and maintaining customer billing files.

Accounts Receivable demand your attention on a regular basis. The longer an account remains in arrears, the less likely that it will be paid in full. Also, if you are borrowing money and utilizing Accounts Receivable as collateral, outstanding Accounts Receivable become less valuable to your lender as they age because older accounts are more difficult to collect. Do not neglect past-due accounts. When the economic environment becomes unpredictable, past due accounts should be visited more often and with greater urgency.

Accounts Receivable Aging Report (Figure A-6). Accounts receivable are displayed on an Accounts Receivable Aging Report, often called a Dunning Report. At a minimum, the Aging Report should include the information shown on the form. Many Aging Reports are void of customer contact information, but I suggest including that information on your Aging Report so it is always at your fingertips. Other information, such as order number, invoice date, original invoice amount, and amount paid to date should be included in the customer file. Email addresses may be added to your email files. You will also want to include new orders that are not yet invoiced. Your Aging Report will include all your customers' outstanding invoices. Each column is labeled with the number of days that an invoice has gone unpaid (0 – 30 Thru Over 120 days). To broaden the depth of this example, the following sample past-due accounts are not true to Accounts Receivable reflected in the foregoing Balance Sheets or Cash Flow Statements.

The ABC Company Accounts Receivable Aging Report tells us that collection activity is a bit sporadic. Jones Aircraft Sales is a sizable account that should receive immediate attention. Notice that Jones has $2250 in the 91 – 120 column. Jones paid $2250 upon purchase, but has not made a payment since. This may be a billing error, but the fact that they have paid nothing on their later invoice in the amount of $1500 begs questions concerning their ability to pay. ABC Company should contact Jones Aircraft Sales, correct any billing errors and get a solid commitment for payment.

Melton Rental Aircraft has paid $250.00 on a $500.00 invoice over a period of nearly 6 months. They also owe $150.00 on a more recent $1,000 purchase that sits in the "Over 120" column. Considering the small amount due and the time that has elapsed, an attempt should be made to settle both invoices with Melton immediately. The oldest accounts may be forgotten by Melton and the most recent account may have gone unpaid for lack of cash or an error on the invoice.

The fact that ABC Company has a small number of open accounts speaks well for the salespeople. They are apparently letting their customers know that open credit is not the norm at ABC Company and they are not offering credit unless it is demanded by the customer.

On the other hand, the small number of accounts that are past-due are going unnoticed and are eventually going to create losses if they are not addressed regularly.

Figure A-6

ACCOUNTS RECEIVABLE AGING REPORT
ABC Company
December 31, 2015

Customer	Contact	Phone	Invoice Number	Invoice Date	Invoice Total	0 - 30	31 - 60	61 - 90	91 - 120	Over 120	Total Due
Melton Rental Aircraft	Amy	330-555-7890	10485	7/4/15	500					250	250
Melton Rental Aircraft	Amy	330-555-7890	10685	8/5/15	1,000					150	150
Jay's Aircraft Repair	Scott	330-555-6524	10950	12/2/15	500	500					500
Jones Aircraft Sales	Joan	216-555-9874	10324	9/19/15	4,500				2,250		2,250
Jones Aircraft Sales	Joan	216-555-9874	10796	11/27/15	1,500		1,500				1,500
Fly Away	Mike	404-555-1010	10899	12/22/15	5,000	5,000					5,000
Cloud Nine	Keri	440-555-8881	10592	10/3/15	1,500			1,500			1,500
					14,500	5,500	1,500	1,500	2,250	400	11,150

WHAT SHOULD I DO? Stay current with your Aging Report and work it regularly. When a debt hits 90 days past due, the odds of collection diminish considerably. See the section on *COLLECTIONS for specific help with collection activities.*

Additional Resources: Accountant, collection agency.

Accounting Software: Most small businesses that employ less than 10 people do not require a full-time accountant or bookkeeper. An office assistant can gather all receipts, vendor payables, receivables, deposit slips, billings, etc., on a daily basis. Backup paperwork should be attached to vendor invoices to provide the necessary information to pay all bills once or twice a month, depending on your cash flow cycle.

An inexpensive accounting software program will allow you to neatly assemble your accounting information into a format that will generate a daily snapshot of the state of your business. Most programs provide the ability to issue checks, balance your checkbook, process payroll, track sales, invoice customers, purchase goods and services, and track payables and receivables.

Programs such as Quicken, Accounting Plus, Peachtree, and QuickBooks Pro are fairly easy to learn and have plenty of power to handle day-to-day bookkeeping functions for small to medium businesses. Specialized software is available for dentists, attorneys, doctors, manufacturers, and a host of other businesses. If you need software training, numerous classes are offered to acquaint you with these programs. Many are free.

WHAT SHOULD I DO? When selecting accounting software, get your accountant and bookkeeper involved. Selecting, installing and setting up your accounting software should be a team effort. Make sure everyone is on the same page before software is purchased. Your accountant should have the final word in software selection. When you involve your CPA from the start, you make life easier for everyone, which helps to minimize your present and future accounting fees.

In-House or Contract Bookkeeper? I know of a small business owner who paid a full-time bookkeeper to handle the accounting function for his business. The bookkeeper had no formal training and developed a multiscreen, spreadsheet agenda to handle all bookkeeping functions. Granted, the bookkeeper performed functions other than bookkeeping, but the major portion of his time was dedicated to duties that could have been handled more cost effectively. His most glaring error was the creation of a spreadsheet system that was easily outperformed by any number of small business software programs available for less than a few hundred dollars.

When the bookkeeper left the business, the business owner contracted with an outside service that performed the same bookkeeping functions, on a monthly basis, for less than the weekly cost of the employee. Often, a startup business may not have the budget to hire an in-house bookkeeper, thus putting the function outside until cash is available to transition the position in-house.

WHAT SHOULD I DO? Assuming that you do not have an accounting background and are not familiar with the day-to- day functions of a bookkeeper, take the safe route. Sources are abundant, but your best sources are your accountant and other business people you know and trust.

There are numerous examples of questions that might be asked of prospective bookkeepers on the Internet. The problem is that you must have an ample knowledge of the bookkeeping function to intelligently ask the questions and follow up on the prospect's answers.

Ask your accountant for a list of bookkeepers she trusts and would recommend for your business. Also ask for a list of typical bookkeeper functions. Call the prospects she provides, as well as those recommended by business friends. Talk to each prospect and ask the questions provided by your accountant. Ask your accountant to narrow the list, based on your conversations with the bookkeeping prospects. Interview the final prospects with your accountant and make a selection. You should come away with a bookkeeper who is on the same page with you and your accountant.

Additional Resources: Your banker, search firm, your accountant.

ADVERTISING

Advertising is paid or free communication to a target market to persuade prospective customers to become involved with a company's product or service. Advertising can take numerous forms and can be delivered through an endless number of vehicles. Advertising is not a pure science and nearly always represents a capital risk of some degree. Advertising is also necessary and should be utilized continuously.

When should I advertise? I once asked a seasoned advertising executive when we should advertise our boating products and services. He said he was not aware of the best time to advertise boats. I, of course, suggested that boats are seasonal products and that warm weather may reap the best response. He reminded me that most boat shows take place in January, nationwide, and that people actually start thinking about buying boats long before warm weather is a factor. In fact, he said, a lot of people buy boats in the winter months when prices are a little more attractive. I suppose I knew all this, but did not take the time to properly process my knowledge base.

What is the point of all this talk about boats? Most products and services are unique in some way. Create a chart featuring the top product(s) and service(s) that form the backbone of your sales. Determine the seasonal dips and rises in sales. Look for new market opportunities. Determine when customers really make buying decisions. Then put together your advertising campaign, based on solid information.

How much of my budget should be spent on advertising? It is extremely difficult to gauge the amount that you should spend on advertising. Generally speaking, spend 2-10 percent of your revenue. Some industries, of course, will fall outside these parameters, but 2-10 percent is a reasonable initial benchmark.

Consider the maturity of your business, the amount and type of effective advertising done by your competition, and the length of your season. If you are seasonal, strike while the iron is hot.

Most business people do not have an advertising plan. Mr. Advertiser stops by the office with dozens of vehicles for putting your name in front of the people who are going to knock down your door to purchase your products or services. You decide to put your business name on any number of calendars, signage, decals, cups, pens, pencils, paper weights, rulers, yardsticks, bumper stickers, television ads, radio ads, Yellow Page ads, Internet ads, social media sites, websites, refrigerator magnets, billboards, bus ads, scratch pads, bags, hats, sweatshirts, T shirts, and so on. The list is as long as your imagination allows.

Regardless of the amount of money you invest in advertising, be sure to give a selected advertising vehicle an opportunity to become successful. Most pundits say that six months is a good trial run. If it isn't working to your satisfaction after six months, switch vehicles.

How much should I spend on advertising each product or service? Pick the low-hanging fruit. Spend your advertising budget on the product(s) and services(s) that give you the biggest profit bang for your advertising dollars. If 30 percent of your profits come from product sales and 70 percent from servicing those products, you are going to want to spend similar percentages of your advertising dollars telling each story, unless market studies demand that you do otherwise.

The automobile market is a good example. A dealer usually makes a profit on the sale of a new or used automobile. If the dealer can capture that customer as her service provider for the duration of the customer's ownership of that automobile, the dealer will profit over and over again, on an ongoing basis. If the customer is satisfied with the service rendered, the cycle starts again when the customer buys her next car from the same dealer. Weigh your products and services in terms of unit numbers and profit margins and spend your advertising dollars accordingly.

Then again, if a vendor is willing to share your advertising bill, you may want to push his product a little harder AND advertise the balance of your products and services according to profit percentages. Do not make the mistake of spending your advertising budget on a slow-moving product because your vendor is kicking in a portion on the expense.

Should I hire an agency? Most advertising media salespeople can provide small businesses with a solid advertising campaign. If your campaign takes you out of your state or municipality or involves multiple advertisers and media, you may want to hire an agency. If so, be prepared to expand your advertising budget. An advertising agency will add approximately 15 percent to your advertising expense. Be sure that all quotes are turn-key and include extras such as creative fees, typesetting, express mail, printing costs, long-distance calls, postage, presentation and ad placement. Agree to the length of a campaign and a maximum expenditure. Include a clause that allows you to walk away from the contract if results are not up to your expectations. An agency should be given sufficient time to develop a decent campaign. Some campaigns show results immediately. Others may require months to produce desired effects. Determine your strategy up front and stick to it. The six month rule should apply here.

Who is my target market? Your target market is comprised of consumers, organizations, and businesses most likely to purchase your products or services when they see or hear your name in an advertisement. The trick is to put together a real plan that reaches *your* target market. Most business people think about advertising when a salesman walks through their door with a handful of pens. Keep in mind that a salesman typically does not have a clue about your business or how to effectively put your name in front of your target market. He is likely cold calling until he finds someone who is interested in his products and services.

Assume that you are selling automobile lifts and associated products and services. Who buys automobile lifts? Garages, automobile dealerships, people who work on their exotic cars, high-performance shops? All of these - and more. At least, that is how it appears to the average consumer. But if you are in the automobile lift business, you know that the list goes a lot deeper.

Every Regional Transit Authority in the United States has buses. These departments have large buses, small buses, and trucks. Decisions for such products and services are generally made locally. Most public school districts and private schools in the United States have at least one bus. Some have dozens. Many districts repair their own buses. They too need automobile lifts. Every city of any size in the United States has at least one garage in town that repairs large trucks. Lifts are manufactured that can handle trucks of any size and ilk. However, garages that specifically service trucks generally have pits. Their mechanics work under trucks in these pits and may not require lifts.

Can you see a target market developing here? You must do your due diligence and locate your target market accordingly. You must spend your advertising dollars where that investment reaps the greatest benefits. Ask the right questions. Do I advertise to truck garages and attempt to convince them of the efficacy of tearing out their pits and installing lifts? Or do I spend my dollars on advertising to entities that use my products and services regularly? You may want to do both, but the lion's share of your advertising budget should be directed toward existing and potential customers that will do business with you now, as well as in the future. Once again, pick the low-hanging fruit. Budget a small percentage of your advertising dollars for the market that is harder to reach, realizing that it may take time and effort to develop a market that no one else has tapped.

What about all those pens, pencils, flyers, websites, newspaper ads, and so on? What will your potential customer recognize as a good advertising piece? I can't give you the answer, and in most cases, neither can the salesperson who walks through your door with a handful of pens.

Real estate companies have relied on newspaper advertising, signs, and open houses as generators of prospective buyers for decades. They found a good method of advertising that works and they've stuck with it. Home security companies are currently enamored of telemarketing, newspaper ads, and direct mail. Landscapers like newspaper and direct mail. Credit card companies seem to depend on direct mail.

The point here is that you want to find something that works for you and put your money into that advertising vehicle(s). If your current advertising campaign is creating business, spread your wings with that vehicle. If not, keep looking. There are no patented answers to your advertising needs.

Take the information generated in the preceding paragraphs and apply it to discovering your target market. Ask yourself: Where and how are my competitors advertising? If it works for them, it may work for me. Where would I look to find the kinds of services that I offer? Experiment with various concepts and track your results. Ask your customers how they found your products and services. Once you find the right advertising combination, change it slowly, as necessary.

How often should I advertise? The answer is *often enough*. Most business owners try advertising, do not see immediate benefits, and quit advertising altogether. Advertising is a game of exposure and constant repetition. If you decide to implement a newspaper campaign, you cannot measure your results unless you stick with it for at least six months. In fact, the six-month rule applies to most advertising. Human beings require repetition to become comfortable with new ideas. Prospective customers must get used to seeing your name, logo, and products and services—it's called establishing a brand.

I attended an advertising seminar several years ago. I cannot tell you the names of the speakers, the name of the agency, or why I attended, but one thing sticks in my mind. Someone asked an advertising agency executive how and when he knows that an ad will generate sales. His answer? "I'll tell you after we run the ad. I really don't have a clue until the results roll in. We're as creative as any other agency. The truth is, I just don't know and neither does anyone else until after the ad has run."

Common theme in advertising. Everything the public sees from your company should have a common look, feel, and theme that are part of establishing your brand. Include your company name, logo, website, and phone numbers on your business cards, stationery, brochures, advertisements, promotions, signage, and anything else that bears your company name. The theme must be common to all advertising pieces and carried consistently in the same style, color, and likeness. You are creating recognition among your customer base and prospect base. Keep it simple with a common theme.

Logos in advertising. Logos are symbols or designs that are unique to a particular company or organization. You may not realize it, but when you shop you often look for the logo that represents the particular product you want to buy.

Your business logo, if you choose to develop one, should become an essential part of everything the public sees, from invoices and business materials to signage on your vehicles and advertising in the newspaper. The name of the game is repetition. Repetition equals recognition.

Advertising vehicles? You will find many different vehicles, or ways, to advertise to your target audience. Possibilities include a website, Yellow Pages, newspaper, radio, TV, card decks, word of mouth, mailers, door hangers, telemarketing, billboards, flyers, sponsorships, testimonials, point-of-purchase displays, signage at your business, vehicle signage, and newspaper articles featuring your business. The list is nearly endless.

WHAT SHOULD I DO? Look at the standard advertising vehicles in your market area and determine what other businesses in your field of expertise are doing with their advertising dollars. Check rates and compare. Do your homework and be smart with your advertising dollars. Start with your typical customers and ask them where they look first when making a buying decision for your product or services. Ask every new customer or prospective customer how he or she heard about your company.

AGE DISCRIMINATION

The Fair Labor Standards Act (FLSA) has an entire litany of laws covering working hours and wage and safety requirements for minors. Go to www.dol.gov for more information.

There are also age laws regarding discrimination against the elderly.

See also **www.eeoc.gov** (*specifically the section on* **Age Discrimination in Employment Act of 1967 [ADEA]**).

Note: Stay in touch with the basics of age discrimination. Investigate further if you have any doubts or questions. Making a mistake here can cost big bucks.

AMERICANS WITH DISABILITIES ACT (ADA)

Here is the purpose and breadth of ADA, as defined on the EEOC website:

"Title I of the Americans with Disabilities Act of 1990 prohibits private employers, state and local governments, employment agencies and labor unions from discriminating against qualified individuals with disabilities in job application procedures, hiring, firing, advancement, compensation, job training, and other terms, conditions, and privileges of employment. The ADA covers employers with 15 or more employees, including state and local governments. It also applies to employment agencies and to labor organizations. The ADA's nondiscrimination standards also apply to federal sector employees under section 501 of the Rehabilitation Act, as amended, and its implementing rules."[2]

Do not overlook ADA requirements in your business. Failure to comply can be costly. Regardless of your business type, investigate compliance with ADA and provide everything required by law. Ignorance is not an excuse for noncompliance.

***Additional Resources*:** www.eeoc.gov or www.ada.gov. ADA specialists can be reached at (800) 514-0301.

AMORTIZATION

Amortization is defined as: 1) retirement of debt, in regular installments over a given period of time, or 2) the retirement of the value of intangible assets, such as patents or copyrights, in regular installments, over a given period of time. Depreciation, often confused with amortization, refers to the same process but deals with tangible assets such as machinery, vehicles, and other capital equipment.

ANGEL INVESTORS

Unlike venture capitalists who typically manage pooled funds belonging to others, angels invest their own funds. Angels usually invest near home. They usually invest in businesses they understand. Angels will generally invest between $150,000 and $2,000,000 to provide the second round of funding after you have exhausted your seed money. The average angel investment is less than $500,000. They are generally looking for a return of 25-30 percent per year, for five years.

Angels vary widely in their expectations. They are somewhat easier to approach and require less time to bring a deal to fruition than venture capitalists. Their due diligence is less intense, and the money is available sooner. Angels will want up to 25 percent ownership in your business, more in some cases. Like venture capitalists, an angel will also want preemptive rights to maintain a percentage ownership in your company by participating in future stock issues.

At the outset, an angel will want board representation, so it is important to realize that you are really taking on a business partner for a number of years. Make sure you and your angel investor are compatible. The last thing you want is a hostile board member who has a good deal of control over your business operations. You are looking for a business partner who will bring more than dollars to the table. Your angel should be your confidant and sounding board. Pick someone with good, sound advice and goals that are common to your own.

Angels are not a lot different than venture capitalists, with the exception that a more personal relationship may develop with an angel. Both angels and venture capitalists want control, hockey-stick projections, huge returns, and ownership to some degree.

ARBITRATION (See also MEDIATION)

Arbitration is a process in which two or more parties agree upon a neutral person(s) to settle a dispute. The arbitrator is given the power to settle the dispute with terms that are legally binding to the disputing parties. Arbitration is generally a last resort when disputing parties fail to settle their differences via friendly agreement or mediation.

Why should I consider arbitration? Arbitration should be considered when all other avenues of negotiation are exhausted. Even though professional arbitrators are paid for their services, the arbitration process is generally more cost effective and less disruptive to your business than the involvement of attorneys to settle disputes.

*Additional Resources***:** Labor attorney, human resources specialist, American Arbitration Association.

ASSET-BASED LOANS

Also called equity-based loans, asset-based loans are secured by assets. If you fail to repay the loan, the assets you pledged as collateral against the loan are forfeited to the party holding the loan. Real estate, machinery, accounts receivable, and inventory are commonly utilized to secure asset-based loans. Asset-based loans are usually employed when normal loans, at normal interest rates, are no longer available, due to the subpar financial status of a company.

ATTORNEYS

You will notice a number of references to attorneys as you read through this book. Attorneys provide a valuable function in business when dealing with the tough issues, such as contractual matters, law suits, business creation, mergers, IRS tax disputes, buy-sell agreements, non-compete agreements, employment disputes, business formation and human resource issues.

Consider also, that attorneys are not created equally. The attorney you want on your team is one who is active with other businesses like your business and has a deep enough understanding of your operation and business philosophy to realize your needs and financial limits. You do not want an attorney who specializes in bankruptcies, divorces and nuisance suits.

WHAT SHOULD I DO? That said, attorneys can be very expensive and should be utilized as a last resort in most cases and a first resort in matters that could devastate your business. Always look at other, less expensive lines of defense before calling an attorney.

AT-WILL EMPLOYMENT *(See also TERMINATION / FIRING)*

According to the National Conference of State Legislatures, "Employment relationships are presumed to be "at-will" in all U.S. states except Montana. At-will means that an employer can terminate an employee at any time for any reason, except an illegal one, or for no reason without incurring legal liability. Likewise, an employee is free to leave a job at any time for any or no reason with no adverse legal consequences."[3].

That being said, there are still limitations to terminating an employee without reason. All 50 states have imposed additional legislation governing the ability of an employer to terminate an employee "at will." Consequently, it is in your best interest to be intimately familiar with the laws of your state before attempting to terminate an employee without cause.

The most common causes of wrongful termination lawsuits are as follows:

Terminating an employee for refusal to commit an illegal act.

Violating the termination procedures in your company handbook. For instance, you have outlined a four-step procedure requiring a verbal warning, a written warning, and a suspension prior to terminating an employee for violating your unexcused absence policy. You accelerate the procedure and terminate the employee after one verbal warning and one written warning. You have just given a terminated employee grounds for a lawsuit.

Terminating an employee for taking leave under the provisions of the Family Medical Leave Act (FMLA). If you employ 50 or more people within 75 miles, you are bound by the rules of FMLA, which guarantees employees up to 12 weeks of (unpaid) medical leave annually to care for medical needs of the employee or the employee's family *(See also FAMILY MEDICAL LEAVE ACT [FMLA]).*

The most common source of employee lawsuits is the collection of federal anti-discrimination statutes that should be common knowledge among all employers and employees. You may not hire or fire anyone on the basis of race, color, religion, sex, national origin, age, or handicap status. Age discrimination begins at 40.

WHAT SHOULD I DO? An at-will firing should be treated like any other termination. If you feel that an at-will termination is going awry, the time to call your attorney has already arrived. Do not attempt to handle a termination lawsuit without involving an attorney. You are not equipped to do so. The price of an attorney could be a fraction of the costs you may incur, should you decide to handle the case without legal representation.

Additional Resources: Human Resources specialist, attorney who has expertise in "at will" employment.

AUDITS

There are internal audits and external audits. It is important to know the difference:

Internal audit. For lack of a better term, an internal audit is a *discovery process* and may be implemented for a number of reasons. The internal audit is undergone at the request of management and/or the Board of Directors of your company to investigate the validity of your internal procedures. An internal audit is often performed prior to an external audit.

An internal audit is usually conducted by a professional firm that specializes in internal audits. If you are large enough to support an in-house internal audit team, that team may perform your audit(s), providing there are no conflicts of interest and the team remains independent from internal pressures. Most small businesses hire outside firms, due to the inability to fund an internal audit team. The following is a short list of reasons you may want to conduct an internal audit.

Compare actual inventory to book inventory.

Accounts Payable: Compare procedures regarding payment of bills, such as matching each purchase order to its accompanying requisition form, pricing information, shipping document, and approval process before submitting payment to the appropriate vendor.

Purchasing: Account for inaccuracies and inequities that result in unnecessary inventory, or goods that are passing through your system while creating benefit for someone other than your company (employee theft).

Human resources: Account for inaccuracies or poor procedures that may create potential lawsuits or losses due to the mishandling of employee relations, including notification of benefits, policies and procedures, actions resulting in termination, post-termination dialog, and termination packages.

Payroll: Account for inaccuracies in wages, commissions, and payroll deductions. Watch for unapproved overtime and phantom employees.

Accounts Receivable: Investigate your collection process for cost, procedure, treatment of customers, accuracy and legality of penalties, interest charges, and customer discounts. Also consider the validity of doing your own collections vs. hiring an outside agency.

Fraud: Investigate potential manipulation of facts and figures for financial gain – embezzlement or misappropriation of company funds.

OSHA Simulation: If you are a potential target for an OSHA audit, you may want to consider hiring a legitimate outside firm to simulate an OSHA inspection. The firm will visit your business under the guise of OSHA. The exercise is designed to detect deficiencies that could result in OSHA penalties. Employees are not told that the inspection is simulated. After the simulation, the inspecting firm presents a platform to management for preparing your operation for an actual OSHA inspection. This is perfectly legal and may be a useful tool if you are concerned about your company's ability to comply with OSHA requirements.

Additional Resources: CPA, The Institute of Internal Auditors.

External audit. At some point, you may want to hire an independent firm that specializes in business audits to examine the financial fitness of your company. External audits are typically utilized to discover specific problems with your business procedures or ethics.

Then, of course, there are external audits that are not elective, such as those conducted by the IRS to investigate the validity of your tax returns. In many cases, an independent external auditor can help you to improve your company procedures, thus reducing risk and keeping unwanted external auditors away from your door.

IRS (Internal Revenue Service). You just received notice that you are going to be audited by the IRS. You hurry to your bookkeeper and accountant and discover that you have done a poor job of keeping track of mileage, travel costs, entertainment, and a host of other items that you decided to ignore until the day of reckoning has arrived. You burn the midnight oil, attempting to construct an accounting of past earnings and expenditures that you hope will satisfy the IRS auditor. Finally, you give up and search for an alternative. Your company is in jeopardy. You are in big trouble.

WHAT SHOULD I DO? The first rule: Do not panic. Set up a meeting with your accountant; include your bookkeeper if your accountant agrees. Do exactly as you are told. If you are going to be audited, you want a CPA in your corner. This is a key reason to hire a CPA from day one. CPA's carry more clout with the feds than non-CPAs. When the time comes to meet with the IRS, your accountant does the talking. Not you. If you do not like the way your accountant is handling the process, say so in a private conversation. Ask the pertinent questions and give the necessary answers. Be sure to discuss strategies with your accountant before the audit. Provide guidelines to settle inconsistencies or indiscretions equitably and quickly. Why? Because your IRS auditor will find inconsistencies and indiscretions. This is a fact of life. Pay penalties promptly and alter your in-house accounting methods until you are following acceptable procedures.

Additional Resources: CPA, www.irs.gov.

AWARDS (See also INCENTIVES)

For business purposes, awards are planned, announced, weekly, monthly, quarterly or annual honors that are traditionally bestowed upon the most outstanding people in your company. Company awards should be plentiful, meaningful, and eventful. Awards are coveted by many and can be a powerful method for keeping your employees with you, year after year.

Types of Awards. Here are a few categories that are universally popular.

Safety awards: You have seen the signs—263 days without a workplace injury. The number changes every day. When an injury occurs, you start over at Day 1—1 day without an injury.

Safety is the number one priority in every industry. Some experts say that customer satisfaction is number one. I disagree. Reward your workers for safety, and they will stay safe. The business you save may be your own.

Quality awards: This is your number two priority. Reward quality. Quality extends directly to your customer—and to your bottom line. Quality should permeate every facet of your business. Produce a quality product or service, and everything improves, from profit to employee turnover. Lack of quality employees, quality products and services, and quality management can cost you your business.

Perfect attendance awards: Poor attendance always has an underlying motive. It may result from poor hiring practices, poor or unsafe work conditions, poor pay structure, poor management, or any number of personal reasons. Regardless of the nature of poor attendance, it can devastate a small business.

If your business is suffering from poor attendance, find the reason now and fix it now. Reward perfect attendance with a bonus, whether it is cash, a day trip, or even a day or two off with pay. Do not tolerate poor attendance. Poor attendance is insidious and expensive. Fix the problem. Start by rewarding top performers.

Performance awards: Poor performance is right up there with poor attendance. Poor performance is as entrapping as poor attendance and is usually spawned by the same set of circumstances. Poor performance must be stamped out. Get to the root of the problem. Reward excellence.

Sales awards: Sales are the lifeblood of your business. Without growing sales, your business is dead or dying. Reward sales performance. Great salespeople are tough to find. Reward extraordinary sales performance extraordinarily. Without sales, there is no business.

When should I present awards? Make awards immediate. Do not let great performance get stale. Surprise your employees. Do not be stingy. Award time is show time. Make everyone feel good about working for you and achieving personal and company goals. This is not a one-on-one event. Reward your employees in a group setting. Be sure to invite everyone, including managers and employees who work outside the building, such as service and sales personnel. Let others see what awards are available and that you stick to your word and pay out.

Note: Keep costs within your budget parameters. Be creative, not cheap.

Additional Resources: Internet and Yellow Pages (look for businesses that provide everything from trophies to vacations). Let your fingers do the walking or surfing, and you will come up with a program that is ongoing and effective.

Chapter B

BACKGROUND CHECKS

There are companies out there that perform background checks for a reasonable fee, and they are responsible for their errors. If you hire such a company, secure a copy of their license and insurance certificate for your files. Background checks are so inexpensive that you cannot afford to use your valuable time to do checks in-house. Background checks also may save your company from aggravating and embarrassing preventable incidents, simply because you took the time to have applicants investigated.

BANKS

Where should I bank? Banks specialize in a variety of areas. Some are interested in attracting home loans and small consumer accounts, but only dabble in business accounts. Others actively solicit customers for a wide range of business services. Many banks specialize in specific types of business loans, such as those guaranteed by the Small Business Administration (SBA). Some banks go one step further and deal only in specific SBA loans that are collateralized with real property. Some get involved in businesses that present greater risks.

Most full-service banks have a business group, staffed with individuals with backgrounds that qualify them to attract and deal with business accounts. Today's business group representative is usually armed with a degree in accounting or finance and may even be a CPA. Choose a bank that does business with businesses like yours on a daily basis. Consider your needs for a minimum of five years into the future.

Many small business owners feel they are not worthy enough or large enough to deal equitably with a full-service bank. Your bank does not choose you; you choose your bank. The days when bankers had business customers knocking down their doors to open new accounts are in the past.

WHAT SHOULD I DO? Meet with your potential banker. Consider convenience of location, banking hours, rates, hidden charges, incentives, services offered, lines of credit, and business loans. Ask pertinent questions: Do they regularly handle business accounts? Do they have a single point of contact for all your business needs? Do they provide e-commerce and credit card services to business owners? Are they a Preferred (PLP) SBA lender? You may not have a need for a SBA loan, but banks that have achieved preferred status with SBA usually employ personnel who possess more business savvy than those that do not carry the preferred designation.

You can never have enough friends at banks or other lending institutions. Freshen your bank connections constantly. Bank employees and positions are continually in flux, as are areas of expertise. Get to know the key players at a minimum of three institutions so that you are ready to do business elsewhere if your contacts or sources become limited or dry up at your current institution.

Ask your potential banking partner for references from business owners whom they service. If you are a manufacturer, ask for references from other manufacturing businesses, and so on. If a banker says his business customer list is confidential, ask him to make the call to the customer. He can introduce you to his customer and ask the customer to call you. Banks are continuously running advertisements that offer special deals when you open a new business account. Cover the most important bases first, and then give consideration to incentives. If the bank does not cover the basic essentials, the incentives are insignificant.

BARCODES/UPC's

Nearly everything you purchase today has a barcode stamped on it somewhere. In many cases, there are multiple barcodes. A barcode may be referred to as a Universal Product Code, or simply a UPC. A UPC looks like this:

Whether you offer products, services or both, UPCs are a valuable asset to your company.

Purpose. The UPC is a method of identifying a product, its genesis, and its description. The UPC code may identify your product as model MT5028, maple table, 28 inches high, 5' X 3', colonial style, varnish finish, manufactured by XYZ Company.

UPC's provide a method for identifying products without taking the product out of its packaging to learn its model, dimensions, color, etc. Furthermore, when the product arrives at its final destination, pricing can be added to the UPC information to allow store clerks to scan the UPC at the time of sale.

UPC's have a sizable litany of advantages. They are helpful in tracking and maintaining inventory control, accounts payable, accounts receivable, product function, sales events, numbering, warehouse organization, service, returns, warranty, handling multiple currencies, and other important product information. Most importantly, UPC's are universal and utilized by just about every business in some way.

WHAT SHOULD I DO? If you have plans to sell to any large distributor or retailer, you must have UPC codes on your products before they will be accepted for sale. Be sure you understand the purpose of UPC's and know exactly what you need before choosing your UPC system. Your expenditure is dependent on the number of products and variations you intend to produce or sell, as well as your plans to add products in the future. You must select the correct UPC-producing software and suitable application machinery to apply UPC labels to your products, packaging, and print materials. There are numerous companies that provide everything from label printers to sophisticated scanning machinery.

To get started, go to GS1. They are a not-for-profit organization that sets the global standards for UPC codes. Find GS1 on the Internet at www.uc-council.org or call them at 937-435-3870. They are willing to help in any way necessary to get your company on board with a UPC system.

BENEFITS

Employee benefits fall into two categories: those mandated by law and those that are optional. Three examples of mandated benefits are Social Security, Workers Compensation, and Unemployment Insurance. According to *Money-Zine.com* (2010)[1], optional benefits include a long list of employee favorites with the most popular being health care insurance, disability insurance, life insurance, retirement and pension plans, flexible compensation, and paid leave. Health insurance may be a mandated benefit, depending on the number of people you employ on a full-time basis.

Should I provide optional benefits? Some small business owners look at benefits as an expense they cannot afford, while others look at benefits as necessities that they cannot afford *not* to offer. If an employee feels that she will receive equal pay and equal treatment at more than one company, she will probably opt for the company that offers the best benefits. In fact, many employees settle for lower wages because a company provides superior benefits. The bottom line is that optional benefits make sense as soon as you can afford to provide them.

When and to whom? Most private sector employee benefit plans fall under Title I of the Employee Retirement Income Security Act (ERISA) and are subject to specific laws governing the offering of benefits and to whom benefits may, or may not, be offered.. Regardless of the depth of the benefits you decide to offer employees, be absolutely certain that you are cognizant of all laws governing benefits *prior* to discussing an offering with anyone other than a qualified attorney or human resources specialist.

False Promises. I have consulted with a number of firms where the owners or managers have promised future optional benefits to employees or new hires. In a few of those cases, employers lost employees at some point due to failure to follow through on past promises. This sounds rudimentary and unnecessary to discuss. It is also an extremely common practice to promise benefits before investigating the costs to a company. If you cannot provide it, or do not intend to follow through, do not promise it.

Vacation. I have never been affiliated with a company that does not offer some sort of paid vacation to attract and retain full-time employees. Some companies offer vacation benefits to employees who work 30 hours or more per week. Some offer paid vacations for full-time employees, only. This is your call.

Vacation is accrued as of the employee's hire date. A typical rule of thumb is as follows, for full-time employees:

1 full year of service	1 week paid vacation
2-5 full years of service	2 weeks paid vacation

6-15 full years of service	3 weeks paid vacation
16-25 full years of service	4 weeks paid vacation
26+ full years of service	5 weeks paid vacation

Based on these guidelines, an employee is entitled to one week of vacation after concluding a full year of service. Your employees should be given clear instructions for requesting vacation. Information should include details about how vacation is granted (seniority is most common). Supervisors should approve vacation requests, based on workload, as well as seasonal and operational needs. Vacation is based on straight time or base pay, excluding overtime, commissions, and bonuses. Most companies require a minimum number of days worked in a year to qualify for vacation. Excused absences are generally included as days worked.

If an employee quits or is terminated, he accrues vacation up to his last day of employment. For example, based on the chart above, if an employee quits or is terminated after five and a half years of service, he accrues vacation based on his sixth year. In other words, he is eligible for a total of two weeks for year five, plus one and a half weeks for year six, minus vacation already taken.

Holiday Pay. Full-time employees receive holiday pay. Employees who work holidays should be paid double-time. Holiday pay is straight time or base pay, excluding overtime, commissions, and bonuses for employees who do not work the holiday. Your employee handbook should include a clause requiring all employees to work the regular workday before and after a holiday to qualify for holiday pay. However, if an employee takes an approved vacation the day before or after a holiday, he automatically qualifies for holiday pay. Employees on medical leave should also receive holiday pay.

Typical holidays are New Year's Day, Memorial Day, July 4th, Labor Day, Thanksgiving plus the day after, and Christmas plus one additional day. Other optional holidays may include birthdays, floating holidays, Good Friday, other religious holidays, and President's Day. Government and bank employees enjoy a number of other paid holidays that are not typically included in your schedule.

Insurance. Laws regarding the offering of health, life, and disability insurance are numerous and straightforward. Benefit structures vary from business to business but must follow federal guidelines. Favoritism and discrimination are not tolerated.

Insurance is a costly benefit. It is also a key benefit in hiring and retaining valued employees. If you fall into a category where you must offer insurance, or if you feel that insurance is a necessary benefit, contact an insurance professional who knows the rules and can help you as you grow your business.

You may want to assume the entire cost of insurance or you may want your employees to pay a portion of the cost. You may want to provide basic health, life, and disability insurance to your employees and allow them to increase their benefits to include additional life, disability, and family coverage, at their expense.

Sick Days/Sick Leave/ FMLA (Family Medical Leave Act). The Family and Medical Leave Act of 1993 became law to allow unpaid, job-protected leave for people who find it is necessary to temporarily care for their families or themselves. The act covers companies with more than 50 employees. FMLA provides up to 12 weeks of unpaid leave per year for care of serious conditions of the employee, certain family members, and newly adopted or newborn children.

Most businesses offer a number of paid sick days. For further discussion, see ***Paid Sick Days*** in the section entitled ***PERKS (PERQUISITES).***

For more information, visit www.nationalpartnership.org and www.dol.gov

Sick Leave *[See **SICKDAYS / SICK LEAVE** and **FAMILY MEDICAL LEAVE ACT (FMLA).***

Stock options. Many companies allow employees to participate in programs to purchase company stock. Some provide discounts for some levels of employees but not for others. Some match 401K plans with stock rather than cash. Stock options should be reserved for high-value employees or individuals who you see as future partners in company ownership.

Pension plans. Pension plans are designed to provide retirement income to eligible employees. Pension plans that are offered to non-government employers are subject to the Employee Retirement Income Security Act of 1974 (ERISA) and IRS guidelines and restrictions. You may want to consider options such as profit sharing, gain sharing, or a 401K. Start by contacting your bank, human resources administrator, financial planner or insurance professional. Pension plans should be discussed with your attorney and CPA before proceeding.

401Ks. A 401K plan is a nice benefit for you and your employees. A 401K is expensive, but the expense you incur may attract and retain higher quality employees. Check several sources before getting involved. Know the law.

WHAT SHOULD I DO? If you are new to business or very small, mandated benefits are definitely a concern. Beyond mandated benefits, however, you will want to provide vacation to all employees, based on the vacation schedule mentioned above. You may also want to provide a minimum number of paid sick days per year – say three to five days. FMLA does not come into play until you have 50 employees within a 75-mile radius of your business. Health insurance may be necessary to hire and keep valuable employees and/or mandated by government regulation when you exceed a minimum number of employees who are eligible. Stock options, pension plans and 401Ks are not something a new or very small business will offer until growth and earnings allow.

If you remain small, your bookkeeper and accountant can track vacations, sick days and similar benefits. As you grow, involve a human resources specialist to keep you within the confines of the law.

Additional Resources: Human resources professional, your local Regional Development Board (they can compare you with similar businesses. Get on the board's mailing list, fill out the Development Board's annual employer survey and receive your community statistical analysis free so you can adjust your thinking annually.

BETTER BUSINESS BUREAU (BBB)

The BBB operates in the United States and Canada. The BBB is a private, neutral, not-for-profit, multi-franchise corporation that is in business to promote an even and ethical playing field between businesses and consumers. While acting as a liaison between both groups, the BBB provides reports concerning fraud, unethical business practices and scams that directly affect both sellers and buyers.

The BBB has adopted an A to F rating system for businesses. If you are willing to meet a special set of standards touted by the BBB, you may be eligible to become an "accredited" member, which requires payment of dues and provides a special logo for your business stationery.

If you believe that membership will improve your profit and community standing, check out the BBB website and consider membership.

Additional Resources: www.bbb.org.

BILLS

When to Pay Bills. If you are new in business, you may find that you are paying your bills when cash is available to do so. Many of your vendors will put you on COD until you have proven your credit worthiness. Once you have cleared this hurdle, you want to establish a payables routine. In a best-case scenario, you should pay your bills twice a month, on the 15th and 30th of every month. February bills, of course, are paid on the 15th and 28th. This allows you to stay current with 30-day terms and maximize early payment discounts. Payables are time consuming and more easily handled if you plan the event and allow your payables person to stay within the parameters mentioned above.

Who Pays Bills? Select someone whom you trust to be accurate in assembling the necessary information to proof payables and write the checks. You approve the items to be paid and then you endorse the checks. Do not use a signature stamp.

Your Role. Your role is to make absolutely sure that nothing is paid unless it is legitimate and due. Pay attention and scan bills for errors and duplicate payments. You are the last stop before the money goes out the door. I always tell business owners that they need to take the time to sign checks to vendors. I am not sure when this function becomes so time-consuming that it requires delegation. I do know that no one is going to watch your money as closely as you.

Who Gets Paid? Here are the rules:

> *Rule #1*: Never pay any bill before it is due unless an extra discount is available. Money is a commodity and is tied to a cost. If you pay a bill early, your vendor is reducing her cost of borrowing by using you as her bank.

> *Rule #2*: Take advantage of all discounts. If the terms are 2/10, Net 30, why wait for 30 days to pay the bill? Take 2 percent off the bill and pay it within 10 days. Your check must hit your vendor's

doorstep, at the latest, 10 days after the date on the invoice. Do not play games with vendor discounts. This is unethical and unfair to your vendors. If you are not going to honor the terms of a vendor's discount schedule, pay the bill on the undiscounted due date. Remember that you are building sound, long-lasting relationships. Treat your vendors with respect and they will reciprocate. Your reputation lasts a lifetime.

Rule #3: Never pay a bill from a statement. If you do not have the invoice, ask your vendor for a new invoice.

Rule #4: If you dispute any amount on an invoice, ask your vendor for a correct invoice or a credit memo to adjust the difference. You are not expected to make immediate payment as long as you contact the vendor regarding the billing error, upon receiving the incorrect invoice. Inform the vendor that the invoice will be paid when a corrected invoice or credit memo is received, based on the original payment terms.

Past-Due Fees: Past-due fees take two forms: Interest and late fees. Past-due fees remain unpaid 80-90 percent of the time. The vendor sends a monthly statement and piles interest on top of unpaid balances, interest and late fees. This turns into a nightmare for your bookkeeper. Stay in touch with vendors and discuss past-due fees. Let your vendors know from the get-go that you pay your bills on the 15 th and 30th of each month.

The majority of vendors will invoice you on the day of shipment. Most vendors also pay their vendors just like you, twice a month. Reach an understanding with troublesome vendors and the problem will likely disappear. The idea is to never pay interest or late fees on any bill. No one else does.

Additional Resources: Your bookkeeper, accountant, your errant vendor.

BOARD OF DIRECTORS

Who should be on my board? I am a magnet for names and numbers. I have a host of friends and acquaintances who I call on when I need advice. Some are absolute business geniuses. Some are authors of business lore. They range from past partners, employers, and employees to best buddies and relatives.

Those who know my business and know me are my advisors. I like people who challenge me and tell me when I am misguided and making a mistake. Sometimes I am not sure of what I don't know. When this happens to you, turn to people who are in-the-know and can provide genuine advice.

If you lack a knowledgeable circle of advisors, get out and meet people. Talk to your current business friends and ask for referrals. With a little constructive research, you can build a team.

You may get pressure from your banker, stockholders, attorney, accountant, or family members to add specific individuals to your board. You are entering into an informal marital agreement with everyone who sits on your board. Do not let others pressure you into offering board membership unless it makes sense. If you are considering a relationship with an investor, make sure you can live with board members who may not have your best interest at heart. Your board members, collectively and individually, have a fiduciary responsibility to your company, shareholders, and employees. They should not be chosen lightly.

Board Meetings. Board meetings are presided over by the Chairman of the Board, or someone designated by the Chairman of the Board. Board meetings may be inexpensive and held in a half hour over a kitchen table. They may also be very costly and time consuming. It is your choice.

There is no specific number of times per year that a board is required to meet. However, your board should meet at least quarterly, or as determined by your bylaws. Board Source tells us that 17 percent of boards meet monthly and that, on average, boards meet 6.9 times per year. Not-for-profit boards, however, are required to meet at least once a year.[2]

Board meetings should be conducted according to Robert's Rules of Order. If you do not have a copy of the book, go to www.robertsrules.com for information. Best place to purchase is Amazon.com. You can get a hardback copy for around $40 and a paperback for around $20. It never hurts to have the rule book if someone challenges the direction of a board meeting.

Board Agenda. Your board meeting should be guided by a written agenda. The agenda should require that the minutes of the previous board meeting are read and approved before conducting new business. After the minutes are read, you will want to clean up any old business that remains outstanding, followed by new business, and finally, anything that requires discussion that does not appear on the agenda. The board chairman is in charge of the agenda and must decide if any discussion is inappropriate for the meeting.

I have been to a number of board meetings that were not supported by an agenda. They are generally much longer and much less effective than those guided by an agenda. An agenda will help you maintain a business atmosphere. Members can socialize after close of business.

Company Bylaws. Bylaws are rules imposed on a company by its board of directors that require the company officers to follow a specific set of guidelines when conducting business. Bylaws address issues such as board of directors' meetings, locations of annual meetings, special meetings, quorums, voting, number of members on the board, vacancies on the board, term limits of board members, roles of directors, minutes, compensation of directors, stock issues, dividends, annual statements, indemnification and insurance, and fiscal year vs. calendar year. Your bylaws are your creation, established for your company.

How many board members? This depends on you and your shareholders. Try to keep the number of board members to a minimum for simplicity purposes, and odd in number to avoid gridlock when issues come to a vote. I prefer five board members, with a minimum of three and a maximum of seven. The larger the board, the longer it takes to reach a decision or a quorum. At the same time, you want enough board members to cover all facets of the business at hand and provide a quorum in the event members are unavailable.

Board Compensation. Compensation for a director(s) is outlined in your bylaws. The amount of compensation should be decided upon by your board of directors and paid to each director for serving on the board. Most companies pay expenses for board members who must travel to attend board meetings. Many companies financially compensate board members who are not affiliated with the company on a daily basis and must take time away from other endeavors to attend board meetings. Many board members serve on boards without compensation.

Board meeting minutes. The chairman of the board will call your board meeting(s) to order. The secretary will record every item discussed in its entirety from that point until the meeting is concluded. Minutes are not expected to be verbatim. Minutes are expected to be accurate and to include all dialogue necessary to allow a party, or parties, to easily decipher the scope and actions of the board meeting at a later date without the aid of additional parties to translate board members' intentions.

Minutes of board meetings must be recorded and presented to the board members prior to the following board meeting. Board members review the minutes for errors and notify the board secretary of necessary corrections. Corrected minutes are opened for discussion at the next board meeting. Minutes are voted on for approval by a predetermined quorum.

Board notification. Your bylaws should require that board members be notified personally, in a specific manner within a specific period of time, that a board meeting is to be held. Notice should be given in writing, at the board member's address of record, by mail, telegram, e-mail, or hand delivery.

Board proxies. Proxies give someone, or a document, the power to represent, speak, or vote for a bona fide board member. In the event a board member is unable to attend a board meeting, she may give her power of attorney to another or provide a written proxy statement to carry out her wishes as a member of the board.

Board quorums. A quorum is the minimum number of members needed to convene a board meeting, or pass a board issue, as set forth in your company bylaws.

WHAT SHOULD I DO? Your job is to create a board that is knowledgeable, cooperative, available, trustworthy and helpful in moving your company toward planned goals. Talk with your key management personnel, accountant, mentor(s) and attorney with a specific number of members in mind. Avoid "friendship appointments" such as relatives, friends of friends, or people you owe a favor. Choose board members as you would choose managers, supervisors or employees. If you would not hire someone to work for you, why would you put that person on your board?

Additional Resources: Your accountant, attorney, business consultant.

BONDING

A surety bond is insurance, guaranteeing that a party will perform according to a particular contract. If the insured party defaults, the offended party is the beneficiary of financial compensation.

There are three types of surety bonds: 1) Bid Bond: Guarantees that the winning bidder will follow through, enter into a contract, and provide payment and performance bonds upon award of the contract. 2) Payment Bond: Guarantees that the company performing under a contract will pay suppliers and subcontractors according to the contract. 3) Performance Bond: Guarantees that the company performing the contract will abide by the terms of that contract.

A number of rules and regulations exist regarding bonds. There are also a number of insurance companies that provide bonds. If the need for a bond arises, become familiar with a bonding company in your community.

Will bonding be a problem? If you are not well entrenched in your industry, you may have trouble securing a bond. If you have current or past convictions, liens, legal or credit issues, you may experience difficulties in finding a bonding agency. If you wait until the last minute to secure a bond for a project, you may be left without the ability to bid. Remember that an insurance company that provides a bond is telling the world that you are a solid citizen who finishes work on time, in an approved fashion, is fiscally responsible and stands by his work. If you have failed in any of these areas in the past, securing bonding may be extremely difficult.

WHAT SHOULD I DO? If you are considering a business that requires bid contracts, you should immediately investigate your ability to secure a bond(s). Your accountant or attorney almost certainly has a connection with a bonding agency. If they are not helpful, check the Internet or Yellow Pages for local bonding agencies.

If you have problems securing a bond, investigate the problem and ask what needs to happen to allow you to secure a bond. If you have never been bonded, see a bonding agency and determine your fitness for bonding prior to deciding to bid on a project that requires bonding. If you find that you are bondable, always present a new project to your bonding agency on the day you decide you are interested in bidding. This eliminates last minute problems that may prevent you from bidding and ensures that you are able to secure the type of bond(s) necessary for you to move forward with the project.

BREAKEVEN POINT

Do a little research on breakeven point and you will find it spelled as one word or two words, defined in a number of different ways and calculated differently, depending on the definition. For our purposes, breakeven point is that moment in your business when you finally are not losing money, nor making money. You are on a level teeter totter, leaning neither toward loss nor gain. You are selling the number of units necessary to cover your fixed and variable costs over a given period of time – usually a month – that creates a zero income or loss. Selling fewer units makes you unprofitable, and selling more units makes you profitable. Why is this important?

From your first day in business, you will look forward to the moment in time when you can say you are profitable. Breakeven usually occurs between your sixth and eighteenth month. New businesses most often hit the breakeven point around the thirteenth month. As you assemble your business plan, you will establish a breakeven goal, say, the end of your thirteenth month in business. The idea is to increase your sales from that point, moving forward with consistent growth until your profits mature to your business plan goals. Remember that a business plan is a living document, and that you are constantly adjusting to the current and future business climate. Consequently, your breakeven point may change in midstream, depending on the accuracy of your business plan research and assembly.

In essence, your breakeven point is one of the many goals of a well-rounded business plan. Granted, breakeven is important, but it is just a small part of the big picture and dependent on a multitude of other factors that will make or break your company.

Breakeven Point Calculation. Breakeven point may be calculated for a group of products or services – Sales Units - or on a particular product or service. For our purposes, we will forego the calculation of the breakeven point. Like any calculation, breakeven can be cumbersome if you are not mathematically inclined. Most business software will calculate breakeven in a few seconds with entry of selling price per unit, variable cost per unit and monthly fixed costs. I said earlier in this book that you must master Income Statements, Balance Sheets and Cash Flow Statements, individually and in terms of their interactions with each other. It is necessary to understand the basics of the breakeven point, but not necessary to master the calculation.

BURNOUT

You will find a lot of opinions out there concerning burnout and its causes and consequences for the individual and the company. Mark Gorkin, The Stress Doc and a licensed clinical social worker, is a nationally recognized speaker, workshop leader, and author on stress. He defines *burnout* as "the gradual process by which a person, in response to prolonged stress and physical, mental and emotional strain, detaches from work and other meaningful relationships."[3]

You know the routine. You get up at 5 a.m. You hit the office by 6 a.m. with intentions of catching up. By the end of the day, you are further behind than you were when you arrived. You have had a donut for breakfast and skipped lunch. You stay late, until 8 p.m. You get home an hour later. The kids are in their pajamas. Your wife is waiting for you to tell them, "Good night."

After the kids go to bed, you head for the fridge, grab a cold one and the closest thing to real food, sit down beside your wife and tell her about your day. By the way, you do this at least six days a week. Why? Because you cannot afford to hire good help. And if you want things done right, you have to do everything yourself.

Burnout can happen to anyone in your company. It will likely happen to *you* first. Why? Because you are the boss. Bad or good, everything rolls down to your level because you are the one person in the organization who understands how much the company means to you. Throw in the fact that no one else really understands the operation like you do, and BINGO, you are a prime candidate for burnout.

The time has come to face the fact that your current situation can, and probably will, cause at least one of two negative outcomes — and possibly both. It may ruin your company and put you out of business. And just as likely, burnout will damage or destroy family and work relationships.

Bottom line? When you reach this point, things are not likely to magically get any better. The fact is, they are more likely to get worse. Read on and you may find a light at the end of the tunnel.

First and foremost, you may recognize that you are a victim of burnout but refuse to admit it or do anything about it. Bad move! Time is of the essence at this point, and you have no time to spare. Get over that hump and face the music. Then move forward.

Second, you need a mentor, someone you trust who knows more than you know. You want someone who has the ability to understand you and your business. Read it again. I did not say that you want someone who understands you and your business. I said you want someone who *has the ability* to understand you and your business.

This expands your options to include a business consultant, someone you've worked for or worked with in the past, someone whose business skills you admire, or even an employee whom you respect. When I need a mentor, I talk to my wife. She is extremely sharp in business, knows my strong and weak points, and knows she can tell it like it is. If she cannot help, I have a number of other excellent sources.

Become a magnet for telephone numbers. Anyone who calls you for any reason, who may offer assistance on a future subject, goes into your contact database immediately. You will be surprised. When you need assistance with a tough problem, search your contacts first. More often than not, you will find someone you can call for help. Try it. It works.

Third, take action. Discuss your problems, your outlook for your business, your fears and your willingness to change for the better. Put together a roundtable with key customers. Find your weak and strong points. Pull out your business plan, starting at square one. Most of all, admit that you cannot pull it off alone. Admit that you need help.

Fourth, agree to a plan and follow it, keeping your mentor(s) informed as you go. The truth is, you have reached the point in your business career where you see failure at your doorstep and do not know what to do next. Follow the above four steps, and you will find the answer.

Fifth, when you see signs of burnout in others, take action. You will likely save a valuable employee.

Note: Delegation is critically important to growing your business. **Harvard Business Review** *featured an article in January 1990 by William Oncken, Jr. and Donald L. Wass called,* <u>*Management Time; Who's Got The Monkey?*</u> [5] *This is one of the finest articles ever written about delegation of authority. Read it thoroughly and digest it completely. When you learn to delegate authority, you will have learned to grow.*

BUSINESS FORMATIONS / STRUCTURES

Sole Proprietorship. This is the simplest form of business. You are the owner. You can do as you please. Just file a fictitious name form with your state, if your business name is different from your own. This is called d.b.a. or "doing business as." For example, John Doe, d.b.a. ABC Company. Your business cards will simply say ABC Company with your name on the card as president, owner, or whatever you choose as your title. Do not print your business cards until your d.b.a. is cleared with the state in which you file.

As a sole proprietor, you get all the revenue, expenses, debt, profit, liabilities, blame, and rewards. Your protection from creditors is nil, putting all your hard-earned personal property, business property, and cash up for grabs. You have unlimited potential—and unlimited liability. Avoid involvement in a sole proprietorship, in favor of a formal business formation such as an LLC. Most states allow LLC's with a single owner.

General Partnership. A general partnership is simply a sole proprietorship, in terms of debt and unlimited liability, but more than one person owns the business. In a general partnership, there must be at least two partners. Unless limited by agreement, there are no boundaries for any one partner. Every partner has unlimited liability, unlimited power, and an unlimited potential to make or break the business.

Although there are some tax advantages, this is absolutely the worst possible form of business. If your partner disappears with the goods and cash, you are saddled with 100 percent of the responsibility. Like a sole proprietorship, choose a formal business formation such as an LLC. You may also consider an S Corporation or C Corporation.

Limited Partnership. A limited partnership is essentially a general partnership with the addition of one or more limited partners. Limited partners have no management authority. Limited partners receive their compensation in the form of a dividend. Limited partnerships limit the liability of limited partners to an amount equal to the partner's investment.

Limited Liability Company (LLC). A limited liability company shares characteristics of partnerships and corporations. Only one person is necessary to establish an LLC in the majority of states. Liability is limited, and the benefits of pass-through taxation are still available. There is no double taxation unless the LLC elects to be taxed as a C Corporation.

S Corporation. Unlike a C Corporation, an S Corporation does not pay corporate taxes, thus eliminating double taxation. The profits and losses of an S Corporation are passed through to its shareholders. The shareholders then file individual tax returns. The S Corporation enjoys the benefits of partnership taxation and gives the owners limited liability protection from creditors.

C Corporation. A C Corporation is a legal entity. C Corporations are taxed entities because the C Corporation has the same status as an individual person. A C Corporation has its own tax return on which profits and losses are reported for purposes of taxation. Remaining profits are then distributed to shareholders in the form of dividends. Shareholders then pay taxes on these dividends at the individual level. Thus, taxes may be paid twice for a company operating as a C Corporation.

Why would I want to register as a C Corporation?

S Corporations are allowed only one class of stock. C Corporations may have multiple classes of stock. S Corporations are allowed a maximum of 100 shareholders. C Corporations have no such restriction. C Corporations allow non-US resident stockholders. S Corporations do not. C Corporations can be owned by C Corporations, S corporations, LLCs, partnerships, and some trusts. S Corporations cannot.

WHAT SHOULD I DO? All business structures have advantages and disadvantages. Rules for business structures may vary among states. Always get your accountant and attorney involved when setting up, or making changes to, any business structure. If you initiate any type of business entity through your state's official website, talk to your accountant or attorney before moving forward. If you have involved a venture capitalist in your business, the VC will demand that you are a C Corporation. Do not decide at the outset that you want a full-fledged C Corporation. Get smart. Get help. Seek the correct solution for your business enterprise. Always involve your accountant and attorney if any entity suggests a change in your business structure.

Additional Resources: Accountant, attorney.

BUSINESS PLAN

I once attended a seminar where the presenter asked how many people in the room were doing what they intended to do with their lives. About 5 percent raised their hands. Then he asked the other 95 percent how many of them had a life plan. Again, about 5 percent raised their hands. You may know where you want to go, but odds are that you will not achieve your goals without a plan.

Do I really need a business plan? Yes, you really need a business plan. If you were applying for a job, your prospective employer would expect a resume featuring your experience, past performance highlights, key strengths, and future direction. A business plan is your company's resume.

Consult your plan monthly, at a minimum, making adjustments as you go, so that you will achieve your goals. Do not get lost. Stick to your business plan and adjust as often as necessary to ensure success.

Who wants to see my business plan? If you are seeking an investor(s) or want a bank to extend credit, you will definitely need a business plan. If you are not seeking investors, you will still need a business plan to successfully manage your business and maximize your profits. If you seek counsel from a consultant, a business plan will probably be a requirement. A solid business plan shows that you understand your business. The business plan can also help you with a "Go" or "No Go" decision to move ahead with a chosen business.

What should I include in my business plan? Typically, a business plan covers five years. A lender generally requires two to five years. Among other things, your business plan should include complete financials and forecasts. The financials include Balance Sheet, Income Statements, Cash Flow Statements, and sufficient backup to support every figure and calculation. The first two years should be presented monthly. The last three years should be presented quarterly. A typical business plan runs 20-30 pages and includes every facet of the business.

Should I utilize a business plan template? I prefer New Venture Creation, Third Edition, by Jeffrey A. Timmons. Timmons' business plan format still stands the test of time, though it originally hit the bookshelves in 1977.[6] It includes an executive summary, industry information, market research and analysis, business economics, marketing plan, design and development plans, manufacturing and operations plan, management team, risks and assumptions, financial plan, and proposed company offering.

Timmons, however, does more than presentation of a plan. Unlike most business plan authors, he asks the questions that are pertinent to each section of the presentation. You pick the questions that are germane to your company, industry, products and services and mold them into a presentation. You may need some help with the prose, but you will definitely have the basis for assembling a first class business plan.

At first glance, you will probably think, "You must be kidding me. I'm not familiar with most of these terms. It would take weeks to put all this information together." Actually, it will probably take a bit longer. And, if you are not familiar with business plan terminology now, what are you going to do when you finally get into business?

Start your business plan now. Most of the information is easily obtainable. Your accountant can get you started on the number crunching. You will learn so much from the process that you will be forever thankful that you took on the challenge. You may even decide to alter your chosen business or consider an altogether different business, once you have finished your business plan.

The Internet is literally loaded with business plan templates, which can cost anywhere from free to several hundred dollars. Start your search with SCORE or SBA. Both sites are free, packed with information, and provide numerous templates and insights into a successful business plan.

What are financial projections? Projections are educated guesses. Your business plan financials are essentially a set of projections, based on research, designed to provide a roadmap for your future. You calculate revenues, profits, and losses that become your goals for the next five years. If you are already in business you will utilize two years of actual financials and three years of projected financials.

Should an expert check my business plan? It is always a good idea to formulate your business plan with your banker and CPA in the loop. These sources can lend assistance, making the process easier. You have a much better chance of securing a loan if your business plan is formulated according to your lender's guidelines.

Some of us can easily string words together and formulate ideas and facts on paper. Others are challenged when it comes to writing. A big part of a business plan is the ability to put your thoughts and facts down in a concise and organized manner. Many of us believe we write well until we discover that a banker, other lender or potential stakeholder expects something more. If you have any misgivings about your abilities as a writer, get your thoughts together, write the first few pages of your business plan and run it past someone at SCORE, SBA or a mentor. In doing so, you may save countless hours of composition that ultimately requires heavy editing.

WHAT SHOULD I DO? Obviously, I am convinced that every business should be founded with a well-documented, intelligently assembled business plan. The truth is that most business founders think about assembling a business plan, find it challenging and time consuming, and eventually punt. So, I ask you? Would you invest tens of thousands of dollars in a lottery ticket with the understanding that you risk losing everything – your life savings, home, and maybe your family - if you are not holding the winning ticket?

Sure, there are examples everywhere of companies that were founded without business plans that have made millions. There is also at least one company for each of those that flopped, leaving a trail of unpaid bills, bankruptcies and broken families. Read and reread this entire section and then call your accountant and local SCORE or SBA office and ask for help with your business plan. You will be surprised at the things you will learn about yourself and your business.

NOTE: I repeat, do not go into business without a complete business plan.

Additional Resources: Business consultant, business services group contact at your bank, accountant, Small Business Administration, SCORE.

BUY-SELL AGREEMENT

Let's suppose that you and a principal, or principals, own a company. All of you are active in the business and are dependent on one another to make the company a thriving and successful enterprise. If one of you is no longer able to work because of retirement, disability or death, who will take up the slack for the lost principal?

If the principal is deceased, his spouse will automatically inherit his percentage of the business. The spouse may know nothing about the business and cannot possibly fill the shoes of the deceased principal. Due to lack of any sort of agreement, the spouse now owns a percentage of the business, possibly a controlling interest.

Other possibilities have a principal retiring or quitting the business to go to another business. He owns shares in his present company and decides to sell those shares to someone or some company that is at odds with his present company. The situation should have been addressed long before the event.

These unpleasant situations can be avoided with a Buy-Sell Agreement that is financially backed by Key Man insurance *(See also INSURANCE: Key Man Insurance).* The Buy-Sell agreement is a legally binding instrument that supersedes all other agreements in the event a principal leaves the business for any reason. The Buy-Sell agreement determines who may or may not inherit or purchase the past principal's stock, who may or may not become affiliated with the business, and addresses insurance proceeds.

Most Buy-Sell agreements are supported by key man insurance. The life of each principal is insured, based on the value of his company stock and his intrinsic value to the day-to-day operations of the business. Premiums are paid by the company. When a principal dies, his spouse (insurance beneficiary) gets insurance proceeds equal to the value of the principal's stock. The stock is returned to the company and the company (insurance beneficiary) gets insurance proceeds equal to his intrinsic value to the company. The company insurance proceeds are designed to offset the loss of the principal until arrangements are made to replace him. The spouse is out of the picture. All insurance proceeds are tax-free.

If a principal leaves the company for any other reason, the Buy-Sell agreement spells out the terms for dealing with any stock owned by that principal. The Buy-Sell agreement may say that the principal's stock must be sold to the company upon the principal's departure, at a predetermined price. It may say that the principal may keep his stock but loses voting rights. In any case, the Buy-Sell agreement is the instrument that spells out stock distribution and stock rights when a principal leaves the company for any reason.

Additional Information: Business attorney, your life insurance agent

Chapter C

CAPITAL (RAISING MONEY FOR YOUR BUSINESS)

It is easy to burn through $20,000 to $50,000 in seed capital before you get off to a running start in your new business. I can assure you that every relative and friend who hands you a check in exchange for stock in your company absolutely expects to make a killing on that $5,000 you took in good faith. The same goes for your spouse, who may now be facing life with an empty savings account and a depleted 401(k).

For an investor, return on investment (ROI) can mean a number of things. For banks, ROI emanates from earned interest and fees on loans. For relatives and friends, cash is king. They love owning a piece of your company, but most believe they will get rich as a result of your business genius. Some of your friends may expect a lofty position in your company, qualifications aside. Anything less is unacceptable.

For venture capitalists and business angels, ROI can take the form of an ownership stake in your company and a seat on your board of directors. Both would prefer a day-to-day management presence. The message is clear. Before accepting capital, know the rules and understand the outcome if you win—or lose.

Seed Money. Seed money is usually $20,000 to $50,000, provided by a second mortgage, savings vehicles, friends, relatives, or others interested in investing in your new startup business. Seed money will be utilized for your business plan, business formation, setting up your financials, patents (if you invent a product), research and development, market research, and a working model of the product you intend to patent and manufacture.

Seed money is only the beginning. It represents the startup costs for your new venture. You want enough financing beyond seed money to carry your business for at least the first two years. For most new companies, the breakeven point is between six and eighteen months. The most common breakeven point is thirteen months. Breakeven means that you reach a point where you are not making or losing money *(See also **BREAKEVEN POINT**)*.

Next, you want to borrow sufficient capital to carry you into the growth phase of business, beyond breakeven and into years three through five. This new round of capital usually requires funds from a bank, venture capitalist, business angel, or other lending source. In a perfect world, you would prefer to always work with someone else's money and keep your savings intact. But, like my CPA, Randal Longacher, says, "Investors want skin in the game." *Skin* refers to the value of your cash, property or equipment that you personally put into the business. They want to know that you have something to lose if your business goes awry. Even though you want to utilize someone else's money, there is no money like your own money, or skin in the game, to help attract capital growth.

How much capital should I raise? After you have formulated your company and successfully completed your five-year business plan, you are ready to discuss capital formation. The key is your financial forecast. Focus on the first two years, month by month. Account for every cent necessary to earn your forecasted profit. Consider a worst case scenario. You need sufficient financing to get through rocky times, seasonal and economic fluctuations, and other opportunities or threats that may present themselves. Multiply your projected needs by a minimum of 1.5 and a maximum of 2. In other words, if you project a need for $100,000 over the next two years, consider $150,000 to $200,000, just to be safe. Most business people with tell you to borrow 20% to 30% more than your calculated capital needs. I suggest that you at least consider the worst case scenario.

Borrow what you need now, and make sure the balance is available when necessary. Do not borrow a lump sum that you may or may not utilize over the coming years. Money costs money. Borrow the cold, hard cash that is necessary to immediately move forward. Guarantee the availability of the balance. Expect your lender to demand your personal guaranty for every cent you borrow until your business is profitable enough and has enough acceptable collateral to borrow through your company.

Many emerging entrepreneurs open a home equity line of credit *(see also **HOME EQUITY LINE OF CREDIT / HOME EQUITY LOAN**)*, utilizing their homes for collateral. Your lender will typically allow a maximum of eighty to ninety percent of the equity in your home as a line of credit. Assume your home is appraised at $200,000, and you owe $100,000. Your equity is $100,000. Eighty percent of $100,000 leaves $80,000 available for a line of credit. If you have good proof of income and a good credit rating, a home equity line will typically bear an interest rate of ±1% below prime to ±1% over prime.

How should I raise capital? When your business plan is tweaked and you are satisfied with your capital demands, make your rounds to several potential lenders, including banks, SBA locations, and other possible sources. Remember that the SBA does not lend money but rather guarantees bank loans. Other sources to consider include business angels, venture capitalists, government assistance, and a long list of private lenders who are looking for places to invest. Some will want to loan you a minimum of $50,000 to $250,000.

I am constantly asked about grants. There are literally thousands of grants available, but they are not generally available to small business enterprises for any purpose. A word of caution: never pay anyone a fee to help you seek out a grant. You are wasting your money *(See also **GRANTS**).*

If you are looking for a larger amount, many investors are not interested in investing less than a million or even more. Seek out an investor who is familiar with your business type, ask for references, and talk to others in similar businesses who have experience with your potential investor. Money is not hard to find if you are willing to do the work to find it. It is the price of the money that will make or break a deal if you have a solid plan and a good product or service. Banks are your best bet because their money is less expensive than most other sources.

Who should I ask for money? Here is the rub: There are a lot of sources, but many of those sources are not compatible with your needs. Banks are the most common source of funds for businesses, however, most banks want you to be in business for two years and show a profit before considering you for a loan. When the market is down and unemployment is up, banks are not lending to startup businesses unless the new business is supported by a well-known entity and a proven management team. Hence, when things are bad, money costs more and the sources are fewer.

You are out there trying to find a source that is compatible. You run out of options and consider doing what too many first-time entrepreneurs might do. You get frustrated and pay too much for capital. That overpayment usually converts to a reduction of ownership in your company.

In some cases, you may be willing to give up control just to get into business right now. Remember, she who controls 51 percent of a company's stock controls that company. If at any time you own anything less than 51 percent ownership, you may lose control of *your* company. It also means that you no longer control your destiny. If the new majority owner decides that you are no longer necessary, she can terminate your employment.

Mezzanine Capital *(See also MEZZANINE CAPITAL)*

Venture Capitalist *(See also VENTURE CAPITALISTS)*

How many shares of stock do I need? Many small businesses start with 600,000 to 1,000,000 shares, depending on future plans for growth. Get your attorney and CPA involved. Do not attempt to sell stock without legal advice. The laws governing stock are plentiful and complex.

Should I select a business formation before I seek capital? Your business plan comes first, because the process will convince you to go—or not go. Once you decide to proceed, select a business formation, and then start seeking capital. Most states have a website dedicated to small business that will walk you through business formation and the acquisition of a federal I.D., tax license, business license and any other necessities for getting started. Your banker and CPA are other alternatives. The cost to file your documents is minimal.

Some consultants will tell you to seek seed money before selecting a business formation. I disagree. It is easier to find money once you have a business name and a legal entity. If you are planning on utilizing venture capital money, your venture capitalist will undoubtedly demand that you register as a C Corporation.

CASH DRAWER/CASH REGISTER

A cash drawer is any device that securely contains the cash and checks that are exchanged for payment of goods and services. Most retail businesses have cash registers that keep track of all transactions, segregating taxable and nontaxable sales. If you are going to utilize a cash drawer, invest in a cash register that calculates the amount of change returned to the consumer at the time of purchase. Even better, select a register that automatically sends change down a chute and into a cup where the customer will retrieve the coins.

State-of-the-art cash registers come with integrated credit card technology that allows you to accept any credit card. Of course, this arrangement is accompanied by various credit card fees. Negotiate the best deal possible. Start by surfing the Internet; utilize a local vendor if feasible. Be sure to select a company that provides 24/7 customer service and a technical support line.

What if my cash drawer does not balance at day's end? The first step is to make sure the till is actually short. Check and double check. The next step is to look for the obvious reasons. Be calm. Do not make accusations unless you can prove them beyond any reasonable doubt. Do not threaten the suspected employee or thief. Get Human Resources or your attorney involved before you call the proper authorities. An imprudent action could cost you a lot more than the stolen property *(See also **THIEF IN THE HOUSE**).*

Should I always handle my own money? This is a tough question to answer. I have a friend who owned a restaurant some years ago. He told me that the only way to make money in the restaurant business is to make sure no one else handles your money. Is he correct?

There are more ways to steal from a business than you can count. The lion's share of business theft is initiated or carried out by employees. If you are a one-person operation, handle all the money. If not, hire the right people. Do background checks on all potential employees. Put up deterrents, such as cameras. Keep safes locked. Do an accounting of your intake every day. Do not give people a reason or opportunity to steal. Utilize the same precautions with relatives and friends that you would utilize with any other employee. Set the rules in advance. Stick by them.

Who is responsible for the cash drawer? Each individual is responsible for the cash drawer during his or her timeframe at work. One person = one drawer. Two people = two cash drawers, and so on. Any other method puts too many hands in the till to draw any meaningful conclusions if the drawer is short or over. Cash registers are available with more than one drawer.

Should two people count the cash drawer? Count the drawer(s) before the shift starts and after the shift is over. If you take walk-in business, invest in a smart cash register that requires passwords and has multiple drawers for multiple employees. Cash should always be counted by at least two people. Even if theft is not a problem, two heads are better than one when a cash drawer is short or over. Whether you are dealing with a pre-shift or post-shift drawer, the money is always counted by two people.

Should I watch the cash drawer with a camera? Cameras are deterrents; always record the action. Put cameras over your register, in your money room, and looking at your safe.

Watch your customers on the other side of the counter if you have a business with a cash register. Put up signs reminding everyone that your business has camera surveillance.

Sweetheart Rings. A sweetheart ring is a sale that is not recorded. A clerk purposely passes merchandise through a register without ringing up a sale. The recipient of the merchandise walks away without paying.

Of course, a cash register is not necessary to be a thief. Be on the watch for merchandise that finds its way out the door with an employee's help. The best deterrent is a camera over your sales counter and all entry and exit doors. In absence of a sales counter, count inventory often, limit access to inventory, bar tag merchandise and keep track of everything that leaves your business. You are going to experience shrinkage. Keep it to a minimum. Do not aid the process with inaccurate bookkeeping and carelessness.

Should I prosecute thieves? The best policy is ***prosecution of thieves.*** Never threaten unless you intend to follow through. Once the message is on the street, employee and customer theft should slow considerably.

Prevention: The best medicine is prevention!!! See the section on *SECURITY / SURVEILLANCE.*

Additional Resources: Your attorney, bookkeeper, accountant, security company.

CASH RESERVE

Cash reserve is a rainy day savings account that you tuck away over a period of time. Initiate your cash reserve account after you have paid down your debt, since debt interest will cost more than the interest you would earn on a cash reserve account. The funds in this account are not earmarked for any particular expense or emergency. You should consider putting the money into short-term CDs, money market accounts, government bonds or other liquid funds that convert to cash immediately, at a minimal cost.

How should I utilize my cash reserve? Cash reserves can be utilized for emergencies. Or they can be utilized for a good deal you cannot refuse. Cash reserves are not earmarked for a particular project unless you choose to do so.

> *Example #1:* Your high-speed, automated powder coating line went down two hours ago. To make matters worse, you are halfway through an emergency order of 250,000 pieces. You can fix the problem for $22,000 and be up and running by tomorrow afternoon. Your cash reserve account is earning less interest than the cost of borrowing from your credit line. Utilize your cash reserve account to pay for repairs on your powder coating equipment.

> *Example #2:* You need a welding machine. A competitor just went under and needs the money. He has the machine you want. It is only two months old. You need $30,000 and would rather not finance if at all possible. Utilize your cash reserve if it is earning less interest than you would pay if you borrowed the money from your credit line.

How much should I keep in cash reserve? The amount of necessary cash reserve is different for every business and every situation. As a rule of thumb, a 90-day cash reserve should be sufficient. A 90-day reserve will carry your business up to 90 days if the need arises. Remember that cash is a commodity and has a cost associated with it. Your cash should always go where it does the most good now and in the future.

WHAT SHOULD I DO? Your accountant understands the relationship between your interest-bearing debts and a potential cash reserve. Seek your accountant's advice and make sure you fully understand the alternatives before coming to a decision. A credit line may suffice for a cash reserve.

CELLULAR PHONES

It is tough to do business today without a cellular phone. Cell phones were once considered necessary evils because of the huge cell bills that were often associated with their use. Today, you can control cell phone usage and cost by adding and deleting services via your contact with your cell provider.

Make sure that one person in your organization is responsible for distribution and usage of cell phones. Discuss cell phone limitations before that person takes over the program. Provide a wall charger, a car charger, a hands-free earpiece, and a good quality holster for the phone. Provide penalties for damaging or losing the phone or extraneous equipment. Put everyone on the same plan so that minutes are shared among the group.

Who owns the cellular phone(s)? Your company owns the phone(s). You want to maintain control of all cell phones and all cell phone usage.

Whose name is on the account? Your company name is on the contract for the account. All bills are paid by your company.

Limits on cellular expenses. Be careful because minutes add up quickly! You would not believe the horror stories that I have personally witnessed with the misuse of cellular phones. I have seen bills in excess of $1,000 the first month a new user gained access to a cellular phone. The amount may seem miniscule to some, but it was gigantic and unexpected with this particular user. Cellular phones can become expensive toys in the hands of the wrong people. Cut your losses by limiting your responsibility upfront, contractually, and in writing.

The bottom line on cell service is the bottom line. Demand fixed pricing on everything. No surprises. If you do not understand what you are getting for your money, keep asking questions until you are comfortable with the jargon and the program. Cut off services that are unnecessary so accidents do not occur, such as accidentally logging onto the Internet and creating a huge bill. Remember, services such as texting, Internet access, sending and receiving pictures, roaming and three-way calling may be extra, depending on your program. If it is unnecessary, do not include it in your package. You may want unlimited voice usage. If an employee abuses the system, you know your potential expenses; budget accordingly.

Driving while talking on a cell phone. No one should be on a cell phone while driving. Dr. David Strayer, a psychology professor at the University of Utah, says the level of impairment while driving and using a cell phone, including hands free, is similar to driving while intoxicated.[2] You do not want to be responsible for an employee's accident because he was talking on a cell phone.

Put a directive in writing. No one is to talk or text on a company or personal cell phone while driving on company business. Nor is anyone to drive while talking or texting on a company cell phone at any other time. Have the directive signed by every employee, whether or not the employee has a company cell phone. This directive may save your company in the event an employee has an accident while driving and talking or texting on a cellular phone.

Employee Cell Phone Contract: Each cell phone user must endorse a simple agreement that makes him responsible for the phone. If the phone is damaged, lost, stolen, or used by someone else, the responsibility belongs to the user. If an employee uses the phone for personal business, treat it like any other violation of company policy.

Employee-owned cell phones. Some companies prefer to utilize employee-owned cell phones. Do not let your employees use their personal cell phones in your business unless you and the employee agree to a predetermined, fixed cell phone expense. In this case, the cell phone is in the employee's name. The employee pays for the cell phone bill, regardless of the amount. The employee also signs all other company cell phone directives. This almost never works. The employee agrees to a fixed expense, then exceeds the expense and asks for more. If you pay the employee more than he spends on the phone, you feel as though the amount should be lowered.

Also, beware of employee cell phones that play messages that are detrimental to your business. If you must have cell phone access for your employees, contract for company phones that are controlled by you.

WHAT SHOULD I DO? Talk to several cell phone vendors. Negotiate for the best available contract. The larger the need, the better the deal. National companies have gobbled up most of the pretenders. Depending on your location, a particular company may give better service than others. In my travels, I have found areas where my business phone (vendor "A") gets great reception and my personal phone (vendor "B") gets poor reception. In a different location, the results are just the opposite. Most national systems have good reception along major highways and in major cities, but fail in outlying areas.

Buy what you need, not what each employee wants. Stay within your budget. Everyone wants a smartphone, today. If you do not require a smartphone, investigate other options. Be aware, however, that cell phone providers will eventually probably do away with everything but smartphones.

Deals on cell phones can be found in your local newspaper, on the Internet, at store kiosks, and at Sam's Club, Costco, and dozens of other outlets. Check out the large companies. They normally offer the best coverage. Design *your* plan for *your* usage. Do not waste money on unnecessary extras. Keep your expense accounts in check with good common sense.

CHARITIES

Ask yourself if giving makes sense for your business. In each case, think it through and make your decision based on the negative or positive effects on your company, in terms of dollars and cents, as well as the public eye.

Give whenever possible. Keep all gifts legitimate and above the table. Be sure your gift is deductible. Be generous if your budget allows it. Weigh the efficacy of the act. Give gifts that benefit your company. If you want to give to a cause that does not benefit your company, give from your personal checkbook. If you receive something in return, all, or a portion of your gift may not meet IRS criteria for charitable deductions. Budget charitable gifts, and stick to your budget.

Receiving. Thank the giver(s) profusely. Do not accept forbidden fruit. Do not accept anything with strings attached. Stay within IRS boundaries.

How much should I give? An overly expensive gift is not necessarily a better gift. Size matters to the extent of your relationship with the receiver. Always consider the state of your company when considering any gift. Your financial solvency is a function of your ability to give.

Additional Resources: Talk to your account about the deductibility of charitable gifts.

CHECKING ACCOUNTS

Where should I open my business checking account? What will your bank do for your business? I prefer banks with national exposure. You may prefer a regional bank because you have an inside track to better rates and great service. Small banks may offer free checking but may not provide the other services necessary to make them a good choice for business banking.

In the final analysis, select a bank that routinely deals with businesses, has a preferred status with SBA, provides online banking, has enough branches to easily service your needs (nationally if necessary), and charges reasonable fees.

Your bank will require you to obtain a federal Employer Identification Number (EIN) before allowing you to open a business checking account. EINs are 9-digit numbers that are issued by the IRS for tax purposes. Sign up for your EIN at www.federal-ein-application.com, or investigate your Secretary of State's website for instructions.

When considering a credit union, be sure that their hours of business are compatible with your hours of business. Credit unions may also provide valuable benefits to your employees, such as free checking accounts, low-interest loans, higher interest rates on savings accounts and CDs, and low-interest credit cards. These benefits are great for your employees and add no cost to your company. Credit unions are not currently affiliated with SBA. You may want a relationship with a bank and a credit union, with certain transactions reserved for each institution.

How many checking accounts do I need? I did some work a few years ago for the owner of a firm that utilized two checking accounts. He wrote checks from one account for 60 days, and then switched to the other account for the next 60 days. His theory was that each checkbook self-reconciled during the 60 day usage of the other. Not a bad idea.

Most companies utilize a single checkbook for all transactions. If you own multiple entities, utilize a separate checking account for each entity. Do not co-mingle funds among companies. Do not co-mingle personal and business funds. The IRS is not fond of this practice.

How many signatures on a check? You, as company owner, will definitely sign checks. Your Chief Financial Officer (CFO) will also sign checks. If you feel a third signer is necessary, based on your continual absence due to travel, a minority partner who is active in the business can sign checks in your absence, but only with your permission.

If your spouse holds one of the above-mentioned positions in the business, he or she should be considered. Nonworking spouses should not have signature access. You will probably want to require two signatures on checks that exceed a predetermined amount, say $5,000, if you are a very small business. A larger business will require two signatures on much larger amounts.

The requirement for two signatures is not just an in-house rule. Your bank will require your written approval. A number of banks will not accept two-signature checking accounts because of the additional monitoring necessary. Some banks will only accept two-signature checking accounts for specific industries and organizations. It may take some research to find a bank that will accommodate a two-signature account.

How much money should I leave in the company checking account? Leave enough in your checking account to cover day-to-day operations. Money is a commodity and bears a cost. Many banks provide free checking if you leave a pre-determined minimum in the account. Some banks and credit unions do not require minimums in free checking accounts. Interest on business checking accounts is miniscule, so you are better off parking your unutilized funds in an interest-bearing savings account, or reducing your credit line during the periods between payables and payrolls. Put your money where it reduces debt or adds value at the most profitable percentage.

Who should make checking account deposits? Choose someone you trust. Check bank receipts to detect alterations or errors. Lock up your deposit slips along with your checkbook.

What kind of deposit slips? You may opt for multiple-copy, NCR-deposit slips. NCR stands for *no carbon required*. NCR deposit slips come in loose leaf books. Each page contains three or four slips, depending on the structure of the book. This system provides a permanent hard copy of every deposit slip, from day one.

Many companies utilize voucher checks. Each check has a voucher attached that explains all transaction particulars. The voucher is torn from the check and is utilized by the receiving party as a record of the transaction.

Laser checks are another alternative. Purchase laser checks that are compatible with accounting software, such as Quicken®, Peachtree® or QuickBooks®.

How careful is the bank with deposits? Banks do not have time to add up a stack of checks for a deposit that you take to a teller. The same goes for night deposits or deposits that are picked up by an armored truck service. The deposit is later counted at a clearing house and reconciled. Any discrepancies will be accounted for and recorded by the bank's clearing house.

Does the bank really pay attention to signatures? I have seen checks get through the banking system without any signature at all. Bank tellers do not know if the signature on a check is valid. I have never banked where a teller has a sample of my signature on hand. Bank tellers do not know if a check requires two signatures. I have personally seen a number of checks that have gone through the banking system that required two signatures but were processed with only one. Do not depend on your bank to check signatures.

Should I put everything on one deposit slip? Put as many checks on a deposit slip as possible. There is less paper to handle when you are reconciling your checking account, preparing for an audit, or preparing for taxes. If you have a particular reason to separate a group of checks – example: you may feel strongly that they will bounce – put them on a separate deposit slip from your other checks.

Should deposits be written in ink only? The bank does not require ink. But for your safety, you should always use ink. It is not foolproof, but it helps to prevent alteration of your deposit slips.

Should I bank online? Online banking is here to stay. It is generally a safer and more efficient use of your time than making multiple trips to your branch bank to move funds and pay bills. My bank is nationwide and claims that online banking is extremely safe. Banks must answer to the federal government if safeguard standards are violated.

Here are a few caveats:

Utilize complex account IDs and passwords that have absolutely nothing to do with you, your family, or your business. Utilizing birthdates and middle names, or things that are remotely familiar are taboo. Do not be lazy when creating passwords. Use letters and numbers. If your banking system allows symbols, utilize them. Example: Jj5Eo08kxX3. I know, you want a password you can remember, but if you can remember it, someone else may figure it out.

Change ID passwords frequently. My banker suggests that I enter new IDs and passwords every quarter.

Do not write down your IDs and passwords and keep them in sight. If you must write down an ID or password, make the information unavailable to others.

Never, never, never share your ID or password with anyone. This means family members and business partners. First, if someone steals from your account, everyone is suspect, including you. Secondly, people have difficulty remembering complex passwords. If you share your password, the other person will probably write it down. If you cannot recall your User ID or password, your bank provides on-line help.

Log in only if you expect to make an online transaction or update your accounts.

Log out immediately upon finishing your banking business. My bank also suggests that after I log out, I close and re-open my Internet connection before I log in again.

Never leave your computer while you are logged in.

Watch your accounts daily. If you have a bookkeeper or CFO in your organization, that is wonderful. Watch your accounts. Watch your money.

I prefer that two people in an organization have access to online accounts; you, plus your bookkeeper or CFO. If your CFO prefers that he and your bookkeeper have access, the CFO must accept responsibility for himself and the bookkeeper.

Take advantage of your bank's online alert capabilities. Set up your accounts so that you are notified of any extraordinary transactions that are overly large, generated overnight, ATM-generated, overdrafts, or unscheduled payments. Most banks have a laundry list of activities that spawn instant alerts that are sent to selected email addresses or texted to a your smartphone.

Should I sign blank checks in advance for convenience? Absolutely not! Never sign a blank check for anyone or anything. This is a steadfast rule. If the check lacks a payee or a specific written amount, it is not to be signed.

Should I utilize a computer-generated signature or a signature stamp? Call me old fashioned, but if it is not a payroll check that is generated and auto-signed by a company or program that specializes in payroll, I want to see that check and personally endorse it before it is mailed. I realize that many CEO's do not have time to sign checks. If that is the case, designate your CFO or another qualified employee or associate to endorse all checks up to a predetermined amount. Anything over that amount, or any expenditure that is out of the ordinary, should come to your attention before the check is disbursed.

Signature stamps have no place in business and should be forbidden. They usually reside on a stamp carousel or in the top drawer of the owner's or CFO's or bookkeeper's desk. Do not use a signature stamp under any circumstances.

Who is really in charge of the checkbook? You make the rules, designate a single individual to control the checkbook, and then abide by your own rules. Typical choices are your CFO or bookkeeper. If you have a CFO, she will decide who controls the checking account(s) – with your blessing, of course.

What backup should I require to sign a check? Always require a purchase order, a packing slip, and an invoice before agreeing to sign a check. Never allow a bill to be paid from a statement. No invoice = No payment.

Checking account floats. In the days before the prominence of computers, it was common practice to assume that a check would not clear the bank until a few days after it was deposited. That is no longer the case.

Be sure the money is in your checkbook the day the check is written. If your check bounces, you are sending a negative message to the employee or vendor who received the check. The message? Your business is in deep financial trouble. You have created a stigma that will pass through your company at lightning speed and will not go away for quite some time, not to mention the extra expense incurred.

Checking account fees. Bank checking account fees are numerous, at an all-time high, and continue to increase in price. A mismanaged checking account can easily result in hundreds of dollars of fees monthly. Before opening a checking account, ask the bank for a list of bank fees. The list will surprise you. The prices will surprise you. Be aware and be informed.

NSF checks. NSF stands for *nonsufficient funds*. The NSF check may be generated by your company or received as payment from another source. The NSF check has been presented to the bank and the account from which it was written does not have sufficient funds to cover the check. The check writer is charged a NSF fee for writing a bad check. NSF fees can pile up quickly.

Most businesses charge the customer a hefty fee for handling a NSF check. NSF fees generally range from $25 to, as high as $50, depending on the size and frequency of bad checks. Post a sign at each register if you intend to charge a fee.

A host of unpleasant situations may arise from receipt of, or writing, a NSF check. If a customer's NSF check is large enough, it may affect other checks written from your account. I know of a company that performed a large percentage of its work for a single customer. The customer paid weekly. Every Friday, the owner would wait for the mail delivery, deposit the check immediately, and hand out payroll checks to a dozen employees. You guessed it. The customer's check bounced. The company's payroll checks bounced. Not a pretty sight. About half his employees also bounced personal checks as a result of their NSF payroll checks. To his credit, the company owner paid for all NSF fees incurred by all employees. As you may imagine, fees amounted to several hundred dollars.

When you are the victim of a NSF check. If you are victimized by a NSF check, you may choose to take civil or criminal action against the check writer. Most municipalities have a division, or a person dedicated to dealing with NSF checks.

Contact the person or company that issued the check and request immediate payment, including any fees assessed by your company or your bank. Be sure you are aware of all the potential damage before settling the NSF. Tread lightly until you are sure that the NSF was intentional.

During the process of funds recovery, you will want to ask pertinent questions about the reason for, and meaning of, the NSF check. This is not a subject to be discussed with a payables clerk or a salesperson. Get in touch with the company controller, CFO, or a principal before proceeding. NSF checks are taboo in business and often create an atmosphere that quickly converts to distrust among employees of both companies involved. If the NSF check was written in error, you do not want to stir up dissension among the employees or owners of another company by talking to the incorrect party.

If you find that a company is in trouble, you may want to let their checks clear prior to delivering additional goods or services. If it happens twice, you may want to change their terms to C.O.D. Regardless, a NSF check should always be investigated with a specific procedure, being sure to completely understand the situation before coming to a decision.

When you write a NSF check. If you write a check that bounces, contact the affected vendor and make immediate restitution. Assure the vendor that the overdraft was caused by an oversight or error and that your business is financially sound. Offer to pay any fees that may have resulted from your NSF check.

Contact your bank and explain what happened. Assure your banker that all is well financially and that the situation will not recur. If you are a first-time offender, your banker may agree to reverse penalties and fees that resulted from the overdraft. Revisit overdraft protection and be sure that the bank is exercising this option appropriately. Banks also make mistakes from time to time.

Revisit your checking account procedures. Have your bookkeeper, CFO, or whoever is in charge of your checking account walk you through your checking account routines. Ask if there are any procedures that are not being followed. Be firm. This cannot happen again.

Overdraft Protection. Talk to your banker about an automatic link to a savings account, credit line, or credit card in case of an overdraft. If your checking account is in danger of overdraft, funds will be transferred from the linked account to cover your shortage. There is usually a fee for overdraft, regardless of the vehicle that feeds the necessary funds to the over drafted checking account. Credit cards should be a last resort since the fees and interest for cash withdrawal from credit cards are much higher than other available choices.

You can also provide overdraft protection by carrying additional funds in your checkbook to assure that an overdraft will not occur. Depending on the size of your business, instruct your bookkeeper or CFO to put an extra amount in your checking account that is substantial enough to cover potential overdrafts. This is not a solid practice and should only be utilized on a short-term basis if no other solution is available. Checkbooks should be handled with great care and should not require such tactics to guard against errors.

Should I post-date checks? No! It is not illegal to issue a post-dated a check. However, the potential problems outweigh the efficacy of doing so. First, the odds of having a post-dated check cashed prior to the date written on the check are the same as the odds that a teller will actually notice the date on the check—

about 50-50. That means that half the time the check will be cashed immediately, leading to a potential NSF problem.

Second, you can notify the bank that a post-dated check has been issued. Bank officials may say they will watch for the check, but they can also refuse or charge you a fee to do so. Once again, there are no guarantees.

Third, there is a law against issuing a check against insufficient funds. This gives the person or business accepting the post-dated check recourse if the check gets through the system early and becomes NSF. You will argue that you made the company aware that you were paying with a post-dated check, to no avail. If you issue a post-dated check, you are always at fault in the eyes of the bank and the law.

Should I accept post-dated checks? Now I am going to reverse my stance. I said that you should never write a post-dated check. However, there is no harm in accepting post-dated checks if you do the following. Bank the post-dated check on the date written on the check. Do not utilize the funds until the check has cleared. Hold delivery of product or services until the check clears.

I once accepted a series of four post-dated checks from a customer. One was dated immediately. The others were post-dated at three-month intervals. Each check was deposited as the customer wished. Each check was good.

WHAT SHOULD I DO? Your checkbook should be secured under lock and key, preferably in a file cabinet, desk or safe, when not in use. Instruct the individual who is responsible for your checking account that the checkbook is not to be on the desktop unless she is in the room. No one is to view the checkbook without permission. This includes family.

Examine the checkbook daily, even if you just glance at it. If any entry appears unusual, investigate immediately. No one writes a check except the person in charge of the checkbook. This includes you, unless an emergency occurs that requires instant checkbook access. You would feel awfully foolish if you wrote a check and found that you committed an error that jeopardized your business. Stranger things have happened.

Additional Resources: Your banker, accountant.

COLLECTIONS

What is Days Sales Outstanding (DSO)? DSO refers to the average number of days it takes your company to collect an outstanding receivable. DSO is an excellent calculation for determining the effectiveness of your collections department. DSO varies among different types of businesses.

What is a normal DSO? The norm for businesses in the United States for the past couple decades was about 45 days for an invoice with 30-day terms. That is 45 days from the day the invoice for a particular account is entered. In bad times, that number may increase to as much as 60 or 70 days.

If you sell to government and receive payment in 30 days, that should be your expected DSO. If you normally receive payment within 60 days, that should be your expected DSO. The key is the trending. Is

DSO consistent? Or is it rising? If DSO is rising, you should have a look at your accounts receivable base and pay special attention to those accounts that are trending toward longer DSOs.

Why should I care about DSO? DSO is a guideline for measuring your effectiveness in collecting outstanding accounts. As your business progresses, you will get a feel for customers that pay promptly and those that constantly need prodding to make payment. You will extend credit to some and require C.O.D. from others. If your DSO is increasing, it may mean that you are doing a poor job of collecting delinquent accounts, not conducting sufficient credit checks on new credit accounts, not conducting credit checks on existing accounts that are lagging behind in payments, or allowing credit to companies that should be paying C.O.D., or with a credit card. A rising DSO may also mean that your company is doing a poor job of invoicing, consequently creating late payments due to incorrect invoices.

DSO should also be utilized when projecting cash flow. An increasing DSO translates to a greater need for financing to replace poor cash flow. For example, sales that are normally converted to cash in 45 days may now require 60 days. That converts to 15 extra days without that cash in your checking account.

How is DSO calculated? For our purposes, basic DSO calculation involves three numbers:

1. Total annual credit sales (ex: $1,200,000)

2. Average annual accounts receivable (ex: $150,000)

3. Number of days in a year (ex: 365)

The equation is as follows:

$$(\$150,000/\$1,200,000) \times 365 = 45.6 \text{ Days Sales Outstanding (DSO)}$$

The calculation may involve any number of days. Just adjust total credit sales and average accounts receivable accordingly. Your accountant may opt for variations in this calculation if your business is seasonal or if he deems it necessary to derive a more accurate assessment of accounts receivable.

How can I reduce accounts receivable? Reduce accounts receivable by accurately invoicing your customers immediately upon shipping goods. Include an interest penalty for late payment. Respond immediately to any problems a customer may have regarding invoicing or payment. Send out statements requesting immediate payment of past-due invoices. Send increasingly stern demand letters to delinquent accounts. Call all past-due customers regularly and discuss the reason(s) for late payment. Resolve *all* reasons for late or short payments immediately. Cut off further shipments until payment is received, if necessary.

When calling a frequently delinquent customer for payment, you must resolve any questions regarding the accuracy of the invoice, extract agreement to pay immediately, and get the check number, date, and amount of the check that is being sent. Request that the check be sent overnight so that it can be tracked for next-day delivery. Email the customer with specifics of your conversation if you feel it is necessary to do so. If your customer is required to go to extra expense for overnight payment, she may consider paying you on a timely basis in the future.

How can I speed up payments to my business? The easiest way to speed up payment is to get your money when your goods or services are delivered. Credit cards are a wonderful way to get your money up front. There is a small fee involved, but this is offset by the increase in business you will experience by taking credit cards.

Stay on top of collections. Most late payments are because your customer received an incorrect invoice or no invoice at all. Call customers a week after an invoice is past due and ask for payment, then deal with any problems promptly.

Bill your customers promptly. Money costs money. If you must dive into your credit line because you are delinquent in sending out invoices, you are not choosing your priorities wisely. Invoice immediately.

I have seen a number of situations where a company is performing work and the invoices are stacking up in a tray on a desk. When I asked the reason for delays in invoicing customers, the answer was always the same. "I've been so busy, I just haven't had the time to sit down and send out invoices." As time passes, invoices become tougher to collect. Late invoices are tougher still. Invoice every day; you cannot afford to do otherwise.

Should I send statements, invoices, or both? Send an invoice for a sale the day the goods are shipped or delivered. When you set up a customer's account, ask if the customer requires a monthly, quarterly, or annual statement. If a company does no business in a time period and owes nothing, do not send a statement unless requested.

If a customer is in arrears, send a monthly statement. Call before sending the statement and inquire as to the reason for the delinquency. Offer to send a corrected invoice(s) with the statement. Remember, no seasoned business person makes payment from a statement. She makes payment only when she has an invoice, matching purchase order and bill of lading for the transaction, in hand.

Should I accept partial payment from a customer? Never turn down payment of any type or amount, unless it is not owed. You can direct payment to the correct invoice when the money arrives.

Should I charge interest on past-due accounts? Yes, charge interest for all past-due invoices. You have the right to waive interest if you feel the necessity to do so. Typical interest is 1.5 percent per month, commencing with the first day of delinquency. Example: You are owed $1,000. Payment is due 30 days from the date of the invoice. If you do not receive payment on the 30th day, interest is added to the bill in the amount of 1.5 percent, or $15. The debtor has used your money for 30 days.

Some customers will argue vehemently about interest charges. Many will refuse to pay. In this sense, interest may become a deterrent to customers that habitually pay late. Be liberal in your assessment of interest charges unless the customer is constantly past due.

Collection agencies. I prefer to utilize in-house collectors up to the point where the debt is obviously uncollectable. This gives you control over the customer service aspect of collections and dispenses with poor treatment of the debtor. The best advice is to stay on top of collections so that an outside agency never becomes a necessity. Even better, get payment at the time of sale and collection problems evaporate.

Once you feel that collection of a debt is hopeless, you may want to sell the debt to an outside agency. Understand that an outside collection agency is going to utilize every possible motivation to collect the debt from your prior customer. The treatment received from collection agencies is not always gentle and may create a good deal of resentment from your debtor. Collection agencies will test the limits of the law to get money. Be careful about putting your current or prior customers in such hands. It is a small world.

Liens. A lien is a legal encumbrance that is filed against a property to collect a debt. The lien may encumber all of a debtor's property or just the property connected directly with the debt.

In all my years in business, I have come across a handful of companies that file liens against properties as a collection tactic. Stay away from this practice unless absolutely necessary and you are willing to give up the debtor's business. Filing a lien against a customer will definitely create an abundance of hard resentment. The word travels fast. Be very careful and very selective about filing liens.

How often should I contact past-due accounts? Select an employee who is familiar with your accounts and your billing procedures. Pick someone who is firm but friendly and is not afraid to ask for payment. Follow up with past-due accounts a week after they become past due, again at 30 days past-due and again at 45 days past-due. If you are not paid within 45 days, follow up weekly until payment is secured. If you have an understanding with a customer that allows some leniency with payment dates, make sure your collector or collections department is aware of the agreement.

Make sure your salespeople are aware of nonpayers so they do not make matters worse by promising something that is undeliverable. Make sure salespeople know the rules. Make sure salespeople follow the rules.

That said, the salesperson probably has the best relationship with, and best understanding of, the customer. The salesperson is also concerned about losing an account that puts commissions in her pocket. If you feel that she can be a positive influence, ask her to get involved in obtaining payment from her customer and possibly saving the account.

Who should I call at a past-due account? It is typically a waste of time to call the clerk or supervisor who ordered a product or service. Call the accounts payable supervisor. If the accounts payable supervisor is not helpful, talk to the controller or CFO. If the situation demands contact with the owner, make the call. These are the times when you recognize the value of the solid relationships that you have built with your customers. Exercise cautious pressure, and obey the law.

What should I say when calling past-due accounts? You should say something like this, "Mrs. Davis, this is Jill Smith from XYZ Enterprises. I am calling to let you know that we have not received payment for invoice # 55555, dated May 5th, in the amount of $638.14. It was due a week ago, on June 4th. Is there a problem with the invoice?" If the invoice is in the customer's hands, ask if it is correct. If the customer does not have a correct invoice, immediately resolve any problems emanating from your company and obtain a commitment date and payment amount. If post-call investigation is necessary, show your enthusiasm for collecting the debt by following through completely on each outstanding account as soon as possible after terminating the call. When calling back to a debtor, get a commitment date and payment amount.

What should I request/demand from a past-due account? Request immediate payment. If late payment is unusual for this particular customer, ask when you should expect a check, and say thank you. If this is just another incident in a string of past-dues, ask for the check number, the amount of the check, and when it will be mailed. If you are concerned about the sincerity of the customer, tell him you will pick up the check. If a troublesome customer is located in another city, you may ask for the check to be sent overnight.

You must ask for payment and get specific about date of payment, method of payment, amount to be paid, delivery or pickup, and when the money will hit your door. Do not threaten to cut off the customer or put her on C.O.D. until she requests future deliveries. Doing so may create an even greater problem with collecting past-due funds.

Should I send nasty notes to past-due accounts? I am not fond of nasty notes. It is okay to firmly request payment on the face of an invoice or statement, but limit remarks to *past due*, *please pay upon receipt*, *second request*, or *third request*. Hand-write remarks in red, for affect. Stamps are often utilized but are not nearly as effective as a hand-written request.

When an invoice reaches 90 days past due, the customer is aware of the situation. A nasty note will do nothing more than add tension to an already tense situation. It is time for you or a manager to call or visit your past-due customer with an expectation that the invoice is paid immediately.

Factoring and past-due accounts? Factoring is the sale of accounts receivable at a discount. The factor buys the past-due accounts and owns the same rights to the receivables that you owned prior to selling them. The factor gets all the benefit and all the risk. Depending on the terms established between the seller and the factor, the seller may be involved in collecting some, or all, of the debt.

The factor's profit is the difference between the price paid for the receivables and the amount ultimately collected from the factor's efforts. Your loss is the difference between the original invoice amount and the discount afforded the factor.

Note: Stay away from factoring if at all possible.

How does Accounts Receivable affect my overall business? The simple answer is that receivables represent money that should be in your hands and is being utilized by someone else. In short, you are acting as someone else's bank. And, you may be borrowing money to pay your own bills due to your uncollectable accounts receivable.

Accounts receivable may have a number of profound influences on your business, beyond tying up capital that should be paying your bills. Probably the most important is the fact that lenders are usually willing to allow 80 percent of accounts receivable to collateralize term loans and operating lines of credit. If accounts receivable gets out of hand, collections are poor, and past dues begin to reside in the 90-120 days category, your lender will likely disallow a portion of your accounts receivables as collateral.

An unexpected rise in accounts receivable often signals other difficulties inside your business, such as poor products or services, lack of confidence in your ability to deliver, poor billing procedures, poor collection practices, or poor credit investigative practices.

WHAT SHOULD I DO? The key to keeping past-due accounts in check is consistency in three areas. First, never extend credit to anyone unless you have absolutely no other choice. Even the US Government can pay with a credit card for approved services. Second, never extend credit to anyone, regardless of size or status, until you run a credit check that tells you that the company is credit worthy. There are a lot of large, well-known companies out there that consistently pay late. Third, follow up all past-due accounts a week after they become past-due and continue to follow up until the account is paid. Once again, the key is consistency. Do not turn your past-due account collections into an ongoing endurance race.

Additional Resources: Human resources consultant, business consultant.

COLLEGE TUITION REIMBURSEMENT

Why does an employee make the effort to earn a college degree? The answer is obvious. He wants to earn more money or find a job in his chosen field. Keeping that in mind, what part should you play in furthering your employees' educations? College degrees are expensive. Most employees are forced to take out loans to pay for tuition. If they could afford to quit work and go to school full time, they probably would. So why would you be interested in investing in an employee who expects you to pay for college and provide him with a healthy pay increase upon graduation? Ask four questions before agreeing to pay all or a portion of college tuition:

Is the employee likely to excel in a curriculum that will be beneficial and profitable to your company? Excel, by definition, infers superior performance. That performance will probably extend to the employee's work habits.

What is the likelihood that the employee will stay with your company after graduation? Require the employee to endorse a legal agreement that obliges him to stay with the company for a given period of time after graduation. A two-year degree converts to a two-year commitment. A four-year degree converts to a four years. An advanced degree requires five years. If the employee agrees and decides to leave prior to fulfilling the contract, you recoup the portion of tuition equal to the percentage of the contract that is not honored.

Is the employee the type of person you want on your team?

Does the cost make sense? Your payback is in the future. It may make more sense to let the employee move to a company that regularly reimburses college expenses. It may be less expensive in the long run to simply hire a person with a college degree.

Start the process by requiring the employee to complete an application with all the particulars, including the name of the college, names of classes, hours per class, and rates. Require a copy of the syllabus for each class. Have the student tell you, in writing, why each class is relevant to her job at your company.

When contracting with a college bound employee, put everything in writing. Will you pay for all tuition or a portion of tuition? Are books, materials, and lab fees included? You will want to stipulate minimum grades. Pay for "C" and above for undergraduate work and "B" and above for post-graduate work. Require proof of classes and grades. Do not pay for repeated courses. Pay after the fact.

WHAT SHOULD I DO? Pay tuition only if the college of choice is accredited. Most businesses pay a maximum of two-thirds of hourly tuition. Books, materials, labs and housing fall to the student. This is only a guideline. Many businesses pay a flat amount per employee, annually, because that is what they can afford. This varies widely among businesses. The actual percentage or amount is up to you. Never pay more than you can afford.

Most colleges and universities include classes and tuition rates on their Internet sites. Do not make any decision until you are completely aware of your costs and responsibilities. Do not make any promises that may be difficult to keep. Look at the total costs if the employee intends to stay with you for the duration of college matriculation. Weigh the costs against your potential profitability from that individual. What does she bring to the table now? What will she bring to the table after she earns her degree?

COMPENSATION

Compensation takes many forms, be it salary, hourly, exempt, nonexempt, bonuses, perks, gifts, incentives, prizes, automobiles, mileage, life and health insurance, disability insurance, pension plans, savings vehicles such as IRAs and 401Ks, to name a few. Some compensation is taxable and some is tax-free. Some, such as your company's portion of your employees' Social Security, are required by law.

Salary. Salary may be defined as "regular compensation received by an employee as a condition of employment". Salaries are composed of a basic wage, based on performance, and include fringe benefits, usually computed on an annual basis." [3]

There is no law that determines that certain parties are paid according to hours worked, piece work, per job, per week or per month. Salaries are usually paid to employees such as managers, supervisors, office workers, clerks, salespersons, and others who are not directly related to the manufacture, installation, and maintenance of a product or service.

Many companies pay salaries to workers who may be paid an hourly wage if they were to perform the same type of work elsewhere. The choice is yours. Determine an employee's job description and pay accordingly. Most companies in a particular industry pay similarly to other companies in that industry.

Salary range. Salary ranges exist because employees in similar positions do not necessarily possess equal education, experience, tenure, or work drive. Salary ranges should be assembled for each job description in your company. For instance, you may hire a salesperson. You determine that he has good potential but is untrained and should have a starting salary of $40,000 plus commission.

Your top producer has a history of outstanding sales, excellent customer retention, and 10 years with your company. She earns $100,000 plus commission and a performance bonus. You have just created a salary range of $40,000 to $100,000 for salespeople, exclusive of commissions and bonuses. All other salespersons will fall somewhere between the bottom and top of the range. Salary ranges should be revisited during annual budget preparation.

Hourly wage. Hourly wages are usually paid to labor employees who are involved in manufacturing, installing, or maintaining products, services, and production facilities. Hourly employees are paid for actual hours worked, where salary employees are paid a flat rate per work period and may work more, or less hours, week to week. Hourly employees are entitled to at least minimum wage. Overtime is typically paid to employees for all work in excess of forty hours in a predetermined week of seven days or less. I utilize the word "typically" since states individually regulate the types of businesses and employees that pay or earn overtime. California, for instance, requires employers to pay overtime (1-½ times the hourly rate) for all work in excess of 8 hours in a single day, and double-time (2 times the hourly rate) for all work in excess of 12 hours in a single day. Be sure to investigate wage laws in your state before making any decisions pertaining to areas such as minimum wage and overtime.

Grade and rank. A number of businesses and organizations designate grade or rank as a definition of pay structure. The grade or rank is usually combined with time on the job to define the amount of compensation paid within a specific job description. The military, police, and fire departments commonly utilize this type of structure to determine compensation. Airlines, colleges, universities, civilian government employees, and employees of companies that provide physical security are all reliant on some type of grade and rank structure to determine compensation.

Pay raises. Many companies negotiate raises for specific groups of employees via collective bargaining agreements. This occurs quite commonly in government and union environments. In these environments, any employee who is still working for the company at year's end automatically receives a raise, usually a percentage of wage or salary, regardless of performance. Try to stay away from this type of arrangement. Employees should be regularly and fairly evaluated. Every evaluation and pay increase should reflect the true value of the employee to the company.

Raises should be based on merit. Anything less than total pay for total performance involves antiquated thinking. Set aside a percentage of your profit every year for employee raises. The best performers earn the largest raises. Those who perform very well earn something less. Improved performers get the next best share. Subpar performers get no raise and are encouraged to improve, and may even be at risk of being replaced. This practice may be prohibited if your employees fall under the auspices of a union or other collective bargaining agreement.

Incentives *(See INCENTIVES).*

Commission/Bonus plans. Commission and bonus plans should always be in writing and signed by you and the commissioned individual. Equality among plans for all salespeople makes things easier in the long run. If you have a real star, you may want to add something extra to the pot to emphasize his importance to your business. Keep side deals confidential or air them publicly, whichever works better for your business and the morale of your employees. Be aware that the secrets you keep are usually common knowledge a short time after the event that spawns the secrets.

Bonuses are calculated on overall quarterly or annual sales and should be paid on the next normal pay day after the end of a bonus qualification period. Year-end bonuses should be paid on the first normal pay day of the following year. Many businesses argue that it takes at least a month to close out year-end sales, creating a waiting period for employees to collect bonuses. If this is the case, tell employees well ahead of year-end that bonuses will be paid on a specific date.

Do not promise a sales commission or bonus you cannot deliver. This sounds elementary, but it happens quite often. A salesperson sells a job at an acceptable profit level. Labor and material costs were underestimated by the individuals who engineered the job. The easiest way to recoup a portion of the lost profit is to reduce the salesperson's commission or bonus. Keep your promises and suck up the loss. Put the blame where it belongs. Make sure the mistake is not repeated on future jobs.

How much is enough commission? Commissions are all over the board. Large sales, in the millions, usually support commissions of 1-5 percent of the sale, excluding freight, special packing, port taxes, special charges, excise taxes, and duties. Smaller sales generally support commissions of 6-12 percent. Check the numbers for your industry and act accordingly.

How much is enough bonus? Bonus is reserved for those salespeople who go above and beyond. Bonus can be based on total sales, a percentage of salary and commission, a percentage of salary only, profit margins, or simply whatever you agree upon. I prefer a bonus based on a percentage of total sales. Bonuses typically max out at 25 percent of total commission for the period in question.

Bonuses are paid for superior performance in excess of quota. If a salesperson's quota is $500,000 per year, bonus is not paid until that amount is reached, then incrementally as that figure is exceeded. Assume a commission of 4 percent on $500,000, or $20,000 commission. The salesperson will also get 25 percent of $20,000, or a bonus of $5,000 at year end.

If the salesperson exceeds $500,000 in sales, you may want to increase her commission by 1 percent (not retroactive) for each additional $100,000 in sales over and above her $500,000 quota. For example, if your salesperson sells $600,000, she still receives 4 percent of the first $500,000 ($20,000) + 5 percent of the next $100,000 ($5,000) + 25 percent of the total commission ($6,250), for a total annual commission and bonus of $31,250.

What is a Draw? Some companies start new salespeople with draws. The draw provides a livable income during the ramp-up period. As the salesperson builds sales and commissions, the draw is gradually reduced. Depending on the company, the draw will go away completely in six months to three years.

If your salesperson is selling into an established territory with imbedded, long-term customers, you should shorten the length of the draw to six months or a year. If the salesperson is selling heavy equipment into a new, unworked territory, his sales will be few, but large. You may want to provide a draw for up to two years, until he is securely established in your industry and his territory.

For example, assume that a seasoned salesperson will make $75,000 a year. You may want to issue a draw based on half that amount, or $37,500. The first quarter the salesperson receives $3,125 as a monthly draw. The following quarter, he receives 90 percent of that amount, reducing the draw by 10 percent of the original first-quarter draw until it ceases after a predetermined number of quarters. If he exceeds his draw in commissions (figured retroactively to prior months), he receives the difference in a separate commission check. Provide a statement to each salesperson monthly. Include draw and commission calculations and balance due.

Draws may be recoverable (paid back to the company) or non-recoverable (not paid back to the company). Recoverable draws are becoming a thing of the past. You really cannot expect a salesperson to come on board, take a draw, and pay the amount back if he does not make the grade. A draw is your cost of doing business and providing training. A draw is the salesperson's reward for time and effort spent on your behalf. Draws should be spelled out in a contract that is endorsed by you and your salesperson.

Salary-Only Pay Plan. Salary-only is quite popular in retail businesses. The clerk works for a salary and may receive a bonus at year end if sales in her department are outstanding. Bonus is not discussed or expected. It is paid at the discretion of the business owner.

You may want to pay salespeople straight salaries. If you are in an industry that typically pays commission, your sales salaries will tend to be higher than those of companies that have salary-plus-commission pay plans. Since there will be a tendency for your sales compensation to be somewhat lower overall, you may want to pay a bonus at year's end to those who exceed forecasted sales quotas.

Note: Consider a pay plan that gives a salesperson incentive to work hard and make as much money as possible for herself and the company. Solid salespeople are equally motivated to increase sales and earn more money. It's a win / win situation. Consequently, salary-only pay plans limit pay and often dampen motivation.

Salary-Plus-Commission pay plan. I prefer this type above all others. The salary is adequate but not high enough to satisfy a top flight salesperson. Commission is paid monthly and makes up the balance of a fair and equitable compensation plan. A bonus may be added for outstanding production, and paid on a quarterly basis.

Commission-only pay plan. A salesperson agrees to work only for commissions that are earned on each valid sale. This is a hard plan to sell to salespeople. Confident salespeople will often opt for a commission-only pay plan because companies that offer commission-only compensation usually pay a far greater percentage, per sale, than those that pay salary plus commission. New, or less confident salespeople, on the other hand, will usually opt for a salary or non-refundable draw *(See also **What is a draw?** in this section)*, in addition to commissions.

Most insurance companies operate on a commission-only basis. A new agent, in absence of a clientele, could wait weeks or months before making a commission. Some companies still provide decreasing draws while the new agent acclimates to her surroundings and builds a clientele. In the first year, the agent collects earned commission, plus additional commission, based on 90 percent of the earned commission. In the second year the additional commission drops to 50 percent of the earned commission amount. In the third year, it drops to 20 percent. At the outset of the fourth year in business, the agent receives earned commission, only. If you place a salesperson on straight commission, provide a plan that offers a livable wage until she is able to adapt to the market and produce consistent sales.

Should I offer a choice of pay plans? Why not? Many companies offer a choice of salary plus commission, or straight commission. Adjust the commission scale so that a salesperson who is receiving straight commission is earning a higher percentage of sales than those who earn salary-plus-commission.

When should commissions be paid? Pay commissions monthly, on the first payday of the month after the commissions are earned. This allows time to ensure that the numbers are correct and the sales that generated the commissions are completed.

Chargebacks on commission sales. A chargeback is a commission that has been earned or paid and must be reversed because a sale is lost, altered, or does not go as intended. If a sale is altered because the customer changes his mind about the size or mix of the order, the salesperson should be paid according to the final price for that particular sale. If the customer receives product and decides not to take it after examination, the same rule applies.

If a salesperson sells a product or service and the sale is canceled or altered due to your company's poor performance, which cannot be controlled by the salesperson, you should allow the salesperson to collect full commission or bonus without penalty. Poor performance does not include the lack of availability of a product or service. If a salesperson sells a product or service and the sale is canceled or altered due to poor performance or misinformation by the salesperson, you should charge back the salesperson, accordingly.

Any chargeback based on subjective circumstances will probably raise a bone of contention. Be sure to clarify chargeback rules in your commission plan. Be sure you have all the facts before you charge back any sale. Discuss every chargeback with the salesperson before it hits his paycheck. Surprises are not an option.

Note: When you lose a sale due to poor performance, follow through so that the problem never recurs. Selling is all about building relationships. If you have sold to a customer, a relationship has been forged. It may be easier, and less costly, to reestablish a past relationship than to find a new customer.

Sales reversals. Sales reversals are a fact of life. People buy things and then change their minds. Some companies, like Costco, Nordstrom and Sam's Club, have a total return policy. There are some caveats, but their overall return policies are incredibly liberal. The companies that exercise these policies usually have an agreement that allows for special treatment by the vendor if they must accept a return. Some companies charge a 25 percent repacking fee if the product is returned without packaging. Some charge a restocking fee of 15-25 percent.

The decision is yours. Repacking and restocking create costs that reduce your bottom line. Maybe you should load your pricing to offset any potential repacking and restocking costs, probably an additional 2 percent. This means that every customer pays a little toward the cost of restocking.

WHAT SHOULD I DO? Approach this area from a cost vs. profit perspective, with an overview that includes competitors' pay scales. Let's take a moment to recap. Laborers should earn an hourly wage or should be paid on a piece-work basis. Bonuses should be considered for extraordinary production. Management, supervisory, office and administrative personnel should be paid salaries. In addition, these personnel should earn bonuses for surpassing predetermined goals. Sales personnel should be paid salary plus commission plus bonus, or commission only plus bonus. New sales personnel are usually paid a non-refundable draw to start and are switched to salary plus commission plus bonus, or commission only plus bonus once they produce at a predetermined rate.

Categorically discuss payroll with your accountant while you are assembling your business plan. Your business plan will determine your ability to hire, providing you make your profit goals. Of course, all this is dependent on affordability.

Additional Resources: Your accountant; check industry standards; check your competitors' policies.

COMPETITION

There are two types of competition, direct and indirect. Direct competition is the company that sells products like yours. You sell hamburgers, and another company sells hamburgers. Will your customer buy a burger from your corner coffee shop or will she go to a signature fast food restaurant?

Indirect competition involves a competitor that has a dissimilar product. Your coffee shop may sell hamburgers. But you may not offer fried chicken, thus sending your prospective customer to the neighborhood KFC chicken franchise for dinner.

Competitors come in all shapes and sizes. What was it that Sun-tzu, the Chinese general, said way back in 400 BC? "Keep your friends close, and your enemies closer."[4] Sun-tzu may have been talking about competition.

Get to know your competition. Have lunch with them, visit their businesses, and talk to your vendors about them. Attend trade shows and become a member of industry trade organizations. Visit your local and nearby Chambers of Commerce. They are often hotbeds of information and they want you to be successful. Know your competition's pricing strategies. Never do anything illegal to get competitive information, but do everything legal to compare your company and every product and strategy you put out there with your competition. Compare strengths and weaknesses and adjust, adjust, and then adjust again.

WHAT SHOULD I DO? Never say anything negative about your competition to anyone - not your employees, your kids, your friends, or your business associates. If someone asks about your feelings toward your competitors, simply say that they seem like a good company and you wish them well. If you talk poorly about your competition, it will get back to them someday, some way. If your competitor speaks poorly of you, consider it as a heads up that they are taking notice of you as a competitor, and adjust if necessary.

COMPUTERS

A computer is an absolute necessity for bookkeeping, payroll, communication, online research, and meetings and presentations. Today's computers are relatively inexpensive, starting at only a few hundred dollars, and readily available. They are relatively simple to operate and available in desktops, laptops, pads, pods and a host of other styles. Even if you are computer shy, there is an abundance of experienced users out there, just like you, who never touched a computer until the need arose. Modern computers are operationally friendly, very forgiving and make the difference between slogging through mounds of paper, or taking the easy route to modern bookkeeping.

Extended warranties for computers. Typically, extended warranties are not a worthwhile investment. Most warranties include exclusions for the most common failures. However, if you purchase a laptop, the screen represents the greatest cost of the computer. If your computer is going to experience rough use, you may want to purchase a warranty that covers the screen against breakage.

I have owned a number of desktop and laptop computers. I ceased buying extended warranties some years ago and have never regretted it. If electronics are going to fail, they usually fail right away, in the first 90 days of use, during the existing warranty period. By the time a computer wears out, your old unit is outdated and it is time to invest in a newer model.

Software bootlegging. Standard software packages are quite sufficient for most small-to-medium-sized businesses. Bootlegging software is the act of using original or copied software on your computer, which was purchased for use on another computer. Most software companies allow you to utilize your software on three of *your* computers, but forbid multiple users, much the same as publishers forbid a reader from making copies of books. Bootlegging is common and illegal. Buy legal software and license it in your company name, for your use, only.

Hardwire or wireless Internet connection. Computers can send and receive information via hardwire or wireless Internet connections. The advantages of hardwire are that it is faster than wireless and somewhat more secure.

The advantage of a wireless connection is transportability, because your computer is not reliant on a wall connection for Internet. Most laptops include a built-in wireless modem that allows a connection to the Internet via Wi-Fi. If you do not have a wireless card, they are widely available at most local electronics stores. You can operate on battery and take your computer on a business trip or use it on a plane, in a car, the airport, an Internet café, a hotel or a fast-food restaurant, to gain free Wi-Fi access.

The disadvantages of wireless are that it is not as secure as hardwire and signal strength can be questionable, depending on your physical surroundings and distance from the signal source. If you are operating via your own modem, your Internet provider should offer wireless security. No system, hardwire or wireless, is completely safe or foolproof.

Company programs on employees' computers. Never! This is a bad practice. Once you put your program on anyone else's computer, you are leaving yourself open to an array of potential problems, such as bootlegging, having company information fall into the hands of competitors, losing the program if the employee's computer is stolen, contracting a virus, having the program fall into the hands of former employees, or employees seeing information they should not have.

If you give any program to an employee for company use, put it on one of your computers and give the computer to the employee with the understanding, in writing, that the information is proprietary and that prosecution will follow any attempts to steal or distribute the information or program without your written permission.

Although many companies allow proprietary information to be taken outside the business, usually in the form of pricing programs on laptops, smartphones and smartpads, it is still best practice to keep proprietary information in-house to the greatest degree possible. It is really easy for an employee to plug a flash drive into any computer that is not password protected and walk away with priceless information. Total protection and prevention are impossible. So why make it any easier to take your proprietary information outside the company unless absolutely necessary?

Proprietary software programs. Proprietary software programs are those that you develop in-house, in lieu of off-the-shelf programs. Proprietary software systems cost more. You are paying for the research and development to create the program. Off-the-shelf programs pay for research and development by spreading the cost among millions of buyers. Investigate off-the-shelf programs first. You may cut your costs by thousands of dollars.

Users. If an employee's job does not require use of a computer, do not provide a password. Tell employees who use computers three things: 1) Never let anyone else use your computer unless the user has the proper permissions to do so. 2) Never tell anyone else your password. 3) Never walk away from your computer without logging out.

Computer viruses. BusinessDictionary.com defines a computer virus as a, "Small but insidious piece of programming-code that attacks computer and network systems through 'contaminated' (infected) data files, introduced into a system via disks or internet. As a digital equivalent of biological microorganisms, it attaches itself to the target computer's operating system or other programs, and automatically replicates itself to spread to other computers or networks."[5] Computer viruses are insidious and dangerous to the health of your computer, in various degrees, and should definitely be avoided, detected and removed as quickly as possible.

Computer viruses are usually contracted from the Internet or bootleg programs. Use certified software. Do not download from questionable sources. Utilize proven anti-virus software on all computers.

Computer backup. Computers crash or wear out. This is a fact of life. Backup is not a choice, but a necessity. Pricing for backup systems is really reasonable. You may own or lease a PC, Apple, or mainframe. You may have multiple locations. You may have computers in your company vehicles. There is a common thread among all these systems. They all require you to back up information and data that is valuable to your business.

Highly valued information must be stored in a manner whereby destruction of your plant or computer system(s) will not interfere with the safety of that valued information. There are far too many storage methods, on and off site, to discuss, in total. So let's mention a few. The least costly backup devices are CDs, DVDs, BLU-RAY discs, flash drives and data sticks. Prices range from a few dollars for a simple flash drive to $100 for 128GB data stick. CDs, DVDs and BLU-RAY discs fall somewhere between these prices, depending on quantity.

Another choice is an external drive. This is a unit that attaches to your computer, but is independent of your computer's hard drive, in the event of a crash. It plugs into your computer's USB port. You can purchase a 2 Terabyte external drive for less than $100.

You also may want to try online storage, which takes the backup system out of your facility, gives you 24/7 access to your data, which is backed up multiple times and encrypted to protect you from computer hackers. You also gain peace of mind because you do not have to worry about failure of your backup system.

There are an abundance of online backup systems. A few that may interest you are, in alphabetical order, Backup Genie, Carbonite, CRASHPLAN, Just Cloud, My PC Backup, SOS, Sugar Sync and Zip Cloud. All are less than $10 a month, dependent on the amount of storage you need. All are PC and Mac compatible. Some are more business oriented than others. Some allow sharing and some do not allow sharing.

If you are going to utilize a backup system, employ a proven and highly regarded source. If your storage source is in-house and your building burns down, you will lose your backup system along with your computer. If you are absolutely frightened that you may lose valuable information, there is always the tried and true method - paper backup in a fireproof environment.

Hard copy vs. disk space. If you cannot afford to lose it, back it up with a hard copy. Tax records are a good example.

Computer repair costs. Ask the cost *before* anyone works on your computer. You may be surprised. It is not always possible to get an exact estimate because detecting computer problems is not always 100 percent predictable. Most computer repair services charge by the hour. Try to derive a maximum cost if an exact cost is not applicable. I have a computer geek friend who works on a number of friends' computers. He is reasonable, reliable, and refrains from nickeling and diming me to death. Better yet, I trust him with my proprietary information. Finding someone you can trust to work on your computer system can be extremely valuable when you are faced with an emergency.

WHAT SHOULD I DO? Do yourself a favor. Get involved in the world of computers. Most computer sellers will also arrange for classes at a reasonable cost. Many provide computer training on specific programs for free.

Note: Company-purchased software should be the only software permitted on company-owned computers. Make it a rule. Put it in writing.

Additional Resources: Yellow pages, your business friends, Internet.

CONFIDENTIALITY AGREEMENT / NONDISCLOSURE AGREEMENT (NDA)

These are the common names for a written agreement between your company and another company, or individual, that spells out the consequences of disclosing proprietary or restricted information to unrelated third parties.

When do I need a non-disclosure agreement? Any time you discuss proprietary information with anyone, that party should first endorse a non-disclosure agreement (NDA). The NDA notifies parties to the document that they will be held responsible for any activity on their part that allows company confidential information to fall into the hands of anyone not specifically covered by the NDA, under penalty of law. Employees should endorse NDAs as part of their orientations.

WHAT SHOULD I DO? Ask your attorney for a boiler plate NDA. You can find NDAs on the Internet, but your attorney should still approve the contents. Over the years, a number of business people and clients have indicated that asking someone to endorse a nondisclosure agreement shows a sense of distrust among the parties involved. Not to worry. Seasoned business people are well aware of the need to protect proprietary business information.

Additional Resources: Your business attorney.

CONSULTANTS

Should I hire a consultant(s)? Consultants are almost always contracted because a business lacks a short-term or long-term solution to a problem. Consultants are typically subcontractors who are not seeking employment. They charge by the hour, week, month or project. Consultants are usually much more expensive than any employee. The answer is, hire a consultant when there is no other way to fix the problem. This may sound a little harsh, but the majority of consultants are niche oriented and not generalized in their business knowledge. A consultant can be extremely valuable to resolve a specific problem, but can become extremely expensive if utilized improperly. Properly utilized, a consultant may become a valuable mentor and business associate.

Where can I find a consultant? Last time I searched the "business consultant" category on the Internet, there were 86 pages with an average of 10 consultants per page. That is just the business consultant category. What about all the other specialized business categories, like "computer consultant" or "consulting services"?

If possible, locate a local consultant through SCORE, your banker, your CPA or a business associate. Always obtain and check out at least three references before employing a business consultant.

References from consultants. I am a consultant. I am also the first one to tell you that all consultants are not created equally. Most consultants have a very narrow niche. Thoroughly vet a prospective consultant. Obtain and check out at least three references. Most people that take references never call them. Be a winner. Call each reference with a list of questions concerning the consultant's ability to serve your needs at a price you can afford.

Specialties among consultants. I am a generalist. There are not many of us around. Most consultants rely on professional or job specialties to get them in your door. As a group, consultants are niche players who are knowledgeable in a particular segment of business such as engineering, finance, human resources or operations. Find a consultant who matches your needs and has the talents that compliment your skill sets. If you and your consultant are drawing from the same bank of knowledge, you are wasting your time and money. If you cannot reach a comfort level with a consultant, keep looking.

Paying Consultants. Consultants should be hired as independent contractors. Paying a consultant is like paying for anything else in business. You want to know the complete cost before you say yes. You want to know exactly how much time the consultant will need for the project and exactly what you will receive for your outlay - and you want it in writing. If your requirements necessitate a long-term relationship, it may be more palatable to make the consultant an employee. This gives you greater control, but necessitates the payment of benefits. Weigh the possibilities and choose the most profitable route.

Pay in a manner that is convenient for you and your consultant. Personally, I like to pay consultants per project, unless the tenure is longer than a month. Then, I like to pay half at mid-month and half the last day of the month, until the project is completed. When I am the consultant, I want to be paid in the same manner.

CONTRACTS

Are all contracts legal? Not all contracts are legal. For example, if you enter into a contract under duress, or if you enter into a contract to do something illegal, or if you enter into a contract that lacks clarification, the contract may be illegal and unenforceable.

Always have your attorney examine a new contract before you endorse it. Always have your attorney examine a contract that you utilize in the normal course of business if it has been altered in any way.

Are oral contracts legal? Oral contracts may be legal, but not enforceable, due to a lack of witnesses to the contractual event. Do not enter into oral contracts or handshake contracts. If something unforeseen happens to you or the other party, no one but the survivor and the witnesses really know the terms of the contract. If an issue is important enough to be supported by a contract, it is important enough to be supported in writing.

Written Contracts. Always! *(See also **Oral Contracts**)* in the above section.

Amendments to contracts—yours or theirs. You will occasionally run into situations where you do business with companies that want to utilize *their* contract rather than *your* contract, or want to strike language from, or add language to, your contract. Have your attorney examine the contract if you have any questions at all. It may save you a good deal of embarrassment.

Who should write a contract? Attorneys should write all contracts - period. If you decide to utilize a contract template, you should still pass it by your attorney for approval.

Sample contracts/templates. The Internet abounds with sample contracts of every ilk. Some of the most popular contracts are confidentiality agreements, promissory notes, sales agreements, and a whole litany of contracts typically used in business. Most sample contracts require some alteration before they can be utilized. Sample contracts also come with a disclaimer that says that you, the buyer of the sample contract, are responsible for the outcome of any transaction that utilizes the instrument.

It is occasionally less expensive to have an attorney check out an existing contract than it is for him to create a contract from scratch. Just make sure you are on safe legal ground before utilizing a sample contract. The money you pay your attorney to approve a contract is pocket change, compared to the alternative if your contract will not stand up in court.

Additional Resources: Attorney.

CREDIT

When should I extend credit? If you extend credit, plan on spending between 30 and 90 days without payment, regardless of the terms. Extend credit only if you can afford to do so. Do not offer credit unless absolutely necessary to earn your customer's business. You may have to pass up some of those huge deals during your early years in business simply because you cannot offer attractive terms to your customer, or demand attractive terms from your vendors to make the sale fly.

How much credit should I extend? What kind of credit terms are your competitors offering their customers? What can you afford, based on 30 to 90 days, or more, without payment? If you are C.O.D. (Cash on Delivery) or C.I.A. (Cash in Advance) with your vendors, your ability to offer credit to your customers is very limited. If you have 30-day terms with your vendors, you may want to offer something less than 30 days to your customers. Allow for the occasional customer that may drag you out for 60 to 90 days. Once again, do not extend credit unless absolutely necessary.

Credit applications. Obtain a credit application from every new customer, regardless of terms, and regardless of the projected length of your expected relationship with the customer. Most word processing programs include a sample template of a credit application. Free templates are also available on the Internet. Run any new application by your attorney, just to be safe.

Obtain an updated credit application any time a customer wants you to extend beyond his normal credit limit or when a customer appears to be in financial trouble. Also get an updated credit application from every credit customer on January 1 of every year. We live in a fast-paced economy. Company health can change dramatically in a short period of time. Do not make the mistake of foregoing annual credit applications because you have *always* done business with a customer or because they always pay their bill. The same rules apply to *all* customers when you are extending credit.

You will need the customer's business name, contact person, business formation (such as corporation, partnership, sole proprietorship, or limited liability company), federal I.D. and/or Social Security number, trade references, and bank references. Be sure to include a line on your application that requests permission to do a credit search and contact references. Never initiate a credit check until you have a signed credit application. A faxed copy is legal, if signed.

Credit references. Require a minimum of three credit references. You want the business name, telephone number, fax number, and contact name of companies that currently supply goods or services to the customer requesting credit. You do not want references such as credit card companies, landlords, utility companies, or vendors that deal with your prospective credit risk on a cash basis. Calling credit references is generally tedious and time consuming. Most companies call the first reference on the list and skip the rest. Call *all* credit references.

The function of a credit application is to limit your exposure to people and companies that are unable or unwilling to pay their debts in a timely manner. The credit application becomes a useless tool unless you take the time to contact vendor and bank references and ask the hard questions.

How long have you done business with the company in question? Does ABC Company pay in a timely manner? Have you had collection or delivery problems with ABC Company? Are you currently extending credit to ABC Company? Have you ever put ABC Company on a C.O.D. basis? If so, why?

When requesting credit information from a prospective customer, explain with absolute clarity that nothing will be shipped until credit is extended, and that credit will not be extended until the potential customer's credit worthiness is fully investigated.

Note: In essence, when you extend credit, you are loaning your money to your customer.

Credit reporting agencies. There are numerous credit reporting agencies; Dun & Bradstreet, TRW, Experian, and Equifax, to name a few. Depending on the sizes of your accounts and the amount of credit regularly extended, you may decide to utilize a credit-reporting agency to determine the credit worthiness of your customers. There is an incremental cost for such services. This is a common sense call. Based on your risk, does it make sense to get a credit-reporting agency involved? Ask your CPA for guidance.

Deposits on account. Always ask for a deposit when you sell anything to anyone on credit. The worst-case scenario is that the customer says, "No." Once you receive a deposit, you reduce the chance of losing the order to a competitor to near zero. You also reduce the amount that must be borrowed or drawn from cash reserves to pay your vendor. If you are asking for a deposit on a large sale, be sure to check your cash flow ramifications before making a decision on foregoing the deposit.

In the case of special-order merchandise, the sales contract should provide that the customer forfeits the deposit and must pay in full if the sale is canceled after you have placed the order with your vendor. Never, never place an order for unusual or special-order products unless you have a deposit, equal to your cost of materials, and an endorsed, non-cancelable agreement that requires payment in full once the product is ordered by you. If a special order requires design changes on the part of your customer, be sure that the customer signs and dates a document outlining the changes and specifications to the product before accepting the order.

Note: Most government and municipal entities issue purchase orders and do not issue deposits or partial payments on contracts for goods or services. If you choose to do business with these entities, take this into consideration.

Late charges on past-due accounts. (*See also* **COLLECTIONS: Should I charge interest on past-due accounts?**)

How much credit can I afford to extend? Extending credit to your customers represents a cost to you. When you extend credit, you are forced to borrow the money to pay your vendor to produce your product, or you are tying up cash reserves that could be utilized elsewhere in your business. The question you should be asking yourself is, "Can I afford to be my customer's bank?" If you must extend credit, price your products so that you can afford to do so.

Terms. The most common terms offered to customers today are Net 30. This means that your customer has 30 days to get her payment to your door from the date of your invoice.

You may want to sacrifice a small portion of your profit to urge your customer to pay more quickly. Terms would be 2 percent 10, Net 30. This means that your customer has 30 days to pay if she chooses to stretch terms to the limit. However, your customer may deduct 2 percent from the invoice if payment reaches your door 10 days from the date of the invoice.

WHAT SHOULD I DO? Extend credit when it makes sense to you. Ask yourself, what are the consequences if I am not paid? Do I really need this sale? Do I have enough in the sale to pay for the interest on the money I may have to borrow to stay afloat between now and when I get paid? If I am not paid by my customer, will I be able to pay my vendor? More importantly, will I be able to stay in business? Do not shoot from the hip. Calculate all the costs of extending credit before making your decision. When the final shoe drops, you must also make your projected profit – in spite of the amount expended to extend credit.

Additional Resources: CPA, Attorney, Fair Credit Reporting Act (FCRA) and Fair Debt Collection Practices Act (FDCPA); these acts fall under the auspices of the US Federal Trade Commission and together, they provide the foundation for consumer rights in the United States.

Credit cards for business purchases. In today's market, credit cards are routinely accepted by a wide variety of businesses. Credit cards can be a profitable way to earn cash back, airline miles and a whole assortment of other freebies if you utilize a credit card when you purchase from your vendors. Get a credit card in your company name and utilize it *only* for company purchases. Accepting credit cards is a great way to reduce reliance on offering credit terms to your customers.

Note: Do not co-mingle company purchases with your personal or household purchases. The IRS is not fond of this practice.

Credit cards for customer transactions. Your customers expect you to accept credit cards. This includes business-to-business customers. Credit card acceptance will actually increase your sales. Whether you like it or not, we are a credit card society.

CreditorWeb.com says, "Thanks to direct payroll deposit and debit cards, 50 percent of Americans carry 'a few singles and maybe a five or a ten' and 40 percent carry 'around $5 or less including coins. . .'" The article goes on to say, "Statistics indicate that the average American carries at least four credit cards and nearly all Americans carry a debit card. You're missing a lot of purchase opportunities if those cards aren't welcome at your business."[6]

Which credit cards should I offer? In my part of the country, we see VISA and MasterCard everywhere. American Express is widely used, but nothing like VISA and MasterCard. Discover Card is here and there. If you are engaged in the sale of high-end goods, American Express may work well for your company. I would still utilize VISA and MasterCard as well, since VISA, MasterCard, and American Express account for all but a small percentage of total credit card business.

Bank vs. independent merchant account vendors. Banks usually cost a little more than independent merchant account vendors. The independent vendor can tie your credit card account directly to your bank account. Pick an independent that has local representation. When your credit card machines goes down, you do not have time to deal with a merchant company at a distance.

Proceeds. Proceeds are deposited directly to your checking account, usually within two working days.

Credit card fees. Read your contract carefully. The credit card merchant will send a representative to your business and expect you to make a decision on the spot. Ask the merchant to fax the contract to you so you can read the requirements before meeting with a salesperson. Fees run from 1.5-7 percent, depending on the card, type of business, dollar volume, and program offered by your credit card processor. American Express routinely charges a higher percentage per sale than other credit card services.

Your costs may include a retail transaction fee, batch fee, monthly statement fee, voice transaction authorization fee, PCI Compliance fee, chargeback fee, annual fee, application fee, programming fee, setup fee, maintenance fee, over limit fee, gateway setup fee, and swipe or phone software. Some vendors will waive all or most of these fees if you have clean credit, an established business, established product or service. The more the vendor wants your business, the more they will bend. Negotiate for the best deal.

Credit card companies have access to your checking account and permission to deduct all fees from that account. Before opening a credit card account, be sure that all fees and amounts are spelled out in your credit card contract. Be careful. Read your contract thoroughly.

Chargebacks to credit cards. Customers have the right to reverse a transaction up to six months after purchase with most credit cards. The burden is on you to prove your case and recoup your payment. Swipe transactions carry a more reliable guarantee than non-swipe transactions.

WHAT SHOULD I DO? You cannot afford to *not* accept credit cards. They are deeply imbedded in our global culture and are a necessity to do business in all but a handful of companies. Price your products and services to cover the small percentage that credit cards add to your cost. If you elect to do business without accepting credit cards, prepare to give open credit to customers and suffer the consequences of collecting outstanding credit balances.

Additional Resources: Your banker, Internet.

Credit Lines. A credit line is an account that allows you to write a check for anything at all, up to a contracted amount, against the net worth of predetermined collateral. You are charged interest on the amount borrowed from your credit line account.

Who provides credit lines? Banks, credit unions, and a host of private lenders.

Used for what? Anything you desire; there typically are no strings attached.

How much should it be? Credit lines are based on a percentage of the collateral you are able to put up to secure the line. You may utilize your home, building, accounts receivable, inventory, etc.

A home may be worth 80 to 90 percent at your bank. If you have $100,000 equity in your home and your credit rating is excellent, you may be able to get a credit line of $80,000 to $90,000. Talk to your lender about a loan against inventory, accounts receivable, or other real or personal property. Try to limit collateral to business holdings.

What is the cost of a credit line? Credit lines can cost ± 1 percent over prime rate to several percent over prime rate, depending on your credit rating and the economic state of your business.

What happens if I use the credit line irresponsibly? Your lender may freeze, reduce, call in, or term out your credit line. The term *call in* means that you must pay off your credit line now. Odds are, your lender is not going to loan you the money to do so. *Term out* means that your lender will convert your credit line to a mortgage. The interest on the line will be increased several percent for a fixed term. The length of the term depends on the amount outstanding, your income, your credit rating and the state of your company.

What happens if my lender *terms out* my credit line? You just lost your credit float and your ability to borrow money at a moment's notice and at a reasonable interest rate. Your lender feels that you are in financial trouble. Loss of your line reduces your financial flexibility.

↳ **WHAT SHOULD I DO?** Everyone should have a credit line (private, business, or both) for those inevitable emergencies, or for a great deal you just cannot afford to pass up. Credit lines are convenient for that new punch press, a great deal on a volume inventory sale, or that delivery truck that is not in your budget. You can always convert the expenditure to a term loan later. Just make sure you can fit it into your cash flow projections.

Additional Resources: The business services group at your bank, venture capitalist, business angel, private sources.

CUSTOMER RELATIONS

Is the customer really always right? Right or wrong apologize, apologize, and apologize! First, look at the situation in a vacuum. Does it make sense to do what the customer requests, purely from a profit standpoint? Next consider the customer's value to your bottom line in the long term. Then marry the two and make a decision. Look for win/win; split the difference if necessary. Try to stabilize future orders. Do not forget that you are in business to secure a long-term, predetermined profit margin.

Is the customer worth keeping? Do what your gut tells you is right. Look at the long term. You may have to eat a little humble pie. On the other hand, if the customer is overly demanding and creates constant unrest, you may want to cease doing business with him.

What if I am right? The same rules apply. You have the right to *fire* your customer. Remember, once fired, the customer will tell his story over and over and over. Be sure you are right. Exhaust every effort to make the situation work for you and the customer before resorting to firing. By the way, most customers are fired because they are becoming a regular fixture on your accounts payable ledger or are eating into your profits because they are impossible to please. Stick to business. Do not make it personal.

↳ **WHAT SHOULD I DO?** Remember the 10/80/10 rule. Ten percent of your customers are high maintenance, but they have been with you forever and comprise the lion's share of your business. You understand them and you love them. Eighty percent of your customers are serviced day-to-day with nothing more than the typical customer problems. The other ten percent complain constantly, pay late and demand, demand and demand more. Fire the bottom ten percent and your competitors will love you for a little while—until they realize you are shifting your headaches to them.

Additional Resources: Talk to the sales representative who handles the customer. Follow your gut and do what is best for your company. Expect major push-back from the salesperson.

CUSTOMER SITE BEHAVIOR

The rules of working at a customer's site are simple. Clean and neat. No smoking. No swearing. No unpleasant behavior. If the customer allows smoking, your employees may enjoy the same treatment within the boundaries of the customer's policies. Your employees should ask permission to smoke, even though smoking appears obvious.

Most of us have a tendency toward parroting the behavior of others in a group atmosphere. If another party swears, we believe that swearing is acceptable. If someone else lights up, we believe smoking is acceptable. Caution your employees to stay within the boundaries you would expect at your premises, even when they are working elsewhere.

Caution your employees about carrying on conversations with employees of your customers. Sidebar chats during working hours interfere with each party's production. Conversations should be kept to the job at hand.

Last, and possibly most important, concerns conversations among your employees within earshot of your customers or their employees. Your employees should not voice their disagreements, disappointments and shortcomings regarding anything that may upset the customer unless they have complete privacy – away from the customer. I recall an incident where a serviceman was telling a customer that the service department was severely overworked because his fellow installers made so many errors during the installations of products. The customer parlayed that statement into a handsome discount on later work. Loose lips can be costly, particularly in the presence of customers.

WHAT SHOULD I DO? Get out of the office and visit customers. If you have a business that sells and installs or maintains products or services, arrange to drop in and ask questions while a project is ongoing. It's a feather in your hat when you visit your employees on the job. They really do not expect to see you away from the office, but they know that you care when you take interest in their work. Sure, some will complain that they are being watched, but the bottom line is that you should have an occasional presence among your employees, especially if they are working at customer sites. And, if you are able to turn a timely stop into a customer visit, you may get an additional sale. All customers love to talk to the boss.

CUSTOMER SITE PREPARATION

Have your salesperson and/or project manager visit the customer site prior to costing out a project. They should discuss permits, parking availability, entrance(s) to be utilized, available electrical outlets and available voltages, Wi-Fi availability, loading dock availability, advanced clearing of work areas, days and hours available to work, ingress/egress access, hazardous areas, explosion proof areas, chase access, roof access, and any local ordinances or concerns that may affect the cost and efficiency of successfully completing a project.

This is certainly not a complete list. It is a good start toward a checklist that should always accompany a project that includes delivery or installation of a product or service. Arm your sales, installation, and service departments with anything and everything that will make costing out a project and delivery of a sale easier on your company and your customer. The end result is the realization or your forecasted profit.

WHAT SHOULD I DO? Assemble knowledgeable members of your sales, installation, and maintenance departments and create a template, based on your business products and services. Adjust the template as necessary. Have the project manager check off items as they are investigated. Leave a section after each item for notes and remarks. Utilize a spreadsheet to make later adjustments easier. Create or purchase *your* template for *your* particular business type. Create a written plan so that profits will not fall through the cracks.

Chapter D

DAY ONE

The first thing on your agenda is compliance with all federal, state, and municipal statutes, rules, regulations, and certifications that affect your business. I have seen a number of companies that opened their doors for business and were shut down in the first few days of operation when a fire marshal or other local authority dropped by to examine the premises for violations. In many cases, the business owner was aware of the violation(s) and opened up for business without the proper licenses or permits. Do not ignore or violate statutes that can create confusion and chaos for your business. Ignorance of the law is not a valid excuse for breaking the law.

Safety First. Enact all safety rules from Day One. Never relax safety. Every time someone is hurt, you and your business suffer, not to mention the suffering among the injured parties and their families. You just cannot tolerate employees who do not put safety first.

What systems should be in place? Dissect your paper flow from the moment your service or product is sold until you receive payment. Look for obvious weaknesses. Do not duplicate efforts. Do not open your doors until every facet of your company is ready to do business.

Accounts payable/accounts receivable. If you are a small operation, i.e., fewer than 20 employees, your bookkeeper can double as accounts payable clerk and accounts receivable clerk until orders start to pile in. When your doors open, you should already have a plan in place to handle every possibility.

Payroll. Send out your payroll from day one if you have more than 20 employees. If not, have a company in the background that can take over payroll at a moment's notice. You will know when it is time to have someone else handle the payroll function. Consider paying employees every other week or twice monthly, rather than weekly. This simply reduces the payroll function and accompanying costs by half. If you can get away with monthly payroll, go for it.

Inventory. Have minimal inventory on hand. You should already have orders when you open your doors. Keep your risk at a minimum until you have a feel for production and sales.

Accountant or bookkeeper. If you can afford an accountant from the start, do so. It is a real pain to switch horses in midstream three to six months down the road. Worse yet, you will be hard pressed to find a bookkeeper who will come on board, knowing that replacement with an accountant is imminent. Even if the bookkeeper sticks around, her working relationship with the accountant will probably be rocky.

Receptionist. In many very small businesses, the bookkeeper doubles as receptionist. Pay a little more and get someone capable of keeping the balls in the air. When profits allow, hire a receptionist and give the bookkeeper additional duties.

Voice mail. Most business owners will tell you that they detest voice mail. You know the reason. Voice mails go unanswered. Customers tell you they left five voice mails for service. You know very well that a customer is stretching the truth to get your attention. Voice mail is a necessity today. If you are alone in the office, a second call will inevitably go unanswered while you are on the other line with a customer. That single call may cost you a sale. Hence, you need voice mail. Install a policy that all voice mails are returned same day, or next day if left after a specific time, say 4 p.m. If you are out of the office, have voice mail messages forwarded to your cell phone.

Business software. QuickBooks, Peachtree, Microsoft Professional, Microsoft Office Groove, Quicken, Money, Versa Check . . . the list is long and the packages are versatile. Pick your accountant. Then pick your software, based on your accountant's input.

WHAT SHOULD I DO? Undoubtedly, you will find something was overlooked when you first open your doors for business. Opening a business is a lot like cooking a dinner for the entire family. Once you procure the ingredients, timing becomes your toughest adversary. The family is arriving at five. Dinner is at six. Appetizers are first, then the main course, then dessert. Everything must be ready when the prior course is finished.

   The first rule of opening a business is to make a checklist of all the items you must have accomplished before you can lawfully and confidently open your doors. Double check each item a week before the grand opening.

   The second rule is to have a couple extra pairs of hands on board for your grand opening, just in case something major pops up. You may need someone to watch the shop or take care of unexpected business away from your business. This will increase your expenses slightly, but only for opening day. Plan for the extra person(s) and add the expense to your forecast.

   The third rule is to open when you are ready. You will feel pressure because the rent clock is running, building improvements are not quite finished, the fire department inspected the premises and found a few things that are needed to attain a green tag and the inventory arrived a little late and will barely make it to the shelves when the doors are ready to open. I repeat, plan to be ready a week in advance. Check and double check every item on your list again. You will miss small items, but the things that can shut you down or delay your grand opening will be handled in advance.

Additional Resources: Your bookkeeper, accountant, business consultant.

DECISIONS

If you are not ready to make business decisions, then you are probably not ready to go into business for yourself. Owning a business is not for the faint of heart. You will be making hundreds of decisions a day, most of them crucial to your success.

Then again, you may have a large enough bankroll to hire a proven manager who knows the ins and outs of your business and industry. Many business owners take years to realize that they are poor managers. Then they hire professionals to manage their companies. Why not hire a professional at the outset and learn to manage as you go?

There is no harm in putting off a decision until you are certain that you have all necessary information to move forward. If a potential decision pushes you out of your comfort level, you are either talking to the wrong folks or lacking information. If you feel like you are being forced into an unpleasant situation or responding to an ultimatum, it may be time to put on the brakes and revisit your options. Do not shoot from the hip.

DELEGATION

Delegation is the process of awarding a responsibility and its commensurate authority to another. Of course, the receiving party must possess the wherewithal and trust to carry out that duty. In fact, you will never be a complete manager until you learn to delegate. Delegation is absolutely necessary to your growth and your company's growth, and is the lynchpin that connects the average manager to the next generation manager who has discovered that he cannot do everything for himself.

Delegation involves trust and the necessity to pass authority down the line to your managers and supervisors so that you can multiply your efforts and grow into a strong, profitable company. Never delegate unless you are willing to part with the commensurate authority that is necessary for the manager to perform her job.

DEMOTIONS

Demotion, for our purposes, is a reduction in rank from manager to supervisor or a reduction from supervisor to a nonsupervisory position.

Demotion vs. Termination *(See also **Termination/Firing**).* If you must make this decision, you are entering pretty tough management territory. This is a test of your management skills and your intestinal fortitude. Demotion is always tough on you, as well as the demoted employee and the employee who replaces the demoted employee. In most cases, a demotion will also cause unrest at home for the demote employee.

Here are two examples. I once demoted an installation manager and promoted his assistant. The ex-installation manager accepted his transition back to the workforce and eventually became the unofficial leader in his old department. He supported the new installation manager, who did a great job, and production and profits increased dramatically.

Some years later, I demoted a manager who was in over his head. I promoted an operator who turned out to be an efficient and effective department manager. The demoted manager was unable to accept the transition to another department, complained constantly and caused so many problems in his department that he had to be terminated.

In retrospect, the first example is highly unusual. I lean toward termination first, and toward demotion only if a mistake has been made with a promotion that can be reversed before any harm is done. A failing manager who has been in his position for more than a few months has probably created an uncomfortable relationship with one or more employees or departments. If you are in touch with your business, you know the decision that must be made.

Pay reduction with demotion. If your business is under a collective bargaining agreement, this is any easy decision. The demoted employee makes the prevailing wage for his skill level. If not, this can be a tough decision. The demoted employee may not be willing to accept a decreased rate of pay. We do have a tendency to live at the outer edges of our earnings. It could be that the demoted employee, even though valuable and cooperative, simply cannot afford the demotion and must take a position with another company.

Repercussions. If you demote an employee and decide to allow her to stay with the company, you cannot tolerate any undermining or negative actions from that individual. Lay out her choices at the time of demotion and make it absolutely clear that she is on probation, just like a new employee. You expect her to act as a new employee and do everything possible to fit into her new position. Promise your complete support. Have a three-way conversation with the demoted employee and her new supervisor. If you are uncomfortable with the situation after the conversation, terminate rather than demote.

What if a demotion involves family? Family members occasionally continue to own a portion of the business after being demoted. The problems that ensue if the demoted family member stays with the business will eventually result in a mess you can do without. The rule of thumb is, do not get into business with family members. If you must terminate a family member, prepare for the inevitable and proceed, based on what is best for your business. Be prepared to suffer the consequences of your decision at a personal level.

WHAT SHOULD I DO? Why are demotions so tough? Because you are dealing with peoples' lives and the lives of their family members. If you promote from within, you know someone pretty well by the time you decide to promote her to a supervisory or management position. When you finally decide that it's time to demote that person, you really know her well, and it's really unpleasant to break the bad news.

So, if you have done your homework and have done everything possible to help that person to be a better manager, that manager knows that she is in trouble, has had multiple conversations and events surrounding those troubles and should be fairly well prepared for the bad news on the horizon. Furthermore, everyone who works for that manager knows that things are not up to par in the department in question and most are well aware that a change is in the wind. No, you have not been public with your feelings, but the grape vine is active and the manager of the department has probably told other managers that things are tense and that she is unsure of her status.

Now is the time to do the right thing. Have a final look at your findings. Huddle with your HR manager or contact, make sure you are on solid ground, review each step of the process, write up the necessary paperwork, and break the news to the embattled manager. You are in for a few rough nights. You will worry that maybe you could have done something different to alter the situation. But, deep down you will know that you did the right thing. Not everyone is cut out to lead others. Nor, will you make it through the balance of your career without demoting or terminating another manager.

Additional Resources: Human resources consultant, attorney.

DEPRECIATION *(See also SECTION 179 OF THE IRS TAX CODE)*

According to the IRS, when you purchase a qualified business asset that has a useful life of more than a year, the value of that asset declines over time, thus creating a tax break for your business. The IRS provides a schedule that determines which assets may be depreciated, over what period of time, and via what method. For example, you may purchase a punch press that is deemed to have a depreciation period of 10 years, at $5,000 a year, excluding salvage value. Salvage value is the amount that the press is worth at the end of its useful life. This does not mean that your punch press can only be used for 10 years or that it may not last for 20 years. It does mean that the IRS has deemed that, on average, the useful life of the press is 10 years. Therefore, IRS will allow you to depreciate that press, based on their depreciation schedule, thus giving you an annual tax deduction of $5,000, over a 10 year period. When the item is fully depreciated, you can continue to use the asset as long as you like, refurbish it, or replace it if necessary. If you refurbish, add to, update or otherwise improve the asset, it may be eligible for further depreciation.

WHAT SHOULD I DO? Your accountant should be well aware of IRS depreciation schedules. She should also have a list of all your assets. Let her decide which assets may be depreciated. Do not tackle depreciation on you own. Always involve your accountant.

DISCIPLINING EMPLOYEES *(See also TERMINATION/ FIRING)*

The act of disciplining or counseling employees is a book in itself. In the purest sense, employee orientation is a form of counseling. During orientation, you will communicate your expectations in oral and written forms. Your new employee will deliver an agreement, in oral and written form, that he will obey the policies and procedures of the organization and do his best to be a model employee.

What causes counseling and disciplinary situations? The reasons are as numerous as they are varied. Company policies are not clarified up front. Who has time for orientation? You are a small business. Your new hire just worked for a company like your own. He has experience repairing the same brand of machinery. What can possibly go wrong?

Your new employee left his last job because he was dissatisfied. Most of the time, a new employee is going to bring his past company's values and procedures to his new job. He brings what he knows. He needs time to develop a persona within your business culture. You knew that when you hired him. His values do not change overnight.

Expect a break-in period. That is why we let all new employees know that the first 90 days are probationary, followed by an evaluation to decide if the employee is to be retained, and what, if anything, he can do to improve his performance.

When should an employee be disciplined? Discipline an employee immediately, if possible. Always discipline during the employee's regular working hours. If at all possible, never discipline on a Friday. You want the employee to work the next day after discipline. If you discipline on a Friday, the employee may go home and spend the weekend talking to family, friends, and fellow employees, and brewing to the boiling point. If he works the day of the disciplinary session and the day after the disciplinary session, you will have a chance to calm any misunderstandings and create positive change. The best days for disciplinary action are Tuesday, Wednesday, and Thursday. Never discipline on an employee's day off.

Who should discipline an employee? An employee should be disciplined by his direct supervisor. The supervisor should feel free to ask her manager to sit in on the disciplinary session. If you feel that the supervisor may have difficulty disciplining an employee, you or your Human resources manager should definitely sit in on the session. If the supervisor has not been trained in disciplinary measures, you may want to give the manager a crash course in the things she may or may not say. Sit in on the session and take the lead if necessary. Poorly managed disciplinary sessions can lead to unwanted, costly results.

Who should be present for a disciplinary session? There are two schools of thought. The first school says that you always discipline without a third party present because the third party can vindicate or condemn the supervisor or employee in a later meeting. Of course, a union will always demand that a union representative is involved if the disciplined employee is a union member.

The second school says that a third party, selected by the supervisor holding the meeting, should always be present to record and validate the disciplinary session at a later date, if necessary. Make it a threesome, stick by the rules, and keep good records. If you are sued for unlawful termination, it's your word against the employee's word when your one-on-one disciplinary meetings are discussed.

If the disciplinary session may involve termination, include your human resources manager. Rehearse the meeting in its entirety, being sure that all bases and legalities are covered. If you are not completely comfortable, involve your attorney. Termination is always a three-party affair (*See also* **Termination/Firing**).

Where should an employee be disciplined? Some managers prefer their own offices. Some prefer a conference room because it is nonthreatening, neutral territory. Either is fine, providing that you will not be interrupted by inside or outside interferences. Discipline is a private matter. The door should be closed. The meeting should only be discussed at a later date if absolutely necessary, and only with the appropriate parties for appropriate reasons.

You have undoubtedly heard about the power of one's own office. When disciplining, forget about sitting the employee in a seat where he must look into sun-lit, glaring windows. Forget about putting a management barrier between you and the employee. Sit in a side chair opposite the employee. No barriers in this meeting. The idea is to create an atmosphere that respects your rights and the employee's rights. You definitely want to control the session, but intimidation will create an unwanted outcome.

Note: Please understand that many employees will discuss their disciplinary sessions with anyone who will listen. This should be expected.

Should I record a disciplinary session? It should not be necessary to record an employee who is being disciplined. Check with your attorney first. If your employee asks to record a disciplinary session, the answer is "No."

WHAT SHOULD I DO if I feel threatened, directly or indirectly, by an employee? There are two things to remember when you are threatened, either face to face with the employee, or via rumor. First, the company grapevine is 80 percent accurate. Second, you are better off safe than sorry.

Note: If you feel threatened, involve the appropriate authorities.

When should an employee be appraised? An employee should be appraised constantly by her direct supervisor. This does not mean that the supervisor takes the employee aside at every opportunity for an evaluation. It does mean that the supervisor is constantly observant and makes mental notes when the employee displays good or poor performance. Formal appraisals should start at 90 days after hire.

Appraise your employees annually, or more often if you feel it is necessary. If you hire an employee in May, appraise her after 90 days. Her next appraisal will take place in December of that year, and every December thereafter. This gets all your appraisals out of the way in December. All raises are effective January 1st for all employees, with exception of those offered for exemplary performance during the year.

Who should appraise an employee? An employee should be appraised by her direct supervisor.

Who should be present? The supervisor and the employee should be present for a formal appraisal, unless the appraisal may result in discipline or termination. A third party should be present for an appraisal that may result in a termination.

Evidence file. Be organized. Have your notes in front of you, whether it's an appraisal or a disciplinary session. Utilize bullet points. Stick to your plan. Make sure you are on firm legal ground.

Warnings. There are three parts to a warning. First, provide proof that the offending employee has broken a company policy. Second, provide proof that at some point in the past the offending employee was made aware of the policy, orally or written. Third, the offending employee is to be disciplined for the infraction.

Warnings may be oral or written. Most companies provide an oral warning the first time a policy is violated. Record of the oral warning is entered into the employee's file – in writing. The second and succeeding warnings are written. The employee is requested to sign and date a written warning. If the employee refuses, make a note to that effect on the warning. If the violation is one that results in termination for a first-time offense, for example, using drugs in the workplace or theft of company property, the termination is prepared in writing prior to the meeting *(See also **Termination/Firing**)*.

Absenteeism. This is a tricky area. Absenteeism may involve sick leave, paid sick days, tardiness, Family Medical Leave (FMLA), paid time off, military leave, funeral or bereavement leave, personal paid or unpaid leave. There are also other reasons for missing work not listed here *(See also FAMILY MEDICAL LEAVE ACT [FMLA]).*

Many state and federal laws exist that involve leave. If you are a union shop, know your contract inside and out. Lack of knowledge on your part does not constitute a legal defense if you are sued by an employee.

Many of your employees know the state and federal laws, and their union contracts, as well as you know them, or better. You must pay to be defended by an attorney. An employee can usually find free representation. The employee pays only if his attorney wins, which means that the employee's attorney gets a percentage of the settlement if you lose in court, giving the employee's attorney great impetus to win a fat settlement.

WHAT SHOULD I DO? Two things come to mind. First, when dealing with any of the items in this section, the best policy is to confront a troubled employee only after you are absolutely certain that you have properly followed all procedures legally and completely. If you are uncertain about anything at all, seek help. Secondly, take any potential law suits seriously. This does not mean that you call your attorney every time something pops up on your radar that has potential to turn into a lawsuit. It does mean that you should pick up the phone and call your HR manager or contact if you feel that a lawsuit has real potential. Use common sense. If a troubled employee or former employee is spreading the word that he is about to sue your company, let HR know about your concern. Lawsuits are untimely, tiring and expensive. If you can avoid a potential suit by being proactive, do so.

Note: Know the rules. Follow the rules. Stay out of court.

DISCOUNTS

Every customer wants to know that he is your most important customer. You cannot give discounts to everyone, all the time. Try to discount *only* products that are discounted to you from your vendors. Keep your gross margins where they belong. You must fulfill projected profits to stay in business.

Payment terms. Payment terms on an invoice describe the date payment is due and any terms that may apply to the payment. Example: The invoice shows a total of $1,000 due. The terms are 2 percent 10, net 30.

Here is the breakdown. Net 30 tells you that the entire $1,000 is due on the 30th day after the date of the invoice. 2 percent 10 tells you that the payer is invited to pay the invoice early, within 10 days of the invoice date, and receive a 2 percent discount for doing so. That represents a savings of $20. The savings is awarded only if the payer's check is in the hands of the payee within 10 days of the invoice date. Otherwise, the payer's next statement will include an invoice for the $20 that was discounted from his original payment.

You may want to offer such discounts to encourage your customers to pay their invoices more quickly. You will find that customers will try to take advantage of your discounts even though their checks arrive after the due date. You will find this to be particularly true among very large customers who know that you heavily depend on their business. Sometimes it is better to tread lightly and suck up the 2 percent, even though the discount is obviously outdated. The customer is aware of the situation and takes the discount because he knows he can do so without pushback from you.

Next-sale discount. Many companies offer a discount on the sale following a sale that is already in hand. The discount is offered for a limited time. Example: You sell a customer a new riding lawnmower. You probably make a larger percentage profit on a number of accessories such as grass collectors, spare blades, and tune-up kits than you make on the riding lawnmower. You want your new customer's repeat business for years to come.

So you offer dated coupons for accessory items. Some must be used within the next 30 days. Others are dated for use later in the season. If you are a successful dealer, your manufacturer or distributor will probably provide you with coupons and special sale pricing.

Coupons. Retail operations have been utilizing coupons for decades. The manufacturer provides coupons. The end user gets the discount when he uses the coupon. The coupon is collected by the retailer. The retailer collects the value of the coupon from the manufacturer.

Some businesses even take competitors' coupons. They are worthless to the taker, but are considered a vehicle that coaxes the competitor's customer into your door. Calculate the cost of acquiring a new customer. The money you lose on your competitor's coupon is well worth that cost.

Freebies and giveaways. If you are going to give something away, try to convince your vendor, distributor or manufacturer, to foot the bill for all, or a large portion of the cost. Example: You give away a free set of poles with every snow ski package you sell. Price the entire package so you make a reasonable profit. Include the poles at your cost. Convince the ski manufacturer to discount his skis an extra percentage to cover the profit you would otherwise lose on the poles. The ski manufacturer makes out because you sell more ski packages.

Loss leaders. Probably the greatest loss leader of all time is Miracle Whip. The product was often sold at a small loss because it was ultra-popular and was a big draw at the grocery store. A loss leader represents a small investment to draw a crowd. The crowd spends money on other, profitable items while in the store. Think about it. Are you more interested in going to the ball game on bat day when you receive something free? Make small adjustments in the prices of more profitable products to offset the cost and lost profit of the loss leader.

⤺**WHAT SHOULD I DO?** Watch your competition; be creative; ask your vendors and suppliers about programs to help your sales; take the initiative. You never know what doors may open if you ask your vendors for help.

DISTRIBUTORS

What is a Distributor? You may be familiar with the 4 Ps of Marketing. They are Product, Price, Place and Promotion. Place refers to the distribution of a product. Distributors are intermediaries, meaning that they move product through the distribution chain, from manufacturers to sellers. Distributors differ from merchants – they are also intermediaries – because distributors are agents or brokers who do not buy and resell products. They are middlemen that have the necessary business connections to put sellers together with buyers. They charge a fee for performing their services, based on a percentage of the sales price to the distributor's contacts.

How do manufacturers sell their products? Some industries utilize specific distribution methods throughout. They sell via distributors or sell directly to a retailer or the end-user. Some sell through more than one distribution channel, possibly dealing through distributors and also selling directly to the end user via alternate methods. The point here is that most industries have a formula that works for them. Be sure you understand the distribution channels in your industry before coming to a decision regarding distributors.

How do distributors operate? Distributors perform a valuable function. Manufacturers typically know the ins and outs of the manufacturing business but have little knowledge of selling to the end user. Distributors fill this gap. They have a stable of outlets that they constantly contact, putting manufacturers' products in front of intermediaries that would otherwise have to be contacted by the manufacturer. Distributors may carry a book of thousands of products from numerous manufacturers who are trying to present their products to their specific target markets.

Advantages of utilizing a distributor:

Distributors relieve manufacturers of the necessity to put a sales force on the street.

By utilizing a distributor, the manufacturer can immediately reach hundreds or thousands of outlets for their products.

The salespeople for the distributor are usually familiar with the products in their books. They occasionally receive a modicum of training to allow them to make the sale.

Distributors usually have an inside staff, as well as a street presence, allowing their customers to instantly fill orders and discuss problems or opportunities.

Distributors will visit their customers on a regular basis, maintaining a pulse on the market.

Disadvantages of utilizing a distributor:

Distributors are usually area dominate. They may serve a particular community, state, region or territory. Depending on your product(s), you may require several distributors to reach your target markets.

Distributors do not necessarily receive an abundance of training on your product. Training sessions introduce new products but salespeople typically get a sketchy product orientation. Details are at a premium until a new product shows signs of becoming a hot seller.

Salespeople are usually paid on commission and have a tendency to play it safe, selling proven products and ignoring new products, to safeguard their commissions. If the salesperson convinces a customer to try a new product, and it does not move well, he may jeopardize his relationship with that customer.

Distributors can take hefty fees for their services, between fifteen and twenty-five percent, depending on the industry. Their fees may put your product out of the price range of similar products and/or reduce your margins unacceptably.

Distributors agree to represent products only after the item has gained some popularity, acceptance and sales.

Although distributors visit their customers regularly, their salespeople chase the money. They visit their best customers quite often, while smaller customers may only see a salesperson once or twice a year.

WHAT SHOULD I DO? If you are interested in contacting a distributor to discuss your products, just go to the Internet and surf the categories, such as, distributors dry goods, distributors electronic components, distributors leather goods or distributors hair products. Directories and companies are abundant. Determine your margins and pricing limits prior to arranging a meeting. Insist on a visit to the distributor's place of business. If you and a distributor have a mutual interest in each other, ask to spend a few days riding with a few of their salespeople and gain an understanding of their ability to move your product. Your decision to do business through a distributor will eventually boil down to dollars and sense. Can you afford to mark up your prices to meet the distributor's needs and still meet your sales and profit goals?

DRESS CODES

Businesses have dress codes for several reasons:

First, you know how you are being represented on the street and inside your business.

Second, you need not be concerned about dress that may offend your employees, or dress associated with gang colors or other offensive organizations.

Third, it is easy to recognize your employees in a group. Everyone with a vest belongs to your organization; those without vests are shoppers.

Fourth, if properly dressed, concerns about safety issues such as wearing loose clothing around machinery, are abated. This also applies to fire retardant and other types of protective clothing and gear.

Fifth, if you have a uniform service, your employees will always look sharp when visitors enter your business.

Sixth, you can put employees' names on their uniforms. You will look like a hero when you finally can call all your employees by their first names when you walk through your building(s).

Seventh, you can issue one style uniform to supervisors and a different style to nonsupervisory personnel.

Eighth, you can provide clothing that will keep your employee's safe in unpredictable outdoor environments. Surely, you have seen those bright orange or yellow-green shirts on employees who do road work or work around loud and dangerous machinery.

Retail environment. Find something that sets your employees apart from customers. It can be a hat, vest, shirt, blouse, badge, or a tie. It can be just about anything that cries out that the employee works for your business.

Ties. Ties should not be allowed in an environment where the tie can become entangled in a piece of machinery and/or injure the employee. Also, nothing looks quite as bad as a tie that is hanging down from an unbuttoned shirt collar. If you require ties, require that they are worn properly. Show some class.

Office environment. Most businesses have something in their handbooks regarding dress. The most common involve cleanliness, clothing common to the particular industry and not offensive to any other employee or to a company's customers.

Most companies do not allow women to show midriffs, cleavages, or legs above the knee. Anything that is sexually provocative is not allowed. This applies to males, as well as females. Shoes must be worn at all times. Flip flops, slippers, socks, and bare feet are prohibited. Bare feet are magnets for paper clips, staples, and anything else that can cause foot injuries. Tank tops, cut-off sleeves, cut-off jeans, cut-off shorts, and any clothing that has been altered unattractively or in a manner that would cause danger or is inappropriate for the employee or others is forbidden. Some companies, such as UPS, do allow shorts for men and women when the environment calls for such wear.

Do customers come to you or do you go to them? Dress appropriately for your customer base. Not everyone is enamored by a salesperson who is dressed to the nines. If you sell golf equipment, dress for golf. If you sell insurance, wear a suit, sport coat, or dress. Give your customers the image they expect to see. Always dress as though a customer will visit your business today.

Factory environment. Safety first. Check with OSHA. Contrary to popular belief, it is better to make friends of the OSHA people up front. They know what dress is appropriate around machinery, chemicals, heavy equipment, and dangerous work environments. OSHA does not recognize lack of knowledge as an excuse for violating the rules. They will generally give you a chance to correct problem areas within a reasonable amount of time before levying fines.

Shoes. If you intend to require a particular type of shoe wear, be sure it is adequate for the environment and meets requirements and standards for your business. Do not require a grocery store clerk to wear black dress shoes if he is responsible for corralling grocery baskets. That would be hard on his feet in any environment.

Check OSHA standards for your business. All or some of your employees may be required to wear steel-toed, reinforced, heavy duty, or fire-retardant shoes or boots. Go to www.osha.gov for more information. A few of the areas that may be helpful to check on the OSHA site are hard hats, foot wear, eye protection, flame retardant clothing, ear protection, lifting protection, inhalant protection, and so on. You get the idea.

NOTE: Safety first! Safety first! Safety first! Safety first! Safety first! Safety first!

Additional Resources: OSHA (Occupational Safety & Health Administration). Your business associates will tell you that you are crazy to involve OSHA. However, OSHA will be happy to answer your questions and is often quite helpful.

Drug-Free Workplace *(See also **HIRING: Drug-free workplace**).*

DUE DILIGENCE

During the process of launching your business, you are going to hear a lot of talk about due diligence. Due diligence is simply an investigation into various areas of a company to determine that company's overall competence. Due diligence is separated into two key areas: *Yours* and *Theirs.*

At the outset, *yours* refers to the compilation of information that will comprise your business plan. You will go through the elements of your business plan with a fine tooth comb. Look at your company from an investor's point of view. An investor wants to know that your management team is strong, clean, and available. Do a background check on every member of your team, including yourself and your spouse, even if he or she will not be involved in the business.

Is there anyone who may present a problem for potential investors? Are you getting into a market where you or another management team member may have endorsed a non-compete agreement that prevents that person from becoming involved until that agreement expires? Is a member of your team along for the initial ride but up for replacement once the business is well underway?

Know everything possible about your competition, your industry, and your present and potential suppliers. Are you counting on a supplier or manufacturer that is at risk of going under? Are you counting on a supplier that may have an exclusive arrangement with your competition?

Go over your numbers again and again. Investors love hockey stick projections, the kinds of numbers that reach for the sky. The question is, are your projections blue sky and unattainable, or realistic with a little extra if things go just right? Are you over projecting profits just to attract investors?

Theirs refers to the due diligence of another entity that intends to do business with you, such as a lender, potential business partner, venture capitalist, or business angel. In these cases, you will likely be dealing with an attorney who represents the investigating enterprise. The documents they require are numerous. Involve your attorney and follow her advice to a fault. No documentation should be given to the investigating company until approved by your attorney.

Chapter E

EMPLOYEE DEDUCTIONS / GARNISHMENTS (OTHER THAN THE STANDARD DEDUCTIONS)

From time to time, you may find it necessary to deduct various items and amounts from employee paychecks, in addition to the standard deductions required by law. The government may instruct you to garnish an employee's wages. You may enter into an agreement with an employee to deduct for items that are required for his work, such as tools, uniforms, products, or equipment. You may offer health insurance, life insurance, or disability insurance above and beyond standard coverage. Occasionally, you may honor a request for a short-term loan to an employee in need.

Written contracts for employee deductions. Contracts for deductions should be signed by the employee and the company, in writing, with specific amounts and dates for repayment. The exceptions are garnishments and other deductions that are demanded and approved by local, state, or federal authorities.

When should I deduct loan repayments? Take the shortest possible route to repayment. Evenly deduct an amount that is reasonable for you and the employee. Utilize the same program for all employees if possible.

WHAT SHOULD I DO? If you are ordered to garnish an employee's wages, just follow the rules. Playing games with any governmental agency is hazardous to the health of your business. If your employee agrees, in writing, to a deduction, follow through like you would with any other contract.

Garnishments *(See Garnishment)*.

Additional Resources: Attorney, accountant.

ENTREPRENEUR

Barron's defines entrepreneur as an "individual who initiates business activity. The term is often associated with one who takes business risks."[5] Business Dictionary defines entrepreneur somewhat differently, as "someone who exercises initiative by organizing a venture to take benefit of an opportunity and, as the decision maker, decides what, how, and how much of a good or service will be produced. An entrepreneur supplies risk capital as a risk taker, and monitors and controls the business activities. The entrepreneur is usually a sole proprietor, a partner, or the one who owns the majority of shares in an incorporated venture."[6]

Entrepreneurs form the backbone of small business in America. They are the business people, just like you, who put their life savings at risk to make something more of themselves by creating companies, jobs and profits. According to the Small Business Administration, there are roughly 26.8 million small businesses in the United States. They account for "99.7% of all employers and employ 49.2% of the private-sector workforce." Over 78% have no employees and most employers have less than 20 employees.[7] As you can see, without small business entrepreneurs we would lose nearly half of the jobs in the U.S. and the buying power produced by those jobs.

EMPLOYEE HANDBOOK

Employee handbooks vary in style, content, and size as widely as the companies that use them. A handbook is a company orientation and a compilation of its policies and procedures, neatly packaged for the employee, whether new or a veteran of the organization. If you operate in more than one state, keep in mind that many of the items included in an employee handbook are state specific.

Purpose. The employee handbook defines your company and employee expectations. It also defines the employee's role in bringing success to the workplace. The employee handbook reduces potential lawsuits against your company from employees, former employees and from outside entities. The last page of every employee handbook should be a signature page, where the employee signs stating that she has read, understands, and agrees to abide by all company policies and procedures. A new employee's signature is required to gain employment.

Do I need an employee handbook? Yes, you need an employee handbook. Set up your employee handbook before going into business. Update it as your business grows and changes. Most of the language is common. Internet-based companies are abundant, featuring do-it-yourself kits and customized handbooks that are state specific. If you want to stay closer to home, see Human Resources specialist for help with drafting your employee handbook.

Should I be directly involved? Most employers are at a loss when faced with challenges that involve EEOC, drug testing, harassment, confidentiality, at-will employment, discipline, benefits, and ADA. Getting involved in the employee handbook process makes you aware of the areas that can create legal discomfort for you and your company. If you become fully involved with assembling your handbook, you will learn enough to recognize when and how to take action when sensitivities arise in a given area.

What is covered? There is usually a short history of the company and an introduction that explains the purpose of the handbook. Next is a disclaimer explaining that no handbook can encompass all possible situations that may arise during employment. This is usually followed by an Employee Code of Conduct section that spells out dos and don'ts such as EEOC, drug testing, harassment, confidentiality, attendance, workplace violence, types of employment (such as full-time, part-time, exempt, non-exempt, at-will, etc.), discipline, benefits, compensation, performance appraisals, types of leave offered, and safety.

What kind of document? Employee handbooks may have a few typed pages or dozens of loose leaf binders that are updated on a regular basis. Your document should cover all the pertinent aspects of your business and should be as long and intricate as necessary to give your employees sufficient guidelines to be happy and successful during their time with your company. The handbook should also spell out and clarify anything that will help you and your employees abide by company and legal policies that will help you stay out of legal trouble.

Breaks. There is no federal law requiring breaks,[2] but federal law does require that breaks provided by an employer must be compensated at the applicable pay rate, whether straight time or overtime. Check your state statutes, just to be safe. If breaks are customary in your industry or workplace, pay your employees their customary wages or salaries for break periods.

State the lengths of breaks and the exact times that breaks must be taken. Employees are not to be compensated if they take breaks that are longer than stated in the employee handbook or taken at a time that is different than the break time stated in the handbook. Breaks are included as hours worked during the week and also included when calculating overtime.

Holiday Pay. There is no federal law requiring compensation for vacations or holidays that are not worked.[3] Agreements for such compensations are made between you and your employees, or an employee representative, such as a union. Employee benefits are discussed in the interview process and spelled out in an offer letter. If you choose to forego payment for nonworking holidays, you may lose valuable employees to a company with a more lenient view of holiday pay. You may want to limit holiday pay to full-time employees and those who work the day before and after the nonworking holiday. This is a common practice in the United States.

Lunch Hours. Lunch hour is generic for the hour, half-hour, or whatever amount of time you allow employees to take off for lunch - without pay. You pay for breaks. You do not pay for lunch hours.[4] Lunch hours are not mandated by federal law. Our local bus drivers are union. They work without a lunch hour. Some pack a lunch and munch outside the bus if they get ahead of schedule. A few minutes here and a few minutes there are usually enough to grab a quick sandwich and a beverage.

The truth is that people work better with occasional breaks, and certainly when they have the opportunity to take between a half hour and an hour for lunch. Your hourly employees should work half a shift, take lunch, and then work the remaining half. Make sure they work right up until lunch time. Make sure they are back on the job on time. Washing hands and cleaning up is on their time, not yours. You set the time that hourly employees take lunch. If they are working more than eight hours, an extra half hour may be in order after the eighth hour.

Salary employees typically take lunch at will. There is no need for you to set their hours unless you are concerned about leaving all workstations unattended during lunch. There is a need to let your employees know the length of their lunch hours (30 minutes or an hour) and that you expect them back on the job when that time expires. The rules apply to all, whether in the plant or on the road. You expect a fair day's work for a fair day's pay. You may want to stagger lunch hours to keep production consistent.

Overtime pay *(See OVERTIME).*

Sexual harassment *(See also SEXUAL HARASSMENT).* Your employee handbook should include a section on sexual harassment. Consult a human resources specialist for a boiler plate sexual harassment section for your handbook.

Vacation Leave *(See also BENEFITS: Holiday Pay and Vacation Pay).* Federal law does not require employers to provide vacation leave, paid or unpaid. However, if you do not provide these benefits, you may lose employees to a company that provides such compensation.

Sick Days *(See SICK DAYS / SICK LEAVE).*

Sick Leave *(See SICK DAYS / SICK LEAVE and FAMILY MEDICAL LEAVE ACT (FMLA).*

Working hours. Working hours should be described for exempt and non-exempt employees. Exempt employees are not paid overtime and typically include executives, sales staff, and support staff. Exempt employees are paid by the week, the job, or the sale. Non-exempt employees, which usually includes laborers, are paid by the hour and also qualify for overtime.

Most companies require that employees work a base week of 40 hours. The week may be comprised of a number of different combinations of days and hours. The most common work week is Monday through Friday, eight hours per day, with a break for lunch of a half-hour to a full hour. Some companies prefer employees to work four days of ten hours each. Some companies that are open more than five days a week, or have extended hours on given days, may require employees to work any of the seven days in a week. When business is good, shifts may be added that require employees to work nights or weekends. There are no federal laws that require specific work weeks, days, or hours for workers. Your state may have laws that limit certain practices regarding working hours in specific industries or circumstances.

WHAT SHOULD I DO? Some states have laws pertaining to many of the areas covered in this section that are stricter than the federal laws. Be sure to acquaint yourself with state laws, as well as federal laws, when assembling your employee handbook.

ENVIRONMENTAL PROTECTION AGENCY (EPA)

"The mission of the U.S. Environmental Protection Agency's Office of Small Business Programs is to support the protection of human health and the environment by advocating and advancing the business, regulatory, and environmental compliance concerns of small and socio-economically disadvantaged businesses, and minority academic institutions".[8] There you are, straight from the source itself. This is a powerful agency. If you see any indication that you may be sidestepping EPA's compliance boundaries, take care of the problem immediately. Get in touch with EPA and ask for help. Do not wait until EPA discovers your lack of compliance and decides to call you.

WHAT SHOULD I DO? If you are not sure of your status, contact the appropriate agency directly, or contact a consultant familiar with your problem. Either of them can conduct an in-house mock review. It is your responsibility to know the rules; ignorance is not an excuse and can be expensive. If you have a violation, get it out in the open and come to an amenable agreement with the agency. Agency officials will provide a document that summarizes your offense(s) and a procedure and time schedule for correcting the violation(s). If you have a reasonable defense for overlooking the offense, most agencies are reasonable in their approaches. A consultant is more expensive in the long run because you must eventually involve the agency in question.

EQUAL PAY ACT

This law prohibits employers from paying dissimilar wages to men and women who perform essentially the same work under similar working conditions. The Equal Pay Act of 1963 falls under the auspices of the Fair Labor Standards Act of 1938.[9] The message here is clear and concise and should not be ignored or violated under any circumstances. Penalties are substantial.

If your business operates under a collective bargaining agreement that differentiates earnings based on seniority, production standards or a merit system, you are on legal ground, as long as sex is not a factor.

Additional Resources: Human resources expert or look for "Equal Pay Act of 1963" on the Internet.

EQUITY-BASED LOANS (See also ASSET-BASED LOANS)

EXCLUSIVITY (See also FRANCHISING)

For our purposes, exclusivity refers to the right to a protected territory for a product and/or service. You are guaranteed that you are the only business selling that product or service within a specific area, defined by boundaries or distance from your business location. For example, you may control *all* sales and service for a particular brand of water softeners in your county and counties adjacent to your county boundaries. Or, your territory may be defined as everything within a 50-mile radius of your business headquarters.

Exclusivity is a two-way street. You may be granted exclusivity for *your* sales area from a vendor or manufacturer, or you may grant exclusivity to vendors of your company's products or services. In either case, calculate the profitability and closely assess the negative and positive attributes of the endeavor. Exclusivity is not always positive, regardless of the direction of flow.

Why should a business seek exclusivity? The greatest advantage to exclusivity is the opportunity to enter and control your target market ahead of the rest of the pack. Other potential advantages are a protected territory, an exclusive right to purchase at a special price, the right to offer genuine name-brand parts and services, the right to display official brand-name signage and advertising, an advertising program that may offer financial reimbursements from the vendor or manufacturer, and rapid market growth in the absence of genuine brand name competition.

Exclusivity also has its disadvantages. If you fail to find success with an exclusive product or service – for whatever reason – you may be considered a failure among your customers and competitors. Your failure may also make it difficult to contract with a vendor for a favorable replacement product or service.

Some vendors and manufacturers offer exclusivity only if you agree to purchase and sell minimum quantities of a product or service. If you fail to achieve these minimums, you may be forced to pay a higher price to retain your exclusivity rights.

Companies that enjoy exclusivity also may be forced to train their technicians and salespeople to sell and maintain their products. Training is usually ongoing and necessary as new products and services enter the market. The training you offer to your staff sets them apart from your competition and creates an entry barrier that discourages competitors from entering the market. Be sure to understand the costs involved with such training before entering into an exclusive agreement.

You also may be forced to forgo the sale of competitive brands. For example, restaurants typically sell Coca Cola or Pepsi products. Neither Coca Cola, nor Pepsi will tell you that you cannot sell a competitive brand in your store. They may tell you that they will provide all dispensing equipment, including free set up and maintenance, if you contract to utilize their equipment for their products, exclusively.

There are many reasons to seek exclusivity. Investigate potential opportunities with your vendors. They will probably require you to become skilled and certified in handling their products and services before exclusivity is granted. You may be asked to purchase a starter package of products and/or purchase and install specific machinery or equipment to service the product(s) you sell. Exclusivity may bear a cost, but the rewards may be very attractive.

WHAT SHOULD I DO? If you are interested in offering exclusive products, services and territories to your vendors, look at both sides of the profit puzzle and strike a deal that is mutually beneficial to you and your customers. If you do not understand the contract completely, call your attorney and follow her guidance.

Additional Resources: Attorney.

EXEMPT VS. NONEXEMPT EMPLOYEES

The Fair Labor Standards Act (FLSA) governs the exempt or nonexempt status of employees.[11] There are a few exceptions to the law. A number of truck drivers, for instance, are governed by the Motor Carriers Act[10], while a majority of railroad workers are governed by the Railway Labor Act[12].

Those employees who fall under the umbrella of FLSA are either exempt or nonexempt. Exempt refers to employees who do not receive overtime pay, while nonexempt employees do receive overtime pay. According to FLSA, exempt employees generally differ from nonexempt employees in three different categories. They are: 1) amount paid, 2) method of payment, and 3) kind of work. FLSA provides three tests to determine the exempt vs. nonexempt status of an employee. They are the: 1) Salary Level Test, 2) Salary Basis Test, and 3) Duties Test. Go to www.dol.gov (US Department of Labor) and navigate to FLSA for further guidance before determining if an employee should or should not be paid overtime.

Additional Resources: Human resources specialist, www.dol.gov.

EXIT INTERVIEW

An exit interview should be accomplished by a neutral, nonthreatening party who understands what she may, or may not, say. Utilize human resources personnel whenever possible. Exit interviews can be carried out before the former employee leaves the premises for the last time, or they can be conducted by phone, on line, by mail, or by a third party who is unrelated to the company. The interview may be verbal or written.

Some companies offer exit interviews for all employees who quit or are laid off. Others offer exit interviews to all former employees, including those who are terminated for cause. Utilize the exit interview to spot areas in need of improvement. Investigate problems that come to light. Take criticisms seriously, but cautiously.

The exit interview should generate feedback regarding the former employee's feelings about her reasons for leaving, as well as her opinion of the company in general, company policies, compensation, benefits, company culture, and management as a whole.

Exit interviews should be available for all former employees unless a crime was involved that prevents a normal course of events. The exit interview is a tool to help you learn more about your company culture and discover methods to improve. A successful exit interview can also aid in neutralizing some of the bad feelings that a former employee may harbor toward your company.

WHAT SHOULD I DO? The information in exit interviews should be viewed as a tool to help you improve your company. Sure, you will occasionally find information that is implausible, but as a whole, the material presented in exit interviews can be converted to positive action. Whether positive or negative in nature, absorb the facts you are given in exit interviews and put it to good use.

EXIT STRATEGY

An exit strategy is designed to sell all or part of your interest in your business at one or more specific times in the future. You may want to divorce yourself from the business completely, or you may want to downsize to a more suitable position, at some time in the future. An exit strategy may follow a planned or unplanned event.

When should I consider an exit plan? You should consider an exit plan when you assemble your original business plan. The idea is to exit on your terms. Thus, it is important to construct a set of terms and conditions that would indicate your need or willingness to exercise your exit strategy at a specific time.

Such considerations may include the ability to purchase another similar business, but you cannot do so without first selling your existing business. Ill health may be a concern since it is one of the leading factors that force entrepreneurs into early retirement. You may want to sell your business or pass it on to a valued employee, all at once or over a period of time. You may be starting a new business at age 25 and plan to retire at age 50. You may recognize that your business may slow down at some time in the future because your new invention has a limited economic growth.

The reason for exiting is not as important as your recognition that future specific events may present the need or opportunity to exercise your preplanned exit strategy. The key is to be ready when the opportunity presents itself.

How should I get ready to exit? Remember what you read just a moment ago. Your exit strategy starts with your original business plan. Once you have completed an acceptable five-year plan, it is time to look to the internal and external reasons that may present opportunities or necessities to exit. Even though you want to exit on your own terms, you must consider other forces that may present reasons to exercise your exit strategy, such as stiff competition, a failing or growing economy on the horizon, death or disability (yours or a partner or employee), or loss of a critical contract.

Provide the ultimate shape of your exit strategy before something else or someone else provides it for you. From the start, identify individuals and companies that may be potential buyers. Develop key principals and employees who may have the wherewithal to eventually take over your business. Investigate key man life insurance policies that insure you and your key partners and employees. Have your attorney draw up a contract that passes life insurance proceeds and company ownership to the appropriate parties, providing the funds for a seamless transition of your business *(See also INSURANCE: Key Man Insurance)*.

WHAT SHOULD I DO? The perfect exit strategy has you exiting: 1) when you plan to exit, 2) on your own terms, 3) debt free, while recouping your investment and planned return on investment, 4) when selling to a financially solid buyer with an experienced management team, and 5) with a solid tax and investment plan that secures your financial future.

Talk to a solid investment counselor when you first get into business. Tell her when you plan to exit, the amount you need to exit, and your method for exit. Invest wisely and safely and follow your plan. Revisit your exit strategy annually and adjust for changes in your family life, the economy, the state of your business and the state of your investments.

Additional Resources: Accountant, attorney, banker, insurance professional.

EXPENSE ACCOUNTS

An expense account reimburses employees for preauthorized, work-related expenses. Notice the terms, *preauthorized and work-related*. When an expense meets both criteria, you are obligated to pay that expense unless you previously made it clear that the item is forbidden entirely or allowed only if approved in writing.

Reimbursable expenses. Certain expenses are always going to be reimbursable—with your pre-agreement. For example, if you reimburse your employees for travel, expenses such as flights, meals, entertainment, hotels, automobile rental, and fuel are your responsibility as long as your employees stay within company guidelines. If you have agreed to reimburse coach class flights and your employee elects to fly first class, the extra expense becomes the employee's responsibility. Have your employees endorse an agreement that limits company credit cards to company purchases only. Company purchases *do not include* extras such as first-class upgrades. Forbidden purchases must be handled with the employees' personal funds and personal credit cards. Do not put yourself in a position where you must negotiate payment for non-reimbursable expenses from an employee.

When you first go into business, you will want to handle all business air, rail, and automobile reservations for your employees. Employee travelers are not always diligent about finding the best deals. Put all air, rail, and automobile charges on the same credit card so you can amass the points, miles, or cash benefits of the card. Choose a company that does not reduce or cancel benefits after a given period of time. When you are large enough that travel becomes more prevalent, select an employee or agency to handle all travel arrangements.

The following is a typical employee expense voucher (Figure E-1). Expense vouchers come in hundreds of varieties, from very simple to very complex. Select something from the Internet or your word processor and adapt it to fit your needs.

EXPENSE VOUCHER

Figure E-1

	Monday	Tuesday	Wednesday	Thursday	Friday	Total
Location:	Okla. City	Enid, OK	Enid, OK	Enid, OK	Okla. City	
Date:	2/6/12	2/7/12	2/8/12	2/9/12	2/10/12	
Purpose (Sales, Install, Maint.):	Sales	Sales	Sales	Sales	Sales	
Vehicle Rental	686.14					686.14
					582.49	582.49
Parking	15.00	10.00	10.00	10.00		45.00
Fuel			55.35		38.97	94.32
Breakfast		15.00	15.00	15.00	15.00	60.00
Lunch	22.00	17.00	16.00	18.00	21.00	94.00
Dinner	23.00	18.00	17.00	19.00		77.00
Ground Transportation						
Mileage @ _____ ¢ per mile						
Lodging	141.90	158.60	158.60	158.60		617.70
Tips / Gratuities						
Tolls						
Miscellaneous Expense						
Entertainment						
Total Expenses	888.04	218.60	271.95	220.60	657.46	2,256.65
						2,256.65
						0.00
						2,256.65

I certify that all expenses are true and accurate.

Signature: _____ Date: _____

Approval: _____ Date: _____

*** Attach all receipts ***

~ 123 ~

Entertainment. Entertainment can be expensive. Some companies purchase tickets to sporting events, the theater, and so on. Tickets are doled out to top customers and top prospective customers with your permission. Entertainment expenses should be designed to produce a profit for your company. Salespeople will spend all the entertainment money you throw their way, without regard to cost and profit. This is just a fact of life. Sure, it takes money to make money, but stay smart. Stay profitable. Require a written requisition from employees who want to provide the above items for clients, in excess of predetermined amount.

Note: This Expense Voucher is based on a 5-day work week. Just add Sunday and/or Saturday if necessary.

Expense Reports. The usual expenses are easy to track. However, you must be more resourceful in tracking expenses for those employees who are working in the field. Salespeople travel and entertain. Installers and service personnel occasionally find it necessary to make a trip to a neighborhood store to purchase a part. Employees who drive personal vehicles are asked to track mileage. For these expenses, an expense report becomes a necessity. Get together with your bookkeeper and assemble an expense report that is simple and that includes typical items for your type of business. Examples abound on the Internet.

Who should have an expense account? Anyone who spends company money on a regular basis should have an expense account. Small, incidental amounts for occasional purchases should be reimbursed via petty cash *(See also PETTY CASH)*.

How often should expense reports be turned in? Expense reports should be turned in on the first business day of every month, for the prior month. Make a rule that provides that expenses will not be reimbursed unless they are included in the report for the month in question, i.e., July's expenses must be included in July's expense report. This prevents employees from turning in late expense reports. Let employees know that expense accounts will not be reimbursed beyond a specific date, say, more than 30 days after the specified turn-in date. Put it in writing.

What is included? If there is no receipt, reimbursement is not approved. Some companies allow payment of expenses under a certain amount or for certain types of expenses (parking meters come to mind) without receipts. Try to avoid this type of grey area.

Accuracy of expense reports. Check every expense report for accuracy and the employee's signature before issuing payment. If the report is incorrect, give it back to the employee for correction. You do not have time to run down expenses for your employees.

Approval. You or qualified accounts payable personnel should approve every expense account after approval by the employee's direct supervisor. Most errors will be mathematical. Encourage employees to avoid erasures and overwriting.

Payment. Expenses should be paid with the first payroll after the expenses are incurred. Expenses should be on a separate check from payroll. If you are providing company credit cards, it is the responsibility of the employee to keep payments current and to present monthly proof of payment. All items purchased on a company credit card should be expensed like any other. Surely, an employee will eventually ask why it is necessary to put an expense on a report since it already appears on the company credit card, creating double entries and unnecessary work. The answer is that the expense report details the nature of the expense, including the reason for the expenditure and the account to which the expense is applied.

WHAT SHOULD I DO? Your budget should include a line or section that deals with expense accounts. The key here is to budget properly and stick to your budget. This is accomplished by clearly communicating the guidelines for expense accounts to those who are creating the expenses. As long as you abide by expense account guidelines with all personnel, you will experience only occasional bumps in the road, usually associated with an unexpected expense that causes you to make an executive decision. Last, you also should follow the rules you created.

Additional Resources: Bookkeeper, CPA.

Chapter F

FACILITY

Should I rent, lease, or buy a facility? Rent refers to a short term, one year or less. Lease refers to a term of two or more years. Owning your facility is almost always better than renting or leasing if everything else in your business fits into place.

For our purposes, assume that you will have a rent, lease, or mortgage payment until such time that you can afford otherwise. The following includes a discussion of facility needs. The choice between rent, lease, or buy should be discussed with your business partners, banker, and CPA.

Location. Regardless of whether you are going to rent, lease or buy, location is the most critical question. The criteria for choosing a place of business is similar to the criteria for choosing a home. Location, location, location come first. Then give consideration to the physical attributes of the property, inside and outside.

Size. Consider room for your current operation, plus expansion for the next five years, at a minimum. Think about markets that you may decide to enter in the future. You may want enough space to sublet a portion of your building with plans to grow into the sublet space at a later date. The sublet portion of your property may offset a substantial portion of your monthly payment. Calculate additional space that will be necessary over the next five years as your business expands. Consider parking for yourself and those companies that will occupy your sublet areas. These are only a few of the questions that should be answered prior to getting involved in a property. Get with your staff and your CPA and crunch the numbers.

Accessibility. Shipping is expensive. Look into the future. Is your potential property in the best overall location for the long term? Do you require rail, roadway, air, pipeline, water, phone lines, cable, satellite, high-speed Internet, private or public means to transport your product or service? Should you be on a main artery that benefits walk-in traffic or delivery concerns?

Utilities. Use an expert to carefully inspect the physical plant's utilities. How is the building heated? Does the electrical load center supply sufficient power for your needs? Is there room for growth for a minimum of five years? Does the building have up-to-date cabling, gas, electric or solar? Is the equipment outdated and likely to add unnecessary expense to your utility bills?

Alarm system. An alarm system is a plus in any business establishment, large or small. If your building does not have an alarm system, invest in one. An alarm system may not keep an unwelcome visitor out of your building or prevent a fire, but it will limit the amount of time that a visitor can stay inside your building without being caught. It may also alert authorities when a fire starts, long before someone near your business is alerted by smoke or flames.

Proximity to customer base. If you require a retail storefront, you want to locate your business in close proximity to your target market. Try to find a retail space where other stores will invite the kind of customer who will also be interested in your business. If you are a machine shop, you want to be closer to businesses that utilize machine shop services. If you are a clothing store or grocery store, look for a space where walk-in traffic is abundant. The rest is easy. Use common sense.

Proximity to competition. If you own a dollar store, you probably prefer an area that does not currently include such an enterprise. If you own an auto dealership, you may want to locate at the city auto mall or the automobile miracle mile. Know your competition and locate accordingly.

Paying for Improvements. It is rare to find a building that is perfectly suited to a specific operation. Your landlord's or seller's willingness to pay for all or a portion of necessary improvements may be the deciding factor in your willingness to do business with him. Your portion of the cost of improvements should be spread over the term of the lease, or included in your mortgage, to reduce your move-in costs. Of course, any improvements that are included in a mortgage are subject to interest, thus increasing your costs over the long term.

EPA concerns. If you have any reason to believe that any part of a property may be contaminated in any manner, have the EPA inspect the property prior to further involvement. Cleanup can be incredibly costly and you may be held responsible even if you are not at fault.

When should I move? Many businesses are operated from an owner's home for the duration. Many neighborhood restrictions do not allow businesses to house employees in private residences. Some do not allow customers to be serviced from private residences. You will know when your business is too large or too restricted to continue operating from your home. If you operate a home-based business, remain there until you have sufficient need and profit to move to a different location.

When moving from your home or a location you have outgrown, ask the same questions you asked when you first began looking for a place to house your business. Are you ready financially? Will the atmosphere of your new location help or hinder your customer traffic? Do not forget that your customers are also relocating with your business. Are you making your customers' life easier? Are you really making your life easier? Can you really afford to move? Can you really afford not to move?

Build to suit. The rules are essentially the same as locating a building for purchase. Now you can find the right location and build a facility to your exact specifications. Keep the cost within your financial limits. Do not spend unnecessarily. Build for function, not whims. Build for the future.

WHAT SHOULD I DO? Do not get involved in overly large spaces with unsustainable costs or overly long leases. Of course, you are sure that your business prospects are bright and that everything will proceed as planned. Forecast facility costs based on planned profits, but leave some room for error or market adjustments.

When moving into a new space, lock in one or two years and opt for the remaining years, usually through the fifth year. A longer lease term – options included - should convert to a lower monthly cost for you. The lessor is looking for a long-term deal that relieves him of hunting for a new lessee every few years. Use this to your advantage. If your business grows more slowly than anticipated, you can opt out at the end of year one or two, and go to a smaller facility. If business grows more quickly than expected, you can opt out and go to a larger space. If you feel that you want to remain indefinitely, renegotiate the cost of your lease when an option year is on the horizon.

Once you find a suitable facility, contact the previous owners or tenants and satisfy your curiosity regarding any unanswered questions. In a rent or lease situation, be sure to meet the owner and clear up any questions regarding improvements, care of the property or plans to sell or modify the building. In any case, do not rely on the real estate agent to convey all the good or poor attributes of the property.

Additional Resources: Commercial realtor, Accountant, business bank contact.

FAMILY

This includes your immediate family, relatives, in-laws, boyfriends, girlfriends, and fiancés.

Should my family be involved in the business? Wow! This is a tough question. Generally speaking, family members are more in tune with your core values, willing to work when others will not, and more likely to work for less, until your business is profitable and paid help is affordable.

That said, the negative side of working with family can be . . . well . . . very negative. First off, when the workday is over you go home with the same people you worked with all day. You are with your family 24/7. And, when vacation rolls around and you are ready to escape your business for a week or two, you vacation with the same people you work with every day. If you employ a family member who is not part of your immediate household, expect that eventually a discussion about that family member will be part of your household conversations or debates.

Jealousy is a terrible thing, especially when it is directed toward a family member from the nonfamily workforce. When a family member is less than perfect in any way, it is *your* fault. You are a failure because, in the eyes of your employees, you should recognize that a family member is not suited for the job at hand. Or, you do recognize the weaknesses of a family member and hired that person in spite of his shortcomings – just because he is family.

I consulted with a company some years ago that was owned by a talented man. His wife wore the pants in the family. She routinely walked in and wrote a check to herself for obscenely large amounts of money. She was responsible for the household bills, which she failed to pay. Bad combination. I've seen the same situation with a woman-owned business and a husband who provided consulting services to her company. He regularly created havoc by pitting one management team member against another.

Think long and hard before inviting your family to work in your business. Be sure to apply your standards to a family and non-family - equally. It may be one of the most important business decisions of your life. It may also be one of the most important decisions of your marriage.

Should my spouse work in the business? You probably already know if you and your spouse are able to put family aside and prosper. If you do not believe that a spousal business partnership will work for you, be strong enough to admit that it will not work. The hard part comes when your spouse reminds you that she or he is a co-owner of the business. This may or may not be the case, but it can be a real stumbling block if it is true.

The same rules apply to your partner(s). If you do not want a partner's spouse in business with you, say "no" and stick to it. And, get the problem resolved *before* you agree to the partnership. You might decide to forego the partnership, and even the business. Harmony is not absolutely necessary to manage a business, but it certainly makes things go more smoothly. Business should be fun. Tension-filled relationships are not. You should get into a business you love, but not necessarily with someone you love.

Should I pay my kids? If your kids work in the business, they should be paid the same wage that anyone else would earn to do a similar job. You can have your children on your payroll, but the key word is *need*. You should not create nonessential jobs for your kids. If you hire your child to work, the position must be one that would be filled if your child were not available. Know the laws when you hire your children. Many jobs are not fit for a child under age 18. View the Fair Labor Standards Act (FLSA) website at www.dol.gov.[1]

There are multiple tax benefits associated with hiring your children to work in your business. The reasons do not override the basic premises set forth in the previous paragraphs. See your accountant for particulars.

Access to equipment and supplies by family members. Family members should be held to the same set of rules as any employee in regards to using business equipment and supplies. If the family member does not work in the business, he should not have free access to business equipment and supplies – period.

Computer access for family members. Family members have no business playing on your business computer(s). If you take family members to work, purchase a laptop for their use that has a wireless package. If you have Internet at work, you should also have Wi-Fi. Do not cave in and give family members access to business computers.

Vehicle usage by family. Use common sense. Your insurance company insures your vehicles and expects them to be utilized only for business purposes. Do not put yourself in a position where you must defend your actions to an insurance investigator. Business vehicles should be driven by business employees only.

Family Attitudes. Employees often develop distrust for family members in a business. This distrust may include relatives of *any* employee or employer. Distrust emanates from the belief that family members receive favorable treatment from each other, often at the expense of nonfamily members. If you must hire relatives of anyone in your company, put them in positions where they cannot influence each other's behavior in any way.

Phantom family employees. A phantom employee is one that exists only on payroll. Suppose that you want to provide income for your daughter while she is away at college. You add her name to your payroll and send her a bi-weekly check to pay all her expenses. She works for you, doing miscellaneous office work during summer breaks. She never provides enough work to make up for her wage or salary.

Anyone who is familiar with your payroll understands the situation. Within a few days, everyone in your business knows what is happening. This creates bad feelings throughout your company. If your bookkeeper or accountant created a phantom employee, she would be terminated immediately. The solution? An honest day's work for an honest day's pay.

Additional Resources: You already know most of the answers. Let common sense be your guide. Be strong.

FAMILY MEDICAL LEAVE ACT (FMLA)

This comes straight from the U.S. Department of Labor website (February, 2013): *"Currently, there are* **no federal legal requirements** *for paid sick leave," (http://www.dol.gov/dol/topic/workhours/sickleave.htm). For companies subject to the* Family and Medical Leave Act (FMLA)*, the Act does require unpaid sick leave. FMLA provides for up to 12 weeks of unpaid leave for certain medical situations for either the employee or a member of the employee's immediate family. In many instances paid leave may be substituted for unpaid FMLA leave.*

Employees are eligible to take FMLA leave if they have worked for their employer for at least 12 months, and have worked for at least 1,250 hours over the previous 12 months, and work at a location where at least 50 employees are employed by the employer within 75 miles.[2]

WHAT SHOULD I DO? FMLA is far too complex to address in its entirety. However, a small error may cost you tens of thousands of dollars. If you are unsure of anything concerning FMLA, contact a human resources expert or an attorney who is well versed in FMLA prior to making a decision concerning an employee.

Additional Resources: Human resources consultant, attorney specializing in human resources, and www.dol.gov.

FICTITIOUS BUSINESS NAMES (DBA's)

Many companies carry out business under an assumed name that is different than the legal name of the business. For example, your legal business name may be Joseph Jones, Inc. You may prefer to call your business something other than Joseph Jones, Inc. You decide to name your business Jones Retail Sales. This is referred to as a DBA[3], or doing business as, Jones Retail Sales. You must file a certificate at the courthouse in your jurisdiction to be sure that no one else is using the name you have selected before utilizing that DBA. Most counties and states have an Internet site with DBA listings. Some jurisdictions refer to DBAs as fictitious business names.

FINANCIAL STATEMENTS (See ACCOUNTING: Key financial statements)

FIRING EMPLOYEES (See TERMINATION/FIRING)

FLEX TIME

Flex time involves a work schedule that is set by the worker rather than the employer, with the employer's approval. The Department of Labor has conducted surveys and published articles and reports regarding flex time, but currently has no laws or restrictions to the practice.[4] An employer may put constraints on flexible schedules, limiting work hours to times when the company is open for business, such as weekdays only, weekends only, nights only, and so on.

Flexible scheduling introduces a whole new set of complications that come into play when employees are able to come and go as they please. The most obvious is the manager's ability to track time and output. Also, flex time for one employee generates requests for flex time from other employees, making accountability tougher and tougher as schedules fluctuate. Flex time should be allowed only when absolutely necessary. This is your call. No law says flex time must be available to employees.

WHAT SHOULD I DO? If you do choose to provide flex time, it should be limited and never used unless absolutely required by circumstances. Flex time is typically allowed for valuable employees who have inflexible schedule conflicts for a limited time period. Some businesses have been successful allowing a majority of employees to work flexible schedules. In the United Kingdom, flex time is quite common. In the United States, flex time is not common.

Additional Resources: Human resources specialist.

FORECASTING

A forecast is your version of tomorrow, next month, or next year, in financial terms. A forecast is a projection, assembled by you and your staff that defines the route to your company goals. Your forecast tells you, your banker, and your stakeholders how you intend to make your bottom line, where you must make adjustments, and why.

Why should I forecast? When you are taught to drive, the instructor usually starts your first lesson by telling you to keep your hands on the wheel and your eyes on the road ahead. The same goes for any business, regardless of size, including your business. If you could look into the future, you would probably want to know how much you will sell, if you will prosper, when you should expand or contract your business and when you should increase or reduce your workforce. The businesses that do the best job of predicting the future are usually the businesses that make it through the good and bad times and prosper at the end of the day.

Take time to construct a forecast, even if it is just your best guestimate of the months or year(s) ahead. This simple act will put you light-years in front of that business owner down the block who cannot figure out why he is failing to make a profit, even though he works 75 hours a week.

What should I forecast? You can forecast future sales, expenses, cash flow, workforce size, department budgets, or any number of items that determine your future. Regardless of the nature of a forecast, there are two variables, the actual numbers and the projected numbers. For our exercise, we will assemble forecasts for an Income Statement and Cash Flow Statement, add actual numbers, and then re-forecast.

Many bankers and other lenders prefer that you present two forecasts. The first is a normal forecast, as close to what you believe to be the real numbers, as possible, two years out. The second is a worst case possibility, a forecast that assumes that sales are off – let's say - by 20%. This is a little more challenging, in that you will be forced to make a number of decisions that are avoidable if you were to make your sales numbers. It may be necessary to cut back on expenses as early as the first or second month of business. When you go into survival mode, all the rules change and your banker or lender will want to know how you will respond under pressure.

Forecasting for a new business. If you are involved in a new business, you have no past performance figures and must rely on research, knowledge and experience to predict future performance. This sounds intense and difficult, but is fairly easy, even if you have no accounting background, whatsoever.

Fixed Expenses, such as Checking Account Fees, Dues & Subscriptions, Insurance, Legal & Accounting, Office Supplies, Rent, Salaries, Taxes & Benefits, Telephone, Trade Shows, Utilities, Vehicle Allowance and Website are easy to predict. It usually takes a phone call or two to come up with an accurate number for these expenses. Variable expenses, such as Advertising, Credit Card Costs, Commissions, Travel and Warehouse Supplies are usually a percentage of Sales and are a bit harder to predict. If your sales are off, so are your variable expenses.

WHAT SHOULD I DO? The idea is to predict your business future as accurately as possible. Exhaust all options before resorting to guessing at the value of any number. And, when you make an educated guess, you should be plus-or-minus 5% of your true estimate, or you have not done your homework.

Consult the library, the Internet, your competitors, potential vendors, the utility companies, your accountant, your banker, your mentor(s), or anyone or anything else that will provide accurate figures for your research. Input your numbers as they become available. If you are not familiar with Excel or a similar spreadsheet program, ask your accountant to help you to enter numbers and formulas. Once the formulas are in your spreadsheet, you will be able to make changes, and watch your program recalculate your Income Statement or Balance Sheet, thus changing your outcome with the stroke of a key.

Of course, you and your accountant will eventually abandon your Excel style spreadsheet for a software program that will handle all financial facets of your business *(see also ACCOUNTING: Accounting software).*

Forecasting for an existing business. If you are involved in an existing business, you will utilize recent Income Statements, Balance Sheets and Cash Flow Statements to extrapolate forecasted numbers. Past performance provides a very strong basis for future performance. If your company has been affected by any dynamic changes recently, such as a change in management or ownership, past performance may have a lesser effect on future performance.

WHAT SHOULD I DO? Forecasting for an existing business is identical to forecasting for a new business – with one exception. An existing business should offer actual information in the form of Income Statements and Balance Sheets from prior years, thus eliminating a lot of the research that accompanies new business forecasts. If you do not have access to prior numbers, you will have to use many of the same sources that are available to those who are forecasting for new businesses.

That said, be careful that the numbers you are given when shopping for a business or buying a business, are real. Some business people misrepresent revenues and expenses in their financials to gain an advantage at tax time, thus leaving you with numbers that are not accurate. Such information is not reliable when forecasting comes into play.

If you feel that this is the case, approach your actual numbers with a modicum of uncertainty and prepare for adjustments in the future. The good news is that you are probably dealing with financials that are heavy in unwarranted expenses and are reporting less than actual revenue. The bad news is the fact that you will never really know the accuracy of the prior business owner's numbers until you get your feet wet and operate your business for a number of months. Do your best with the information you have and be prepared to adjust as often as necessary.

Last, do not get hung up on industry norms when forecasting. I have done my share of forecasts over the years and have learned that companies have a tendency to get in a forecasting rut. I worked with one company that forecasted 15% growth every year for a decade. The question here is, how can this be correct in a constantly changing economic environment?

When you forecast, have a strong look at your strengths and weaknesses in terms of your team's capabilities, your competitors' capabilities and the economic environment for your product or service. Many companies look at numbers only, without regard to strengthening their teams and finding ways to improve every aspect of business while stretching for the best they can achieve. In short, look deep and make the necessary changes to achieve more. Do not be strangled by past performance when forecasting. Forecasting is not just an exercise to come up with *the numbers*. It is an opportunity to improve your business, top to bottom.

Income Statement Forecast. Let's take another look at ABC Company's Income Statement (Figure F-1) for their first full year in business – 2015. Notice that ABC's Sales were $702,500, which converted to a Net Profit of $ -364. Utilizing these actual 2015 numbers, we will walk through the forecast for the year, 2016. But first, we will review a list of forecasting tips.

INCOME STATEMENT FORECASTING TIPS

Forecasting is not a science. It is a "best guess with maximum effort" exercise.

If you are a new or existing company, the first number in your forecast is your salary. If your forecast does not allow you to take home enough money to be comfortable, this may not be the business for you.

Many items are fixed costs, such as rent, utilities, phone, salaries, taxes, benefits and cost of goods sold. No guessing. Fill these in before identifying more difficult costs.

Your pricing should be driven by your competition. You should be at a maximum of plus-or-minus 5% of your key competitors' prices. Plus-or-minus 2% is better.

Forecasting for a new or struggling business is often a matter of what you can afford, rather than what you want or need.

Forecasting is only as good as the effort and energy you put into researching your numbers. "Garbage in = garbage out."

Forecasting is a moving target. If a period falls short, it may be necessary to re-forecast the balance of the year – or the next few months.

Forecast 2-years out initially, then at least a year out once you show a profit in two consecutive quarters. Many businesses forecast 5-years out.

Do not get in a rut. When your numbers speak to you – listen. If your numbers tell you that sales are not up to par, correct the problem. If expenses are out of control, correct the problem. You must learn to convert your numbers to positive action. Continually adjust until you get it right.

If you are not sure, call your accountant.

Forecasting, for lack of a better term, is backwards. Really! You start with the salary you intend to extract from the business, then pencil in a profit number you intend to reach at the end of year one, and then year two, month by month. Most business owners forecast years three, four and five by the quarter, calculating only major numbers, such as Sales, Cost of Goods Sold, Gross Profit, Total Expenses and Net Profit.

So, we just said that forecasting is a *backwards* process. Decide where you want to go, and then construct a plan to get there. Some first-time entrepreneurs leave out a line for the owner's salary, favoring a bottom line profit number that becomes the owner's pay. Add a line (Salary – Owner) so that lenders know that you intend to get paid. Lenders need to know that you will earn enough to keep you in the business. They also know that all businesses must make a profit above and beyond the owner's salary to remain prosperous, and to grow. In the case of ABC Company, their minimum goal is a Net Profit of at least 15% of Sales in 2016. They show a projected Net Profit of $223,224, at 15.46% (Figure F-2).

Next, focus on ABC Company's fixed expenses (Figure F-1) in 2015. Fixed expenses are those that are expected to remain constant throughout the year. They include Checking (under Bank Expenses), Dues & Subscriptions, Insurance, Legal & Accounting, Office Supplies, Rent – Building, Rent – Inventory Storage, all Salaries, Taxes & Benefits, Telephone, Trade Shows & Exhibits, Utilities, Vehicle Allowance and Website.

ABC has decided to utilize the 2015 Consumer Price Index (CPI), defined as "the weighted average of prices of a basket of consumer goods and services, such as transportation, food and medical care[5]," that tells us that most goods will experience a price increase of 4% in 2016. Therefore, ABC Company will utilize the CPI projection to calculate increases in selected fixed expenses for the year 2016. This is a common practice among many businesses. The only fixed expenses that will experience 4% increases in 2016 are Insurance, Office Supplies, all Salaries, Taxes & Benefits and Trade Shows & Exhibits.

The remaining fixed expenses were not increased. Checking (under Bank Expenses), Dues & Subscriptions, Legal & Accounting, Rents, Telephone, Utilities, Vehicle Allowance and Website are expenses that should remain static in cost throughout 2016.

Note: Rent for 2015 (Figure F-1) is $4,500 in January. January rent includes an extra $3,000 for a one-time charge for a 2-month security deposit, plus January's rent of $1,500. Also, Website for 2015 (Figure F-1) is $4,000 in January. January includes $3,750 to develop the website, plus January's monthly hosting / maintenance fee of $250.

This leaves us with only five expenses that fall into the variable expense category. Advertising is 5.5% of Sales, and increases and decreases as Sales fluctuate. Credit Card Costs are 2.8% of all sales that are paid by credit card. In our example, half of all sales are paid by credit card, thus making credit card expenses 1.4% of Sales. Commissions – Sales are 5% of Sales. Travel is 1.5% of Sales and Warehouse Supplies are 3.1% of Sales, essentially the same as 2015. These variable expenses rise and fall with Sales and will not be affected by the CPI.

As you can see, forecasting expenses is not a mystery. It just takes time and investigation, but it is well worth the effort. Please keep in mind that the percentages expressed here are standard for this particular type of business. Your business may require a different set of standards, based on your industry.

The last items to be added to ABC Company's Income Statement are Sales and Cost of Goods Sold. In 2015, total Sales amounted to $702,500. Cost of Goods Sold was $386,375, or 55% of total Sales. ABC Company has an agreement with their contractor that guarantees that the cost of each unit will not increase before 2017. Therefore, there is no need to increase the sale price of each unit, if it is possible to maintain that price and still achieve ABC's Net Profit goal of at least 15% in 2016.

After careful consideration, the owner of ABC Company decided that it was possible to achieve $1,444,000 in Sales with the current sales team. Since Cost of Goods Sold will remain at 55% in 2016, a solid sales year will allow ABC Company to make a Net Profit of $223,224. This is 15.46% of Sales, the bottom tier of Net Profit for companies in ABC's industry. That is a pretty good performance for only their second year in business. If all goes well in 2016, they will likely add another sales person and attempt to achieve 18% in 2017.

So, you have walked through your first forecasted Income Statement. With a little practice, you should be able to assemble a forecast and push your business forward with a viable plan and realistic goals.

INCOME STATEMENT
ABC Company
December 31, 2015

	Jan	Feb	Mar	Apr	May	Jun	Jul	Aug	Sep	Oct	Nov	Dec	Totals	Rev. %
Sales	44,000	38,000	40,000	42,500	47,500	49,500	57,500	65,000	62,500	81,000	82,500	92,500	702,500	100.00%
Cost of Goods Sold	24,200	20,900	22,000	23,375	26,125	27,225	31,625	35,750	34,375	44,550	45,375	50,875	386,375	55.00%
Gross Profit	19,800	17,100	18,000	19,125	21,375	22,275	25,875	29,250	28,125	36,450	37,125	41,625	316,125	45.00%
Expenses														
Advertising	2,420	2,090	2,200	2,338	2,613	2,723	3,163	3,575	3,438	4,455	4,538	5,088	38,638	5.50%
Bank Expense														
Checking	100	50	50	50	50	50	50	50	50	50	50	50	650	0.09%
Credit Card Costs	616	532	560	595	665	693	805	910	875	1,134	1,155	1,295	9,835	1.40%
Commissions - Sales	2,200	1,900	2,000	2,125	2,375	2,475	2,875	3,250	3,125	4,050	4,125	4,625	35,125	5.00%
Dues & Subscriptions												450	450	0.06%
Insurance	735	0	0	735	0	0	735	0	0	735	0	0	2,940	0.42%
Legal & Accounting	250	250	250	250	250	250	250	250	250	250	250	250	3,000	0.43%
Office Supplies	50	50	50	50	50	50	50	50	50	50	50	50	600	0.09%
Rent - Building	4,500	1,500	1,500	1,500	1,500	1,500	1,500	1,500	1,500	1,500	1,500	1,500	21,000	2.99%
Rent - Inventory Storage	100	100	100	100	100	100	100	100	100	100	100	100	1,200	0.17%
Salary - Administrative	2,500	2,500	2,500	2,500	2,500	2,500	2,500	2,500	2,500	2,500	2,500	2,500	30,000	4.27%
Salary - Owner	4,000	4,000	4,000	4,000	4,000	4,000	4,000	4,000	4,000	4,000	4,000	4,000	48,000	6.83%
Salary - Sales	4,000	4,000	4,000	4,000	4,000	4,000	4,000	4,000	4,000	4,000	4,000	4,000	48,000	6.83%
Taxes & Benefits	1,905	1,860	1,875	1,894	1,931	1,946	2,006	2,063	2,044	2,183	2,194	2,269	24,169	3.44%
Telephone	550	550	550	550	550	550	550	550	550	550	550	550	6,600	0.94%
Trade Shows & Exhibits			5,000							5,000			10,000	1.42%
Travel	660	570	600	638	713	743	863	975	938	1,215	1,238	1,388	10,538	1.50%
Utilities	554	563	573	562	558	613	652	701	601	550	576	785	7,288	1.04%
Vehicle Allowance	800	800	800	800	800	800	800	800	800	800	800	800	9,600	1.37%
Warehouse Supplies	132	114	120	128	143	149	173	195	188	243	248	278	2,108	0.30%
Website	4,000	250	250	250	250	250	250	250	250	250	250	250	6,750	0.96%
Total Expenses	30,072	21,679	26,978	23,063	23,047	23,391	25,321	25,719	25,257	33,615	28,122	30,226	316,489	45.05%
Net Profit	-10,272	-4,579	-8,978	-3,938	-1,672	-1,116	554	3,532	2,868	2,836	9,003	11,399	-364	-0.05%

Figure F-2

INCOME STATEMENT FORECAST
ABC Company
January 1, 2016

	Jan	Feb	Mar	Apr	May	Jun	Jul	Aug	Sep	Oct	Nov	Dec	Totals	Rev. %
Sales	101,000	102,500	111,000	112,000	116,500	133,000	136,500	138,500	133,500	125,000	118,000	116,500	1,444,000	100.00%
Cost of Goods Sold	55,550	56,375	61,050	61,600	64,075	73,150	75,075	76,175	73,425	68,750	64,900	64,075	794,200	55.00%
Gross Profit	45,450	46,125	49,950	50,400	52,425	59,850	61,425	62,325	60,075	56,250	53,100	52,425	649,800	45.00%
Expenses														
Advertising	5,777	5,863	6,349	6,406	6,664	7,608	7,808	7,922	7,636	7,150	6,750	6,664	82,597	5.72%
Bank Expense														
Checking	100	50	50	50	50	50	50	50	50	50	50	50	650	0.05%
Credit Card Costs	1,414	1,435	1,554	1,568	1,631	1,862	1,911	1,939	1,869	1,750	1,652	1,631	20,216	1.40%
Commissions - Sales	5,050	5,125	5,550	5,600	5,825	6,650	6,825	6,925	6,675	6,250	5,900	5,825	72,200	5.00%
Dues & Subscriptions												450	450	0.03%
Insurance	765	0	0	765	0	0	765	0	0	765	0	0	3,060	0.21%
Legal & Accounting	250	250	250	250	250	250	250	250	250	250	250	250	3,000	0.21%
Office Supplies	52	52	52	52	52	52	52	52	52	52	52	52	624	0.04%
Rent - Building	1,500	1,500	1,500	1,500	1,500	1,500	1,500	1,500	1,500	1,500	1,500	1,500	18,000	1.25%
Rent - Inventory Storage	100	100	100	100	100	100	100	100	100	100	100	100	1,200	0.08%
Salary - Administrative	2,600	2,600	2,600	2,600	2,600	2,600	2,600	2,600	2,600	2,600	2,600	2,600	31,200	2.16%
Salary - Owner	4,160	4,160	4,160	4,160	4,160	4,160	4,160	4,160	4,160	4,160	4,160	4,160	49,920	3.46%
Salary - Sales	4,160	4,160	4,160	4,160	4,160	4,160	4,160	4,160	4,160	4,160	4,160	4,160	49,920	3.46%
Taxes & Benefits	2,396	2,407	2,471	2,478	2,512	2,636	2,662	2,677	2,639	2,576	2,523	2,512	30,486	2.11%
Telephone	550	550	550	550	550	550	550	550	550	550	550	550	6,600	0.46%
Trade Shows & Exhibits			5,200							5,200			10,400	0.72%
Travel	1,515	1,538	1,665	1,680	1,748	1,995	2,048	2,078	2,003	1,875	1,770	1,748	21,660	1.50%
Utilities	554	563	573	562	558	613	652	701	601	550	576	785	7,288	0.50%
Vehicle Allowance	800	800	800	800	800	800	800	800	800	800	800	800	9,600	0.66%
Warehouse Supplies	315	320	346	349	363	415	426	432	417	390	368	363	4,505	0.31%
Website	250	250	250	250	250	250	250	250	250	250	250	250	3,000	0.21%
Total Expenses	32,308	31,722	38,180	33,881	33,773	36,250	37,568	37,146	36,311	40,978	34,011	34,450	426,576	29.54%
Net Profit	13,142	14,403	11,770	16,519	18,652	23,600	23,857	25,179	23,764	15,273	19,089	17,975	223,224	15.46%

Cash Flow Forecasting (Figure F-3). Now let's discuss cash flow forecasting. Utilizing the information from the prior three months (Figure F-3), we can forecast ABC Company's cash needs for the next 3 months, and beyond. We are looking for irregularities that may arise, thus disturbing normal cash flow. Our job is to manage those abnormal cash demands.

The left portion of Figure F-3 is a historical account of ABC Company's actual cash flow over the last 3 months of 2015. The right portion of Figure F-3 is a forecast of ABC's cash flows over the first 3 months of 2016.

Notice that ABC Company is projecting decreases in Cash Receipts in January, February and March of 2016. They intend to collect $6,000 in Accounts Receivables in January and March. Additionally, they will make a quarterly insurance payment of $765 in January and a payment of $5,200 in March for a trade show that they will attend in April. Quarterly taxes are due in March, in the amount of $7,274.

At the beginning of January, ABC has $35,422 in cash, February shows beginning cash of $20,942 and beginning March cash slips to $13,463, if ABC's predictions are accurate. At the end of March, cash further decreases to $12,321. March, however, has an unusual expense since $5,200 for Trade Shows & Exhibits is due only twice a year. Without this unusual expense, ABC would finish March with $17,521 in their checkbook.

In any case, there is no need for the owner to dip into his personal credit line for additional cash as long as cash inflows and cash outflows remain stable through the end of March. On February 1st, when January's actual Cash Flow numbers are available, ABC Company will compile an up-to-date forecasted Cash Flow Statement that includes April. February and March will almost definitely change at that time, unless the January forecast is absolutely perfect.

If you take the time to complete a Cash Flow Statement regularly, you will always be prepared to respond to any cash flow emergency before you are blindsided by an unforeseen event. During your first year in business, look at your Cash Flow on a daily basis. Be sure to have a cash source, such as a credit line *(see also HOME EQUITY LINE OF CREDIT / HOME EQUITY LOAN)*, to prevent cash interruptions that may harm your business and your credibility. And, remember that if you are out of cash, you are out of business. Do not let it happen to you.

CASH FLOW STATEMENT PROJECTIONS ABC Company December 31, 2015						
Figure F-3						
	Actual - 2015			Forecast - 2016		
	October	November	December	January	February	March
Beginning Cash Balanc	14,000	16,143	31,716	35,422	20,942	13,463
Cash Inflows						
Cash Receipts	76,000	82,500	86,500	101,000	96,500	111,000
Owner Contributions	0	0	0	0	0	0
A/R Collections	0	5,000	0	6,000	0	6,000
Total Cash Inflows	90,000	103,643	118,216	107,000	96,500	117,000
Cash Outflows						
Inventory Purchases	(41,800)	(45,375)	(47,575)	(55,550)	(53,075)	(61,050)
Advertising	(4,446)	(4,528)	(5,077)	(5,777)	(5,863)	(6,349)
Checking	(50)	(50)	(50)	(50)	(50)	(50)
Credit Card Costs	(1,132)	(1,153)	(1,292)	(1,414)	(1,435)	(1,554)
Commissions - Sales	(4,042)	(4,117)	(4,616)	(5,050)	(5,125)	(5,550)
Dues & Subscriptions	0	0	(450)	0	0	0
Insurance	(735)	0	0	(765)	0	0
Legal & Accounting	(250)	(250)	(250)	(250)	(250)	(250)
Loan Payments	(646)	(646)	(646)	(646)	(646)	(646)
Office Supplies	(50)	(50)	(50)	(52)	(52)	(52)
Rent - Building	(1,500)	(1,500)	(1,500)	(1,500)	(1,500)	(1,500)
Rent - Inv. Storage	(100)	(100)	(100)	(100)	(100)	(100)
Salary - Admin.	(2,500)	(2,500)	(2,500)	(2,600)	(2,600)	(2,600)
Salary - Owner	(4,000)	(4,000)	(4,000)	(4,160)	(4,160)	(4,160)
Salary - Sales	(4,000)	(4,000)	(4,000)	(4,160)	(4,160)	(4,160)
Supplies - Whse.	(243)	(247)	(277)	(315)	(320)	(346)
Taxes & Benefits	0	0	(6,641)			(7,274)
Telephone	(550)	(550)	(550)	(550)	(550)	(550)
Trade Shows & Exhib	(5,000)	0	0	0	0	(5,200)
Travel	(1,213)	(1,235)	(1,385)	(1,515)	(1,538)	(1,665)
Utilities	(550)	(576)	(785)	(554)	(563)	(573)
Vehicle Allowance	(800)	(800)	(800)	(800)	(800)	(800)
Website	(250)	(250)	(250)	(250)	(250)	(250)
Total Cash Outflows	(73,857)	(71,927)	(82,794)	(86,058)	(83,037)	(104,679)
Ending Cash Balance	16,143	31,716	35,422	20,942	13,463	12,321

Out of Cash = Out of Business

What if my actual business performance is better or worse than my forecast? Regardless of the accuracy of your forecast, you will almost definitely find that your actual numbers do not duplicate your forecasted numbers. This is why forecasts are considered living documents and moving targets. As time progresses, forecasted numbers are replaced with actual numbers, creating the necessity to re-forecast coming months and years so that you are always in a position to fulfill you original goals.

Let's bring ABC Company's 2016 forecasted Income Statement (Figure F-4) forward and discuss the necessity to re-forecast when our original forecast numbers appear to be too low or too high. In figure F-5, ABC Company has worked through the first two months of 2016. We have replaced January and February of 2016 with actual performance numbers.

The first thing we notice is that Sales are less than predicted. ABC Company posted Sales of $90,500 (Figure F-5) in January against forecasted Sales of $101,000 (Figure F-4). Then, in February Sales fell further behind with actual Sales of $97,500 (Figure F-5) against forecasted Sales of $102,500 (Figure F-4). In January and February, notice that all the categories associated with Sales also dropped. Both months show decreases from forecasted Cost of Goods Sold, Gross Profit. Variable Expenses, such as Advertising, Credit Card Costs, Commissions – Sales, Taxes & Benefits, Travel and Warehouse Supplies also showed decreases. All these items are forecasted as a percentage of Sales. When Sales decrease, Variable Expenses decrease accordingly.

Fixed Expenses, however, remain stable. Items such as Checking, Insurance, Legal & Accounting, Office Supplies, Rent, Salaries, Telephone, Utilities, Vehicle Allowance and Website are not affected by Sales. These costs must be covered, regardless of Sales revenue.

Figure F-4

INCOME STATEMENT FORECAST
ABC Company
January 1, 2016

	Jan	Feb	Mar	Apr	May	Jun	Jul	Aug	Sep	Oct	Nov	Dec	Totals	Rev. %
Sales	101,000	102,500	111,000	112,000	116,500	133,000	136,500	138,500	133,500	125,000	118,000	116,500	1,444,000	100.00%
Cost of Goods Sold	55,550	56,375	61,050	61,600	64,075	73,150	75,075	76,175	73,425	68,750	64,900	64,075	794,200	55.00%
Gross Profit	45,450	46,125	49,950	50,400	52,425	59,850	61,425	62,325	60,075	56,250	53,100	52,425	649,800	45.00%
Expenses														
Advertising	5,777	5,863	6,349	6,406	6,664	7,608	7,808	7,922	7,636	7,150	6,750	6,664	82,597	5.72%
Bank Expense														
Checking	100	50	50	50	50	50	50	50	50	50	50	50	650	0.05%
Credit Card Costs	1,414	1,435	1,554	1,568	1,631	1,862	1,911	1,939	1,869	1,750	1,652	1,631	20,216	1.40%
Commissions - Sales	5,050	5,125	5,550	5,600	5,825	6,650	6,825	6,925	6,675	6,250	5,900	5,825	72,200	5.00%
Dues & Subscriptions												450	450	0.03%
Insurance	765	0	0	765	0	0	765	0	0	765	0	0	3,060	0.21%
Legal & Accounting	250	250	250	250	250	250	250	250	250	250	250	250	3,000	0.21%
Office Supplies	52	52	52	52	52	52	52	52	52	52	52	52	624	0.04%
Rent - Building	1,500	1,500	1,500	1,500	1,500	1,500	1,500	1,500	1,500	1,500	1,500	1,500	18,000	1.25%
Rent - Inventory Storage	100	100	100	100	100	100	100	100	100	100	100	100	1,200	0.08%
Salary - Administrative	2,600	2,600	2,600	2,600	2,600	2,600	2,600	2,600	2,600	2,600	2,600	2,600	31,200	2.16%
Salary - Owner	4,160	4,160	4,160	4,160	4,160	4,160	4,160	4,160	4,160	4,160	4,160	4,160	49,920	3.46%
Salary - Sales	4,160	4,160	4,160	4,160	4,160	4,160	4,160	4,160	4,160	4,160	4,160	4,160	49,920	3.46%
Taxes & Benefits	2,396	2,407	2,471	2,478	2,512	2,636	2,662	2,677	2,639	2,576	2,523	2,512	30,486	2.11%
Telephone	550	550	550	550	550	550	550	550	550	550	550	550	6,600	0.46%
Trade Shows & Exhibits			5,200							5,200			10,400	0.72%
Travel	1,515	1,538	1,665	1,630	1,748	1,995	2,048	2,078	2,003	1,875	1,770	1,748	21,660	1.50%
Utilities	554	563	573	562	558	613	652	701	601	550	576	785	7,288	0.50%
Vehicle Allowance	800	800	800	800	800	800	800	800	800	800	800	800	9,600	0.66%
Warehouse Supplies	315	320	346	349	363	415	426	432	417	390	368	363	4,505	0.31%
Website	250	250	250	250	250	250	250	250	250	250	250	250	3,000	0.21%
Total Expenses	32,308	31,722	38,180	33,831	33,773	36,250	37,568	37,146	36,311	40,978	34,011	34,450	426,576	29.54%
Net Profit	13,142	14,403	11,770	16,519	18,652	23,600	23,857	25,179	23,764	15,273	19,089	17,975	223,224	15.46%

INCOME STATEMENT BEFORE RE-FORECAST
ABC Company
February 29, 2016

Figure F-5

	Jan	Feb	Mar	Apr	May	Jun	Jul	Aug	Sep	Oct	Nov	Dec	Totals	Rev. %
Sales	90,500	97,500	111,000	112,000	116,500	133,000	136,500	138,500	133,500	125,000	118,000	116,500	1,428,500	100.00%
Cost of Goods Sold	49,775	53,625	61,050	61,600	64,075	73,150	75,075	76,175	73,425	68,750	64,900	64,075	785,675	55.00%
Gross Profit	40,725	43,875	49,950	50,400	52,425	59,850	61,425	62,325	60,075	56,250	53,100	52,425	642,825	45.00%
Expenses														
Advertising	5,177	5,577	6,349	6,406	6,664	7,608	7,808	7,922	7,636	7,150	6,750	6,664	81,710	5.72%
Bank Expense														
Checking	100	50	50	50	50	50	50	50	50	50	50	50	650	0.05%
Credit Card Costs	1,267	1,365	1,554	1,568	1,631	1,862	1,911	1,939	1,869	1,750	1,652	1,631	19,999	1.40%
Commissions - Sales	4,525	4,875	5,550	5,600	5,825	6,650	6,825	6,925	6,675	6,250	5,900	5,825	71,425	5.00%
Dues & Subscriptions												450	450	0.03%
Insurance	765	0	0	765	0	0	765	0	0	765	0	0	3,060	0.21%
Legal & Accounting	250	250	250	250	250	250	250	250	250	250	250	250	3,000	0.21%
Office Supplies	52	52	52	52	52	52	52	52	52	52	52	52	624	0.04%
Rent - Building	1,500	1,500	1,500	1,500	1,500	1,500	1,500	1,500	1,500	1,500	1,500	1,500	18,000	1.26%
Rent - Inventory Storage	100	100	100	100	100	100	100	100	100	100	100	100	1,200	0.08%
Salary - Administrative	2,600	2,600	2,600	2,600	2,600	2,600	2,600	2,600	2,600	2,600	2,600	2,600	31,200	2.18%
Salary - Owner	4,160	4,160	4,160	4,160	4,160	4,160	4,160	4,160	4,160	4,160	4,160	4,160	49,920	3.49%
Salary - Sales	4,160	4,160	4,160	4,160	4,160	4,160	4,160	4,160	4,160	4,160	4,160	4,160	49,920	3.49%
Taxes & Benefits	2,317	2,369	2,471	2,478	2,512	2,636	2,662	2,677	2,639	2,576	2,523	2,512	30,370	2.13%
Telephone	550	550	550	550	550	550	550	550	550	550	550	550	6,600	0.46%
Trade Shows & Exhibits			5,200							5,200			10,400	0.73%
Travel	1,358	1,463	1,665	1,680	1,748	1,995	2,048	2,078	2,003	1,875	1,770	1,748	21,428	1.50%
Utilities	554	563	573	562	558	613	652	701	601	550	576	785	7,288	0.51%
Vehicle Allowance	800	800	800	800	800	800	800	800	800	800	800	800	9,600	0.67%
Warehouse Supplies	282	304	346	349	363	415	426	432	417	390	368	363	4,457	0.31%
Website	250	250	250	250	250	250	250	250	250	250	250	250	3,000	0.21%
Total Expenses	30,766	30,988	38,180	33,881	33,773	36,250	37,568	37,146	36,311	40,978	34,011	34,450	424,300	29.70%
Net Profit	9,959	12,887	11,770	16,519	18,652	23,600	23,857	25,179	23,764	15,273	19,089	17,975	218,525	15.30%

January's Net Profit was forecasted at $13,142 (Figure F-4), against an actual Net Profit of $9,959 (Figure F-5). February yielded $12,887 (Figure F-5) against a forecast of $14,403 (Figure F-4). Now, have a look at our prospects for our annual Net Profit. If the balance of ABC's forecast holds up, they will still yield a Net Profit of $218,525 (Figure F-5), or 15.3% of Sales revenue, against a forecasted Net Profit of $223,224 (Figure F-4), or 15.46% of Sales revenue. So, how can ABC Company make up the Net Profit differential, created by early failures?

What are my choices? ABC essentially has three choices. 1) Meet forecasted Sales and leave Expenses as forecasted. 2) Decrease Expenses and settle for a poor Sales performance. 3) A combination of Sales increases and Expense cuts.

If they opt for choice #1, either the existing sales force of two people must get on the ball and increase Sales output to meet forecasted numbers, or additional sales people must be hired to take up the slack. This will increase Sales Salaries, Commissions, Taxes & Benefits, and Vehicle Allowance. Considering the fact that the shortage of Sales amounts to $15,500, which equates to only 31 units, at $500 per unit, year-to-date, it is probably a little early to panic and begin hiring additional sales people. ABC Company carried over last year's sales people to 2016, giving us the impression that they are confident that the sales team can accomplish the job as forecasted.

If ABC Company opts for choice #2, and simply decreases Expenses to accompany a poor sales performance, management will be showing their employees that poor performance is acceptable. Granted, ABC's forecast may be above actual expectations, but once again, it is too early to panic and accept a sub-standard performance, based on numbers that are on the low end of an expected 15% to 18% Net Profit.

If ABC Company chooses to opt for choice #3, a combination of Sales increases and Expense cuts, they are once again jumping the gun. Unless the economy has tanked since the end of 2015, there is a good to excellent chance that ABC Company can make up the difference in forecasted vs. actual Sales by the end of the year.

What is the best choice for ABC Company? There are certainly more questions that we must ask of ABC Company before deciding to move forward with choice #1, #2 or #3. For our exercise, we are going to move forward with choice #1. The business year is still young, the sales people met their goals for 2015 and the sales goals for 2016 appear reasonable, based on data that tells us that a 15.46% Net Profit is certainly within realistic boundaries for this industry

The next question is, when do we make up our lost sales? The answer is, immediately. ABC Company could evenly spread 31 extra sales units over the remaining months of the year. But as they get further into the year, the odds of making up the difference gets tougher and tougher. So, we will add 15 sales units to the quota of one salesperson and 16 units to the other, spread over the next three months. ABC Company's owner will monitor individual sales more closely, beginning immediately, and investigate every possible way to squeeze those extra sales out of the system. Let's go to Figure F-6 and look at the newly forecasted Sales numbers for March through May.

INCOME STATEMENT AFTER RE-FORECAST
ABC Company
January & February Actual Numbers

Figure F-6

	Jan	Feb	Mar	Apr	May	Jun	Jul	Aug	Sep	Oct	Nov	Dec	Totals	Rev. %
Sales	90,500	97,500	116,000	117,000	122,000	133,000	136,500	138,500	133,500	125,000	118,000	116,500	1,444,000	100.00%
Cost of Goods Sold	49,775	53,625	63,800	64,350	67,100	73,150	75,075	76,175	73,425	68,750	64,900	64,075	794,200	55.00%
Gross Profit	40,725	43,875	52,200	52,650	54,900	59,850	61,425	62,325	60,075	56,250	53,100	52,425	649,800	45.00%
Expenses														
Advertising	5,177	5,577	6,635	6,692	6,978	7,608	7,808	7,922	7,636	7,150	6,750	6,664	82,597	5.72%
Bank Expense														
Checking	100	50	50	50	50	50	50	50	50	50	50	50	650	0.05%
Credit Card Costs	1,267	1,365	1,624	1,638	1,708	1,862	1,911	1,939	1,869	1,750	1,652	1,631	20,216	1.40%
Commissions - Sales	4,525	4,875	5,800	5,850	6,100	6,650	6,825	6,925	6,675	6,250	5,900	5,825	72,200	5.00%
Dues & Subscriptions												450	450	0.03%
Insurance	765	0	0	765	0	0	765	0	0	765	0	0	3,060	0.21%
Legal & Accounting	250	250	250	250	250	250	250	250	250	250	250	250	3,000	0.21%
Office Supplies	52	52	52	52	52	52	52	52	52	52	52	52	624	0.04%
Rent - Building	1,500	1,500	1,500	1,500	1,500	1,500	1,500	1,500	1,500	1,500	1,500	1,500	18,000	1.25%
Rent - Inventory Storage	100	100	100	100	100	100	100	100	100	100	100	100	1,200	0.08%
Salary - Administrative	2,600	2,600	2,600	2,600	2,600	2,600	2,600	2,600	2,600	2,600	2,600	2,600	31,200	2.16%
Salary - Owner	4,160	4,160	4,160	4,160	4,160	4,160	4,160	4,160	4,160	4,160	4,160	4,160	49,920	3.46%
Salary - Sales	4,160	4,160	4,160	4,160	4,160	4,160	4,160	4,160	4,160	4,160	4,160	4,160	49,920	3.46%
Taxes & Benefits	2,317	2,369	2,508	2,516	2,553	2,636	2,662	2,677	2,639	2,576	2,523	2,512	30,486	2.11%
Telephone	550	550	550	550	550	550	550	550	550	550	550	550	6,600	0.46%
Trade Shows & Exhibits			5,200							5,200			10,400	0.72%
Travel	1,358	1,463	1,740	1,755	1,830	1,995	2,048	2,078	2,003	1,875	1,770	1,748	21,660	1.50%
Utilities	554	563	573	562	558	613	652	701	601	550	576	785	7,288	0.50%
Vehicle Allowance	800	800	800	800	800	800	800	800	800	800	800	800	9,600	0.66%
Warehouse Supplies	282	304	362	365	381	415	426	432	417	390	368	363	4,505	0.31%
Website	250	250	250	250	250	250	250	250	250	250	250	250	3,000	0.21%
Total Expenses	30,766	30,988	38,914	34,615	34,580	36,250	37,568	37,146	36,311	40,978	34,011	34,450	426,576	29.54%
Net Profit	9,959	12,887	13,286	18,035	20,320	23,600	23,857	25,179	23,764	15,273	19,089	17,975	223,224	15.46%

We added $5,000 (10 units) of Sales to March and April, and $5,500 (11 units) to the month of May. In the event that the sales team cannot make up at 31 units by the end of May, the remaining units can be made up in the months of June, July, August and September, which were the best Sales months of 2015. If ABC makes up the lost sales, the re-forecast tells us that Net Profit is once again $223,224, or 15.46% of Sales.

Is re-forecasting always this simple? Re-forecasting is a monthly event. If you miss your forecast on the low side, you want to improve, which further alters your forecast. If you are doing better than expected, you want to hold the line and maybe even improve on your future numbers.

WHAT SHOULD I DO? Whether you are behind, or ahead of your forecasted numbers, always follow the *INCOME STATEMENT FORECASTING TIPS* that appear at the beginning of this section. Accuracy is the key to a great forecast. Follow-through is the key to making that great forecast a reality.

Forecasting regularly and accurately is a major difference between the successful business person and the *also-rans*. Read the entire section on *FORECASTING* and respond accordingly – ADJUST, ADJUST , ADJUST.

Additional Resources: Department Managers, Accountant, Business Consultant.

FOREIGN ACCOUNTS

The requirements and regulations that accompany foreign trade are numerous and necessary. Unfortunately, trade in foreign countries can be frustrating and costly if you are not careful. Many foreign lands do not follow the rules that are in place to protect American enterprises. If you are serious about foreign trade, do not cut corners. Contact a consultant who understands the foreign market you intend to enter. Ask for references and follow through with a visit and Q&A session. Going global is a gigantic step for most small businesses and should not be taken lightly.

Additional Resources: Attorney or consultant with expertise in foreign trade, www.importexportcustoms.com/importrequirements.html.

FORMS

All popular word processors contain a number of free boilerplate templates that can be modified to suit your company needs. QuickBooks, Peachtree, AccountEdge, and NetSuite Small Business are just a few of the financial systems out there, ranging from $19.95 to more than $2,000. Most of these systems include all financial forms necessary for your business.

If you prefer to purchase locally, most office store chains have a full section of software dedicated to business forms. These are usually boilerplate templates that simply require you to add your company information. Avoid production of forms from scratch. The cost is far greater than converting boilerplate forms for usage in your business

WHAT SHOULD I DO? Most forms can be generated from your company computer and printer. Do not purchase mounds of forms that may be useful in your business. Talk to your CPA and/or bookkeeper and determine your needs, and then take the least expensive route toward providing necessary forms. As your business grows, you may find that more – or less - forms become necessary. When you add a new form, try to integrate it with an old form to save paper and space.

Some companies create a master copy of each form. When a particular form is needed, the master is copied, thus producing a copy of a copy. This is a poor practice. As the original is copied, over and over, it becomes worn, thus reproducing copies that appear soiled and crooked. Always print a new form for each usage. This ensures that you will present a crisp, clean, straight form every time.

Check for similar or duplicate forms at least once a year and shed unnecessary paper. No one enjoys extra or duplicate paperwork. Ask your CPA or bookkeeper for guidance.

FRANCHISING (See also EXCLUSIVITY)

According to Entrepreneur.com, franchising is defined as, "*A continuing relationship in which a franchisor provides a licensed privilege to the franchisee to do business and offers assistance in organizing, training, merchandising, marketing and managing in return for a monetary consideration. Franchising is a form of business by which the owner (franchisor) of a product, service or method obtains distribution through affiliated dealers (franchisees).*"[6]

In essence, franchising is a type of exclusivity with additional bells and whistles, most notably; the payment of ongoing royalties and an initial fee to the franchisor. The franchisee also receives the benefit of the franchisor's experience and ongoing training as business progresses. Good franchisors provide franchisees with a familiar brand, a major competitive advantage and a fast start that may not be available in any other startup business.

A good deal of the franchisee's homework should be accomplished by the franchisor in exchange for the initial franchise fee, such as a market analysis, competitive analysis, assistance in finding and negotiating a lease for a suitable business location, traffic and demographic studies and a proven operational procedure. You can skip the major part of that business plan you intended to write because the franchisor will provide it for you. You will also be asked to interview a number of current franchisees to get a feel for the value of the franchisor's operation.

The bottom line here is the bottom line. The amount of help the franchisee receives from the franchisor often depends on the size of the franchisee's investment. The franchisor is in business to sell successful franchises because the franchisee's success provides the royalties that are the mainstay of the franchisor's profits.

To be a successful franchisee, you should follow the same rules you would follow in entering any other business. Is the franchise the right business for you, one that utilizes your experience and fulfills your appetite and desires for success? Can you earn the kind of income you need? Have you selected a business that is economically competitive? Can you envision a long-term relationship with the franchisor and the business? Are your strengths, weaknesses and temperament adaptive to a franchise environment? Finally, selecting a franchise requires the same due diligence as entry into any other business. Do your homework and do not settle for a franchise that does not meet your personal and financial requirements.

Additional Resources: Attorney educated in franchise operations, www.entrepreneur.com/encyclopedia/printthis/82150.html, www.franchise.org, www.franchisedirect.com.

FREIGHT/SHIPPING

For our purposes, *freight* and *shipping* are synonymous. Regardless of your product or service, freight costs will likely impact your business in one way or another. Freight, whether inbound or outbound, is the price that the shipping or receiving company pays to transfer goods from one location to another. Freight is one of the most overlooked costs of doing business. In fact, freight is often overlooked completely when companies negotiate a price for a product or service. Freight is usually 5-15 percent of the cost of goods, inbound or outbound.

Who selects a freight company? Assuming that all your potential carriers are properly licensed and insured, there are four major criteria for selection. 1) You must have on-time delivery. 2) Your goods must arrive unharmed. 3) The cost of shipping must fall within your budget. 4) Insurance and loss & damage claims are clear, concise and reasonable. If you are satisfied that all four criteria are in order, it really does not matter if you or your vendor selects the shipper. Many vendors have great relationships with shippers they utilize on a regular basis. These relationships may convert to better pricing and handling for you.

Who pays the freight company? Prepaid & Add terms come into play when the vendor has a contract with a carrier for a better freight rate. The vendor prepays the carrier and adds the freight charges to your invoice without a markup. If you prefer to pick the carrier and pay the freight because you can get a better rate, feel free. Vendors do not usually care who picks up the order, as long as pickup is timely. Of course, if you pick the freight company, you are responsible for the goods during transit.

Who files claims for damage by a carrier? If damage occurs, the driver should sign the Bill of Lading and enumerate the damage. Take pictures before the freight is moved off the vehicle, if possible. Damages must be explicitly noted on the front of the Bill of Lading. If you accept the freight, do not move, repair, or assemble until pictures are taken and the carrier sends someone out to inspect the damage to the goods. Each carrier may handle damage claims differently. Keep original cartons and packaging for the insurance adjuster to review.

Never depend on the driver to handle a claim. If freight is damaged, ask the driver to call the carrier immediately. If the driver will not call the carrier, you make the call before moving forward. Always talk to the carrier about damaged goods before the driver leaves your premises.

Freight costs. Freight costs include transportation, packing, and handling. Here is the breakdown. Product must be placed in a carton, crate, special container, bin, or bag. Larger quantities are usually shipped on pallets. Cartons or containers may require special materials, safety standards, labeling, bar code(s), wraps, ties, staples, tape, inner and outer cartons, structural supports, coolants, ventilation, refrigeration, and a number of other specialty items not mentioned here. Hazardous materials and live product add an entirely different level of special handling concerns. Hazardous materials may be subject to additional mileage charges due to restrictions for transporting such products, while live product may be able to withstand certain weather conditions, and not others. All the foregoing costs must be recovered when you price your products or services.

Learn the difference between FOB Origin and FOB Destination. FOB Origin, often referred to as FOB Shipping Point, holds the buyer responsible for shipping costs and the safety of the goods at the moment they leave the shipper's door, until they arrive at the buyer's door.

FOB Destination: Shipper is responsible for shipping costs and the safety of the goods until they reach the buyer's door.

Freight LTL shipments. LTL stands for *Less Than Truckload*.[7] Many trucking companies take full loads only. This means that a company that ships a partial load on a full-load carrier is going to pay full-load pricing even though the truck is not full. Consequently, many carriers provide LTL pricing for companies that cannot fill up a 48-foot or 53-foot trailer.

The advantage of LTL shipping is that you may reduce freight costs for partial loads. The disadvantages are that your freight may be loaded with goods for one or more destinations, and may be unloaded and reloaded several times and may arrive later than those loads that are hauled by full-load shippers. All this loading, unloading and reloading may result in higher than normal damages and / or losses of your goods.

LTL carriers also may have specific shipping requirements that are uncommon to full-load haulers, due to the fact that LTL haulers may put different types of goods, which require protection from each other, on the same truck. These restrictions may increase your packaging costs significantly.

Fuel surcharges. These are costs that are routinely added to shipping costs to make up for the variation in fuel prices. Fuel surcharges are usually updated weekly and are sometimes unpredictable. Be sure you understand that fuel surcharges are constantly in flux, especially when you are quoting shipping prices for goods that are scheduled to be shipped in future weeks or months.

Inbound freight charges. First, assume that the selling party is going to pay for your inbound freight. If you are negotiating the price of inbound goods, discuss the cost of the goods, independent from freight, before introducing freight into the process. When a fair price is reached, say, "And of course, the price is all inclusive." If you fail to nail down the responsibility for shipping costs, the seller will automatically assume that you, the buyer, will pay for all shipping.

If the selling party says that freight is extra, reopen negotiations. When you endorse the order, be sure that the words "FOB destination" appear on the sales document and on the bill of lading when the shipment arrives at your door. This designation means that the seller pays all shipping costs and is responsible for any damage or loss of the goods until they arrive safely at your destination. If you do pick up the tab for freight, be sure to include it in your cost of goods sold.

WHAT SHOULD I DO? Always inspect and count every incoming shipment as soon as it arrives at your dock. Never move goods from the dock until this step is accomplished. If goods are damaged or if the count is over or under, notify the shipper immediately. Do not keep overage. It does not belong to you. That said, vendors will occasionally tell you to keep overage, simply because it is not economically feasible to return the goods.

Outbound freight charges to your customer. Once again, assume that the other party is going to pay for freight. Ask how he intends to pick up his order. Always ask if the buyer has a vehicle large enough or small enough to pick up at your premises. Put the onus on the buyer to make the decision.

Most companies that ship goods automatically add outbound freight charges to the buyer's invoice without prior discussion, assuming that the buyer will pay for freight. If your customer refuses to pay the freight, put your negotiating hat on and strike a new deal. Know your costs. If you intend to add charges for loading and packaging, put the entire charge on the invoice under "Shipping and handling."

WHAT SHOULD I DO? Never pay freight *out* to your customer unless the customer asks you to do so. Always recover the cost of the freight in the price of your product. Calculate the gross margin of your product and add freight to the price. Example: Your product sells for $83.99 per unit. Freight is $5.00 per unit. Add $5.00 to $83.99 for a total sale price of $88.99 per unit. If your customer demands that you include freight as a separate line item on his invoice, do so.

You are not permitted to make a profit on freight unless your customer agrees to that profit in writing. If you incur extra costs for Shipping & Handling, add the amount to the customer's bill under a separate line, entitled Shipping & Handling. If you gouge your customer with Shipping & Handling charges, be prepared to suffer the consequences the next time you and that customer negotiate a price.

Additional Resources: http://www.fmcsa.dot.gov/

Chapter G

GARNISHMENTS

A garnishment is a court order that requires an employer to withhold all or a portion of an employee's pay and send it to a court or other party as payment for a legal debt. The court serves your company with a notice that outlines the terms and conditions of the garnishment. A garnishment is not a request; it is a legal court order. You must comply as directed or suffer legal consequences. The word *garnishee* refers to the act of holding an employee's money until the court takes it for payment. The most common garnishment is probably child support.

WHAT SHOULD I DO? I have had employees ask me to fire them and pay them under the table, or cut their pay to a level that cannot be garnisheed and pay the difference under the table. A few have asked me not to abide by a garnishment. In many states, spousal and child support are always garnisheed. Please refer to Lynn Miller's Daily Dozen: *Rule #1 - Never do anything illegal or get involved with anyone who does anything illegal*. Garnishment is a tool of the legal system. Refusal to garnishee an employee's pay is a refusal to follow a court order.

Additional Resources: Attorney.

GOALS

Set goals and accomplish them and—you win. Fail to set goals and—you lose.

Somewhere in your past, someone has mentioned the proverbial uncharted waters. No direction. Forever caught in a circular trough. Circling the drain. That says it all.

If you do not have written goals, do not go into business. If you are in business and do not have written goals, start planning for your future today. It sounds corny, doesn't it? You may have gotten this far without goals or a plan. You may not fail, but you will finish far behind the folks who have set goals for their futures.

Your first goal is easy. Assemble a business plan for today and for the future. You will learn a great deal about yourself and your business as you put your plan together.

Stepping Stones. Make small goals at first. Do your homework. Investigate other businesses similar to your own. Put together a management team and engage in fact finding. Pull together a few business plan boilerplates that are similar to your business. As you develop a team, increase your goals. See an accountant and an attorney. Talk about legalities and numbers now that you have some knowledge under your belt. Do all these things in a deliberate way, setting new goals before and after each step is accomplished.

Your guides to success. Lay out a path to business success. Start developing your business plan. Your goals are a big part of business plan preparation. Set goals for sales, hiring, capital spending, and everything that is important to your success and the success of your stakeholders and employees. Never stop setting goals. Goals are your keys to a lifetime of achievement. There is nothing to fear, nothing to lose and everything to gain.

WHAT SHOULD I DO? The trick is to think out your goals in advance, put them in writing, and make yourself accountable for the accomplishment of each goal. Setting goals will put you at the head of the pack at the end of the day. Be honest with yourself—you set a goal when you decide not to set goals. See the section entitled, **BUSINESS PLAN.**

GRANTS

Most people who attend small business workshops and seminars are looking for investors to provide business capital for startups or expansion of an existing business. Many ask questions concerning government grants, or free government money for business investment. The ads are all over the Internet. "Why borrow money and pay interest when you can get a grant for free?" Go to www.grant.gov. This is a government website, which states:

"ATTENTION! *Grants.gov does not offer money for personal financial assistance or debt. If you are seeking personal financial assistance, such as*:

>*Social Security/Supplemental Security Income, Medicaid or State Social Services, please visit: www.GovBenefits.gov*

>*Student Loans, please visit: www.Studentaid.ed.gov*

>*Small Business Start-up Loans, please visit: www.sba.gov*

This type of individual assistance is NOT available on this website. "[8]

There are numerous organizations that offer grants for numerous purposes. They require full disclosure of your business type and ability to utilize the grant for specific purposes. Some grants are free, some require matching money, and others may be coupled with a loan that requires repayment. Application forms for both construction and non-construction grants may be found on the SBA website at www.sba.gov.

If you are an existing not-for-profit company, you may want to hire a grant writer and consider paying her to formalize your pursuit of grant money. Costs range from zero to thousands of dollars. Be sure the grant writer is reputable. Ask for references and check them thoroughly.

There are people out there who will offer to help you find a grant – for a fee. In my experience, such individuals take your money and arm you with a book or list of numerous grants that are available for the taking. The book promises to teach you how to seek a grant. Walk away from these types of offers. Go directly to the SBA and get the real truth about grants.

Additional Resources: *See **SMALL BUSINESS ADMINISTRATION (SBA),** www.grants.gov, www.sba.gov.*

GROSS MARGIN / GROSS PROFIT

Gross margin is the portion of the sale price, over and above the cost of that sale, expressed as a percentage. Gross profit is that percentage expressed in dollars and cents. In other words, if you sell a product for a dollar and the cost of the product is 60 cents, the gross margin is 40 percent and the gross profit is 40 cents.

The concept is easy. Most people get confused about the mathematics. They cannot decide whether the process requires multiplication or division, or which number is divided by the other.

How do I calculate gross margin/gross profit? Easy stuff. Using the example in the prior paragraph, just divide the profit (.40 cents) by the selling price (1.00) and the product is .40, which converts to a gross margin of 40%. Subtract the cost (60 cents) from the selling price (1.00) and the gross profit is the remainder (40 cents).

To convert your cost to a selling price at a particular gross margin, do the following:

Example: Your product cost is $60.00. That means that you paid $60.00 for the product and want to sell it at a profit. You decide on a gross margin of 40 percent. Subtract .40 from 1.00. The difference is .60, right? So, here's the math . . .

The math: 1.00   This is always 1.00

- .40   This is your desired gross margin

=.60   This is the figure you divide into your product cost

Hence $60.00 ÷ .60 = $100.00, your selling price @ 40 percent GM

Your selling price is $100.00

Thus, $40 gross profit ÷ $100 selling price = 40 percent gross margin

One more example to make sure you understand the math, okay?

This time the product cost is $60. You decide on a gross margin of 50 percent. Subtract .50 from 1.00. The difference is .50, right? So, here's the math . . .

The math:	1.00	This is always 1.00
	$-\ .50$	This is your desired gross margin
	$=\ .50$	This is the figure you divide into your cost

Hence $60.00 ÷ .50 = $120.00, your selling price @ 50 percent GM

Your selling price is $120.00

Thus, $60 gross profit ÷ $100 selling price = 60 percent gross margin

Calculate this over and over until you understand the concept. Not everyone will pick it up the first time. If the concept escapes you, call your accountant and ask for an explanation. Math can be a tough business, but this is one piece of math you want to understand. A lack of understanding can cost you a lot of future profit, especially when a customer or employee wants to debate price.

Adding a profit percentage. This is the most common fallacy regarding gross margin. Many entrepreneurs misunderstand gross margins and add a percentage to product cost, believing that the add-on percentage is the same as the gross margin percentage.

For example: Product cost is $60. You want a gross margin of 40 percent. Multiply $60 X 40 percent (.40) and come up with $24. You add $24 to your cost of $60 and your sale price becomes $84. Is this a gross margin of 40 percent? Let's do the math.

Divide the gross profit ($24) by the selling price ($84) and the gross margin is 28.57 percent, not 40 percent. All this time, you believed that you were calculating a 40 percent margin, but you did not understand why your bottom line was not reflecting the commensurate profit.

Where did you make your mistake? You should have divided your product cost ($60) by the inverse of your desired gross margin (1.00 − .40). Therefore, $60 (your cost) ÷ .60 = $100. The correct selling price for a 40 percent gross margin is $100, not $84. You were selling your product $16 short every time.

If you are still a little shaky on the math, revisit the previous section, entitled, *How do I calculate gross margin/gross profit?*

What gross margin is right for my business? There are a number of variables that determine a company's desired gross margin. Type of business, length of time in business, the economy, the competitive climate in your area, and desired cash flow are just a few.

The first key variable is profit. Is your gross margin healthy enough to consistently offset all your costs and expenses and produce your forecasted profit? The second key variable, your competition, is as important as the first. If your competitors consistently sell for a lower gross margin than your own, you may be forced to make adjustments in other areas to meet your goals. You may have to cut expenses or alter your purchasing policies to acquire product at a better price.

Have a hard look at your business, and then have an equally hard look at your competition. You should know what they charge, their cost basis, and their general philosophies. Try to stay in the same price range as your competitors. Offer solid service and reliable, competitive products. You want to maximize your gross margins without putting your product or service at a price that will not survive the competition. On the other hand, you must set your gross margins at a level that produces your target cash flow and earnings.

Note: No one wins a price war but the customer.

WHAT SHOULD I DO? If you experience problems with mathematics, you are not alone. However, you really need a functional understanding of gross margin and gross profit. A functional understanding means that you can calculate and utilize these figures in the day-to-day management of your company. It does not mean that you should have taken accounting in high school or college, and all is lost if you failed to do so. If you do not understand margins, get help from any of the individuals or entities discussed below under *Additional Resources*.

Additional Resources: Your accountant, banker, business consultant, Internet, public library.

Chapter H

HIRING

Do I need a hiring plan? Your hiring plan should be integrated into your annual business forecast. Your annual forecast lays out your budget for the upcoming year, including increases or decreases in production, sales, and workforce. Based on your forecast, it may be necessary to hire or lay off people to balance your workload against your workforce. You should always plan hiring prior to the need.

Questions to Ask. This is another area that requires more room for explanation than we have available in this book. Obviously, you cannot ask any discriminatory questions that have to do with race, religion, sex, age, national origin, etc. If you intend to do your own hiring, you must know the rules of interviewing potential employees. Talk to a discrimination attorney or contact a human resources specialist for more information. Do not strike out on your own until you know the rules. For additional information, go to www.eeoc.gov.

Drug free workplace. If you are doing business with federal or state government accounts, you may be required by law to create an alcohol-free and drug-free policy. Even outside of dealing with government accounts, alcohol-free and drug-free policies are becoming commonplace in the private sector. Such a program provides you with a basis for dealing with abusers and hiring non-users. It also provides a safer and more predictable workplace for you and your employees. For additional information, go to www.dol.gov/elaws/drugfree.htm

Should I do new-hire background checks? Yes. *(See BACKGROUND CHECKS).*

Offer letters. Everyone you hire should receive an offer letter that spells out the terms of employment with your company. At a minimum, an offer letter should be welcoming and include the necessity for a drug test and background check. In addition, an offer letter should include start date, position description, income (salary or hourly), payment increments, vacation particulars, holidays, sick days, personal days, place to report for work and any other benefits or perks. Include a signature and date line for acceptance or non-acceptance of the position. Indicate the date by which the letter must be returned for the offer to remain valid.

Offer letters abound on the Internet. If you are uncomfortable with that venue, contact any human resources professional for assistance. Regardless of the source, do not utilize preprinted templates with fill in blanks. Make your offer letters professional and double check every item in the letter before putting it in the hands of a candidate.

What if someone fails testing? Let the prospective employee know in writing during the hiring process that passing a drug test is a condition of employment. The employee can be terminated upon failing the drug test, even though he has begun to work. He must be paid for time worked. The easiest way to avoid this situation is to plan ahead and start a new employee only after he is found drug-free and alcohol-free.

Immigration *(See IMMIGRATION & NATURALIZATION SERVICE (INS).*

Reference checks. Take letters of recommendation with a grain of salt. They are often written by the prospective employee and signed by the sender. Shy away from personal references, in favor of prior workplace references. If the applicant is new to the workforce, ask for references from organizations with which the applicant is, or has been affiliated. Organizations are responsible for information disseminated during a reference interview, where personal references may embellish the skills of the applicant with impunity.

There are no federal laws regarding the disclosure of information about former employees. Labor laws vary, state-to-state. Stick to questions that are pertinent to the situation. You are certainly trying to validate the candidate's accomplishments, but you are also on a mission to spot "red flags" regarding any strange or negative behavior.

You are always in danger of attracting a defamation suit if you stray from the facts that are relevant to your inquiry. You could also be on shaky ground later if you fail to discover facts about the potential new hire that indicate that he or she could present a danger to your workplace.

Checking references requires knowledge and skill to be legal and effective. If you are not aware of the laws regarding reference checks, get help *before* you dive into this arena. Mistakes could be lethal to your business and extremely costly. On the other hand, failure to check references can invite all manner of unwanted problems in your workplace.

Additional Resources: Human Resources specialist.

Communicating with Non-Hires. Close each interview with a timeframe and method for getting back to the candidate. "Ms. Smith, we will let you know the status of your application within seven days from today. We will call you or send a letter with our determination." Make up form letters, fill in the blanks (on the computer please), leave the candidate with dignity and move on.

If you are certain that the candidate will not be hired after the initial interview, explain that you are looking for a candidate with a different skill set and thank him for the interview. No letter or follow-up call is necessary.

Keep all resumes in your files in alphabetical order for three years. Check new resumes for duplicates and prevent return interviews of unwanted candidates. Tag resumes of good candidates and file them separately if they are not hired. Do not write on applications. Notes should be on a separate piece of paper and attached. When you need someone, dip into this file and make some calls. You never know who may finally be available.

Warm bodies. Stick to your guns. If you do not find the quality employee(s) you are seeking in the first round of interviews, cut the process short and start over with a fresh group of interviewees. Change your hiring parameters, your ads, or your agency. Do not hire warms bodies. Your decision will haunt you over and over.

More than one interview. The number of interviews depends on the value of the position. A labor position will require a lesser number of interviews than hiring a CEO or company president. Any position deserves at least a second interview for those who make it past the first interview, simply because people do not usually open up during an initial interview, making it tough to effectively identify "red flags." A second interview offers the opportunity to develop a genuine line of communication with the candidate.

As you climb the hiring ladder and interview candidates for higher paying positions in your company, the cost of selecting and training a new hire increases dramatically. Therefore, you can afford to spend more to hire better. Bottom line: Do not stop interviewing until you are satisfied that you have the right candidate for the position. This does not mean that the candidate is a perfect fit. It does mean that the candidate meets most of the necessary qualifications for the position and is trainable and willing to learn the rest in a short timeframe. Everything in business has a cost. Hiring is no different than any other expense. Spend wisely and look at the long-term benefits.

Note: When interviewing a candidate, you talk 10 percent of the time and the candidate talks 90 percent of the time. Control the interview and stay on target.

Pre-Employment Testing. Most companies do not test employment candidates. They assume that the candidate is honest about her past endeavors and has that college degree and multiple years of experience requested for the position. They also assume that the candidate has simple math, writing, spelling and speaking skills. You should be interested in how closely the candidate's aptitude, personality, and skill sets match the position for which she is applying. But, you should first be interested in the candidate's ability to do the simple, daily tasks.

Renee Schoof covers education, colleges, job training and special education for McClatchy Newspapers, based in Washington, D.C. She writes that "As the economy begins to perk up and businesses start to hire, a lack of basic knowledge about mathematics could present a problem to people looking for work."[1] She goes on to say that Eric Hahn, vice president of organizational development of General Plastics Manufacturing Company in Tacoma, Washington gives a basic middle school math test to applicants. "Only one in 10 who take the test pass."[2] All test takers have a high school education. This is not met to be an indictment of today's schools, but it is met to give you a heads-up about the poor skills of many of our high school graduates. Pre-employment testing is something you should consider for your business.

Pre-employment testing can be accomplished by consultants or companies that specialize in testing, or by administering tests that you have devised for your company via research with reliable sources. Pre-employment testing serves two purposes: First you have a better chance of hiring the right person the first time, thus shortening the road to full productivity and decreasing turnover. Second, you have a better chance of matching the candidate's personality to her new work environment, helping her to fit into the cultural mix more quickly and more efficiently.

Companies such as eSkill, Valtera, Criteria Corporation and Saterfiel and Associates, to name a few, offer a wide range of employee tests, to include reasoning, memory, specific skill sets, mathematics, various certifications, and general skills testing. Testing can be very expensive or very inexpensive, depending on your industry and the position that is being offered. Treat testing like any other expense. Weigh the consequences and spend wisely.

WHAT SHOULD I DO? When you are ready to make the final decision on a potential new hire, follow your gut! You will generally get a partial picture of the candidate by the end of the first interview. As time passes, that partial picture becomes a gut feeling for the candidate's ability to perform in the company environment.

Many candidates look great in the first interview, but when they have the opportunity to fully express themselves in the second interview, they begin to show weaknesses. If your gut tells you that your candidate is not a good match for your team, continue looking. Trust your gut—it will rarely let you down.

Note: Hire attitude and enthusiasm! Train skills!

Additional Resources: Human resources consultant, attorney versed in human resources and/or hiring and terminating employees.

HOLIDAYS (See BENEFITS)

HOME EQUITY LOAN / HOME EQUITY LINE OF CREDIT

If you have been in business less than two years, you may not be able to secure a business loan or business line of credit on the merits of your business, alone. This usually leaves you with two choices. You may want to target a personal home equity loan or home equity line of credit.

A home equity loan is collateralized by the equity in your home. If you have a $225,000 home and owe $100,000, the equity in your home is $125,000. Most banks will loan up to 80% of your equity value, thus putting a second mortgage on your home. The bank cuts you a check for 80% of $125,000 ($100,000) that is payable to the bank, with interest, over a specified term, say 15 years. You repay the loan out of your personal checking account. Whether or not you utilize the money for your business, the payment is due every month until the loan is satisfied.

Ask your bank to deposit the loan ($100,000) in your personal checking account. Do not deposit the $100,000 directly into your business account. This is a violation of IRS rules - co-mingling of funds. Write a check from your personal checking account to your business checking account for $100,000. Draw up a simple loan agreement to cover the transaction. Add interest to the loan if you and your accountant determine that a tax benefit will result. Write a monthly check from your business account to your personal account for the amount of the loan payment, plus interest if applicable. Make the bank loan payment from your personal account.

If a home equity loan is your only choice, this route may make sense. The disadvantage of a home equity loan is the fact that you get your funds in a lump sum, whether you need it or not. Interest on the entire loan begins the day the money hits your account. You probably will not utilize the loan amount immediately, which means that a portion of your $100,000 is left in your checking account or a savings vehicle, where it likely earns less interest than you are paying on your loan. But, there is usually a better way.

Consider a home equity line of credit. The exercise is the same as a home equity loan. The bank approves a credit line in the amount of $100,000, based on your home's equity of $125,000. The bank gives you access to a $100,000 credit line, usually at an interest rate that is considerably less than a home equity loan. You transfer the money in and out of your personal checking account as you see fit. You move the money in and out of your business account in the same manner discussed above. The difference is huge. You pay interest on the money you borrow for as long as you possess the funds. Once your need for the funds has passed, you put the money back in the credit line where it resides – interest free – until you have a future need. Some banks charge a small annual free for an equity line, usually less than $100.

A home equity line can be a powerful tool if utilized properly. It is also a nice rainy day fund. When the need arises, the funds are available at a moment's notice. You pay interest, only while you make use of borrowed funds. When your company becomes profitable enough, apply for a business equity line of credit.

Additional Resources: Your accountant, bookkeeper, banker.

HOURLY EMPLOYEES

Pay ranges. If you are a union shop, pay ranges are probably negotiable every two or three years, then etched in stone until the next round of negotiations. Whether union or nonunion, you should be looking at your industry, the competition, and the general economic climate in your area(s) of operation. You may have an office in Akron, Ohio, and another in Chicago, Illinois. The differences in economies, revenues, expenses and wage scales in cities such as these call for vastly different hourly pay ranges.

First, look at your competition. What are they paying for similar skill sets? Do they include benefits in their packages, or do they pay an inflated rate and depend on their employees to provide self-benefits? Are you a small or large operation, relative to your industry in your area? Depending on your size, you may be able to provide more than a smaller operation, thus reducing your employee turnover.

Next, do your hourly employees possess unique, hard-to-find skill sets? If the inventory of skilled workers is low, availability becomes a problem and you may pay more to attract quality employees. You may want to go outside your area to bring in experienced employees. These people will probably demand moving expenses and a higher wage to relocate.

Last, consider the general economic climate in your geographical area. How much do companies in your industry pay for employees with the skill sets you are seeking? Is unemployment on the rise among your target candidate group? Or is unemployment at a low among the group? Do economic factors in your area point toward overall growth or decline?

After examining all the above, devise a pay range that is based on the lowest rate for the least skilled and least senior employees, and highest rate for highly skilled, long-term employees. Other employees fit somewhere in the pay range, based on their skill sets and tenure.

Wage earner's grapevine. You may have encountered employers who warned employees that their earnings were private and were not to be discussed with anyone else in the company. The real truth is that, with few exceptions, everyone wants to know what everyone else earns. As soon as that new employee gets to know others in the company, the subject of compensation comes up full bloom and the truth is out.

WHAT SHOULD I DO? You must have consistency in pay scales. Be fair and be honest. Why? The *wage earner's grapevine*. Assume that eventually everyone knows what everyone else earns. If you feel the necessity to interfere with free speech in your business, odds are that your employees already believe that you are hiding something from them. Pay a fair day's wage for a fair day's work. Let the grapevine take its course.

Pay grades. The military, fire department, police department, federal government, and many others too numerous to mention utilize pay grades. Reach the grade and you get a pay increase, based on skill sets and tenure. Although pay grades are the norm in many industries, common sense says that employees should be paid based on their production: great job, great pay; mediocre or poor job, less pay. We should be paid what we are worth. Equal pay increases to entire workforces are a function of weak management. Poor employees continue to flounder and produce poor results, while extraordinary employees eventually leave and go where their qualities are recognized.

Time recording systems. Time recording systems for small businesses can be purchased cheaply or expensively, depending on the sophistication necessary for your enterprise. Simple time card systems require someone to calculate time data and convert it to payroll. Beyond standard time clocks, there are numerous systems that integrate nicely into your company computer system. The more innovative systems automatically calculate time and eliminate erasures, print-overs and tampering with the system. An employee simply carries a smart card – looks like a credit card – and swipes or waves the card near a sensor. The system records the time and the employee ID number. The system analyzes the information and sends payroll-ready data to your in-house payroll department or an off-site payroll service. Every degree of sophistication adds a little more to your system costs, but reduces the time necessary to record and calculate payroll. If you utilize a payroll service, have a chat about time recording systems before making a purchase.

If you have an unusually large number of employees, you will want a number of time recording stations spread throughout your plant. Otherwise, you will have a mob at the recording station, all trying to clock in or out at the same time.

That said, when you add up the time that employees spend in front of a time clock, waiting to punch in or out, you can literally see your profit going down the drain. If you must have time clocks, eliminate punching in and punching out for lunch. Various employee groups or sections can take lunch at specific times and must be off work stations and back to work stations promptly. Supervisors can deal with employees who lag behind. If you save five minutes a day for twenty people, you save 433 man hours a year (that's 10.8 weeks of straight time production) because people are not waiting to punch in or out before and after lunch. Do the same calculation for the minutes lost when the cattle call affect takes over fifteen minutes before quitting time and you will be astounded at the amount of money you lose around your time clocks each year.

Note: See more below under the area dealing with Clean up Time.

Time sheets. Time sheets are not time cards. Time sheets require the employee to keep track of his time; hence, some time sheets are accurate, while others are not. Most employees dislike time sheets because it is nearly impossible to keep track of every minute of every day. Employees also feel that time sheets are a way of telling them that trust is an issue. If you are using a time sheet to control an employee, you are probably wasting your time. If you want to keep track of piece work, look at the number of pieces per employee shift and derive an hourly average that is acceptable for each work station.

Clean Up Time. Clean up time creates a bone of contention in many companies. For instance, the employee working on the lathe cleans up his area before going home at night. He shovels and sweeps up metal filings and shavings and puts them in a recycle bin. He puts tooling away, wipes down equipment, and lubricates his machinery. It may take 15 minutes or a half hour, but at least his work area is squeaky clean before he punches out and heads home.

If his machine is already clean with 15 minutes left on the clock, he shuts down and heads for the time clock where he catches up on the day's gossip while he waits for the time to punch out. Multiply his 15 minutes times 50 hourly employees and you are losing 12 1/2 hours of production each and every day. Multiply the hours lost per day, times an average of 21 work days per month, and that adds up to 262.5 hours per month, or 3,150 hours lost a year. Wow! What can you do to control this madness?

This is madness, but it is the way of the American worker. Some workers clean as they go. Some clean before they start. We are all individuals and we all develop good and bad habits as life moves along.

Set a production goal for each employee, per shift, per hour, per quarter hour, per day, whatever works best for the machine, the employee, and you. Base production goals on revenue goals. Base hourly rates and bonuses on employees' goals. Pay more for producing more. If goals are met and your employees can still afford to spend the last 15 minutes chatting, don't worry—you have made your numbers for the day.

Tardiness. Tardiness should not be tolerated. In the business world, if you are not on the job and producing at starting time, you are tardy. But what about John Doe Machinist? He is five minutes late every day because he drops off his son at school every morning. He works five minutes longer at the end of the day to make up the time.

Of course, this was not a problem when he signed up to work for you. He was going to be the perfect employee and always be on time. Surely, other employees talk about John Doe Machinist and wonder why you do not take care of the problem. The rules are the same for everyone, and everyone should be treated equally. Manage the employee and explain that he is expected to be on time. Manage from a position of strength. To do so, the playing field must be level for everyone. If you want to be respected, you must earn it.

Union pay rates. Union members are under contract. If you hire union workers, you are under contract with the union that represents those union workers. You negotiate with the union's bargaining unit, not with your employees, and you are bound by the contract you agree to, as is the union. Abide by the union contract, line for line. Do not take non contractual liberties. If you do not like the terms of the union contract, renegotiate during the next round of contract talks.

Additional Resources: Human resources consultant.

HOURS OF BUSINESS OPERATION

Unless you are very small, say a tiny retail business or a cafe, it is nearly impossible to be at your business all the time. You need time to attend to books, banking, and other necessities associated with running a business. However, when you are not in the office, you need to understand the risks. Reduction in profit, inventory shrinkage, loss of money, poor service, lost customers, and lost sales are all possibilities.

Hiring employees is an option, and the key is to hire the best people you can afford. Build a two-way trust between you and your employee. Reduce employees' opportunities to damage your business, whether purposefully or unintentionally.

I have an acquaintance who owns a number of franchise sandwich businesses. He manages one store and his wife manages another. They are producing forecasted profits at the stores they manage. The remaining stores are breaking even or losing money. He forecasts accordingly. Is he getting what he expects? Or is he failing to manage properly? This is a common scenario among businesses with multiple locations. Hire better, pay better, manage better, and you will do better.

Customers may determine your hours. A restaurant owner at a downtown location may be open from dawn until midnight, depending on traffic. Some cities are alive and bustling with activity all day and into the night. Others roll up the sidewalks at five o'clock.

Know your customers' habits and stay open during profitable hours. Pay attention to your competitors. You may copycat their hours of operation. You also may stay open during their closings because you find a niche market that competition has not explored.

Stick to hours. Open on time. Close on time. Open at the time posted on your door. Closing at 9 p.m. means the last customer is in the door at 9 p.m. If you plan to keep irregular hours for vacations or holidays, post a notification to your customers a month in advance. When you get back from vacation, advertise a sale to remind customers that you are open again.

Competition and surrounding businesses. If you do business in a mall, strip mall, or a town square, you will probably have a clause in your lease that sets your hours. If possible, lessors want all the businesses in their units opening and closing uniformly. It doesn't look good to have a business next door that is closed when your doors are open. It gives the impression that businesses in the area are not doing well.

When you are reconnoitering various areas for your business location, lean toward sites that have an *anchor store* in the immediate vicinity. Anchor stores are successful, well-known businesses such as department stores, big box stores or grocery stores that are capable of attracting customers who may also be interested in shopping at other nearby businesses. Without an anchor store in the vicinity, you are solely dependent on your advertising dollars to draw a crowd to your business. Why not take advantage of an anchor store's reputation to bring in additional customers?

Additional Resources: Know your customers' needs and your competition's hours.

HOURS OF WORK (See also BURNOUT)

How many hours should I work? You may be thinking that if you are not at your business, things just are not done in the same, efficient manner. Managing employees comes with being an owner. The better you hire, the more responsibility your employees will assume.

Sooner or later, you are going to learn that your business will not grow unless you hire people you trust and allow them to do their jobs. If you grow into satellite operations, the fantasy of always being there evaporates immediately. So why not hire people at the outset whom you would eventually trust with a satellite operation and wean yourself off those 14-hour days and 70-hour weeks sooner rather than later? This is not to say that you will become a 40-hour employee, but you must delegate or you will burn out *(See also DELEGATION)*.

Time management. Time management may be the number-one reason why owners and managers do not seem to have enough hours in a day. Do yourself a favor. Have a look at the book and the article mentioned under *Additional Resources* below. Hands down, this article from Harvard Business Review is one of the best ever written on delegation. It first appeared in 1999 and still stands the test of time.

Additional Resources: Your gut, your family, valued employee(s). Go to the Harvard Business Review on the Internet. Look for the article, "Management Time: Who's Got The Monkey", by William Oncken, Jr. and Donald L. Wass.[3] Also, look for the book, *Run Your Business So It Doesn't Run You,* by Linda Leigh Francis.[4]

HUMAN RESOURCES (HR)

This is an area where you can really get into trouble if you ignore the rules or are unaware of the rules. If you have any questions about the handling of human resources, take nothing for granted. For example, in some states, holding back wages owed to a terminated employee can result in paying those wages in triplicate. Clearly, knowing the rules is important. Keeping that in mind, the primary areas of concern, regardless of your location, are as follows:

Breach of employee contract. A verbal contract may be as binding as a written contract, particularly if witnessed by a third party. The rules are simple. If you do not intend to uphold a contract, do not make the contract in the first place. Do not assume anything when contracting with an employee. Utilize written contracts that are properly drawn and are normally employed in your type of business.

Demotions *(See DEMOTIONS).*

Discrimination. Discrimination falls into six basic categories: sex, race, national origin, religion, age, and disability. There are subtypes of discrimination, but these cover the basics. If it is happening on your watch, you are responsible. In fact, in many cases, you are responsible even if you are unaware that discrimination is taking place.

You could be fostering discrimination simply because you foster behavior in private that finds its way into your workplace. The concept is simple! Do not discriminate and do not allow discrimination in your business or your life.

Failure to Promote. This is a common sense issue. If you plan on filling a vacancy or creating a new position, post the position and give all applicants the opportunity to apply within a reasonable amount of time. This is a courtesy, not a law. It may be unrealistic to interview all qualified employees. It is, however, a good idea to be prepared to tell qualified and nonqualified employees why they are not being considered for the position if the question is asked.

You do not have an obligation to promote someone from Position B to Position A simply because she has held position B for a certain amount of time, and the last person who worked in that position was promoted to Position A. However, if you tell an individual that her promotion is imminent and then promote someone else with the same or lesser qualifications, you may be in for a fight.

The key here is honesty. Do not make idle promises. If you indicate that a particular person is slated for promotion if certain job-related tasks are accomplished, put it in writing. Lay out a program and a system for accomplishing the tasks within a specific time line. If your employee completes the tasks as outlined, be prepared to hold up your end of the bargain.

Next, your former customer service manager unexpectedly returned from North Carolina where he had decided to spend the remainder of his days. Jobs were tough to find, and he is out of work. He was the perfect employee. Give this some deep thought. He left you once and will probably leave again. Your new manager has been in her position for six months and has gotten control of the department. Your customer service employees have grown to respect their new boss. Maybe you should do the same.

Harassment. Human resources managers shudder and panic over harassment accusations faster than any other discrimination case. Here are the rules:

Rule #1: If you know about harassment and it is happening on your watch, you may be a party to the harassment.

Rule #2: You have a responsibility to safeguard your employees, suppliers, customers, visitors, and anyone who comes in contact with anyone who works for you.

Rule #3: Harassment does not have to occur on your premises for you to be responsible. If your supplier calls and tells you that your afternoon delivery person is saying naughty things, or even making strange gestures, to one of his employees, you had better take it seriously, immediately.

Rule #4: If you have knowledge of harassment in your business, you are required to investigate the possible wrongdoing and take action. If you ignore the situation, you may be included in the wrongful act.

Rule #5: Harassment can be male to female, male to male, female to female, and female to male. Harassment can be sexual, verbal, physical or visual. Harassment can involve disability, gender, national origin, religion, age, and a host of other categories. The genesis may be printed or visual material, offensive actions, innuendo, suggestive comments, jokes, teasing, physical contact, and so on. The bottom line: If someone perceives something as harassment and brings it to your attention, you must investigate, and possibly act.

Rule #6: This may be the most important rule. You may not think it is harassment, so you fail to address the situation. Your opinion does not count when dealing with harassment. If the victim feels that another person's act is harmful, treat the charge as if it is legitimate until you have thoroughly investigated the circumstances leading to the accusation.

Rule #7: Treat rumor as fact until you learn differently. You may be held responsible if you ignore a rumor that may be factual.

Rule #8: When you hear an accusation, seek counsel from an expert in harassment (either inside or outside your company) immediately.

Retaliation. In the event you are investigating an accusation involving one or more of your employees, you are bound to inform all parties (accused and complainants) that everything and anything involving the complaint is confidential and will not be discussed with anyone unless a party desires professional advice.

If anyone who works for you, whether or not they are involved in the complaint, retaliates in any way, against any party, as a result of any action or inaction regarding the complaint, the party must be dealt with immediately. In the event retaliation appears imminent, get council from a Human Resources specialist immediately.

Termination *(See **TERMINATION / FIRING**).*

Whistleblowing. You decided to forego paying taxes on a special cash deal that you gave your buddy, just because he is your buddy, and you gave him a reduced price to induce him to pay cash. You can also use the cash for inventory that you fail to count, and you can sell it again—for cash—and so on. Your salesperson, who gets a percentage of gross, gets annoyed because you are, once again, bypassing your obligation to him, and he decides to blow the whistle on you. You learn from a trustworthy source that he called the IRS hotline. The IRS takes him seriously and you are looking at a possible audit and maybe much worse. Ultimately you decide to get even with the whistle blower. You fire him under the guise of at-will employment. Very bad move!

Retaliation will get you everything—and everything retaliation reaps is bad. If you are unworldly enough to put yourself in a position where you must watch your back because you decided to cheat a regulatory agency of any kind, just walk away from retaliation, beg forgiveness of the regulatory agency and suck it up.

Attorneys love retaliation. It is one of the best sources of revenue for an attorney if it can be proven. What about those pesky attorneys out there who are willing to take on your complainant employee as a client? Attorneys are in business to make a profit, just like you. If an attorney is not going to prosper from the case of the individual who claims to have been injured by a wrongful event, the claim is probably not going anywhere. That does not mean that an attorney will not sue you if he thinks you are in a weak position and may settle out of court. Out of court settlements are fairly common with retaliation suits. Your employee's attorney convinces you that taking your case to court will do irreparable damage to your business, regardless of the outcome, guilty or not guilty. You cave in and eventually agree to an amount that will make the suit go away, along with a guaranty that the outcome will not be made available to the public. This is all well and good with the exception of the stigma that hangs over your company and the handsome settlement that may put you out of business.

WHAT SHOULD I DO? You must be familiar with the events that will trigger unrest in any of the foregoing areas. The best prevention is knowledge of the laws and staying within the boundaries of those laws. Ignorance is not a legal defense. Always involve an attorney who is an expert in the field of Human Resources if you are at all uncomfortable with any of the aforementioned situations or, for that matter, any human resources situation that appears legally troublesome. Stay legal and remain safe.

Additional Resources: Human resources specialist, attorney specializing in employment law.

Chapter I

IMMIGRATION & NATURALIZATION SERVICE (INS)

Form I-9. The Immigration Reform and Control Act (IRCA) of 1986 requires that you verify the employment eligibility status of new employees hired after November 6, 1986. The act also makes it unlawful for employers to knowingly hire or continue to employee unauthorized workers. The I-9 compliance form is used to verify that the prospective employee is authorized to work in the United States.

Every new employee, regardless of race, color, national origin, citizen, noncitizen, or whatever, must complete an I-9 Form and present proper identification. If the new employee is your brother-in-law and born in Cleveland, you submit the form.

You must comply with this law—every time! Noncompliance is violation of a federal act and is punishable by imprisonment, fines, or both.

How do I know if my employees are telling the truth? You don't. However, you're not expected to. You *are* expected to do the paperwork. Hence, you are required to submit an I-9 form for every employee.

How difficult is I-9 submission? The I-9 is a simple, one-page form that requires specific identification on the part of the employee. Occasional re-verification of documentation may be necessary if the employee's current documentation is not permanent. The form can be submitted via mail or online.

↳**WHAT SHOULD I DO?** Remember that you, the employer, are required to complete specific portions of, and personally sign every I-9 form, verifying that the applicant supplied the required information in its original form. You are responsible for submitting the I-9 to the proper authority. According to the U.S. Citizenship and Immigration Services, *"If the employer completes and retains Form I-9 in paper format only, he or she must retain the original Form I-9 with the original handwritten signatures for three years after the date of hire or one year after the date the individual's employment is terminated, whichever is later. Photocopies of the completed Form I-9 are not acceptable."*[1]

Additional Resources: U.S. Citizenship and Immigration Services at www.uscis.gov.

INCENTIVES *(See also AWARDS)*

For our purposes, incentives are unplanned, spontaneous gifts that are given to employees for performance improvement. Incentives can take numerous forms. The most common incentive is cash. It is also the most costly. The perceived value and actual value are identical. In the long term, cash is rarely considered large enough, regardless of the amount. It is also the longest remembered.

So, what is the best incentive of all? "Jeff, you really did a great job with that Jones Rentals account. I just want to let you know how much I appreciate it. I won't forget it." And neither will Jeff. By the way, it never hurts to back it up with a cash reward to seal the deal.

Why should I provide incentives? Your employees see you differently than they see themselves. Regardless of your struggles to keep your business profitable, regardless of good times or bad, most of your employees regard themselves as less fortunate than you. Some employees consider you lucky and some consider you wealthy, regardless of the state of your business. Spread the wealth, even if it is only perceived wealth, and even if it is just a little bit. It makes you a better person, and your employees will respect you for your generosity.

At what levels should incentives be provided? All levels, all employees, even part-timers.

When should incentives be given? The best time to provide an incentive is immediately after an event that deserves special recognition. The second best time is when it is not expected. If your dog rolls over, you give him an immediate treat. Maybe this is a poor example, but you get the picture.

Name a few incentives. My wife is a customer service guru. Here is her advice: Consider anything and everything a vendor or customer gives to you as potential incentives. This may include gift cards to the employee's favorite restaurants or shops, giveaways you pick up at trade shows, seminars or business meetings, coffee and donuts in the morning, pizza for lunch, a bagful of sandwiches from a fast food restaurant, pens, pencils, cups, key chains and desk calendars, just to name a few.

The key here is volume, not dollar amount. Do not be cheap, but there is a limit on what you can afford in your budget. It is better to reach more people than to spend more per incentive and reach a smaller audience. Initiate a practice of giving incentives for the little things that employees do, or for no reason at all.

WHAT SHOULD I DO? The smallest incentive narrows the distance between you and your employees. The absence of incentives has the opposite effect. Cost is certainly a factor. Include incentives in your business forecast and stay within the confines of your forecast.

Additional Resources: Business consultant, human resources consultant.

INDEPENDENT CONTRACTORS

The Internal Revenue Service (IRS) separates employees and non-employees into four general categories: independent contractors, common-law employees, statutory employees, and statutory non-employees.[2] It is worthwhile to have a short discussion regarding independent contractors because they can be a cost savings or a cost creator for your company.

What is an independent contractor? The IRS defines an independent contractor as follows: "people such as attorneys, contractors, subcontractors, and auctioneers who follow an independent trade, business, or profession in which they offer their services to the public, are generally not employees. However, whether such people are employees or independent contractors depends on the facts in each case. The general rule is that an individual is an independent contractor if you, the person for whom the services are performed, have the *right to control or direct only the result of the work and not the means and methods of accomplishing the result.*"[3] This is word-for-word from the IRS website. Notice that the description is ambiguous and actually references the word *contractor* in the definition. So, with that information under our belts, let us continue.

Where are independent contractors most commonly utilized? They are most commonly utilized in the construction of homes and buildings, and in providing the electrical and mechanical backbones common to those structures. Examples are building automation, electrical systems and plumbing. Their services may also include built-ins, specific types of rooms or areas, alarms, card-access systems, closed-circuit television systems, or just about any big ticket item that is secured via bid. Independent contractors are widely utilized in both public and private enterprises.

Why hire an independent contractor? Several reasons. **First, most small** companies do not have the knowledge or skills to be all things to all people. You may not possess the certifications, vendor relations, or connections to perform at every level in your area of business. Contractors are good examples. A general contractor may know how to build a commercial structure or house, but does not directly employ the expertise to install plumbing, electric, heating and air conditioning. His operation just cannot support full-time employees to handle these areas. Consequently, the general contractor sees the necessity to hire independent contractors to perform those functions.

Second, is the question of price. You may want to negotiate a portion of your work at a lesser price than it would otherwise cost your company to do the same job. You may accept a bid where your cost is $100,000. After parceling out the work to independent contractors, your cost may shrink to $85,000. If things go smoothly, your benefit is an extra $15,000 to your bottom line. This is a common practice with general contractors.

Third, the independent contractor relieves you of the burden of withholding federal, state and Social Security (FICA) taxes, or paying unemployment and Workers' Compensation insurance. All those expensive benefits such as vacation, health insurance, and sick leave shift the burden to the independent contractor's company because the independent contractor is a business, just like you.

Fourth is time. You may have the expertise to perform the service, but you may not have the means to finish on schedule. You do not want to hire labor for the job and lay them off when finished. So, you hire an independent contractor to do the job.

Fifth is union labor. For example, a bid may require that all wiring and conduits must be installed by union labor. This is common among many municipalities. Devices may be hung, terminated, and turned on by non-union labor, and your company is non-union. But you must hire a union company to do the union work. Best practice is to withhold your non-union employees until the union laborers are finished and gone from the worksite.

Why not hire independent contractors for all my work? Independent contractors come in all shapes and sizes. Some are very good, while others are just awful. Some companies work exclusively with independent contractors because they know the players and need the labor and expertise provided by those companies. And, the price is right.

For example, a local company hired an independent contractor to install a large system in a 500,000-square-foot building. The independent contractor cut corners, did not meet legal specifications, had several weeks of work to accomplish with only two weeks left until penalties were activated, used inadequately trained labor, and created a rift among the independent contractor, the company and the customer.

The company threw the independent contractor off the job. The project manager pulled company labor off other ongoing jobs for two weeks to finish the work on time. This increased the company's backlog dramatically. The company sued the independent contractor for cost overruns and failure to abide by the contract. The company won the suit, and the independent contractor was forced out of business. In the end, both made costly mistakes and both were harmed. On the bright side, the customer loves the system and is open to doing additional business with the company.

Hiring independent contractors is not much different than hiring employees. Look for quality owners with quality workers and a list of satisfied clients. If you can find a quality independent contractor that satisfies your needs, why not utilize him as long as profits justify doing so?

Do I need a contract with an independent contractor? Yes, and the contract should be all inclusive, meaning that all costs pertaining to the work done by the independent contractor are absorbed by the contractor. Sample contracts are available from your business consultant, your attorney, and on the Internet. Do not reinvent the wheel. Find a contract that fits your business type, and have your attorney look it over. Make the independent contractor responsible legally and fiscally if things do not go as planned.

Once the contract is in place, you will probably find that the customer will make changes to your agreement as the project progresses. Change orders will be necessary with the independent contractor as well. All change orders are to be executed in writing, with a specific price and specific time parameters, as an addendum to the original contract.

Your written agreement with an independent contractor spells out exactly what he intends to do for you, i.e., install a building automation system. The contract fixes the price, includes a drop-dead date to finish all work, identifies who supplies materials, includes parameters for material substitutions, specifies that the work must be done in accordance with all applicable laws and ordinances, outlines inspection routines and final acceptance, includes your customer's wishes regarding hours of work, contains a noise and cleanliness provision, stipulates removal of waste and storage of materials, requires necessary applicable insurance and warranty, and details fines to be levied if work runs over and incurs penalties. You can see the value of such a detailed document.

How much should I pay an independent contractor? The price, of course, depends on the project. You should know the labor rates in your industry and the cost of materials and equipment. Accurately cost out the total project price, based on utilizing your own labor. Seek bids from selected independent contractors. You want bids that show a Bill of Materials, labor and any extraneous costs. Do not accept bids that are do not compartmentalize costs. Check their hours and materials against your hours and materials, and then negotiate price and terms.

You should assemble your original cost estimates and pricing prior to seeing the independent contractor's price. Most companies that utilize independent contractors collect bids from a minimum of two companies for each project. Your profit is the difference between the cost of your independent contractor and your final price to the general contractor or the end user. Build alliances and try to use good, solid independent contractors. The extra profit you earn goes straight to your bottom line.

Note: Always have the independent contractor give you a turnkey price before you divulge the price you are willing to pay for the project (See also TURNKEY PRICE).

Independent contractors-Advantages. One of the key advantages of hiring an independent contractor lies in the fact that the contractor is not an employee and is not subject to all the costs of an employee. In addition to payroll taxes, your company is relieved of overhead expenses such as plant, heat, light, transportation, tools, communications, training, and benefits that are usually associated with employees. Independent contractors are responsible to provide all these costs at their expense. In short, the independent contractor's business works for your business on an as-needed basis.

Independent contractors-Disadvantages. The disadvantages of hiring an independent contractor can be numerous. Ask yourself a few key questions. What is the quality of the employees and the work performed by the independent contractor? Is the contractor reliable and can the independent contractor and his employees work side by side with your employees while creating a reasonable work environment? Can the contractor stay on schedule and produce quality work that is acceptable to you, on time? Is the independent contractor's price palatable and within your profit/cost guidelines?

Additional Resources: www.irs.gov; see Publication 15-A of the IRS Employer's Supplemental Tax Guide.

INFORMATION DISSEMINATION

How much should I tell my employees? Some companies share all financials with employees. Some share nothing. Some companies are tied to regulations that prevent sharing of sensitive or proprietary information with employees. Trade secrets are protected legally and physically.

My feeling is that you share anything that does not compromise your position with your competition, vendors, contractors, customers, and regulatory agencies. The more your employees know, the more they are able to benefit your business. An uninformed employee is typically an unhappy employee. If she does not know the truth, she may propagate her own version of truth via the rumor mill.

How much do employees really know? Have you ever tried to keep a secret? Human nature propels curiosity to unimagined heights. We have a need to know and share. If you are hiring employees who are intelligent and productive, they are already a step ahead of your latest plans, and they know much more than you might think.

Is the company grapevine really 80 percent true? Probably! Employees discuss the things that concern them at home and at work. There are informal leaders and followers. The followers trust the informal leaders to tell them what is happening in the organization. Everyone knows who is close to the boss and forms opinions about the operation based on the information gleaned from others. How do you limit the grapevine? Understand that the grapevine is active in every business, and then do your part to keep your employees informed, thus eliminating the need for the accurate and inaccurate grapevine conversations.

Goals and Results. Stay in front of your employees with goals and results. If you share your goals and your plans to achieve those goals, your employees become part of your desire to succeed. As Jack Welch says, "Leaders make sure people not only *see* the vision, they live and breathe it."[4]

WHAT SHOULD I DO? Be aware that publicly traded companies must share their numbers – publicly. So, it's not a rarity for employees to understand what is happening with their companies. Share results, good and bad, along with the reasons for both. When sharing, be ready to answer tough questions if things are not going as well as expected. Remember that you are the leader. Your employees want to believe that you have all the answers. They are depending on you to take good care of them. Timing is everything. Share and ask for help in achieving positive results. Never lie to your employees.

Are you looking at expansion? What about new products? Targeting new customers? Facing new competition? Doing more hiring? These types of items provide good information for your company newsletter. No need to go to great lengths, but a page or two on a regular basis keeps your employees informed and reduces the rumor mill to a dull roar. Do not forget that your newsletter does not stay within the walls of your business. Assume that the written word will be shared with everyone, including vendors, customers, stakeholders, competition and former employees.

Additional Resources: Trust your gut.

INSURANCE

What kind? You want to protect anything that, if lost, would threaten the health of your business or anyone connected with your business. Meet with your property and casualty agent and insure your plant, machinery, equipment, tools, inventory, vehicles, and the wheels of the business that must turn every day.

Talk to your attorney about patents, proprietary information, formulas, logos, copyrights, trademarks, and anything that–if lost to your competition–may destroy your ability to continue in business without significant temporary or permanent loss.

Talk to your life insurance agent about insuring the lives of yourself and your key employees so that the untimely loss of either will not impact the business negatively from a financial or management standpoint.

Also discuss health insurance for yourself and your employees. Federal and state laws may require you to provide health insurance, depending on the number of employees on your payroll.

Purchasing insurance. Shop your needs among legitimate insurance companies. Insurance companies are rated, and ratings are in the public domain. Typically, cheaper converts to less desirable coverage.

Disability insurance. Disability insurance is intended to aid the employee who acquires a temporary or permanent disability. Thus you want to investigate long-term and short-term coverage for yourself and your key employees. A short-term or long-term disability can wipe out a family's life savings.

Health insurance. If you can afford it, offer it at some level. If you are required to provide health insurance, make it a priority and provide what is required, plus whatever makes sense for your business. Think in terms of costs and employee retention. A quality health insurance policy may retain employees, even though salaries and wages are not above average. In today's market, health insurance is second only to salary or wage in terms of importance. The employee you insure may be the employee who does not jump ship to your competitor.

Life insurance. Stick with the large companies. Ratings and assets are public record. Investigate whole life and term insurance and the long-term benefits and costs of each. If you can afford whole life products, buy them. Whole life insurance gives level protection with a level premium. Only a handful of companies offer quality whole-life products today. Term insurance costs less in the early years, but the costs will eat you up in the later years of life.

Key man insurance. Key man insurance is intended to relieve your company of the burden of losing a key partner, manager, or member of your business. In the event of a principal's death, you may lose an individual whose absence could prevent the company from carrying on. The financial remuneration that is created from key man insurance can help to offset all or most of the loss. The same situation may occur with the loss of a key engineer or an individual whose training and status allow your company to carry necessary licenses and certifications to keep you in business.

In the event a key principle dies, you may be faced with having the deceased party's spouse as your new partner. Key man insurance is usually accompanied by a buy-sell agreement *(see also **BUY-SELL AGREEMENT)*** that provides that the spouse gives up all rights to the company in exchange for all or part of the proceeds from key man insurance. If properly contracted, everyone wins and business goes on without major interruption.

Most insurance companies use a boilerplate contract that is designed to provide you with the amount of insurance necessary to carry on in the event of disaster. Most of the boilerplates are also designed to be generous with your premium expenditure. Get your accountant and attorney involved and be prepared to err slightly toward the high side. Get coverage, but do not become insurance poor. Revisit key man insurance every two years, or when a key player joins or leaves your company.

Additional Resources: Accountant, Attorney, Insurance Professional.

INTEGRITY AGREEMENT

An integrity agreement is a legal instrument that lays out a procedure to diffuse disputes among the shareholders of an organization. A typical integrity agreement offers a series of five stages that begin with one party notifying the other that a state of discomfort exists and that a dispute is imminent. The stages progress through negotiation, mediation, and possibly, arbitration until the dispute is settled. The dispute is always settled at the lowest level of discomfort for both parties and progresses through the necessary stages until agreement is reached.

Why does an integrity agreement exist? The context of an integrity agreement disallows suits against one shareholder by another, thus preserving the integrity of the company and its shareholders. The instrument is designed to address situations that typically arise at some time or another in every multi-owner company, without involving attorneys and the time and expenses associated with litigation.

Who should endorse an integrity agreement? The integrity agreement should be endorsed by every shareholder of the company.

Is an integrity agreement good for my business? The integrity agreement simply defines the steps for resolving misunderstandings and disputes with potential savings for all involved. Check with your attorney to determine if an integrity agreement is good for your business.

Additional Resources: Attorney.

INTERNAL REVENUE SERVICE (IRS)

Never evade or mislead the IRS. Never underestimate the IRS. It can cost you a lot more than your business. Pay your taxes. Always retain a solid, professional CPA who understands business and can keep you out of trouble with the IRS.

Additional Resources: Accountant, www.irs.gov.

INTERNET

Who should have access to the Internet? Access to the Internet should be given to those in your company who require it to do business on your behalf. Eliminate the problem before it starts. Provide an Internet connection to those who require it and make it clear that using Internet for non-business purposes is not permitted.

Internet Banking. Internet banking is really handy. You can do almost anything that you can do during a personal bank visit. Of course, there are limitations. I talked with the IT people at my bank (it has national exposure) and asked about the safety of Internet banking. I was told that hardwire transactions are probably safer than wireless, but that no online banking is truly 100 percent safe. I was also told that FDIC affords online bankers the same protection against theft that is afforded to those of us who walk up to the teller window.

Employee e-mail. Employees use e-mail for any number of purposes. Some create greater efficiency and some create unnecessary bottlenecks. Some purposes are business related, others are not. Some employees prefer e-mail because, for business or personal reasons, they do not want to engage in face-to-face conversations with certain parties. The party may be on another floor or in another building. Maybe there is an ongoing conflict with another employee, customer or vendor. You should not tolerate the use of e-mail when personal contact presents a more favorable alternative.

Access to employee e-mails. Company computers belong to the company. You may want to clarify, in writing, with your employees that personal business is not to be conducted on company computers. Consequently you have the right to inspect anything on any company computer at any time. Password protect all computers and give access to managers and supervisors as you deem necessary.

Your IT manager should have the ability to override all passwords. If you demand that employees use company e-mail for business purposes only, there is nothing to hide. E-mail privacy should be invaded only if an absolutely dire emergency exists. In that case, ask the employee if you may see his e-mails. If he says no, you can exercise your authority and access them anyway.

Viruses. A computer virus can cause disruption and occasionally a complete breakdown or loss of information from your server(s) or standalone computers. Be sure to protect all computer information with a quality antivirus program. My computer guru tells me that computer viruses are a fact of life. A user can follow all the rules and still contract a terrible virus. Set your computers to scan for viruses on a regular basis.

Finding quality anti-virus software. The Internet is loaded with anti-virus programs. The names will probably sound familiar. Some are basic, while others are complex. Some are free, and some are very costly. Examples include Malware, Norton, McAfee, Kaspersky, Panda, Trend Micro, CCleaner, Zone Alarm, and Vipre, to name a few. Talk to a computer expert who is familiar with your business operation and computer system before choosing your anti-virus software.

Cable vs. Phone Line. Cable claims to be faster than phone lines for Internet access. Yet AT&T claims its phone lines are at least as fast as cable. Standard phone lines can be configured with DSL. You can probably do fine with standard cable unless you are using an inordinate amount of bandwidth, in which case you may want the cable company to expand your capabilities for a slightly higher price. Spend wisely and buy what you need. If the phone company does a better job in your area, fine. Some companies provide top-shelf products and service in some areas and do poorly in others. If you bundle your cable, Internet, and phone, you may save a few dollars a month.

WHAT SHOULD I DO? The Internet is one of the greatest inventions of all time. Virtually anything you care to investigate, or anyone you care to contact, is somewhere on the Internet. Just like books, you are not guaranteed 100 percent accuracy on the Internet, but the information is readily available and can save a lot of trips to the local library or bookstore. The Internet is handy for staying in touch with customers, vendors, business news and trends, the political landscape, almost anything at all. You can communicate worldwide in any language, at any time. The Internet never sleeps. You can buy and sell every day of the year.

You may have gone into businesses and noticed employees, and even owners, playing Internet games, buying tickets online, surfing eBay, and keeping up with the latest news. Granted, some of your employees are going to abuse the Internet and you are going to have to handle the situation. But, somehow it is hard to imagine a business today that does not have an Internet connection. There is just too much valuable information out there to forego such an opportunity.

Additional Resources: Your computer guru, the Internet (thousands of sites available; many are free).

INVENTORY

Other than cash, plant and machinery, inventory is usually your most important asset. Not only does inventory represent potential profit, it also may be pledged as collateral for loans or lines of credit. Unfortunately, inventory is often given too little attention, creating a great deal of potential for losses through mismanagement and/or theft. Other than embezzlement, inventory represents the greatest potential for loss in most businesses.

Inventory security *(See also SECURITY / SURVEILLANCE).* You have probably heard the old 13th Century proverb, "Opportunity makes the thief." Actual thieves aside, inventory can disappear, or seem to disappear, in a number of ways. The common suspects are records related, such as putting undocumented extras on the maintenance truck just in case a part fails out of the box, stocking up installation vehicles in case a customer asks for an extra (they are rarely recorded), taking a sample for demonstration and not returning it to inventory, providing a loaner for a customer and forgetting to put it back into inventory when it is returned, providing a loaner and not getting it back from the customer at all, using an inventory part for warranty and failing to record the transaction, telling an employee to take a part off the shelf and forgetting to record it, letting employees into the inventory area after hours when your inventory person is already gone for the evening, returning unused parts to the incorrect inventory , and allowing installers and maintenance people to retain material overages in their vehicles instead of returning them to the inventory room. That was probably the longest sentence you will ever read. Hopefully, it may also be the passage that convinces you to lock up inventory and keep superb records of incoming and outgoing transactions. Missing inventory is equal to missing cash, and as we know, cash is king.

Inventory management. You are ultimately responsible to your shareholders for the safety and accuracy of your inventory. Beyond that, you want to appoint a knowledgeable, organized, responsible inventory manager to distribute and safeguard your inventory. Your inventory manager is the ultimate authority in the inventory area. If she has clerks who stock, organize, and distribute inventory, she is responsible to decide if they will have extraordinary access to the area. She is also responsible for all their actions involving inventory.

Your inventory manager must be given the latitude to decide who may or may not enter, based on agreement with you. She must be guaranteed that she will never be put in a position where she is at risk due to unauthorized personnel in her area. That includes you. If you expect your employees to follow the rules regarding access, the same rules must apply to you.

Inventory access. No one should have access to your inventory other than your inventory manager and her clerks, unless accompanied by the inventory manager or a clerk. Many businesses allow salespeople, installers, service people, purchasing agents, and others to have access to inventory. Remember the first rule of preventing theft: If you present the opportunity to steal, you are as guilty as the thief.

Inventory surveillance. Your inventory area should have sufficient cameras to cover all aisles, ingress/egress points, and your inventory distribution point(s). Recordings should be kept for 60 days. If you are not prepared to opt for a surveillance system, at least lock your inventory in a controlled space.

Inventory distribution. This is actually pretty simple. The person requesting inventory must present a two-part document requesting the parts and items necessary for a job to be accomplished. The document must have been signed by an authorized party. The inventory clerk issues the exact contents requested by the document. The clerk and the requesting party sign the sheet after they agree that the list is complete. Backorders are noted. The clerk takes the original and gives the copy to the requesting party. The requesting party is responsible to return any items that are not ultimately used. The clerk's copy becomes part of the customer sales file. At final invoicing, the inventory sheet is compared with the customer signoff sheet to be sure the inventory signed out matches the items sold or returned to inventory.

This is the least complex system that covers all the bases of inventory security. Whether you have a tiny or very large business, your inventory should be kept in a space that allows for limited access. All paperwork should be filled out, signed and approved before any inventory is taken from or returned to any inventory shelf or bin.

Inventory in company vehicles. Many business owners do not believe in allowing extra inventory on company vehicles. They argue that control is a problem. Vehicle inventory is a must if you are in the business of performing service at your customers' locations. The cost incurred to make trips back to the plant or to the nearest hardware store to pick up necessary parts eats away at profits in a hurry. Over the years, a number of companies have forced service people to return to the company shop or store to pick up necessary parts to perform service. All of them eventually conceded to allowing service parts on vehicles when customers complained of inordinate service bills because they were paying for service people to return to the shop for parts.

Granted, there is never a good time to inventory a service vehicle. It is usually messy and typically pulls the vehicle off the road for two hours, minimum. Service personnel are not always the best housekeepers, and they collect parts in case an emergency may arise. We all know that the average service person has as many extra parts in his garage as he has in his vehicle.

That is why you must designate specific parts, tools, and bins for each service vehicle, as well as an area for miscellaneous parts. Realize that it is unrealistic to demand that a service person clean up his vehicle after every job. It is just not going to happen. But it is not too much to ask that the vehicle is organized for a monthly inventory.

Inventory – High value. This is inventory that is either very expensive or very rare. If you deal in electronics, for instance, you want to protect those high-value circuit boards from theft, unnecessary rattling or jarring, and electrical interference. In some cases, you are repairing old versions of electronics that require rare parts that are worth many times their original price.

If you sell precious metals, furs, jewelry, cigarettes, spirits, medical instruments, electronics, or collectibles, you may want to inventory these items separately in a heavily secured area. In many cases, your insurance company will require that the storage area for high-value items must meet specific qualifications or your insurance will become null and void.

Inventory – No value. No-value inventory includes items that are used and no longer available for sale as new. Example: You rented a company-owned electronic system to a customer for five years. When the contract expired, the customer opted for an upgrade, and you recovered the used system. You have earned your profit on the system, and it is outdated. But the system has a rare power supply that can be utilized for repairs of other rented units. The power supply has no inventory value but is useful as a repair part for other outdated units that are still in the field.

Inventory accountability. You are accountable to your shareholders for inventory. Of equal importance, your inventory may represent collateral to your bank or another lender or investor. You have an agreement with that lender or investor that requires you to count and evaluate your inventory on a prescribed basis. Any obsolete inventory must be reported. A write off of obsolete inventory reduces its value as collateral and may affect the standing of your loans and credit lines.

There are two caveats here. 1) Do not misrepresent your inventory to a lender; the problem can only grow worse. 2) If you discover an inventory problem, before settling for a loss, go over your numbers again and make sure you are not experiencing a paper-flow problem. You may find the overage or shrinkage on the wrong job, on the shelf and uncounted, or staged incorrectly.

Inventory levels. In a perfect world, you will carry just enough inventory to sell and service every customer on time, without constantly experiencing shortfalls of needed product and parts. You will receive or produce inventory at regular intervals and experience consistent on-time delivery to your customers.

Inventory levels can be tricky for the smallest of businesses. Consider a hair salon with a half-dozen chairs. Every time a customer walks in the door a stylist may need shampoo, conditioner, mousse, hairspray, color, dye, perm packages, shaping gels, straightening cream, smoothing balm, and possibly, a number of brands of each. You can see that all businesses have a balancing act when purchasing and maintaining inventory at the correct levels.

Inventory organization. There are three inventory categories. Not all companies require all categories. They are as follows:

> **Raw Materials:** For our purposes, raw materials are those inventory items that must be converted to finished goods with labor. If you are building homes, raw materials may be lumber, dry concrete

mix or nails. If you assemble computers, raw materials are boards, wiring and CPU cases. If you manufacture ceramic art, your raw materials would include clay, water and paint.

Work in Process (WIP) is the inventory that has been partially converted to finished goods. If you own a picture framing business, you may assemble wood into frames, but you may wait for your customer to select glass, matting and frame color before assembling the final product – finished goods.

Finished Goods are the portions of the inventory that are assembled, boxed, labeled, priced and ready for sale to a customer. Finished Goods represent the portion of your inventory that appears on your Balance Sheet. Most small businesses do not have raw materials or WIP inventory. They purchase all their finished goods from their vendors and put them into inventory until they are sold.

Inventory tracking. Every good business accounting system includes an inventory module. Most small businesses start with a generic, relatively inexpensive system. There are also special editions available for construction, manufacturing, distribution, nonprofit organizations, etc. You can track your inventory from arrival until it leaves your door as a sale. Your system should automatically deduct inventory as it is utilized and automatically alert you to order when necessary, from a chosen list of vendors. Have a conversation with your accountant before investing in an inventory tracking system or module.

Inventory Turnover. Inventory turnover is the number of times your inventory is sold and replenished during an accounting period, usually monthly, quarterly or annually. Inventory turnover is typically calculated by dividing average inventory into sales for the same period. Dunn & Bradstreet prefers this method.

For example . . .

Average inventory = (beginning inventory + ending inventory) ÷ 2

Inventory turnover = sales ÷ average inventory

Assume sales are $100,000, beginning inventory is $15,000, and ending inventory is $12,000, making average inventory $13,500 (15,000 + 12,000 = 27,000 ÷ 2 = 13,500). $100,000 ÷ $13,500 = 7.41. Your inventory will turn over 7.41 times during the period measured.

On the other hand, some accountants prefer to utilize the following formula, replacing sales with cost of goods sold:

Inventory turnover = cost of goods sold ÷ average inventory

Assume cost of goods sold is $70,000 and average inventory is still $13,500. $70,000 ÷ $13,500 = 5.19. Your inventory will turn over 5.19 times during the period measured.

This calculation is important because you want to reach a point where your inventory turnover is creating optimum profit for your inventory investment. In a perfect world, you will purchase or produce exactly what you need, in the perfect quantities that allow minimum waste of finances and supply the exact quantity of finished goods for optimum sales revenue. This is a fantasy, of course. You will never be perfect, but it never hurts to try.

Unusually low inventory turnover means that you are leaving goods on the shelf longer than necessary and tying up capital that could be used elsewhere in your business. Low inventory turnover may force you to sell *old* inventory at a reduced price because the shelf date or shelf warranty expires. If you are selling fresh food items, low inventory turnover converts to selling at a reduced profit, selling at a loss, or trashing unusable or expired inventory. Excess inventory is also exposed to the same risks as any other inventory, such as theft, damage and obsolescence.

Unusually high inventory turnover may find you scrambling to keep up with sales production. You also may be producing or purchasing in smaller quantities, which means you are paying too much because you are unable to take advantage of quantity discounts. This puts pressure on sales to deliver product on time and may kill some sales for failure to deliver.

If you manufacture your product, unusually high inventory turnover will create spikes in production when you are forced to increase output. This converts to overtime inefficiencies that increase product costs and reduce profit margins. If you purchase your product, high inventory turnover puts an additional production burden on your supplier, thus converting to a higher cost for each inventory unit you buy.

Try to buy inventory at the best price. Watch trends in sales and in the market. Adjust accordingly.

Inventory turns per year. The ideal number of inventory turns per year depends on your business, your sales, and your industry. For information pertaining to your business inventory turnover, go to www.bizstats.com.

How many vendors per product? The best-case scenario is a minimum of three vendors per product. Try to buy from your number one vendor at all times to take advantage of volume discounts, volume shipping and special payment terms. Occasionally contact your number two and number three vendors for pricing and supply. You never know what you might learn.

Warranty returns. For some reason, warranty returns often fail to make the trip back to the factory to be repaired. Granted, most warranty these days is handled directly between the customer and the factory. The seller never gets involved. But, for the sellers who do get involved with warranty returns, the damaged or broken product usually languishes in the back room until it gets thrown away by someone who has no idea why it is there. More often than not, the warranty item goes directly to the waste basket, robbing your business of any potential for recovery of its cost. In many cases, the warranty item is robbed of parts, making it impossible to recover its original value.

Treat warranty items like any other inventory. They have value. Throwing away a warranty item is no different than throwing away perfectly good inventory. Track warranty items and make sure they are properly recognized, sent back for repair, returned to a sales shelf, or replaced.

Inventory counting. If you are a startup business, count your inventory every Friday, and then dwindle down to monthly counts when you have a feel for your needs. Once you become profitable and feel like inventory is under control, go to quarterly inventory counts. No need to be fancy. Before starting your count, be sure that all existing inventory is on the shelf, labeled and orderly. Count every piece of inventory and compare against your records. Have your accountant walk you through your first inventory count, and then handle it on your own once you understand the system. She will also acquaint you with the materials and procedures that are necessary to ensure an accurate result. After compiling your final figures, she should show you how to investigate discrepancies and account for any apparent losses or unexplained overages.

Inventory management software. Inventory management software abounds. There is something out there for every size and type of business. Your system may be in-house or web based. Inventory management software will allow you to track and manage your inventory, thus reducing paperwork, shrinkage and the time necessary to keep accurate records. Pricing starts around $100 and goes to tens of thousands of dollars. Speak with your accountant and come up with a reasonably priced system that is compatible with your accounting software, your industry and your company size.

Inventory shrinkage. This is a dirty word for any business owner. Shrinkage is an accounting term for loss of product between the time you buy or manufacture it for resale and the time it actually reaches your customer's door. Depending on the information source, employee theft accounts for about 50 percent of all shrinkage. In some industries, this figure could be as high as 75 percent. Other reasons for shrinkage include breakage during shipping or handling, spoilage, vendor fraud, lost goods, warehousing and shipping errors, accounting errors, failure to count incoming product accurately, or not counting it at all.

Shrinkage seems to be at its worst in retail businesses because of the constant exposure of product to employees and shoppers. Total annual retail shrinkage is around 2 percent, depending on your business type *(See also SHRINKAGE)*.

WHAT SHOULD I DO? Experience shows that a business that fails to count incoming product shipments will suffer up to 5 percent overpayment or product shrinkage per year. If you trust your vendors to count accurately or to ship the correct product, you are probably costing your company unwanted shrinkage. Do it right. Count incoming shipments against the bill of lading. Compare the bill of lading to the amounts on your purchase order and vendor invoice. If everything matches and the prices and payment terms are correct, pay the bill.

Inventory obsolescence. This is inventory that is dead. You have no profitable market for the goods, and the inventory cannot be updated or altered for sale. Bottom line? Obsolete inventory has scrap value unless you can find a more suitable buyer. There are buyers in nearly every industry who specialize in helping you unload obsolete inventory.

Do not confuse obsolete inventory with outdated inventory, which may have a very high value because it is rare. Inventory is obsolete only if it has no value whatsoever, except scrap value. Even inventory that is outdated due to technological advances is not obsolete until it becomes totally useless.

Obsolete inventory may present problems beyond its useless status. When the bank offered you that credit line that you utilize to float short-term needs, it gave you up to 55 percent of value against your inventory. If you suddenly realize an obsolescence of, say $25,000, you also may have lost the ability to collateralize $13,750 (55% of $25,000) of your credit line. You also may be forced to establish an obsolescence reserve that lowers the value of your inventory and has a negative effect on earnings.

The roots to obsolete inventory are poor planning and poor communication among departments. Purchasing has poor communications with production, which claims that sales management is providing inaccurate sales forecasts or no sales forecasts at all. Each department operates in a vacuum and makes poor decisions that are based on inaccurate information. Other causes involve inconsistent lead times from vendors and a basic lack of inventory control. Frankly, with all the reasonably priced inventory systems that are available in today's market, there is no excuse for *not* having good control of obsolete inventory.

Obsolete inventory is a costly fact of life. If you have obsolete inventory, contact your vendors about returning the inventory at a reduced value. Sell the inventory to customers at a reduced price. Give tax deductible inventory to a charitable organization. Sell it at auction. Some of your obsolete inventory may be valuable for repairs of outdated systems. Last, just scrap it if you are absolutely certain it is worthless. Any amount of cash you get for scrap is more valuable than letting it take up room on your shelf.

Inventory valuation methods. Prices of goods are changing continuously, usually upward. You may have identical parts in a single bin that were purchased at different prices. The following valuation methods are required to justify those fluctuations.

> **FIFO:** First-in, first-out, which simply means that the oldest inventory is recognized as first sold.

> **LIFO:** Last-in, first-out, which simply means that the newest inventory is recognized as first sold.

LIFO is most common because of the tax advantages of lowering your profit during inflationary periods. Some businesses are born with FIFO and turn to LIFO at a later date. Neither method should be abused. It will eventually catch up with you. Be aware that converting from LIFO to FIFO, or vice versa, can involve a major change in your accounting procedures. Talk to your accountant at length before selecting or converting to either valuation method.

Inventory as collateral. In good times, most banks allow manufacturers, wholesalers, and importers a maximum of 55 percent of the cost of qualified inventory against asset-based loans, usually in the short term. Your bank will want first position, pushing all other investors and lenders to the rear. Bottom line: The bank is paid first.

The number one criterion for utilizing inventory as collateral is the bank's ability to quickly convert the inventory to sufficient net cash to pay off the loan if your company defaults. The bank is not interested in damaged, hard-to-sell, or obsolete inventory. Banks are apt to apply a lesser collateral value to seasonal, WIP, or slow-turning inventory. Your bank is also concerned that the value of your inventory is based on GAAP (generally accepted accounting principles). And, of course, when was the last time your inventory was counted in the presence of a bank auditor?

Additional Resources: Bank, accountant.

Chapter J

JOINT VENTURES

A discussion of joint ventures is far too complicated and lengthy for this venue. However, here are a few points to ponder if you are contemplating such an undertaking.

Purpose? Joint ventures are formed for any number of purposes. Some of the more popular reasons include capital infusion for a project that is too expensive for your company, necessity to expand into a vertical market(s), increase buying power, spread risk over a wider platform, need for expertise or knowledge that is not readily available under current circumstances, attract funding that is otherwise unavailable, capture a large piece of a valuable market quickly, and expand to foreign market(s), just to name a few.

What business formation?. Most commonly, joint ventures are incorporated. The structure is determined by the necessities of the businesses involved. If you are involved in a joint venture, be sure to remember that the venture may not work out. Structure your business so that tax and legal consequences will be favorable if this happens. Protect your assets and reputation for the long term, regardless of the durability of a joint venture.

WHAT SHOULD I DO? Any time you become married to another company, you open up possibilities for a number of opportunities and difficulties. Entering into a joint venture also means that you may give up control of some facet(s) of your company to some degree. If you intend to get involved in a joint venture, work out all the known points of controversy up front. No handshake deals, regardless of how large or small the companies, or how well you know the players. Always leave room to exit the agreement, on your terms, if things do not go according to plan.

Additional Resources: Attorney, accountant, your management team.

Chapter K

KEY MAN INSURANCE (See INSURANCE: Key Man Insurance)

KEYS

Have you ever given thought to the number of keys that are needed to properly manage entry to a business? You may have keys to doors, vehicles, tool cabinets, tool cribs, inventory area, vault, safe, burglar alarm systems, fire alarms systems, fire hose boxes, fire alarm pull stations, Knox Boxes, gates, outdoor storage, money rooms, high-value areas, indoor storage, tow motor(s), machinery, desks, file drawers, guard shacks, machinery lock outs, post indicator valves, gate valves, hydrant locks, computer rooms, recorder security cabinets, roof hatches, and even towel machines in the bathrooms. How many so far? And those are just the keys that are in use on a full-time basis. You need a master for each key for your master cabinet. That is at least two of each key. And, you also need keys to the master key cabinet.

The Problem with Keys. Keys are broken, misplaced, lost, duplicated, occasionally fall into the wrong hands, and are often hard to recover from a former employee. In addition, each key represents a potential for loss. Every time you lose a key you will probably think about changing all the locks associated with that key. And it is costly.

Solving the Key Problem

> **Make sure** you have a back-up key for every key that is distributed. Keep back-ups in a locked key cabinet. Every key is labeled. Keep the cabinet up-to-date. Master keys only leave the cabinet if a duplicate is needed.

> **Mark every** key with the phrase, "DO NOT DUPLICATE." Put your company name, phone number or logo on your master keys. This does not always prevent duplication, but it can help.

> **Put a code** on each key and a matching code on the item that the key fits. Do not code outside doors or gates.

> **Keep a list** of every person in your company who has a key. Anyone who is given a key signs for it, including you. Include a clause in which the person receiving a key agrees to pay $25 if the key is lost or stolen. You will be surprised how few keys come up missing.

If someone loses a key, call in everyone with a similar key before you make new keys. You may find more than one key missing.

Collect all old keys as they are retired and destroy them.

Never give a key to anyone who isn't an employee. This includes shareholders, board members, consultants, and anyone who is not part of the day-to-day operation. This even includes your spouse and children. This can be a hardship with cleaning people and off-hour deliveries. If you have cleaning people a couple nights a week, stick around. Notify all freight and delivery companies of your delivery hours.

*See also **SECURITY / SURVEILLANCE** for other possible solutions*

Should managers have keys? Managers should have key access to all areas under their control.

Should cleaning staff have keys? I do not recommend providing keys to non-employees, including your cleaning staff. This may sound harsh, but someone connected with your business should be at your business when cleaning people are there.

Should security guards have keys? Some security companies still provide response to alarms at extra cost. Most security companies do not want keys to your business. It stretches their liability and insurance costs.

Who should have Knox Box keys? If your municipality requires you to maintain an operable fire alarm system, they probably require a Knox Box outside the main entrance to your building(s). A Knox Box is a security box that houses a key that the fire department can use to enter your building in the event of a fire alarm. The responding fire department will require a key to open the Knox Box.

Who should have alarm system codes? Typically, the same people who have keys. Anyone who opens and closes your business or needs access in the event of theft or fire alarm should have an alarm system code.

Do alarms reduce the need for key control? Yes. If someone with a key enters your business when the burglar alarm is on, she will also need a code or key card to turn off the alarm system(s). Without a code, the key will provide entry and the alarm will alert the authorities immediately.

Who should open or close the business? This is your choice. If you are a one-person business, the choice is obvious.

Additional Resources: Your alarm security company, police and fire departments.

Chapter L

LAYOFFS *(See also* **REDUCTION IN FORCE)**

If you have never been laid off, it is hard to appreciate the stress that accompanies such an action. Try to imagine that you have lost your job and must confront your spouse with the bad news. Unemployment benefits are normally available to the laid-off worker, but the amount usually covers only a portion of the worker's regular earnings. Career transition and education may be necessary. Unemployment benefits usually begin after a week or two. Hard feelings are absolute.

WHAT SHOULD I DO? Choose a layoff strategy as a last resort, and prepare yourself for the upcoming backlash. Regardless of how you try to soften the blow to former employees, there is a price to pay, both to the person who is laid off and to the employees who remain. Right or wrong, in the employee's mind, layoffs are products of management failures.

Additional Resources: Attorney, human resources professional.

LEADERSHIP

Webster's Dictionary defines Leadership, as follows: "1: the office or position of a leader, 2: capacity to lead, 3: The act or an instance of leading, 4:LEADERS."[1] It seems that no one has a realistic definition of leadership. However, there are countless lists of the qualities that define a leader. Jack Welch provides a list of eight characteristics in his book, Winning, and defines leadership as "helping other people grow and succeed."[2] Michael Feiner's book, The Feiner Points of Leadership,[3] provides a fine treatise on the qualities of a leader. Both are on my list of the best books that discuss leadership.

I define a leader as one who encourages a team toward a common goal while persuading that team to embrace the constructive powers of that leader through self-empowerment. Granted, this definition may not cover every facet of leadership, but it covers the basics. People do not follow others because they are paid to do so. They follow others because they believe that their leader will empower them to gain personal and common goals.

LEASING YOUR PRODUCTS TO YOUR CUSTOMERS (See also FACILITY: for leasing a building)

If you are like most business people, you accept cash, checks, and credit cards. You may want to investigate leasing your products to your customers. In fact, some businesses offer all the above choices to potential customers. There are many types of leases. The leasing company you select will be happy to educate you because you will bring business to their doorstep.

Advantages. Leasing your products offers several advantages, including the following:

Your company is paid immediately, plus a commission.

Collection of the debt from your customer is now the concern of the leasing company, releasing you and your company from any further involvement.

Your customer can usually finance 100 percent of the price of the product.

Unless prohibited by law, your customer pays a one-time processing fee and first and last payment in advance.

Leasing is typically faster than a loan. Your customer fills out the credit application, and money should be available in a day or two. Depending on the size of the lease, your customer may be subject to additional disclosures.

You can lease just about any product to a customer.

Your customer can save credit lines for inventory and rainy day or emergency uses.

Lease payments and terms are fixed and are not subject to fluctuations in interest rates.

Your customer may be able to adjust her last payment (balloon payment) to a larger amount, thus reducing her monthly payments.

In some cases, your customer can choose to return or purchase the equipment to the leasing company at the end of the term. She may also be able to extend the lease.

You can negotiate a percentage of the amount of the lease as a fee, usually 2-6 percent, depending on the agreement you negotiate with the leasing company.

You usually receive your money within 48 hours.

There is no recourse once the deal is signed, sealed, and delivered. If you are asked to accept recourse, walk away from the deal.

Leasing is a good option for a customer with tainted credit.

Leasing is a good option for a new, unproven business. Although a lease may cost more, new businesses may qualify for leases when they cannot qualify for a loan.

Disadvantages of leasing.

Your customer will probably pay a higher monthly payment than with a standard loan or a credit line purchase.

If your customer's business goes away, the lease payment is still due.

The lessee is responsible for all repairs and maintenance of the equipment.

Who owns leased equipment? The leasing company owns the equipment until the lease is paid off. Then the buyer takes ownership of the equipment.

Who insures leased equipment? The customer who receives the equipment insures it, as part of the lease agreement.

Who maintains leased equipment? The customer who receives the equipment maintains it. This is also part of the lease agreement.

Warranties on leased equipment. The fact the equipment is leased does not interfere with the equipment warranty in any way.

Lease or Buy. Whether your customer is buying equipment, property, vehicles—whatever—the first choice should always be cash. Second is a line of credit. The third is to finance the purchase with a loan. The fourth choice is a lease. If your customer can afford a cash or credit line purchase, go for it. A loan is almost always less costly than a lease.

Breaking Leases. Breaking a lease is like breaking any other credit agreement—it affects the buyer's credit score. Your customer may find a way to break a lease. Not to worry. You are not obligated in any way to your customer or the leasing company.

Do leases qualify for Section 179? *(See also SECTION 179 OF IRS TAX CODE).* Some leases qualify for tax breaks that are available in Section 179 of the IRS Tax Code. Some do not. If the lease does qualify, it may be a good tool for landing that particular sale.

WHAT SHOULD I DO? Several years ago, a client was having trouble finding credit worthy customers in his industry. His average sale was around $8,000, with an occasional sale that was upwards of $30,000. After struggling with extending customer credit, unpaid accounts receivable and his share of bad checks, he did some homework and discovered leasing. He found that leasing companies were accepting customers who could not find credit elsewhere. The leasing companies were also willing to pay a percentage of every lease back to my client. He increased his sales somewhat dramatically, reduced his accounts receivable and became more profitable. Leasing worked for him. It may work for you.

Additional Resources: Accountant, banker, Internet, www.irs.gov.

LETTERS OF INTENT

A letter of intent (LOI) can serve a number of different functions. For the purpose of our business discussion, it is a pre-contract or pre-negotiation instrument containing binding and nonbinding clauses that outline an agreement to be finalized at a later date. A LOI will contain language that binds all parties to good faith negotiation, including nondisclosure of confidential information shared among the parties of the LOI.

When should I use a Letter of Intent? LOIs may be used in business in a number of ways. For instance, if you are interested in purchasing a business, a building, or an expensive piece of machinery, your lending institution may want you to provide a LOI indicating your intention to purchase before going to the expense of taking your potential loan to committee. If you are considering a merger or joint venture, a LOI can be an excellent way to spell out the intentions of the involved parties.

You may want a LOI to make a prospective buyer's or partner's intent public to test the market for potential future problems with your intended transaction. You may find value in requiring a prospective employee to endorse a LOI to spell out both parties' interests. Or you may require a LOI to protect you in the event a transaction goes awry.

WHAT SHOULD I DO? Do not take LOIs lightly. Do not endorse a Letter of Intent unless you absolutely intend to complete the transaction.

Additional Resources: Attorney.

LICENSES, PERMITS, ZONING

Before you rent, lease, or purchase any piece of business property, check with the appropriate city hall's Building Department to substantiate the information you have been provided by the seller or seller's agent. The burden is on you to know what you need in the way of business licenses, inspections, and permits. Real Estate companies and other sellers of property occasionally make mistakes or possess outdated information about the properties they have for sale. Do your own homework and ensure that all information presented to you is true and accurate.

What will I need at the Building Department? Take your sales tax ID number, federal ID number, and any permits you have acquired from city, county, state, or federal agencies. Your trip to the Building Department is designed to assure that you have everything in hand that will be necessary when the Building Inspector visits your place of business. You do not want to get ready for your first day of business and discover that you lack a critical permit or device that prevents you from opening on schedule.

Additional Resources: CPA, attorney, city, state and federal authorities.

LOANS

Keep the following guidelines in mind when borrowing money:

Borrow money only when it is necessary. Many business owners borrow because "the rate is good and I will have the money when I need it." Wrong approach. If you want money at your fingertips, arrange for an equity line. The annual fee is inexpensive and the interest is zero until you actually pull money out of the account.

Borrow money only when the price and terms fit your budget. Money is a commodity. Generally speaking, when it is readily available, it costs less. When it is not, it costs more. The least expensive way to borrow short-term is a bank equity-based credit line. The most expensive loan is probably via venture capital or mezzanine borrowing. The terms are never right if you can lose your company.

Borrow money only when you can afford to pay it back according to the terms of the contract. If the price of money is too high for you, you should probably forego the loan and forego your prospective purchase. Unfortunately, we make mistakes in business and put ourselves in unenviable positions that leave us with a number of poor choices. This is when the price of money becomes high and odds of getting a loan at a palatable rate evaporate.

Borrow money only when the terms of the contract are in writing and signed by both parties. Forget about handshake deals. You are a business person. If the other party says to take the money and pay it back when you can, say "no" nicely and find another source, even if the lender is a good friend or a relative.

Borrow money from a legitimate source. Never, never, never borrow anything from an illegitimate source. Remember **Lynn Miller's Daily Dozen, Rule #1: Never do anything illegal or get involved with anyone who does anything illegal**, even if your business is in jeopardy.

Borrow from whom? If this is your first business, approach the banker that handles your personal finances. Ask her to hook you up with the business loan specialist in her branch or a branch close to you. If you strike out, check out other banks for a business banking specialist. Do not quit trying if your bank says "no". Some banks just are not interested in, or good at, lending money to businesses.

You can also seek out the Small Business Administration (SBA) representative in your area at SBA.gov. SBA does not loan money to businesses. Your SBA representative, however, is affiliated with a number of banks that have business banking specialists. Loans that are guaranteed by SBA have a tendency to have more strenuous terms than those that are not guaranteed. SBA also charges an additional fee for its services. The SBA loan guarantee is in the form of a contract with your bank that insures that the bank will be paid if you default on your loan. In a manner of speaking, SBA becomes your co-signer on the loan.

Interest rates. Shop around. Interest rates should be printed in the business section of your local newspaper on a regular basis. The prime rate is published daily. If you cannot find the prime rate, go to the Internet and search for *prime rate*. Many interest rates are tied to the prime rate. Interest rates are often expressed as prime plus a given percentage. For example, prime plus 2.5 percent. In this example, if the prime rate is 3.25 percent, just add 2.5 percent. Your rate to borrow would be 5.75 percent per year if you meet the criteria for borrowing at that particular institution.

Loan term. A loan term is the length of time you have to pay off a loan. The term is based on regular payments of a specific amount, on time, each and every month. If you fail to live up to the loan contract, your lender has a right to shorten the term and/or call in the loan for immediate payoff. If you are unable to meet the lender's payoff terms, the lender will immediately initiate efforts to seize any collateral that is obligated to the loan.

Secured loans. If you are borrowing money for your business, it will probably be a secured loan. Your lender will secure his company's interests via contract, which will require you to put up collateral that will be forfeited to the lender if you fail to live up to the terms of that contract. A collateralized loan is a secured loan.

Collateral for loans. Collateral is the additional security that you, the borrower, provide to the lender in the event that you fail to meet the obligations of your loan contract. If you default, the collateral is awarded to the lender to offset the unpaid portion of your contractual obligation.

Collateral items for business loans are often real estate, machinery, accounts receivable, inventory, or vehicles. IRAs, 401ks, CDs and other savings vehicles may also be accepted as collateral, depending on the account contract. Collateral must have a quantifiable value and must be easily converted to cash. Lenders will have a defined list of items that are acceptable.

Annual Percentage Rate (APR). The cost of a loan is rarely just principle plus interest. According to Banking.about.com, APR is defined as "a way to compare the costs of a loan."[1] APR is the combined costs of interest, discount points, closing costs, processing fees, and private mortgage insurance. When you calculate your monthly payment, do not forget to factor in external costs that will increase the amount. APR will be defined in your loan contract.

Late payments. Pay all loans on time. If you look at your credit report, you will find a reference to late payments. This is the same credit report a lender sees when she determines your worthiness as a borrower. A lender's number-one criterion concerns your ability to repay your loan on time. Pay late on one loan and expect higher interest rates or a shorter term on subsequent loans. Pay late often enough and you may be turned down the next time you apply for a loan. Treat one lender poorly and every subsequent lender is aware of your past behavior.

Late fees. Late fees should be spelled out in your loan contract. If you feel that you have made a payment on time, call your lender and argue the validity of a late fee. You may win this argument once or twice. Once lateness becomes habitual, you are targeted as a late payer. This decreases your chances of getting favorable terms on future loans.

Default. *Do not default on a loan*! Loan default is simply the failure of a borrower to meet one or more of the terms of a loan contract. The most common defaults involve late payments, partial payments or no payments at all. At times, this is more easily said than done. Make every possible effort to avoid default. Once you default on a loan, your chances of getting a future loan with decent terms are nil.

WHAT SHOULD I DO? The most common mistake in obtaining a loan is to accept the first offer. Money is a product. Money costs money. Money is bought and sold. When you borrow, you will pay a price for the privilege just as you would pay a price to borrow a spray washer from Home Depot. See money as a product and make your best effort to borrow it as inexpensively as possible. Make your rounds at the banks and other lending institutions, and find the best deal available.

Additional Resources: Business banker, CPA.

LONG-DISTANCE CALLING

Today, most long-distance calls are usually made from cell phones. Your cellular contract probably includes calls to anywhere in the continental United States, as well as Hawaii and Alaska. Some contracts include all of North America, including the United States, Canada, and Mexico. The advantage of cell phone long-distance is your ability to call from anywhere.

But, there may be a less expensive alternative. Many cable companies now offer unlimited long-distance service for land lines inside the continental United States. That usually excludes Hawaii, Alaska, Canada and Mexico. Rates are typically less than cell phone service.

Which carrier should I choose? Look for the best rate from the most reliable primary carrier. Many one-person operations opt for cell phone, only because the owners are out and about and prefer to receive calls immediately, in lieu of depending on an answering machine at their place of business. If you opt for unlimited monthly cell phone service, you can make your long-distance calls from your cell for an all-inclusive, flat monthly price. Stay out of long-term contracts and reevaluate services and pricing annually.

Lockout Codes. If you open up land-line, long-distance calling to your employees, expect abuse. You can require codes for making long-distance calls. Each employee who has a need for making long-distance calls is issued a code in writing. Your billing statement shows the person's code who placed the call, call duration, call cost, the number called, and so on. That person is responsible if unauthorized calls are made with his code via an agreement that requires him to keep his code confidential and obligates him to pay for unauthorized calls.

Toll-free numbers. If you do business outside your city, state or country, you should weigh the cost of an inbound toll-free number against the sales losses you incur if you choose not to include free inbound calls. Toll-free numbers are relatively inexpensive. Your customers expect to call you toll-free. If you advertise a toll-free number as *"For sales calls only,"* expect abuse from customers and prospective customers who just want to ask questions or discuss other matters.

Additional Resources: Check out all available plans. Primary carriers are usually best.

Chapter M

MANAGING YOUR COMPANY

Most business consultants will tell you that your management team consists of the in-house managers who manage your day-to-day operations. I believe that your management team goes beyond your company and includes three tiers of managers.

Tier One: In-House Managers: These are the hands-on managers and supervisors who conduct business on a daily basis. They are the backbone of your management team.

Tier Two: Your mentor, banker, accountant, attorney, board members, and advisors. These are the people who should be available when you need them. This group should be chosen as carefully as Tier One. Everyone in this group should have the pulse of your business and the ability to provide responsible guidance as necessary.

Tier Three: Manufacturers, vendors, consultants, trainers. This group offers specialized help, as necessary. They can provide assistance with special projects, sales training, product training, time studies, product and industry certifications, and so on. This group should use their special skills to keep you and your employees up to speed with your industry and your competition. Choose them carefully and keep them in the loop.

   Why are manufacturers and vendors included in this group? Manufacturers and vendors often require special training and certifications prior to allowing your company to sell and/or service their products. They may also provide training at no charge or on a fee basis. Many vendors and manufacturers will train their sales teams to assist you in assembling projects and pricing at no additional cost. Why? They want you to use their equipment and are willing to provide the expertise to help you with pending sales.

Quick management decisions. Think before you act. Never let anyone force you to act until you are comfortable with your decision. Every decision requires one of the following actions:

> **Make** a decision right now.

> **Wait** and make a decision later.

Do not make any decision; let the situation take care of itself.

If you feel forced into an uncomfortable position, put the decision off until later. Collect additional data and rethink your alternatives. Sleep on it. Do not be pushed into a decision until all the parts are in place.

Ultimatums. Never, never, never bow to an ultimatum for any reason. When you do, your relationship with that person or company changes forever. If possible, take the conversation to a rational level and discuss the request as you would any other situation. If necessary, refuse to discuss the situation until the request is presented on a level playing field. If you do bow to an ultimatum, you may lose control of more than just the moment.

Managing the day-to-day operation. If you purchase an ongoing concern that is well staffed, you may want to leave existing management in place, putting yourself at the helm. However, if you are a startup, short of help and money to staff up, you will be the day-to-day manager. Once you get your feet on the ground and have several quarters of back-to-back profits, you may want to consider hiring key managers to help move your company toward expanded product and service lines, an expanded customer base, and higher earnings.

Business vs. personal relationships. Keep business and pleasure separate. This is not about taking a client to a game or playing a round of golf. Here is the rule. When at work, business is business. When enjoying a nonbusiness event with employees, do not initiate a discussion about work. If the discussion gravitates toward work, fine. Do not interrupt. Be cordial. Sounds easy. Right? Not the case.

Infighting in the company. I was a young general manager when I took over a regional operation that involved selling, installing and maintaining a commercial product. The operation was in a shambles after being mismanaged for a number of years. I visited a jobsite to have a look at a rather large installation when I came upon the site owner, who was having a conversation with one of our maintenance employees. Our employee was telling the business owner that he, the maintenance employee, would have a lot less problems with customers if the "idiots who were installing the system (his fellow employees) had a clue about what they were doing."

This is a classic example of *infighting*. You cannot afford to have employees fighting with one-another, particularly when a customer is involved in the process. Nothing good can come of infighting unless the problem between departments arises and is immediately resolved before it gets out of hand. I define *infighting* as *a continuous disagreement between, or among departments that goes unresolved*. Infighting is detrimental to any operation and should not be tolerated. Problems of this nature should be resolved immediately and completely. Disagreements are expected, but ongoing infighting is not.

In the case of the above example, I told the maintenance employee to leave the site and asked him to meet me in my office later in the day. I included his supervisor in the meeting, resolved the problem to everyone's satisfaction, and then met with the maintenance supervisor and the installation supervisor. We agreed that the situation was unhealthy and that further incidents of this nature would not be tolerated. There were a couple of minor disagreements between the departments in the weeks to come, but nothing that could be called infighting.

Infighting is a function of management failure. In this situation, maintenance employees were – for the larger part - properly trained and managed. The maintenance supervisor was a leader who would go on to become a very successful manager. The installation supervisor was eventually replaced due to lack of performance and the infighting problem evaporated completely. Internal struggles are a fact of business. They should never goes outside the walls of your company.

WHAT SHOULD I DO? If you have infighting in your business, address the problem immediately and make it absolutely clear that such behavior is deeply detrimental to the business, inside and outside, and will not be tolerated. If you cannot eliminate the infighting, eliminate the cause.

Affairs in the office. The word *affair* refers to two individuals who are intimate and at least one of the parties is married to someone else. Affairs in the office can lead to proprietary information leaks, adverse effects on co-workers, costly lawsuits against your company or an employee, and in the worst cases, workplace violence.

WHAT SHOULD I DO? Put a policy in place. Be sure it is legal. Act appropriately. This includes you.

Additional Resources: Let common sense be your guide. Follow your gut. Involve a Human Resource specialist.

When is it time to turn the reins over to someone else? Business owners rarely enjoy turning the reins over to anyone. Two businesses come to mind where business owners were cajoled by their boards into turning over the reins. Each business was poorly managed by the owner and showed no signs of improvement.

In one case, the owner recognized his shortcomings and hired an experienced insider who took the business to greater heights and profits. Everyone involved profited handsomely.

In the other case, after a 6-month turn-around effort the owner regained day-to-day control of his much improved company. The business eventually failed and was absorbed by a larger company in the same industry.

Be strong enough to assess your strengths and weaknesses. If you find an uncorrectable weakness that endangers the company's longevity, it may be time to step aside – temporarily or permanently. In any case, maintain majority ownership if possible.

Do I need someone to manage me? Many entrepreneurs lack the necessary knowledge or time to manage their businesses. Some choose to learn the tasks at hand and take control of the business. Others find a knowledgeable manager to handle daily operations. Some find interim managers who attend to the business while mentoring the owner until he is able to take over.

If you elect to allow someone else to manage your business, have patience and understand that the business culture will not develop based on your personality but the personality of your surrogate. This may appear trivial at the outset but may cause a good deal of unrest if your surrogate eventually departs your business, leaving you in charge. Your employees may need some time and a good deal of understanding to adapt to your management style.

Can I ever walk away from my business *(See also **EXIT STRATEGY**).* When you assemble your first business plan, you should include an exit strategy regardless of how far in the future your exit may occur. You may walk away for retirement, or you may walk away for another opportunity. You may also walk away due to illness, to pass the business to an employee, friend or family, or because you are no longer in love with the business. If you decide to walk away, expect regret and exhilaration possibly lasting for several months, until you adjust or find another endeavor. It is never easy to leave your creation behind - even if you fail.

Can I count on my kids to take over my business? This is a very personal decision. Your kids are going to watch you and your spouse's reactions to owning your own business. They will see either a parent who comes home fulfilled and happy most of the time or a disgruntled, worn, and frazzled parent who comes home but never leaves the business behind to spend time with the family. Your kids will watch and learn and grow up to like or dislike your business, based on watching you. If your spouse and children feel that your business comes before family, they may not be interested in getting involved.

Your kids may have a different mindset and different skill set than you. You have probably worked for someone else at some point, and may see your business as an opportunity to be free of the reins that dictate your hours, pay scale, vacations, and overall opportunities. Your business represents a chance to build a better life. If you are successful, your kids also have the opportunity for a better life. Maybe they can afford a better education. They may feel that they can do as well working for someone else and be free of the aggravation they have seen you work through while they were growing up.

Be honest in your evaluation of your children. Do they really have the stamina and drive to do the things you have done to become a success? You do not want your kids to see your business as an entitlement that they deserve to inherit when you retire. They must see your business as an opportunity, something they can manage and improve. Bottom line? They must bring something positive to the table.

It seems that very few children are successful at working in the businesses their parents built. The reasons are many and varied, and you likely have seen that for yourself. It seems unfair that a parent should *expect* a child to become active in the family business. If you feel that your child has what it takes, make an offer when you feel the time is right. But do not be upset if the answer is "no." We are all driven by different loves, challenges and needs.

Management by Objectives (MBO). Anyone who has taken elementary business courses is probably familiar with Peter Drucker. In 1954 he wrote *The Practice of Management.* In the book he introduced the term *management by objectives* (MBO). MBO is the practice of agreement between a company and its managers regarding targeted objectives.

Drucker requires that the objectives be "specific, measurable, achievable, relevant, and time specific."[1] Objectives must be quantified and monitored. Bonuses should be tied to achieving pre-agreed objectives.

Example: Your sales manager has six salespeople and a departmental quota of $3,000,000 of Class AAA widgets, at 40 percent margin, contracted and delivered between 1/1 and 12/31 of the coming year. You both agree that the quota is fair and achievable in your marketplace. You also agree that if her department achieves $3,500,000 in sales during the same period of time, she will receive a bonus calculated as 5 percent of her pre-bonus earnings. She will also receive an extra one-half percent of total sales, retroactive to dollar one, if her department exceeds $4,000,000 in total sales.

After nearly sixty years, Drucker's ideas about MBO still attempt to motivate people to stretch their efforts and do a better job. It takes a lot more than just dangling the carrot to create and lead a team that will provide superior effort. But, in the short run, MBO stills remains a viable alternative to get the ball rolling.

Note: To some, Peter Drucker's methods may seem archaic. Thousands of books have been written espousing myriad systems for providing objectives for achievement by managers. MBO is simple and effective. It is easy to institute, motivational and easy to understand.

Additional Resources: CPA, Human resources consultant, business consultant.

MANUFACTURING

Manufacturing is defined by Merriam-Webster Dictionary as, 1: something made from raw materials by hand or machinery, 2: the process of making products especially with machines in factories.[2] Carrying this definition a step further, manufacturing in a small business may include assembly of parts purchased off the shelf from an assortment of vendors. I spent a number of years in the boat business. We purchased boats, trailers, dashboard instruments, engines, canvas and numerous other items that required assembly before a boat package was delivered to a consumer.

You will probably purchase most of your products from a vendor. These products will be packaged, bar coded and ready for sale, simply because you may not possess the facility or equipment to manufacture your products.

In the event you decide to investigate the possibilities of manufacturing all, or a portion of your products, take a long, hard look at the complexity of doing so. Manufacturing is a specialty in itself that normally requires a sizeable investment in additional facility, machinery, time, capital, labor and management.

WHAT SHOULD I DO? If you intend to get into manufacturing, approach with caution and seek professional advice and mentorship before doing so. You may be able to partner with a local manufacturer that has unused capacity available for your product(s). There are options out there. Try to remain local, if possible, to reduce transportation and travel costs *(See also PRODUCTION)..*

MARKETING

Marketing encompasses all the buying, selling, promoting, distribution and logistics necessary to get your products and services to your customers.

This is a pretty broad definition. Marketing is very tough to capsulize because it covers such a large spectrum in your business. Of the essential elements of any company, such as Human Resources, Finance and Operations, to name a few, Marketing is close to the top in importance. Marketing presents your business and your products to the world, and includes the four 'Ps', discussed below. You have certainly heard that sales is the lifeblood of any business. Simply put, if no one knows about your products, no one buys your products.

The first 'P', Product, refers to all the products and services you present to your target market. More than that, Product involves the relationship between your market and those products and services. What are your customers' needs, and why do they buy your products and services? What are your potential customers' demographics?

Where do they live, what age group, what are their income levels and how do they pay for the products and services you offer? Are your products and services the right mix and price for your target market? What is the life cycle of your product or service? How long will your product or service present value to your target market? Pay attention to your competitors and adjust accordingly.

The second 'P', Price, refers to setting prices for your products and services. You must consider your offerings versus the offerings of your competitors. Are your products and services higher, lower, or the same quality presented by your competition? How does the price of any one product fit into the product mix of your company and your competitors' companies? You will probably want to be at or near the prices of your key competitors. You do not want to undercut competitors just to make a sale. Sell your offerings at a fair price and defend product quality rather than price alone. If you are selling in multiple markets, you may have multiple pricing schemes for multiple economies.

The third 'P', Promotion, refers to all those things you do to get the word out to the market place, such as advertising, publicity, selling and involvement in community activities. Promotion requires a constant effort to present your company and your products and services to your target market. Available promotional vehicles are almost endless in nature and require constant and diligent research to discover the most efficient methods for market presentation and sales.

The fourth 'P', Place, refers to your distribution methods for getting your products or services to your customer base. Be aware of the logistics and distribution channels necessary to reach your market. Will you be selling directly from a store front or will you ship your products via truck, rail, air, delivery van or some other method? Will you utilize direct sale technics, Internet, website, distributors, dealers, franchises or some other method to reach your end user? Will you locate near a main artery for faster access to your area of influence? Will you build or rent warehouses if you intend to promote and sell in multiple cities or regions? Will you consider doing business in foreign countries? You want to take these logistics opportunities into consideration as you grow, eventually discovering the most efficient, least costly method of reaching your customers.

WHAT SHOULD I DO? Marketing can be an overwhelming endeavor for any business, at any level of maturity. Your marketing plan should be carefully thought out. Seek appropriate mentors and advisors to guide you initially. If you have a new or emerging business, you are probably not prepared to make large investments in advertising, promotion, publicity and sales staff. You will likely be the sole salesperson for your company in your early years in business. Spend slowly at first and increase your marketing efforts as profits allow. Develop relationships in your community to establish a favorable public image. Stay involved. The cost is minimal and should help you to grow into a mature business more rapidly. You absolutely must advertise and promote to draw your target customers to your products and services.

For a more in depth discussion of the various areas of Marketing, *(see also Advertising, Competition, Customer Relations, Discounts, Distributors, Exclusivity, Franchising, Sales, Social Media Marketing and Target Market).*

MATRIX MANAGEMENT

In a standard management model, lines of authority are clearly defined. The general manager works for the owner(s). The sales manager, accounting manager, production manager, installation manager, service manager, customer service manager, and human resources manager work for the general manager. The department names and individual titles may change, depending on the business type and size, but the lines of authority and chain of command are direct and well defined. Each employee is directly responsible to her immediate manager for her performance.

Matrix management abandons singular authority in favor of functional authority. For instance, in the standard management model a salesperson makes a sale, stays in touch with the installation or delivery, follows up with the customer, and may be involved with collecting the final payment. During each phase, the salesperson is directly responsible to the sales manager. The sales manager interacts with the installation manager and the collections department on behalf of the salesperson.

In the matrix management model, the salesperson may work for a number of different managers through the project's duration, depending on her role, be it installation guidance, or assisting with delivery or collections. Division of loyalty may occur, thus diluting the overall effectiveness of the individual employee. Matrix management also tends to involve a number of managers in every project, thus increasing time-relevant costs.

Some managers believe that matrix management convolutes and dilutes lines of authority, increases costs, and often creates conflict among departments. Patrons of the matrix management model feel that it opens up valuable lines of dialogue among departments and merges similar skills for projects.

MEDIATION *(See also ARBITRATION)*

Mediation is a process in which a mutually agreed upon, neutral person (mediator) is called upon to settle a dispute between or among two or more parties. The mediator has the power to settle the dispute with terms that are not binding to the disputing parties. If mediation fails, arbitration is generally the next step in settling the dispute.

Why should I consider mediation? Mediation allows disputing parties to reach a settlement with a nonbinding agreement. This is usually more palatable than the binding agreements that are handed down by arbitrators. Nonbinding agreements usually find the disputing parties at relative peace at the conclusion of negotiations. Binding agreements usually are binding because at least one party has no intention of settling peacefully.

Additional Resources: Human resources consultant, your attorney.

MEZZANINE CAPITAL

Mezzanine capital is normally a subordinated, unsecured, high interest note. Mezzanine debt carries a higher cost because it is not secured by collateral such as property, machinery, or inventory. Other debts may be paid ahead of a mezzanine note, making it particularly vulnerable in the event of business bankruptcy.

WHAT SHOULD I DO? Mezzanine capital is costly and is generally utilized by companies that are unable to secure traditional financing. If you have arrived here, it may be time to sit down with your accountant and management team and take a long, hard look at your company and determine your next step.

MISSION STATEMENTS

We sat in a conference room for an entire afternoon while six visiting grad students (all were in business for themselves) attempted to assemble a mission statement for a business. After four hours and most of the contents of an erasable high liter, we settled on a five- or six-line statement on the white board. After the students left, the owner said he did not like it. We erased it and came up with a new and improved version, three lines long, in less than a half hour. We utilized none of the contents of the original mission statement.

Mission statements should be general in nature and should let you and every business and person you touch, know your purpose, intentions, and values in a few sentences. You may consider looking at other mission statements and craft a similar statement for your business. They all say pretty much the same thing. Relevant mission statements must be *remembered* and *lived*.

Who cares about mission statements? You care, your employees care, and everyone you touch in your business cares that you intend to carry out your mission statement. Review it every now and then, and be sure you are true to your vision.

WHAT SHOULD I DO? A mission statement provides you with purpose and goals to chase. If you believe in your mission, so will your business partners and your employees. Post your mission statement throughout your facility. Some businesses put their mission statements on their business cards, stationery, and brochures.

Additional Resources: Human resources consultant, business consultant, Internet.

MONEY

To many people, money is simply something they have or do not have in abundance. But most people never look at money as a commodity with an associated cost. They look at money simply as a temporary possession that will eventually be replaced by more money.

Money is the lifeblood of your business. Monty is cash. Without a constant influx of money, you have no business. The measure of successful cash flow is simple. On a daily basis you take in more cash than you pay out. At the end of the day, you need enough available cash to pay your bills and yourself.

Pay close attention. We are talking about cash. Money is not accounts receivable. Money is not product that will be finished, sold, and paid for in a week or a month. Money is cold, hard cash. You need cash to pay your bills and stay in business. Bottom line? Cash on hand is your number-one priority. Cash is King.

Out of cash = Out of business.

Manage from your checkbook or go broke. Managing cash involves a constant vigil to determine what comes next. Can you afford to take on a gigantic job that requires a substantial upfront cash outlay for materials, rented tools and vehicles, travel and housing to initiate the project? Can you afford to extend credit to secure a large block of business that will otherwise go to a key competitor? Can you secure and afford a short-term loan if necessary to get the job done?

Look at your cash flow over the duration of a project to make your decisions. Again, cash enters and leaves your checkbook on a daily basis. If you run short, you may be in trouble.

Do not spend money until you deposit it. Sounds simple, right? Unfortunately, too many business people count on that check in the mail and spend the proceeds before the money hits the bank account. A relationship with the owner of a small maintenance company comes to mind. He received a check by mail every other Friday from his largest customer. The check covered his 2-week payroll with a little to spare. He wrote his payroll checks Thursday. He handed the checks to his employees Friday morning. His big check came Saturday, creating a great deal of ill-will between the business owner and his employees. Do not put yourself in this situation. Do not spend it unless you have it. Secure a back-up position, such as a credit line, to cover your cash needs until that big check arrives.

Where can I get cash quickly? You should have a credit line from the first day your business doors open. The cost is usually between $50 and $100 a year. There is no interest unless you use the credit line. There is no transaction charge. Rates vary. Collateral is necessary to secure a credit line.

Promissory Notes. A promissory note is a specific promise to pay a debt to a certain party on a specific date, or a date to be determined. Interest, late-payment penalties, default penalties, and certain other rights, such as the right to foreclose on the maker's assets, may be included in the note. A promissory note is a legal contract.

WHAT SHOULD I DO? Lead by example. If you do not have enough money to pay all your vendors and expenses and pay yourself, then keep your day job until you raise enough cash to open your doors and stay in business. New companies do not generally operate smoothly until they are in business several months. The number-one reason new businesses fail is undercapitalization. If you have employees, they are paid before you are paid.

Additional Resources: Accountant, banker, business broker.

Chapter N

NON-COMPETE AGREEMENTS

For our purposes, a non-compete agreement is a written contract between you and an employee, in which that employee agrees to forego working in, or starting a business similar and competitive to your business within a specific period of time and a specific distance of your business, should he leave or be terminated from your company. A non-compete agreement also includes language forbidding the employee from divulging any proprietary information that may be damaging to your enterprise. Many non-compete agreements are much more complex and dynamic than we have described here, but all are essentially designed to protect the employer from unfair business practices that are fueled by an employee's tenure with a past employer's company.

Are non-compete agreements necessary? Business owners can suffer greatly due to the absence of a non-compete agreement with a past employee. The employee can strike out on his own and encourage his past employer's customers to do business with his new company, armed with proprietary knowledge that is known to him only because of his employment with his past employer. In absence of a non-compete agreement, an employer may have no recourse other than an expensive lawsuit. He may even find that he has no legal grounds for filing a suit against the former employee. In the worst case, such a loss of revenue may drive the former employer out of business.

Are non-compete agreements enforceable? Non-compete agreements have been well-tested in courts of law, even though laws vary from state to state. A non-compete agreement should protect you and your legitimate business reasonably within a given geographic area for a specific period of time, preventing your employee from leaving you and doing specific things that harm or interrupt your business. An individual cannot be barred from engaging in a trade for which he is trained unless it harms his present or past employer.

Most non-compete agreements prevent a present or past employee from setting up shop within a specific radius around your business for a period of one to two years. Agreements also prohibit the theft of proprietary information, solicitation of your employees or customers, and passing any sensitive information to any other person or company.

A non-compete agreement generally becomes unenforceable when it interferes with the past employee's ability to make a living in a field in which he is trained. Some states limit enforceability of non-compete agreements to those employees who hold equity positions in the past employer's business.

WHAT SHOULD I DO? Non-compete agreements are quite common in our litigious society. Non-competes are commonly challenged and often overturned by courts. On the other hand, if you stay within reasonable boundaries and require a non-compete agreement with every employee, you should be on fairly solid ground in protecting your company from being devastated by an ex-employee's efforts. The key word here is "reasonable." What is really necessary to protect the rights of the employer?

Geographic area in a non-compete agreement. Most non-compete agreements cover a specific distance, say a 50-mile radius, around your business. Others cover specific cities, counties, zip codes, customers, or competitors. If a non-compete agreement does not pass the *"fair & equitable"* test, it is probably too strong to stand up legally.

If I terminate someone with a non-compete agreement, does the non-compete still apply? Non-compete agreements are usually unenforceable if an employer fires an employee who has endorsed an agreement, with some exceptions. Example: If an employee is fired for stealing proprietary information, a court may uphold the agreement, regardless. Put a clause in your agreement that says it is enforceable if you fire the employee for cause. Then let the courts handle it.

Should I hire someone who is restrained by a non-compete with a competitor? Most companies have a section in their job application that asks a prospective employee if he has a non-compete agreement in effect from a past or present employer. If so, a human resources manager or attorney for a prospective employer will require a copy of the agreement and make a judgment call. A smart employer will frown on violating another company's non-compete agreement. Many firms forbid the hiring of anyone under the auspices of a valid non-compete agreement that would affect the businesses of their direct competitors.

Signature on a non-compete before a new hire starts? Always require a new employee to endorse a non-compete agreement prior to his start date. You do not want to admit to a judge that the employee endorsed a non-compete agreement after coming on board.

Additional Resources: Human resources consultant, attorney.

Chapter O

OCCUPATIONAL SAFETY & HEALTH ADMINISTRATION (OSHA)

OSHA is part of the Department of Labor. OSHA is a federal agency created to prevent injuries, illnesses and fatalities in America's private sector workplace. OSHA issues health and safety standards, and is a watchdog agency with an enforcement arm that specifies and forces implementation of safety devices and programs for industry.

OSHA Compliance. OSHA promotes voluntary compliance but has the power to enforce its standards and demand compliance. In short, do not play games with OSHA. If you have questions about OSHA compliance, go to www.osha.gov. The website is informative and complete. If you require local assistance, you'll find OSHA offices around the country. It is much better to face OSHA problems in their infancy. The longer you ignore a problem, the harder it will be to explain your disregard for OSHA compliance.

OSHA also "offers Cooperative Programs under which businesses, labor groups, and other organizations can work cooperatively with the Agency to help prevent fatalities, injuries, and illnesses in the workplace. For help on deciding which cooperative programs are right for you, see Find a Cooperative Program,"[1] at OSHA.gov.

WHAT SHOULD I DO? If you are not sure of your status, contact OSHA directly or contact a consultant familiar with your problem. Either of them can conduct an in-house mock review. Ignorance is not an excuse if you are found to be in violation. If you have a violation, get it out in the open and come to an amenable agreement with OSHA. OSHA officials will provide a document summarizing your offense(s) and a procedure and time schedule for correcting the offense. If you have a reasonable defense for overlooking the offense, most OSHA offices are reasonable in their approaches. Generally speaking, a consultant buys time but is more expensive in the long run because you must eventually involve OSHA.

OFFICE SUPPLIES

You would be amazed at the dollars that walk out of the average business each year in the form of office supplies. One way to cut the cost of office supplies is to use computers and sufficient backup systems that severely cut back on massive amounts of paper, paper clips, file folders, printer cartridges, file cabinets, and stacks of old records.

Who should purchase office supplies? Office supplies should always be purchased by the individual who takes orders from the various departments in your business. The individual will also be responsible to learn the real needs of those departments and investigate unnecessary usage prior to ordering from known, reliable sources.

Who should distribute office supplies? Office supplies should be locked in a central cabinet or supply room at all times and should be distributed by the same person who purchases the supplies.

When should office supplies be distributed? Office supplies should be distributed as necessary upon receiving a purchase requisition. Each department should budget supplies annually and be charged for supplies used. This makes each department manager responsible for her departmental office supply expenses.

Why do I constantly run out of office supplies? If you are running out of office supplies, you are probably not following the above procedures. Office supplies truly define the *nickel and dime* concept. They disappear one at a time. In the long term, office supplies account for a good deal of profit that finds its way to employees' homes. This is not always malicious. This is just a fact of life. Some employees carry out all manner of office supplies because they work at home occasionally or just forget to leave a pen or pencil at work.

Where should I purchase office supplies? Check out membership clubs like Sam's and Costco, but keep in mind that corporate deals are not always deals. Office supply catalogs will arrive regularly via U.S. mail. Many have loss leaders but overall pricing may not be a bargain. Most require a minimum purchase before free shipping is included. There is a tendency to overbuy just to get a deal.

Pick up office supplies - or have them delivered to my business? Delivery is more convenient and it is more expensive. Can you afford to send someone to shop for office supplies? Can you call ahead and have the order ready for pick up later in the day? Is it less expensive to have office supplies delivered, rather than sending an otherwise productive employee to do a pickup? You make the judgment call.

Additional Resources: CPA, bookkeeper.

OUTPLACEMENT ASSISTANCE

This is assistance you offer to a terminated employee to help her find another job with the aid of a professional career consultant. Outplacement organizations do not find jobs for people. They train and coach people to hunt for jobs. There is a fee involved and should be paid by the company that is initiating the layoff. Outplacement assistance may diminish the chance of a potential lawsuit if the employee feels she was treated unfairly.

Assistance is typically offered to former executive-level employees. Outplacement assistance can also be offered either to former employees involved in mass layoffs or to those with a great deal of longevity with the company. Smaller companies with fewer than 100 employees are less likely to provide employee outplacement services **(See also REDUCTION IN FORCE [RIF]).**

***Additional Resources*:** Regional Development Board, Human resources consultant.

OVERTIME

Overtime usually comes into play when your business is seasonal or an unusual short-term situation creates a need for additional labor. For example, seasonality creates increases and decreases in production and revenue. Seasonality may force you to lay off excellent employees during the low season and attempt to hire them back in the high season. Some businesses avoid these hiring fluctuations by utilizing overtime when business is flourishing and reducing overtime when business slows down. Plan overtime in advance throughout the year to help offset labor shortages. You may not escape unexpected overtime completely, but you will be a lot better off than a business owner who takes one day at a time, without a plan. Keep in mind that your pricing must support your overtime usage if you intend to maintain your forecasted profits.

Many businesses experience a large order from time to time that puts extreme pressure on the work force. The deadline may be short and fines or fees may be levied for failing to deliver on time. Examine the limitations of your labor force, plan around overtime inefficiencies, and price the job accordingly. Calculate your profit, based on total labor, including overtime, before establishing a final price.

Unfortunately, not all overtime events are planned. When overtime is unexpected, it creates costs that are not projected and cuts into your profits in a profound way. Unexpected overtime is usually a function of poor scheduling and poor forecasting – or unforeseen circumstances, such as employee accidents or sickness. When you forecast, be honest with yourself. Granted, you are not clairvoyant, but if you expect that overtime is in your future, price your products or services to include such costs.

What can I learn from overtime usage? Whether expected or unexpected, overtime usage can provide a fairly accurate gauge of the state of your business. Are you paying overtime because you lost an employee and are temporarily shorthanded? Have you taken on a new account that is eating into your available work hours? Or, are you ignoring the obvious and allowing a situation that will eat away at your profits until you make the necessary changes?

Examine overtime and determine if it is temporary or permanent. If it is temporary, you may be better off with the overtime. If it is permanent, consider hiring additional help when overtime exceeds three-quarters of one employee's straight-time work week for a period of two consecutive months.

Does overtime have other negative affects? Statistics for overtime are widespread and numerous, but they all agree that overall output and the quality of workmanship drop quickly and dramatically if the overtime situation is allowed to continue for any length of time. You are not saving money by living with a long-term overtime situation. It usually creates more work for everyone and less profitability too. The employee who is taking home a fat overtime paycheck will tell you that all is well. However, employees who experience the advantage of taking home a fat overtime check on a long-term basis will expand their expense horizons. When the checks stop, they must readjust their life styles to a straight wage, causing unrest in the workplace.

How can I control overtime? Overtime is approved – in advance - by the manager or supervisor of the individual requesting the overtime. If an employee works overtime without consent, he will be paid overtime for that pay period, just as if it were approved in advance. He should receive a verbal warning about working overtime without permission. A second incident will result in paid time, just like the first time. But that incident will include a written warning with the understanding that a third overtime incident will result in suspension without pay, the length depending on severity. If it happens a fourth time, John Doe will be terminated for failure to follow company policy. This may sound harsh, but it will send a message, probably with the first warning. John Doe will let everyone know what happened. Some will take his side and others will side up with you. Regardless, it probably will not happen again for quite a while.

Note: Some states require businesses to pay overtime, if worked, regardless of the circumstances. Know your state laws.

WHAT SHOULD I DO? You are going to have situations where an employee works overtime without permission because there was no choice. These things happen and you should be understanding and respond accordingly. Yes, a rule is a rule, but there are times when you must bend just because it makes sense.

Additional Resources: *See EXEMPT VS. NONEXEMPT EMPLOYEES.*

Chapter P

PAGERS

Pagers are still out there, but cell phones perform all the functions available in pagers, plus many more. Put your cell phone on vibrate, and you have a pager. Cell phones are a little more costly but provide two-way communication. If you want something inexpensive and you can live with one-way communication, opt for pagers. Otherwise, compare prices and features of both systems and make your decision. You may prefer cell phones because you will eventually end up with cell phones when you tire of paging employees, unable to leave a message or get an answer to your questions.

Buy or rent. Compare and make a decision. Pagers are a fraction of the cost of cell phones, and you'll find a number of available options.

Extra pagers. Like always, purchase to your needs and upgrade if necessary. If you plan to upgrade eventually, you may want to obtain a model that is compatible with future needs.

Personal use of a company pager. Warn against personal use, with the understanding that it is going to happen. If it gets to be a problem, treat it like any other employee indiscretion.

Who supplies batteries for pagers? You do.

What if pages are ignored? This is a fact of life. Pagers are like cellular phones in this respect. Problems with range and dead areas are legitimate. Ignoring a page because an employee is with a customer is also legitimate. You will see patterns form with your employees. Pay attention to the obvious patterns and act accordingly if unusual fluctuations occur.

Written agreement with employees covering loss, damage, ruin, or failure to return pages. Always utilize a written agreement *(See also Cellular Phones).*

PARKING

Parking can be an expensive proposition, particularly if you have a fleet of vehicles near a downtown office in a large city. Rates vary, city to city. Some parking facilities provide ins and outs. This is a policy that allows you to leave the facility and return the same day without paying an extra parking fee. Others require vehicles to park and stay for the entire day or lose the spot to another vehicle. Covered parking exceeds the price of outdoor parking. Often your vehicles will be hemmed in by other parked cars and unavailable until office personnel evacuate parking lots at the end of the workday.

On-premises parking. If you decide to buy or lease a property for your business, be sure that parking for you, your employees, customers, delivery vehicles, visitors, and vendors is ample for both the present and future. If your business is going to reside in a complex that also houses other businesses, be sure your agreement provides for ample parking and ingress/egress after normal business hours. Often, larger truck gates are chained and locked during non-business hours to prevent theft. Be sure you will always have access for small and large vehicles during weekday non-business hours and weekend or holiday non-business hours. The same goes for the times when a guard is present or a card or key is required to gain access.

Off-premises parking. If you are providing services for a hospital, school campus, or other public location, be sure to include parking in the contract. Do not assume that   ample parking is available. Visit the facility. Ask where and when you may load and unload people, equipment and supplies. Check for availability of docks if you will be shipping via tractor-trailer. Check out driveway and road conditions if your equipment includes oversize or overweight vehicles or machinery.

Above all, be specific and investigate the situation if you have any reason to believe that parking, ingress, or egress may present a problem. Be aware of parking that is designated for the handicapped and emergency vehicles only. Sales profits can disappear if someone fails to ask about parking, ingress and egress.

Employee-of-the-month parking. If you believe this is important to potential employees-of-the-month, then provide such a space. Frankly, if parking is tight this may be a bad idea. Depending on the number of hours worked by your star employee and whether she even has personal transportation, the space may go unused a good part of the time.

Handicapped parking. Follow the law and by all means, demand that your employees obey handicap rules. Anyone who has a handicap placard also has a certificate that vouches for the rightful owner.

Reserved spaces (special spaces for special people). Special people may be board members, owners, managers, customers, and visitors. Handicap spaces are required by law. Customers and visitors are special because customers do business with you and visitors are potential customers, potential employees, vendors, and guests. Think it through. Board members are seldom at your business and may park in the visitor parking spaces. You, the business owner, should park in the lot with everyone else. This provides you with the opportunity to greet your employees as you walk from the parking lot to the building every morning and to your car every night. Forego signs that designate special spaces. Park in any empty space, like everyone else.

PARTNERS

There are a number of different business formations that allow for a partnership with one or multiple partners. This discussion is limited to the reasons one may or may not want to form such a union. For further information pertaining to partnerships in specific business formations, please *see BUSINESS FORMATIONS / STRUCTURES.*

Why consider a partner? Reasons for forming a partnership are many. The most common are a need for additional capital, plant expansion, management expertise, specific certifications, vertical or horizontal integration, absorb a competitor, implementation of a new or different technique or operation, or upgrade an operation via buyout of a more advanced company. All of these possibilities may offer potential to take on a partner. In many cases, you may not be able to cut a deal unless you are willing to form a partnership.

Who should I take on as a partner? Do not take on a partner unless it is absolutely necessary. A partner changes your life forever. A partner dilutes your ownership percentage. If you must take on a partner, it must be profitable for you, your new partner and your company. Investigate the person and/or company exhaustively–with written permission, of course.

When should I take on a partner? Take on a partner only when it provides long-term benefits for your company.

Should we have equal shares of the business? No. When you have equal shares, you will be making equal decisions. If you own a business, you want final word on all decisions. Of course you are open to advice and help from others, but you do not want to get into a situation where every decision requires two or more people to agree. *See Lynn Miller's Daily Dozen, Rule #2: Always retain majority control of your business.* You went into business because you wanted to be your own boss. Keep it that way unless you find an offer you cannot refuse.

WHAT SHOULD I DO? If you take on a partner(s) in your business, you should demand that all parties endorse a written partnership agreement to cement the new relationship. If necessary, you should upgrade your business formation to one that supports that partnership. If you are considering a verbal agreement with a partner(s), try to imagine the grief that ensues when one party dies and the spouse of that party gets entangled in a squabble for legal rights to a share of the business. Be fair to yourself, your spouse, and your partner(s). If you form a partnership, see an attorney before you construct a written agreement *(See also BUY-SELL AGREEMENT and INSURANCE: Key Man Insurance).*

Additional Resources: CPA, attorney.

PAYDAY LOANS

Payday loans are not something you want to encourage employees to request. In fact, the employees that ask for payday loans are usually the people that are least likely to have the means to repay them. So here are the rules:

It must be a dire emergency. Example: An excellent employee blew the transmission in his car and is unable to get to work. His car is his only transportation. You may want to make the loan. Example: The employee's car was taken at midnight by the repo man and he cannot get to work. He mismanages his money. Hard decision. You may not want to make the loan.

The loan must be in writing and repayable in a maximum of 90 days.

The employee agrees to allow the payments to be deducted from his payroll check until paid in full. **Do not** charge interest. The employee is probably having difficulty paying back the principal.

Get a signed promissory note that includes interest from day one if he defaults on the loan or leaves without notice *(See also **PROMISSORY NOTE**).*

Do not even consider making the loan unless, based on the employee's history, you are certain you will be repaid.

The employee is long-term and reliable, and you know him well enough to realize that his emergency is real.

PAYROLL

Who should do my payroll? Most small businesses have a bookkeeper handle payroll. There are a number of complete software packages that include a payroll function. Most have a favorable learning curve, allowing the novice to pick up the procedure in a relatively short time. Software classes are abundant and relatively inexpensive.

Once you exceed 20 employees, you may want to investigate an outside payroll service to handle the function. Input can be accomplished online. Talk to your accountant for reputable payroll services in your area.

What is the benefit of using a payroll service? Most payroll services will tailor their payroll options to meet your company's needs. They will handle anything and everything related to payroll. You provide the input online, and your employee receives payment on time, by check or direct deposit, all taxes and deductions handled by the payroll service. If your input is correct, payroll payments will be correct.

How much does a payroll service cost? Costs are dependent on employee head count and the number of services rendered. Most payroll services start at less than $100 a month and increase, depending on your specific needs and your payroll population.

Should I take time to investigate my payroll register? Take a journey through your employee roster and accompanying payroll data at least once every month. Watch for phantom employees, raises that you did not approve, or anything that appears unusual. If you are concerned that a phantom employee resides in your workforce, cut off the uploading of payrolls to employees' accounts for one pay period each year. Require employees to pick up live checks. Require identification and a signature before a paycheck is given to any employee. Any leftover checks may be fraudulent and should be investigated. Checks should be distributed by a neutral party of your choosing.

How often should I pay my employees? Payroll should be biweekly or on the 15th day and last day of the month. However, there are companies out there that pay monthly or weekly as well. Weekly payroll is inefficient. Monthly payroll may be a stretch for some of your employees' bank accounts.

WHAT SHOULD I DO? There is a recurring message throughout this book. Do not play games with local, state or federal governments. It is just not worth the risk. Make sure your in-house accounting people understand withholding. With today's software programs, you just fill in the blanks. There is no mystery or reason to make errors or ignore withholding. The same rules apply to garnishment of employee wages. Once again, ignorance of a law is not a legal defense if you make a mistake. If you do not understand payroll, do not proceed until you have the facts straight.

Additional Resources: Accountant, your bookkeeper, any number of reputable payroll services, the Internet.

PERFORMANCE EVALUATIONS – REVIEWS

Why should I perform employee evaluations? An employee evaluation provides an opportunity to, 1) thank the employee for her performance, 2) discuss any areas that are of concern to you, 3) give the employee an opportunity to present feedback on her ideas and concerns, 4) present a constructive program to relieve areas of concern and 5) determine if the employee's performance warrants an increase in pay, perks or other remuneration.

Who should perform evaluations? Performance evaluations should be handled by an employee's immediate superior.

What are the steps in performing an evaluation? Employee evaluations are a two-way-street if done correctly. The employee should receive a blank copy of an evaluation form two weeks prior to the scheduled evaluation. The employee completes the evaluation form and presents it at the time of the evaluation. The employee's supervisor will also complete a separate, identical evaluation form. When the supervisor meets with the employee, the employee should verbalize her thoughts on each evaluation item, without interruption from the supervisor. When the employee is finished, the supervisor should quietly compare the two evaluations. If the supervisor's evaluation agrees with the employee's evaluation, the parties should talk about any areas that require discussion, such as methods for improving performance, goals and completion dates. The supervisor and employee should sign off the employee's copy and consider it the final evaluation.

If a pay increase will accompany the evaluation, tell the employee the particulars and thank her for a job well done *(see also COMPENSATION)*.

If the supervisor sees major differences in the employee's view of her performance, the supervisor's written evaluation will come into play. There will probably be some disagreement about various parts of each party's evaluation. The supervisor should attempt to create an amicable atmosphere that promotes a positive experience for the employee. Shortcomings should be discussed and solutions should be presented that will allow the employee to improve performance via specific means and actions within an agreed time period. The supervisor should promote a supportive program, moving forward, and tell the employee exactly what will be done to help her to achieve her goals and become a more valuable member of the team.

Additional comments should be cited on the employee's copy and the employee should be asked to sign the evaluation and initial any additions or deletions. If the employee refuses to sign, the supervisor should make note of her refusal and sign the evaluation and initial the additions or deletions. If a pay increase is a consideration, the matter should be discussed at this time.

Where are Performance Evaluations / Reviews available? Jump on the Internet and search for "performance evaluation forms" or "employee evaluation forms" or "free performance evaluation forms." There are hundreds of different evaluation forms available. Some are preprinted. Some may be downloaded. Some are boilerplate and may be altered. Just pick what you need and you are in business. Some states permit items that are not permitted by other states. Have a Human Resources specialist approve any evaluation form before you put it to use.

Who should approve evaluations? Performance evaluations should be approved by an employee's immediate superior and the management level that approves adjustments in pay rates.

How often should employees be evaluated? New employees should be evaluated constantly up to 90 days. At 90 days, evaluate the employee formally, in writing, and make a decision to keep or terminate, depending on past performance. Employees who have been with the company at least a year should be evaluated annually or more often if you notice shortcomings in performance.

Anyone who is elevated to a new position should be evaluated at 90 days, or more often if you question the employee's ability to handle her new responsibilities. When you are convinced that a newly promoted employee is handling new responsibilities properly, continue with annual evaluations unless you notice a reason to evaluate more often.

When should employees be evaluated? Some companies perform annual evaluations on the employee's hire date. Others evaluate employees in December of each year with increases taking effect on January 1st of the following year. The latter method is easier to track and easier to budget.

Why should we evaluate employees annually?

Every manager and supervisor is keenly aware that evaluations that are not performed on time will result in a number of problems in her department if all other departments, except hers, receive their scheduled increases on January 1. Hence, consider the following:

Since all evaluations take place at the same time, it is easy to track any department manager who fails to get performance evaluations finished on time.

When performance evaluations are accomplished throughout the year, managers have a tendency to do evaluations as time becomes available. If an employee does not complain, evaluations can be overlooked for months before the problem is addressed, bringing about the necessity to pay the employee in arrears, dating back to the true evaluation date.

All increases for all employees are initiated on the same date, creating an easier task for payroll.

WHAT SHOULD I DO? Failure to perform employee evaluations on time sends a clear message. You are telling the employee that she is not important to the team. If you promise to evaluate in December, make it happen. The same goes for your supervisors and managers. Evaluations are tedious and sometimes unpleasant. Evaluations are routinely late in most companies. Be smarter. Do better. Your employees deserve on-time evaluations.

Additional Resources: Human resources specialist.

PERKS (PERQUISITES)

The Internal Revenue Service (IRS) defines a perk as a fringe benefit. Perks are not awards or incentives. Perks are part of an employee's compensation package and are negotiated along with salary, wages and benefits. The list of perks is numerous, including bonuses, company vehicles, club memberships, qualified retirement planning, disability insurance, life insurance, long-term care, tuition reimbursement, corporate credit cards, vacations, vacation getaways, personal loans, outplacement services, qualified employee discounts, chauffeurs, employee paid parking, relocation expenses, noncommercial air travel, wealth management, and on and on and on. What do all these items have in common? With a few exceptions, they are all taxable.

Who should receive perks? Some perks must be enjoyed by all your employees, depending on the size of your organization. Others, such as company cars, personal loans, and club memberships may be enjoyed by a few. The decision is yours. Check to be sure you are legal before proceeding.

Tuition Reimbursement. This is a great tool to keep an employee onboard who is interested in obtaining a degree and moving up in your company. Don't forget that other companies are also interested in your degreed employees *(See also COLLEGE TUITION REIMBURSEMENT).*

Vehicles. For years, larger companies outfitted their sales forces with company vehicles. Today, with insurance, fuel, and other vehicle costs rising, many companies are offering monthly car allowances if the employee uses her own vehicle. Yes, you can require that an employee own an operable vehicle, and have adequate insurance and a clean driver's license before hiring her to work in a position that requires a vehicle to perform her job function.

Health club memberships. Health club memberships can be costly but beneficial. Healthy employees cost you less in terms of health insurance, sick days, and medical leave. Healthy employees also suffer less stress than unhealthy employees. You may offer employees a flat fee – say $500 – a year if an employee shows proof that she attended a health club a given number of times per year, say 180 times, or roughly every other day.

Day care for employees' children. The cost of day care can cut deeply into a family's budget. How valuable is the employee who needs day care? The truth is that some moms and dads cannot afford day care and may have to make a decision to find a higher paying job. Weigh the costs to your company and make the best decision for you and your employees.

Expense accounts. Most companies that have salespeople also provide expense accounts. Salespeople endorse an expense account plan upfront that includes all spending parameters. Alcohol is not deductible. You decide what you want to spend in advance and put the rules in writing. Anyone who goes outside the boundaries pays his own way. Talk to your accountant and understand what is considered acceptable by IRS standards.

Flex/time. You may want to allow flexible schedules for some of your employees. If you are a union shop, you must negotiate with the union before you can utilize flextime scheduling. Flextime employees should be among your most trustworthy employees since there is a chance that they may be working a schedule that does not allow for the guidance of a direct supervisor. Lay out everything in writing to include day, hour, and time parameters. You may want to require that flextime employees earn their wages via piecework rather than hourly or salary *(See also FLEX TIME).*

Paid sick days. Most businesses allow three to five paid sick days annually. Be aware that many employees consider paid sick days to be an entitlement. They expect to take the maximum number of sick days every year, even if they do not experience illness. If you have a sick day policy, budget the number of available sick days each year as non-productive and live with the losses *(See also SICK DAYS / SICK LEAVE).*

401K. This has been a staple among retirement plans for many years. Your employees deserve a savings vehicle. You must decide if, and when, you can contribute. There are many choices out there.

Stock. Some companies pay bonuses to their executives in the form of company stock. Some companies allow employees above a specified level of management to purchase company stock at a discount. If the company does well, the stock does well. The thinking on the part of ownership is obvious. If the company is well managed and well represented, everyone does well financially.

Car Allowance. Many companies reimburse employees a flat amount each month if the employee utilizes his own car for company business. You must be sure that the employee has business auto insurance, a safe vehicle, a safe driving record, and no convictions for drug or alcohol abuse before he is awarded an offer letter for employment.

You are not obligated to pay an employee any particular amount per month or per mile. Make the amount large enough to entice him to do business at an optimum level. Provide a mileage sheet with dates and places visited if he is paid by the mile. If you are paying the employee a flat amount, forget the mileage sheet. It is usually not productive to pay an employee by the mile.

Note: Automobile mileage or flat payments are taxable to the employee.

Which perks are deductible? Do not assume anything. Talk to your accountant. IRS rules are always in flux.

Additional Resources: CPA, human resources specialist, attorney.

PERMITS, CERTIFICATIONS AND LICENSES

Permits and Licenses. It is difficult to think of a single legal business that does not require some kind of permit, certification or license to open its doors. Permits and licenses are required for most businesses at some level, be it federal, state or local. If you are not aware of the permits and licenses required for your business, you would be wise to contact your federal, state and local agencies for information.

Start at www.federal-ein-application.com/ to obtain your federal ID number, regardless of your business formation – sole proprietorship, partnership, LLC, S Corp, C Corp, or whatever. Next, go to your state's website and obtain a legal name and whatever your state recommends on their site. Be sure to apply for a state vendor permit and sales tax permit. Visit your county website where you should find a list of all included municipalities and attendant licenses and permits. Determine those that apply to your business location and type. Go to your city website and apply as necessary. You will likely need a business permit. Fire, health and police departments typically require permits or inspections before opening your doors.

This list is a little vague, but licensing and permits vary dramatically from location to location. If websites do not satisfy your search requirements, call each federal, state, county and city department to ensure that you are legal across the board. If your business must meet federal standards or requirements, act accordingly.

Certifications. For our purposes, a certification attests to your company's ability or an employee's ability to perform specific acts or deeds, or possess a certain degree of knowledge about a specific subject or situation. In business, we are generally referring to the ability to service a product, perform an act or do something that requires successful training and testing of the individual performing that act.

For example, many manufacturers require service people to be factory-trained and certified before they are permitted to service the manufacturer's products. Manufacturers are concerned that repair people may not have the expertise to install or repair their products in the field, thus inflating warranty costs and damaging the manufacturer's reputation. Products are wholesaled to dealers that are certified as sales and service businesses for that particular product. Dealers cannot carry the manufacturer's certification or sell the manufacturer's products unless they agree to factory train their service personnel.

WHAT SHOULD I DO? Whether you own a beauty shop, a variety store, a manufacturing concern or a service business, you will require some kind of permit, license or certification. Lack of knowledge is not a defense for operating without proper documentation. Do not risk temporary or permanent shutdown of your business because you lack proper licenses, certifications or permits.

PETTY CASH

You will occasionally have purchases that are not large enough to warrant a purchase order or payment by check. Your bookkeeper will keep a locked box in a desk or safe that includes cash and change in a predetermined amount. The amount depends on the size of a typical purchase and the length of time it takes to deplete the fund. The purchaser presents a receipt. He is reimbursed in cash. No one is to purchase anything via petty cash without prior supervisory approval. The cash box is replenished as necessary. The bookkeeper is responsible for all cash and record keeping. The bookkeeper is the only person permitted to make and record transactions for petty cash.

PHONES *(See also* **CELLULAR PHONES***)*

What kind of phone(s) should I buy? Most in-house phone systems have similar features, including call waiting, teleconferencing, auto dial, etc. Phone systems are a lot like DVRs, cell phones, TVs, and all other electronics out there. As phone systems become more robust, the prices increase. Weigh the extras against your actual needs, then shop for quality vs. price. Stick with standard brands unless you need something really special. Be sure you are able to purchase additional phones singularly.

Off-brands often utilize proprietary parts and are hard to repair when they fail. Sam's Club, Costco, and BJ's (just to name a few) may have a package deal that fits your needs for a reasonable price. If you require encryption, look for brands such as Polycom or Tandberg.

How many phones should I buy? Boxed phone systems are not terribly expensive. You buy a system today and it is outdated within a year. Look at your needs and buy a system that will meet your demands for five years. If it fails, replace it.

Custom-designed phones. Stay away from custom-designed phones unless you have no other choice. When you buy a custom unit, your dealer is probably the only company in town that can provide service. Custom costs more and the potential for headaches is much higher than a standard unit. Also, customization of a known brand will void the manufacturer's warranty, once again putting you in the hands of your local dealer.

Expandability/scalability. You should opt for a system that is scalable. Scalability refers to the phone system's capability for expansion, in the event that your company grows over time. Measure a new system's scalability against the odds that the system electronics will be outdated when you eventually decide to scale up your needs.

How many lines do I need? Look five years into the feature and make your decision. You should have a minimum of three lines when you open your doors. Your best bet is two voice lines, and one line that is dedicated to credit card approval. Fax lines are not as popular as in the past, but you should still have fax capability if you deem it necessary.

Radio Frequency (RF) problems with wireless phones. If you plan to include wireless handsets or wireless headsets, make sure the equipment does not interfere with other sources of RF in your workplace. RF problems are much more prevalent in proximity to airports and military bases. If you have radios in your vehicles, be sure that your radio frequencies do not interfere with the frequencies of your in-house phone system(s).

Should I record employee phone calls? Most call centers record inbound and outbound calls for training purposes and legal protection from customer lawsuits. It is a fact of life that employees are going to use company phones to make personal calls, sometimes to excess. Do not listen to personal conversations unless an employee's calls get to the point where the employee is not performing to expectations. Employee handbooks should make employees aware that business and personal calls are recorded and that those calls may be heard by management. Most companies do not record any phones other than call center phones that involve conversations with customers. Be aware that most phone systems present the option to record a single phone, or a group of phones, as needed.

Do I need a dedicated fax line? Have you ever waited to pay your restaurant bill while the clerk waits for someone else in the building to free up the fax/credit card approval line? Have you picked up the phone to make a call and had your ear blasted by a fax tone? If you have need for a fax, it should be on a dedicated line. Just about everyone e-mails today, but you will be surprised at the number of businesses that still depend on faxes to send hard copies.

WHAT SHOULD I DO? Your phone supplier will probably attempt to sell all the bells and whistles that you do not require. This is just part of the sales pitch and should be expected. Give the salesperson kudos for making the effort. Your job is to purchase for your needs – NOW – and to buy a system that you can adjust to your needs when you grow. Try to lock in today's price for future additions.

Additional Resources: Internet.

PLANNING (see also BUSINESS PLAN and FORECASTING).

While attending a seminar, the presenter asked how many people in the room were doing what they intended to do with their lives. About 5 percent raised their hands. Then he asked the remaining 95 percent if they had a life plan. Again, about 5 percent raised their hands. This is life and, in many cases, business. You may know where you want to go, but odds are that you will not achieve your version of success without a plan.

Is planning necessary? We can repeat everything we have heard all our lives about steering a ship without a rudder. Or we can have a discussion regarding the number of hours saved for every hour we spend planning. Maybe we should go directly to the bottom line instead.

You already know that a written plan is necessary. You also know that you are having a tough time catching up with the things you overlooked yesterday or last week or last month. There are not enough hours in the day to get the job done. Now you are reading a book that tells you that planning may save your business, written by someone who has only a general idea of what you are up against. Wrong! Poor planning is a product of poor management. Been there, done that.

Most business people have never put together a business plan. This includes startups and ongoing businesses. Most do not do well in a stagnant economy because they do not know how to adjust. This may be why nearly half of all businesses are out of business within 5 years.

Census data report that 69 percent of new employer establishments born to new firms in 2000 survived at least 2 years, and 51 percent survived 5 or more years. Survival rates were similar across states and major industries.[1] Is planning absolutely necessary? ABSOLUTELY!

Who should be involved in planning? Involve players in the three tiers of your management team. In the beginning, you may be the only member of Tier One. Tier Two (your mentor, banker, account and attorney) should definitely be involved. Tier Three, any reliable vendors, should also be involved in planning *(See also MANAGING YOUR COMPANY)*.

Additional Resources: See **BUSINESS PLAN.**

PRIME RATE

You may know the prime rate as the prime lending rate or the prime interest rate. Among other things, the prime rate is the benchmark that banks and other lending institutions watch to set the interest rate for loans and lines of credit. A number of interest rates, such as those used for variable-interest short-term loans, adjustable rate mortgages (ARMS), credit cards, investment vehicles, and savings vehicles are based on the prime rate. This, by no means, explains the prime rate in its entirety. It does touch on the areas that are most important to your business. Keep in mind that the prime rate varies with changes in the economy. Prime rate *trending* is a strong indicator of the state of the economy. Changes in the Prime Rate may also cause changes in interest rates that affect your bottom line.

PRODUCTION

In business parlance, production is the act of combining and/or converting raw materials or existing parts to a saleable product or service that is provided to a customer.

Production quotas. Production quotas are normally driven by forecasted profits. Most companies – smallest to largest - initiate business planning with an operating profit number that management deems necessary to satisfy the needs and wants of stakeholders in the company. Management then works backwards from the operating profit number to determine needs in all other areas of the business. Thus, production quotas are born.

Production shifts. If you do not have the necessary equipment to meet production quotas on a regular basis, you may want to add a second, and possibly a third shift to take up the slack. Entrepreneurs who utilize additional shifts must understand that second and third shifts are not likely to turn out the same quantity and quality that one expects from first shift. First shift almost always has the benefit of the most experienced, longest term employees. Management is also more experienced and things run more smoothly.

If you decide to add a shift(s), convince a some of your more reliable daytime managers, supervisors and laborers to go to the later shifts to balance out production. Necessity will probably force you to hire less-experienced help to work later shifts. Offer your experienced day workers a bonus for working night shift hours. Do not pay first-shift workers overtime to work a second or third shift after spending all day working first shift. Production begins to fall off dramatically when an employee exceeds eight hours.

Also, workers who continue to the next shift are making an overtime wage. The people you convinced to go from the daytime shift to the nighttime shift are making a bonus of a dollar or two per hour. This will create hard feelings among the group that is not reaping overtime wages. If first-shift workers want to reap a bonus and are qualified, suggest they go to second shift. It is usually much easier to train new employees on first shift. The key to second- and third-shift production is the manager or foreman. Choose good management and you will reap good production.

Additional shifts include extra costs for electric, heat, management, premium hourly rates, added equipment wear and maintenance, and the high probability of substandard production in terms of numbers and quality produced. If you are considering additional shifts, weigh the value of investing in additional work space, additional equipment and additional labor on your day shift before making your final decision.

Production slowdowns. You may occasionally find that production slows down for one reason or another. You have a new employee who routinely produces more than a long-term employee. The long-term employee feels endangered and is not interested in working harder, so he harasses the new employee, telling him to slow down. This seems to be more predominate in union shops where everyone in a particular job makes the same wage. Typically, this situation will work itself out without intervention. The net effect is that your profitability will suffer in the meantime.

The solution is to prevent such incidents prior to the event. Put workers on quotas. As long as daily quotas are met, your problem is solved. The old hands will let the new person know that they dislike his *over performance* and that you are happy with quotas as they currently stand. The blip eventually goes away without major intervention and you are happy because your goals are achieved.

Raw material availability. In 2002, President Bush imposed tariffs of 8% to 30% on several types of imported steel.[2] The immediate result was a shortage of steel in the American market. The secondary affect was a series of price increases that were staggering. This unforeseen challenge forced many American companies to re-evaluate their forecasts and increase prices accordingly. Always have a secondary and tertiary source for raw materials.

WHAT SHOULD I DO? Stay in touch with your vendors. Always have a stable of at least three vendors for each raw material or product you require. Look at purchases for the next 12 months. Analyze your costs and pricing against your market and make purchasing decisions based on your analysis. You can never be 100 percent sure of the future, but it really pays off to stay in touch with market trends.

Quality assurance *(See **QUALITY ASSURANCE**).*

PROFIT

Profit is not a dirty word. Randal Longacher, CPA and friend, brought up the subject of profit last time we met. He did not coin the phrase, "Profit's not a dirty word," but he did refer to business people who sometimes worry that they may be gouging their customers. A number of those clients baffled Randy, telling him that they had covered their costs in their pricing, but were not making a profit. It is amazing that some business owners do not understand what it takes to make a profit. In fact, many companies seem to make a profit accidentally.

Who cares about profits? You, your employees, vendors, customers, bankers, lenders, and stakeholders in your business all care about profits. There are two kinds of businesses - growing businesses and dying businesses. Profit is the key that gets you into the door to longevity.

Why should I care about forecasting my profits *(See also **FORECASTING**)***?** This is a pretty typical question from entrepreneurs, both seasoned and new. Prior to owning your business, you probably worked for a company that provided a regular paycheck. You had regular bills to pay each month at home. You stayed on top of your checkbook, always sure that you spent less than you were paid in any given month. If you decided to make a purchase with a credit card or extended credit, you looked at your current cash intake and output and decided if you could afford the new purchase. Your profit went into your savings account.

Managing a business is a lot like managing your checkbook at home. For the largest part, entrepreneurs just make it tougher and more exciting by making poor management decisions. If you do not forecast your profits, you have no idea what your business requires in terms of sales, loans, purchases, and wages for the coming months and years.

Why should I bother to track my profits and losses? You track your profits and losses because they are harbingers of the future. We are creatures of habit and have a tendency to continue past practices as we move forward, resisting change. Constantly look at past trends to discover means to improve your future.

Additional Resources: CPA, banker, business consultant.

PROMISSORY NOTE *(see also **PAYDAY LOANS**)*

A promissory note is a legal document and a promise to repay a loan at an agreed rate of interest, or on demand, to the lender. Make sure the note has all pertinent borrower and lender information, such as name, address, date(s), interest rate, late-payment fees, method and address of payment, prepayment clause, attorneys' fees clause, and the borrower's signature. An attorneys' fees clause spells out lender recourse in the event the borrower defaults on the note.

PUBLIC RELATIONS

We are all aware that public relations can be positive, negative, or neutral, depending on the view of the reader. Public relations are extremely powerful and should be handled appropriately and delicately.

Company spokesperson. If you are a very small company, you are probably wondering why you cannot get public exposure. If you are Enron, you are probably wondering if the public will ever again see you in a positive light.

In either case, you need a single voice to speak for your company when positive or negative public opinion is foisted upon you. If you are small, you may be your company's voice. If you are uncomfortable in such a role, you may want to select a well-known voice that is, or is not, employed by your company. If you are constantly in the spotlight, you may want to employ a spokesperson to handle public relations. Your company voice should be educated about your business and must understand the image you want to portray to your customer base and the public as a whole.

WHAT SHOULD I DO? If you are fortunate or unfortunate enough to gain the attention of the public eye, you may find it necessary to hire a spokesperson to project a positive image to your customer base. Golf ball manufacturers usually hire professional golfers. Progressive Insurance hired a gecko. Then there is the Michelin Man. Publicity often goes hand-in-hand with advertising. How about Tony the Tiger? A gecko or tiger is not going to do something unseemly – like the Tiger Woods fiasco – that would shed a poor light on your company.

The public may develop a public image without your help. Discover that image and put it to your advantage or work to redeem your image if it is negative. A good example of a positive image is Reese's Peanut Butter Cups. Do you pronounce Reese's as Reesee's? Just say the word and you can taste it. This is an example of a positive public image. Everyone knows that Reesee's represents creamy peanut butter and chocolate melting in your mouth.

Smart company owners build images before something goes wrong. If the image is tarnished, the company is in a position to rebuild its image, rather than creating a positive image from scratch.

Additional Resources: Seek positive public relations via trade publications, newspapers, word of mouth, advertising, radio or whatever method is cost efficient and projects the proper image for your company.

PURCHASE ORDER FINANCING

Your best business buddy comes to you for help. He has a $2 million project that he wants to dump in your lap. The facts are as follows: The project is right in your wheel house. It is insanely profitable. There is no doubt that you will be paid on time. Your buddy's word is golden. Your team is extremely proficient with the work involved. The project is local. All you have to do is say, "Yes." Small problem! You cannot afford to front the costs of the materials and labor until you are paid. Bummer! This is where purchase order financing may be beneficial if, 1) you have exhausted all other possibilities to finance the project and, 2) if you utilize purchase order financing, your profit is hefty enough to make the project worthwhile.

How does it work? Purchase order financing is a last-ditch effort to obtain fast, expensive money for a project that will, in spite of the financing terms, make a reasonable profit from the project in question.

It works like this. You obtain a signed purchase order from your customer, and then place an order with your supplier for the materials needed for your project. You contract with a working-capital financing company to provide purchase order financing for your project. Keep in mind that the financing you obtain is tied to a particular project, start to finish. As you perform work, you bill your customer as usual. However, your agreement requires that all invoices are paid directly to your purchase order financier.

Your financier pays all invoices pertaining to the project, as contractually agreed, then takes a piece of the proceeds and sends the balance of the payment to you. The total of payments you receive from your financier represents your piece of the project and must cover labor, any ancillary purchases, and general expenses related to your project. The remainder represents your operating profit.

When should I choose purchase order financing? Utilize purchase order financing only if the project is a home run, start to finish, and there is absolutely no other way to obtain the necessary capital.

What does purchase order financing really cost? Purchase order financing rates may exceed 20 - 25 percent.

How does purchase order financing affect my costs and pricing? Purchase order financing will increase your costs and pricing dramatically.

Fees for purchase order financing. Be sure to read the entire contract carefully and have a complete understanding of all terms. See your attorney if you do not understand the *entire* contract – *before* you sign on the dotted line.

Note: If you are thinking about taking on a job that will be funded with purchase order financing, check out all financing costs before you agree verbally or in writing to proceed. Definitely involve your CPA and attorney.

Chapter Q

QUALITY ASSURANCE

Quality Assurance (QA) is a program, or programs, that should systematically and constantly evaluate a product, project or service from inception to the end of its useful life cycle. It has been said that quality assurance is everybody's business. No truer words were ever spoken. It takes only one small mistake to shoot quality in the foot, possibly costing your company thousands, or even millions, of dollars and causing irreparable damage to your reputation.

WHAT SHOULD I DO? Put your quality assurance program in writing. Put your quality assurance program in the hands of an employee who understands your operation and customer demands, and has the respect of the vendors and department managers who produce, sell, and maintain your product(s) and service(s). If you skimp on quality assurance, the price you pay may be your company.

Additional Resources: Quality engineer, business consultant who is an expert in quality assurance.

Quick Decisions *(See MANAGEMENT: Quick Decisions).*

Chapter R

RATIOS

In business, relationships among and between various numbers and values can teach us a lot about the health of a company. These relationships—or ratios—can tell us if we are making good or bad decisions about managing our day-to-day operations. Ratios can also guide our decision-making process. For instance, based on your business capital structure, should you take on a high-dollar, low-margin project or are you just spinning your wheels to keep your employees working? This question and a host of others can be answered by applying the proper ratios and calculations to the decision-making process, thus eliminating guesswork and mistaken assumptions.

We will discuss five of the basic ratios that all business people should know. They are Current Ratio, Quick Ratio, Inventory Turnover, Gross Margin and Days Sales Outstanding (DSO). All of these ratios can be utilized in the smallest or largest of businesses. Portions of this section duplicate the section that deals with GROSS MARGIN / GROSS PROFIT.

Current Ratio. Current ratio = current assets ÷ current liabilities. Both figures are included in your Balance Sheet. This ratio indicates the solvency of your company and the ability to pay off current debt. Most lenders prefer a current ratio of 2/1; that is, your current assets are twice your current liabilities. A ratio of 1/1 is not uncommon, but you should strive for 2/1 as a minimum. Three to one is more desirable.

Quick Ratio: Quick ratio = cash and cash equivalents + marketable securities + accounts receivable (net) ÷ current liabilities. Notice that inventory is not part of this calculation. Also known as the acid test, the quick ratio compares current liabilities to the current assets that are most quickly converted to cash. Lenders are looking for a minimum 2/1 quick ratio. Strive for 3/1.

Inventory Turnover. Inventory turnover = cost of goods sold ÷ average inventory. This ratio tells you how many times you replace your inventory during a given period, usually a year. Some businesses turn inventory several times a year, while others turn inventory less often. There are rules of thumb for inventory turnover. It may be best to ignore them and find a comfortable inventory turnover rate for your business based on experience and industry benchmarks *(See also **INVENTORY: Inventory turnover**).*

Gross Margin. Gross margin expresses profit as a percentage of sales. Gross profit is not a ratio and expresses profit as a dollar amount. We will discuss both because they go hand-in- hand.

If you are one of those entrepreneurs who utilizes add-on percentages to calculate sale prices, pay particular attention to the following calculations. You may not be making the gross margins you expect. Here are both calculations.

Gross margin percentage = 1 - (cost of goods sold ÷ net sales).

Example: Net sale price is $100. Cost of Goods Sold is $60.

Gross margin percentage = 1 - ($60 ÷ $100) = 1 - .60 = .40, which equates to a 40% gross margin.

Gross profit = net sales – cost of goods sold

Example: Net sale price is $100. cost of goods sold is $60.

Gross profit = $100 - $60 = $40 gross profit.

Gross margin on sales varies widely from one industry to another. Financial Projections.com[1] provides gross profit margins for a list of 47 generic industries. They tell us that, on average, legal services gross 93.22 percent, accounting services gross 87.6 percent, beverage manufacturers gross 57.09 percent, clothing manufacturers gross 38.42 percent, and car dealers gross 14.4 percent.

As you can see, the margins are all over the board. Check out the gross margins that are expected for your industry, and set a benchmark (a standard) for your company. If your gross margins are unusually high, you may thwart sales. If your gross margins are unusually low, your bottom line may suffer. Where is the best place to check out gross margins? Your competition. You know their approximate cost and it is easy to discover their sale prices *(See also GROSS MARGIN / GROSS PROFIT).*

Days Sales Outstanding (DSO) *(See also **What is DSO?** under **COLLECTIONS,** for a complete explanation, including formulas and calculations.)*

WHAT SHOULD I DO? Many readers will look over this section, write it off or promise to get back to it later. This is one of the most important sections in the entire book, particularly the segment dealing with Gross Margin and Gross Profit. These calculations are widely misunderstood and can make the difference between a healthy profit and a business failure. If you find the calculations challenging, talk to your accountant or similar source until you understand how to make the calculations and regularly apply them to your business.

Additional Resources: Accountant.

RECRUITING

Recruiting is an ongoing activity. Encourage everyone in your business to keep an eye out for friends and acquaintances who may fit into your company in some way. Excellent employees who invite friends into the fold will want to help the newcomer succeed because the new employee is a reflection on the person who recommended her.

Sources for new employees? Recruiting sources are numerous. Employees, former employees, search firms, vendors, customers, suppliers, Internet, and newspaper are just a few of the thousands of sources for new employees. Tell everyone you respect that you are searching for a quality person to fill a position in your company. Provide a job description and salary or wage range. Explain that you want top quality people.

The recruiting approach. Go to a reliable source or agency and tell them the following: "I am looking for a solid individual to fill a sales position. The position is salary plus commission and annual bonus, with a total compensation package worth approximately $75,000. Salary is 60 percent of the total compensation package, commission is 35 percent, and bonus is the remainder. Product and sales training are provided. I am looking for someone who will cold call and build a territory. Sales experience is not necessary, but I want someone who is hungry and will sell."

Regardless of the position available, utilize the same strategy and assure the source that you treat employees well and are interested in long-term prospects. Don't be surprised if your source eventually gives you a call and is personally interested in a position with your company. Many recruiters routinely call on sources they intend to hire and recruit them as if they are looking for someone else to fill the position.

WHAT SHOULD I DO? You should always be on the lookout for that perfect employee because you should always be looking for ways to improve your workforce. Everyone you know or meet may be a potential star employee for your company. Never stop looking.

Agencies *(See also SEARCH / STAFFING FIRMS).*

Additional Resources: Your existing and past valued employees are almost always your finest source for new hires.

REDUCTION IN FORCE (RIF) *(See also OUTPLACEMENT ASSISTANCE)*

Reduction in force (RIF) is a politically correct term for *layoff*. Both actions result in loss of job and income for one or more employees. Some business people make a distinction between the terms, preferring to use the term *RIF* for a massive layoff.

How should I handle a RIF? A reduction in force should always be handled gently, honestly, humbly and professionally. Do not apologize for the layoff. Stick to the facts. Always tell the truth. Make it as short and concise as possible. Do not say things, such as, "If things pick up, I'll give you a call." or "Check in with me from time to time." These phrases may make you feel better, even though they are probably misleading. But, they give false hope to the former employee.

Always take a company witness with you when you announce a RIF. I was involved in a turnaround situation that required closing a satellite office. I had joined the operation two weeks earlier, and had no prior contact with the 32 people who were about to lose their jobs. The manager of the satellite office had been instructed to say nothing about the layoff or the purpose of my visit. I flew to the satellite location for a prescheduled, mid-morning meeting in a second-floor conference room. I announced the layoff in a group forum and then talked to each employee individually. The company had no money for severance or outplacement services of any kind. The company was in immediate danger of failing. Today was the last day of work for the people in the room.

An overly aggressive, rather large employee pushed through the crowd and threatened to throw me out of a second-story window. Other employees who were also about to lose their jobs held him and calmed him down.

Layoffs are never pleasant. You can never say enough to console someone who is about to walk out of your company for the last time and go home and tell a spouse that the family income just took a gigantic hit and that no severance package is available.

Who should be present for a layoff? In the case of every layoff, you should have a witness present. If the person who is being laid off reports directly to you, your witness is simply an observer. If the person who is being laid off reports to a manager or supervisor who works for you, you should have that manager or supervisor in the room. If you feel that you may encounter difficulty with the explanation of legal areas, include a human resources specialist.

Should I have security for a layoff? This depends on the number of people involved and your gut feeling about the mood of the crowd. Better safe than sorry. If you feel an inkling of distrust or have been told that trouble may be in the offing, take necessary precautions.

Should I pay unused vacation for a layoff? All earned, unused vacation must be paid to an employee upon termination, regardless of cause.

Should I pay unused sick days for a layoff? Unused sick days are not an entitlement and should not be paid in the event of a layoff unless there is a contractual agreement that provides for same.

Should I provide severance for a layoff? If you can afford severance, provide it. Typical severance is one week for each year of employment. If you have been blindsided by a drastic, downward economic spiral, you may not be able to afford severance.

What if a family member is involved in a layoff? Family are treated the same as any other employee. No favoritism.

Should I get advice before I lay off an employee? Absolutely! Talk to an attorney who is well-versed in the legal side of layoffs. Also, speak with a human resources specialist for tips on severance, outplacement assistance and final meeting(s) with your employee(s).

WHAT SHOULD I DO? This is an area where a mistake can cause a great deal of pain if handled incorrectly. Poorly executed layoffs may entangle you and your company in extended legal proceedings and may cost a great deal of time and money. If you are a well-known company, a layoff will make the news and create negative publicity. It is never wise to put yourself in a situation where you are forced to spin a story, but if there is any way to truthfully put a layoff in a positive light, feel free to make the public aware. If you have any questions at all concerning the legalities of your actions, see a human resources expert first, then an attorney who is familiar with the subject. In most cases, the human resources specialist will probably suggest consulting an attorney if there is any chance of repercussions.

Additional Resources: Human resources specialist, attorney.

RELOCATION OF AN EMPLOYEE

Relocation can be a very expensive proposition that can easily cost tens of thousands of dollars. Prior to offering to move an employee, assemble a package and costs and determine if relocation really makes sense.

Relocation agreement in writing. A written agreement between the company and the party to be moved is an absolute necessity.

Employee payback period for relocation. A relocation package should include a clause that spells out all relocation costs and the employee's responsibility in the event he decides he is not happy with relocation, after the fact. Include a 24-month payback period. If the employee leaves your company during the first 24 months after the date of relocation, he must pay back a portion of the total relocation cost, pro-rated to the number of months remaining in the 24-month period. Example: Based on a 24-month agreement, if relocation costs are $24,000, and the employee leaves you 10 months after the date of relocation, he immediately owes you $14,000 for the remaining 14 months of the payback period.

Lump sum payment for relocating. After calculating the probable cost for relocating an employee, you may want to consider a lump sum relocation package. You give the employee a check for the relocation package on his first regular payday at his new location. The employee does all the work and personally organizes and pays for the move. If he decides to travel on work days to find a new dwelling, he does so without pay or using available vacation days. If he decides to rent and buy at a later date, he bears the cost. The same payback terms apply to the lump sum package that would be utilized for a standard relocation package. You are not concerned about receipts or moving costs or if he does or does not make a purchase. Your only concerns are payment of the package to the employee and employee repayment if he leaves your company during the repayment period.

Pre-relocation visit. If you are relocating a family, send the employee and spouse for a long weekend—two days for travel and two days for house or apartment hunting. You pay the tab. Set up travel plans to include flights, automobile, and hotel. Meals are on you. Kids are not included.

Housing assistance. Do not get involved in the sale of an employee's existing property unless the employee asks for help. You may suggest a realtor, but clarify your role and the employee's role in the relocation agreement. Some companies still provide financial assistance in selling the employee's home. Most small businesses cannot afford to do so.

Offer to help with a real estate agent at the new location. Be sure the employee who is relocating has an agent available upon arrival, for house hunting. When the employee arrives, the agent should have a number of homes to show that are properly located and in the correct price range. This is a house hunting trip, not a vacation.

A number of companies have multiple operations in multiple cities, some of which have a condo, home, or apartment at each location. These companies use these short-term residences for visitors or relocated employees. A relocated employee may move to the new location ahead of his family and stay at the temporary residence until housing arrangements are final. Do not let temporary arrangements go beyond a month or two. Relocated employees never feel at home at a new position in a new city until housing ties are cut at the previous location.

Job assistance for a relocated spouse. This is not your responsibility. That said, many companies provide a search firm at the new location for the employee's spouse because it helps to remove some of the pressure that falls on the shoulders of the employee. Relocation can become a sticky process for the employee and the company if the move is not well thought out. You should not get involved with any type of compensation for the spouse's search firm. Search fees are the responsibility of the company that hires your employee's spouse.

Paying relocated employees. If you are relocating a current employee, there is no break in service or pay. The employee is paid at the new rate the day after the last day at the former position. He is paid for traveling to the new location. He starts at the new position the day after he arrives at the new location. You do not pay a relocated employee to stay home, unpack boxes, and set up housekeeping.

If you are moving a new employee, pay commences the day she leaves her previous place of employment. Make transitions easy. To avoid confusion, salaried employees should start on the first day of the month. Hourly employees start the first workday following their exits from their previous positions.

Additional Resources: Chamber of Commerce at both ends of move, accountant, attorney, human resources consultant.

RETIREMENT FOR EMPLOYEES

An employee retirement plan can be a vital factor in attracting and retaining excellent, long-term employees. If you can afford to get involved in an employee retirement plan, and find it beneficial, do so. As economies tighten and profits diminish, many companies cannot afford to retain valuable employees. A retirement plan may be the difference between hiring, or not hiring, a valuable addition to your company.

How much should I invest in employee retirement? Strike a balance between affordability and necessity.

↪**WHAT SHOULD I DO?** Include an employee retirement plan in your business plan. When you become profitable and your debt is under control, start a retirement program. Before getting involved with any retirement plan, talk to your CPA and attorney about applicable laws.

Additional Resources: The Employee Retirement Income Security Act of 1974 (ERISA) at www.dol.gov, attorney, human resources specialist, CPA, bank, insurance agent.

RETIREMENT FUND

You are probably familiar with the saying, "Pay yourself first." Not to be confused with paying yourself last, after your bills and employees. You should put away a nest egg, a portion of your profit, before you walk away with your take-home pay. In short, put a percentage of your personal earnings into a retirement fund before taking your paycheck. Your investments should grow appreciably over time, creating a number of alternatives if it becomes necessary to sell or quit the business. You may not reach a point where you can invest in an employee retirement plan, but you should always invest in your personal retirement plan as early as possible. Your personal retirement plan is one of the keys to your exit strategy *(See also EXIT STRATEGY)*.

RUMORS

Rumors have always been a part of employee interaction. Today, rumors are even more prevalent because just about everyone has a cell phone or other portable device on her person. Communication is swift and inevitable. Expect that any statement of gravity is going to make its way through your company and industry at light speed, true or otherwise. Secrets are not secrets for long.

You have probably heard that the employee grapevine is 80 percent correct. Many believe this to be true. Do not think for a moment that your employees are in the dark, do not understand, or do not care about the evolution of events in your company and industry.

↪**WHAT SHOULD I DO?** Stay on top of rumors. Check them out and set the record straight. Employees have the right to expect you to tell the truth. If the time is not right, make everyone aware that you are on top of things and will get back to them when the situation stabilizes.

Chapter S

SAFETY

You have seen the signs. They tell you how many days a business has gone without an accident or injury. There are complete books written about safety in the work place. Know the Occupational Safety and Health Administration (OSHA) regulations regarding your business. OSHA has people to help you to make safety part of your operation. Safety should be promoted to every employee, over and over. Safety is everyone's first job, every day.

WHAT SHOULD I DO? Do not play games with OSHA. An OSHA representative has the power to walk in your door and shut you down without notice if your plant or work force is at risk, or if you fail to respond to OSHA directives as prescribed. Work with OSHA, not against them. Accidents can cause big problems, big fines, and bad publicity. OSHA people will usually work with you to solve a problem in a reasonable amount of time. You cannot afford to *not* trust OSHA. Bottom Line: A bad experience with OSHA can put a small business out of business.

Additional Resources: www.osha.gov, safety consultant; *See also (OCCUPATIONAL SAFETY & HEALTH ADMINISTRATION [OSHA]).*

SALES

Sales are the lifeblood of your business. Selling is simply the *name of the game*. If you meet your sales goals, every other facet of your business can be fixed. Without sales, you are out of business.

Are sales goals necessary? Sales goals are based on your business plan. To make it easy, let's assume that you need $1 million in sales to meet your revenue goals. Your average sale is $1,000, so you need one thousand sales a year to make your numbers. That equates to 83.3 sales a month; round it up to 84 sales a month to keep it simple. You feel that the average sales person will account for 12 sales a month. Divide 12 sales per rep into 84 sales a month. You need seven salespeople, for starters. You will eventually find that 20 percent of your sales force will produce 80 percent of your sales. Make changes as necessary and you will probably eventually employ between three and five salespeople to make your goal of $1 million in sales a year.

Should I hire salespeople? You may have to do everything yourself at the outset if you are a new business. You may not feel that you can afford to pay a salesperson. Nevertheless, sales are an absolute necessity for your business to remain viable. You may not need that extra sales hand for a few months, or even years. But when you are not making your revenue numbers without a salesperson, the time has come to take the next step and hire a sales force of one or more people.

Who should be selling for my company? Everyone in your company is selling - all the time. This is an age-old axiom and sounds corny. But think about it. You are *always* selling. Are you and your employees selling your products and services with smiles and winning attitudes? Or are they selling prospective customers on doing business elsewhere because their needs are not being met by your company? Whether you are at a customer's site, the grocery store, or on the golf course, people are deciding if they want to be your customers.

The same goes for your employees. You and your employees should always be selling a positive image, not only to your customers, but to each other. Think about the athletes out there who are endorsing everything from Wheaties to Ford F-150s. One little misstep and the endorsement money is gone. Guard your company and personal images. You are always selling, whether you realize it or not.

Additional Resources: Business consultant, sales seminars, Internet, business books.

Sources of new business. Sources of new sales often elude us. Here are a few guidelines:

> **Sales to existing customers**: Existing customers are your best bet when searching for new business. If you are on a solid basis with a customer, visit the customer and talk about additional products, services, and locations. If you know the customer is buying from your competitors, ask why and how much. If you are not sure of her competitive buying habits, do not mention competitors by name. If the *customer* brings up competitor names, ask why she prefers them over you. Then ask her to buy additional products and services. Call, make an appointment, and visit. This is not something that is handled with a phone call.

> If you are not on a solid basis with your customer, you have an even better reason to make a visit. First, investigate the *real* difficulty that exists between you and the customer. You may believe you know the answer, but when you get in front of the customer, things often turn out differently than you might expect. Resolve your differences and ask for additional business. Problem customers who are brought back into the fold often become your best customers. They know your products and services are valuable. Otherwise, why would they continue to do business with you, even though difficulties exist between your company and theirs?

> **Sales to your competitors' customers.** Competition is discussed in your business plan. Competition is part of the due diligence required to present your case to a potential lender. Competition is every business out there that is siphoning dollars off all the customers you have *and want* on your customer list. If you are not calling on your competition's customer list, you are ignoring a huge part of your market *(See also COMPETITION).*

Sales to past or lost customers. Believe it or not, past or lost customers will usually talk to you. Why? Because the problems that curse one company in an industry have a nasty habit of cursing that company's competitors as well. Most companies in the same industry seem to learn to do the same things the same way, right or wrong. Ask yourself this question. "What can we do differently to shift our lost business back to our company?" You know the players. You should know why you lost the business. Why not try to get it back? This strategy is a lot less expensive than cultivating a brand new customer.

Sales to customers you fired. Some customers are just not worth the time and energy it takes to make them happy. Occasionally you get to the point where your profits are continually drained from a sale and you fire the customer. The customer goes to another supplier, finds that life is not greener on the other side, and eventually makes his way back to you. He calls in an order, your employees complain, and you go about reconciling the account – on your terms. Lay down the ground rules and get agreement to do business in a new way. If the customer reverts to his old self, you fire him again, this time for good. Sometimes it works. Sometimes it is another exercise in futility.

Sales to non-customers you called on in the past. All businesses are constantly in flux. Consequently, something may have changed since you last visited a prospective customer. The prospect may have changed product lines, hired a new purchasing agent, changed owners, or added a satellite office. You may have hired a new salesperson who knows the prospective customer. You may have changed product lines. Keep a database of prospective customers who say "No." Revisit them annually, or sooner if something occurs that puts you in the driver's seat. If nothing else, maybe you should invite the prospective customer to your business. Be inventive. Find new ways to approach again and again.

Sales to customers and non-customers who need your brand new service. You have sold a particular type of machinery for some time. You provide warranty and repair service. You have just decided to promote annual maintenance contracts. You charge a nominal annual fee to see each contracted customer once each quarter. Your maintenance specialists will examine and diagnose specific parts and functions, checking for unusual or unnecessary wear. Emergency service calls and customer downtime should be reduced. It is also likely that the overall annual cost to operate the piece of machinery will be lower as a result of regular maintenance. Bottom Line? Your customer saves money and agrees to your service.

Get out in the field. Entrepreneurs usually establish a new business from the field. They are active salespeople in the early years because they simply cannot afford to hire someone to take over the sales function. Once out of the field, there is a tendency to get bogged down inside the business and leave the sales function to others. They get out of touch.

Get out of the office and spend a few days each month meeting and greeting customers and prospective customers. Ride with a sales person for the day and discover the things that are going right and wrong in the sales process. You may be amazed at the things you will learn.

Business to business sales. If you sell business to business, the guidelines are somewhat different than selling to the retail consumer. Here are a few:

When selling to a retail customer, you will nearly always have access to the end user. When engaging in business to business sales, you may deal with a purchasing agent, a department manager or supervisor, or an agent for the buying company. Many organizations are just too large to allow every salesperson to have access to the owner or CEO of the company.

Many end users will buy one time, never to be seen again, but B2B sales may be repetitive and ongoing, sometimes for years. When you are selling B2B, try to make every relationship a lasting relationship.

You may be familiar with the adage that says that people often buy emotionally and defend the buying decision logically. As an example, they may buy a brand new Porsche because they want to be seen driving the car. But, they defend the purchase by saying that the car is high quality and holds its value better than other automobile. Oh, and the deal was too good to pass up. B2B sales often lack emotional enthusiasm on the part of the customer. The bottom line may be the price.

Depending on your product or service, you may be selling something that will be resold by your buyer. Know your competition's strengths and weaknesses, their pricing schemes, their ability to deliver on time and your customers' inventory needs and turnover rates.

When you sell to the end user, the customer generally has to shop around, going place-to-place, trying to find a better deal. When you sell B2B, the customer simply makes a phone call if she is dissatisfied in any way. There is always someone else who is happy to make a call on your current or prospective customer to offer a different perspective on price and service. When you sell B2B, your potential customer community is usually small and under constant pressure from your competitors. Stay in constant contact with your customers, prospective customers and your competition.

Your B2B customer may be in a position to demand special pricing, credit and delivery terms. Fledgling businesses that are desperate for sales occasionally take on a customer that demands more than a new entrepreneur is willing or able to provide. In some instances, the new business tries too hard to satisfy the demanding customer and eventually goes out of business. Be careful and grow sales at a pace that suits your budget.

WHAT SHOULD I DO? B2B sales relationships are often long-lasting. They can develop into friendships that last a lifetime. The friendship can be a positive or negative influence on you and your employees. Regardless of what you hear about separation of business and pleasure, they meet on the golf course, at church, at civic affairs, all around town and, in many cases, all around the world. If you are in business, you must be positively visible.

Sales refunds. If you are a typical shopper, you are familiar with 30-day, money back guarantees. Sales refunds are expected by your customers because most retailers offer refunds of most products within a specific period of time. Some items are refunded in full while others may suffer refund reductions due to shipping charges, usage charges or contractual obligations. Regardless, your customers expect to buy anything and everything with the assurance that they have the right to return an item for any reason. If money back guarantees are the norm among your competition, or in your industry, your sales numbers may suffer if you refuse to follow suit.

Do your homework, study the competition and do what is best for your company. Sales refunds are a fact of life and can often be a source of new business. If the customer fails to present a receipt with a return, the company issues a credit or gift card that must be spent at that business. More often than not, the person receiving the credit or gift card spends more than the amount of the refund, converting a refund to a winning situation for your company.

Note: When you assemble your sales forecast, add a line to your Income Statement – Less Returns & Allowances – to offset potential returns.

Sales contracts. Are they necessary in my business? It is much easier to convince a contracted customer to continue to do business with your company. Even if the customer is thinking of leaving you for another service, you have the advantage because you already know the customer's business dynamics. If the journey has been difficult, start talking new contract at least three months before contract expiration, if not sooner. Straighten out the old problems and get a new contract endorsed early. It is better to lose a few months of the old contract than to lose all of a prospective contract to a competitor.

WHAT SHOULD I DO? Selling is the number one failure area for new entrepreneurs. New business owners should have a minimum of a month's worth of sales on the books the day they open their doors. Many new entrepreneurs have no idea of the difficulties they may experience when they attempt to present their products or services to potential buyers. Few new business owners have made a single "cold call" in their careers. Most have no sales experience, whatsoever. You have surely heard the saying, "sales is the lifeblood of your business." Without sales, you have no business. Cover this base *before* you open your doors or your business venture may be short-lived.

SCORE

SCORE is a national organization headquartered in Washington, D.C. SCORE provides confidential guidance for current and prospective small business owners. Advice is disseminated via online or face-to-face counseling. Business assistance is available through workshops, webinars, and appointments at your business or at your nearest SCORE office. SCORE has over 13,000 volunteers at more than 360 offices nationwide. There is a wonderful cross section of talent among volunteers, covering nearly every facet of business. Experience abounds among members, and advice is free and confidential.

Additional Resources: www.score.org.

SEARCH/STAFFING FIRMS

Search firms play a valuable role in recruiting, interviewing, and providing temporary and permanent employees for businesses. Back in the day, we referred to them as employment agencies. Search firms provide a conduit between you and the millions of people who are looking for jobs. There is a search firm out there that will recruit to nearly any position you have available. Some are local firms with local connections. Others fall under state, regional, national, and even international umbrellas.

Why should I employ a search firm? Utilizing a reputable search firm can fill gaps in your skill sets if you are not familiar with hiring, interviewing, or selecting quality employees. Search firms also have the ability to recruit a passive candidate for a specific skill set. Good search firms have a stable of potential employees who may fill your temporary and permanent needs.

Do search firms specialize? Most search firms can help you with temporary or permanent hires. Beyond that, many specialize in particular segments of the workforce such as accounting, finance, or human resources. Some specialize in administrative staff, such as clerks, administrative assistants, and receptionists. Others place only sales-related applicants. Many search firms deal with executive positions only. Others specialize in labor and blue collar positions or particular industries.

Local vs. national search firm. Many business people prefer a local search firm because they want to see the personality of the firm and its contacts. If something goes awry, a quick face-to-face meeting can often accomplish more than a long-distance phone call. Hiring a search firm is an ongoing endeavor. Employee turnover is a fact of life. A good search firm can reduce turnover by prequalifying applicants and reducing the stress of finding and selecting from a field of unknown quality.

Search firm contracts. Any reputable search firm is going to require you to endorse an agreement for a standard search or a retained search.

Standard search. A standard search requires no front money. The search firm agrees to introduce suitable candidates to your company until you mutually agree on a person for hire. If the firm cannot provide a suitable candidate, you have no further obligation.

Retained Search. A retained search is usually an exclusive search for an executive with a salary in excess of $100,000. The search firm will require 50 percent of their fee at the time of contract endorsement and the balance on the hiring date of the new employee. The upfront payment is nonrefundable. A firm's fee is typically 25% - 35% of the assumed total compensation package that the new hire will earn, including salary, bonus, stock options, and other perks. Example: If the new hire will earn a total package worth $200,000, the search firm's fee will be $50,000, with $25,000 due with the endorsed agreement. If the search firm cannot satisfy your needs, or if you back out of the contract, you lose $25,000. You also receive all the research data developed by the firm during their search.

Temporary employees (temps). You may have need for temporary help for several hours, days, weeks, or months, to fill a position(s) for which you do not wish to hire permanent help. Temporary help may be employed in any business facet, from blue collar to white collar, from laborers to engineers or executives.

When you hire a temp, the search firm takes care of all payroll taxes, workers' compensation, unemployment, and anything else that you would normally deduct from an employees pay. You pay the grossed-up wage or salary, plus a premium of 40 to 100 percent to the search firm for providing the temporary help. This may sound pricey, but when you consider that the search firm recruits, interviews, conducts skill assessments, and guarantees the performance of the temp, you are relieved of a good deal of work that would otherwise cost valuable time and money.

There are advantages and disadvantages of temporary help. The advantage is that they are typically available immediately, and their assignment can be terminated at any time, for any reason. You do not have to advertise, interview, or provide payroll services.

The key disadvantages are the temps' lack of training for specific operations in your business and the knowledge that they can typically walk away at the end of the day without retribution. Treat a temp like anyone else in your company and expect the same work you would expect from a permanent employee.

Temporary to permanent employee. Try before you buy. You hire an employee on a temporary basis, seeking a long-term relationship. If the temp meets your requirements, a permanent position is offered. If the temp does not fit into your plans, request a replacement. If you are sure you want to hire a temp on a permanent basis, you should proceed immediately. If the temp is competent, other companies may also be interested. Some companies charge a conversion fee when you hire a temporary worker for a full-time position. Remember, everything is negotiable.

Permanent Employee. If a permanent hire does not work out, the search firm will usually find another person for the position at no extra charge. Legitimate firms offer a 90-day, pro-rated refund for hires that do not remain with your company. Make sure you understand your contract. Everything must be in writing to be executable.

Cost of search firms. Temporary workers cost total payroll and deductions, plus a margin of 40 to 100 percent. Temporary to permanent workers cost the same as any comparable temporary workers until converted to full time. At the time of conversion, costs occasionally include a conversion fee, which could be 20 to 35 percent of the starting salary, or total compensation package if it is an executive level candidate. Some search firms charge 1 percent per thousand of the starting annual salary, with a maximum of 35 percent, i.e., 25 percent of $25,000 or 35 percent of $80,000. Permanent hires cost a flat fee of 20 to 35 percent of the annual package. Candidates who are hired via retained searches cost 25 to 35 percent of the total annual package. A minimum of half the fee is nonrefundable and due at the time you endorse the agreement with the search firm.

Terms of search firms. All invoices for all transactions are due immediately upon receipt. Invoices for permanent hires are issued on the person's first day of work. Temporary workers are paid weekly, on Friday, one week in arrears. You will receive weekly invoices for temporary workers beginning 10 days after the temp's first day of work.

Guarantees by search firms. Temporary workers are replaced if problems ensue. Permanent hires are replaced or partially refunded if they do not work out.

What makes a good search firm? Good search firms simply do a better job of providing a higher quality candidate, whether temporary or permanent. Search firms develop reputations. Before you hire a firm, ask for references. Talk to your business friends. Good firms have good reputations. Many provide transportation to and from job sites. Many require uniforms for temporary workers. The good firms conduct thorough interviews, complete and thorough reference checks, assess skill sets of potential candidates, and even complete drug screens and background checks per the client's request.

Additional Resources: Area search firms.

SECTION 179 OF IRS TAX CODE *(See also DEPRECIATION)*

IRS Tax Code 179 allows a business to depreciate a qualified item, in total, in the year it is put into use, rather than spreading the item's depreciation over a longer period. Depreciable property must be eligible per IRS Code, must have a useful life that exceeds one year, must be at least 50 percent business use, and must be acquired by purchase. There is a specific list of items that do not qualify. The IRS also provides specific cost and dollar limits for each category of depreciation. Be sure to discuss Section 179 deductions with your accountant when you file your taxes. Items purchased via lease may also fall under Section 179.

Additional Resources: Accountant, banker, Internet, www.irs.gov.

SECURITY/SURVEILLANCE

Do I really need security/surveillance? Yes! The majority of businesses have some type of alarm and fire monitoring system. Criminals shy away from businesses with security systems. Most municipalities require a fire monitoring system.

What security system is good for me? Have two or three reputable companies look over your facility and pick the system you like best. Be sure to have a plan in mind so you know what you value most.

Burglar alarm systems. Burglar alarm systems are pretty inexpensive when you consider the alternative. You can usually buy or lease the system. Central station monitoring is the only way to go. Eighty-five percent of all businesses have burglar alarm systems; get one!

Camera systems (CCTV). Buy or lease good equipment. If you are a very small operation, you may want to purchase a system at Sam's Club, Costco, or BJ's. Installation is simple. If you are looking at growing, get a scalable system from a reliable dealer. Stay off the Internet when buying equipment. You never know what you will get until it arrives. If you want to watch your business cameras 24/7, opt for a system that allows you to eavesdrop via the Internet with your laptop or home computer. Such capability adds very little cost to your overall system and puts you at your business, even though you are at home. If you invest in CCTV, include a recording system.

Card access systems. Card access systems provide another depth of security that you may welcome if you are interested in securing and monitoring ingress and egress within your facility. Every person who works in your building will be issued a card, unique to that individual, which has electronic circuitry imbedded. You can determine who may enter or exit any door(s) included in the system. You can also determine time parameters for each card holder and record those entries and exits for your use. In other words, you gain complete control of all pathways, gates, lanes, parking lots, computer rooms, money rooms and all manner of ingress and egress, inside and outside your facility. If it opens or closes, it can be fitted with a mechanism that is compatible with an access card. Cards with restricted access can also be issued to vendors, cleaning people, maintenance people, delivery drivers, and so on.

Fencing. Fencing stops or slows illegal vehicle entry and unwanted pedestrian traffic. Before erecting a fence with barbed tape, coils of concertina, and wire outriggers, check local ordinances. Some municipalities have strict rules regarding fencing.

Fire alarm systems. Most municipalities have ordinances that will not allow you to open a business until a fire alarm system is installed, inspected, and approved by the local fire marshal. If you are required to have a fire alarm system and ignore the regulation, the fire marshal has the right to shut you down and lock you out – without giving you notice.

Most fire marshals will give you a specified number of days to comply before locking you down. Check with your local fire marshal before you buy or rent your building. Fire ordinances can be surprising and inordinately expensive if you opt to look the other way.

Safes. There is not a safe that cannot be cracked, taken, or blown open if the burglar has the means and time to do so. If something is too valuable to lose at any cost, it should not be kept in your safe. This includes large sums of money, negotiable instruments, patent information, rare or priceless items, and highly confidential documents.

If you have a small safe, bolt it to a concrete floor from the inside of the safe, so that a burglar must enter the safe or pry it off the floor to break it loose. Most safes are small and light. They are simply carried away in a matter of minutes and forced open later. If you cannot afford to lose it, rent a safety deposit box at your bank. If the contents are exceedingly valuable, back it up with an insurance policy.

Shredders. Shred first and ask questions later. Get a cross cut model that cuts the paper in strips, and then cuts the strips into very small pieces, greatly reducing the chances that the pieces can be reassembled. If it has your name or your business name on it, shred it. That includes everything from credit card offers to outdated records.

Security signage. Security signage is a **wonderful** deterrent. You've seen the signs: "Protected by ABC Alarm Company" or "This property is protected by video surveillance." And the most popular by far: "Beware of Dog." Signage works.

Guards. Typically, contract guards are far too expensive for the average small business. However, there are situations that require security personnel on duty while the business is open, closed, or both. If you have a gate that requires inspection of vehicles or individuals, entering and exiting the business, you may need a guard at your gate on a full-time basis. You know your business and your risk. Just be sure to match the risk to the necessity for contract guards.

Barriers. Barriers are usually water, steel, concrete, wire or cable. They include fences, walls, bollards, pop-up devices, pools, moats, bullet-proof panels, bullet-proof windows and gates, to name a few. If you have a reason to believe that someone may be interested in damaging or destroying your building or property with a vehicle or other motorized device, you may want to invest in barriers.

What areas should I watch? Watch high-value areas such as cash registers, money rooms, doors, shipping docks, yards or any inside or outside area where you would expect a potential loss. It is *always* a good idea to watch shipping docks and yards. Have you ever wondered how many pallets are sold each year to the same companies where they were stolen days or weeks prior?

What about additional security lighting? Lighting is your best night deterrent. Lighting can also allow you to view an area as though it were daylight.

Where should I buy security? Save time and money. Go with a national company or a well-respected, long-term, local company for your security needs. If you have multiple locations, you may want to buy security from a nationwide company so that one 800 number services all your facilities.

Additional Resources: www.nbfaa.org, Better Business Bureau, Internet, Yellow Pages.

SEMINARS (See TRAINING)

SEXUAL HARASSMENT

Sexual harassment accusations can be harmful to your business, whether true or false. Your employee handbook should include text that identifies all aspects of sexual harassment, as well as the actions that must be taken in the event that sexual harassment is experienced or observed by anyone in your employ. This includes acts by, or toward your employee, customer, supplier, or anyone affiliated with your business.

Should I provide sexual harassment training for my management staff? Sexual harassment training requirements vary from state to state. Employers and supervisors can be held personally liable for sexual harassment and related crimes in a number of states. Some states hold employers responsible, but not supervisors. Some states require sexual harassment training, often dependent on the number of employees in the company. Other states have no such requirements. Some states clone federal regulations, while others complement federal regulations.

You should be familiar with state and federal laws. Be sure that your supervisors are properly trained. Their actions may save you from a sexual harassment lawsuit.

Who should provide sexual harassment training? Most organizations that provide sexual harassment training include discrimination training in their curricula. Go to the Internet and surf for "Sexual harassment training programs." There is an abundance of choices. The teaching vehicles and prices vary significantly.

Sexual harassment by men and women. Sexual harassment may be committed by anyone toward anyone else. Sexual harassment is not specific to gender. Men may harass women and men. Women may harass men and women.

Sexual harassment in a group. If you are among a group that sexually harasses another, every member of that group may be guilty of sexual harassment. Even if you do not take an active part in sexually harassing another, the mere fact that you stood by as a member of the group and did not report the incident may be enough to convict you of the act.

When do I investigate a sexual harassment complaint? Investigate immediately. You never know the severity or danger involved until the complaint is investigated. Delay will get you nothing but grief. The accuser and accused deserve immediate, unequivocal action. Look at the complaint unemotionally and without bias. If you have firsthand knowledge, do not take sides.

Should I always consider all sexual harassment complaints seriously? Yes. If you feel that the complaint does not involve you directly, call your attorney anyway. Better safe than sorry.

Should I investigate every sexual harassment complaint? Emphatically, yes!

WHAT SHOULD I DO? Always call your attorney first. Tell the person reporting the sexual harassment complaint that you want to contact legal counsel prior to discussing the complaint. Do *not* have the complaining party in the room when you contact the attorney. Use an attorney who has a creditable history with sexual harassment cases. Follow the attorney's advice to the letter.

Additional Resources: Attorney who is adept at handling sexual harassment cases, human resources specialist.

SHIPPING (See FREIGHT/SHIPPING)

SHRINKAGE

Shrinkage is the loss of business inventory, due to any number of causes, from the initial order, until the product goes out your door – paid or unpaid. Consider the journey of any inventory purchase from beginning to end and the possibilities for error. The order may be shipped incorrectly and not caught when received at your company. The wrong product may be shipped and inventoried improperly. Inventory may be damaged and not replaced. Inventory may be stolen before it gets to the shelf. Inventory may be priced improperly, creating a loss at time of sale. Inventory may be stolen by employees or customers. Inventory may be bad out of the box and not returned for a replacement. Customer returns may be improperly warrantied. Inventory may be purposely or accidentally broken or destroyed by employees or customers and not reported. Inventory may be returned by a customer without packing and never returned to the shelf or the vendor. Or, inventory may be robbed of parts to satisfy a warranty and never reported. Surely you can see a plethora of possibilities for inventory shrinkage. Every time your inventory shrinks, your profit margin and bottom line follow suit. Need help with shrinkage? See **SECURITY.**

SICK DAYS / SICK LEAVE (See also FAMIILY MEDICAL LEAVE ACT [FMLA])

Sick days. Federal law does not require an employer to provide paid sick days. However, most companies provide three to five paid sick days a year. If you choose to forego payment for sick days, you may lose valuable employees to a company with a more lenient sick day policy.

Please understand that many employees view sick days as entitlements. Employees will use up their sick days, even if sickness is not an issue. Some companies require a doctor's slip before allowing an employee to return to work after missing three or more consecutive work days. If you provide sick days, suck it up and realize that employees may use sick days as personal time off. If you want to preserve your production time, offer to pay a bonus to each employee with perfect attendance for the year. Or, you may want to give each employee an extra days pay for each unused sick day at the end of the year. Make it worthwhile for the employee and profitable for your company. Consider the overtime that may be necessary to cover sick days. Include costs in your budget forecast.

Sick Leave. There is no federal law that requires American companies to provide paid sick leave. However, the Family Medical Leave Act (FMLA) does require certain companies to provide up to 12 weeks of unpaid medical leave annually for certain employees.

↳**WHAT SHOULD I DO?** Approach sick days, sick leave or any healthcare issue very carefully. Find an expert and make sure you are within the law when addressing healthcare.

Additional Resources: Human resources consultant.

SIGN-ON BONUS

A sign-on bonus is additional compensation awarded to a new-hire at the time she joins the company or at some specified time in the future.

Why should I award a sign-on bonus? Sign-on bonuses are designed to encourage a prospective new hire to work for your company. These bonuses are usually paid to upper level new hires that possess unique skill sets that are rare in a particular industry.

Occasionally an unknown quantity walks in the door. Star potential, fresh out of school, engineering degree, top of the class, unproven, and wants an astronomical salary. Pay a lower salary. Pay a sign-on bonus that is a fraction of the difference.

What kind of sign-on bonus? Most sign-on bonuses are monetary. Be creative.

How much sign-on bonus? A sign-on bonus should be 10 to 20 percent of salary, the lower the better. You know what you can afford. Stay within your preplanned boundaries.

Should a sign-on bonus be in writing? Yes! Include the total bonus amount, payment arrangements, and performance necessities for the employee to collect all increments beyond the initial payment. Include this as an addendum to the new employee's offer letter. The new hire must endorse and date the letter prior to any payment.

WHAT SHOULD I DO? No new hire wants a sign-on bonus that is paid later. No employer wants to get into a grab-and-run situation where the new hire gets full payment immediately and quits soon after because a better offer is available. Pay as little as possible on the employee's start date and make the balance conditional, based on tenure and evaluation. Stretch out payment increments until you have a feel for the employee's skills and work habits.

Additional Resources: Common sense, CPA, Attorney.

SIX SIGMA

"Six Sigma is a quality program that is designed to improve your customers' experiences, lower your costs, and build better leaders."[1] Six Sigma seems to have an answer to almost any problem posed in a business environment. Originally focused on manufacturing processes, Six Sigma now encompasses a wide range of processes that are useful in public and private sectors, on a global basis. Now a global brand, Six Sigma is constantly evolving to improve business performance and deliver the right product or service to the consumer, the first time, and forever.

Is Six Sigma for you? Start by analyzing your opportunities for improvement. Quantify your findings in terms of potential profit. Seminars that will familiarize you with Six Sigma are relatively inexpensive. Implementing Six Sigma is not inexpensive. Attend a seminar, learn the costs involved, and determine if Six Sigma is on your short list.

SMALL BUSINESS ADMINISTRATION (SBA)

Under normal circumstances, SBA does not make loans to businesses. SBA works with affiliate banks that extend loans to businesses. SBA guarantees individual business loans, up to 90 percent of principal. By doing so, loans are made available to businesses that may not qualify for credit without SBA's guarantee.

SBA does provide direct loans to a number of entities during times of national disaster. Such loans are handled by the Federal Emergency Management Agency (FEMA). For more information, visit DisasterAssistance.gov.

Where is SBA available geographically? SBA operates in all 50 states, plus Puerto Rico, the U.S. Virgin Islands, and Guam.

How does SBA work? SBA supports several loan programs that are offered to businesses in all phases of growth, from startup to mature. SBA offers its programs through banks of its choosing, using a fixed criteria to determine the prospective lender's ability to perform. The bank is given a choice of the loans it may offer, based on its status with SBA.

Should I seek SBA assistance? Consider all your choices, including SBA. If SBA is your best choice, be prepared to pay prime rate plus a fixed percentage. If you are short on collateral, SBA may be able to assist you in providing a guaranty that will allow your bank to make a loan to your business.

Who really loans me the money? A SBA-affiliated bank.

Which banks should I consider? Start by calling your regional SBA office. Tell them about your company and request a bank and loan officer that fits your business and personal qualifications. If you would rather search the Internet, go to www.sba.gov. Enter your zip code on the SBA home page and follow the prompts.

Are all SBA-associated banks created equally? No. First, not all banks are SBA lenders. SBA certifies affiliate banks at one of three levels. If you borrow from a *Preferred* SBA lender, your banker handles the entire process, including the decision to offer you a loan. *Preferred* banks have a tendency to be national banks or larger regional institutions. They are tried and tested by SBA and usually have an SBA-certified staff to handle your needs. *Certified* and *Express* lenders follow a different set of SBA standards and may take longer and provide less services than a *Preferred* lender.

Collateral with SBA loans. This is quoted directly from the SBA website. "To the extent that worthwhile assets are available, adequate collateral is required as security on all SBA loans. However, the SBA will generally not decline a loan when inadequacy of collateral is the **only** unfavorable factor.

For all SBA loans, personal guaranties are required from every owner of 20 percent or more of the business, as well as from other individuals who hold key management positions. Whether or not a guaranty will be secured by personal assets, is based on the value of the assets already pledged and the value of the assets personally owned, compared to the amount borrowed."[2]

Startup loans for small business. SBA has programs dedicated to business startups. They are: Basic 7a Loan Guarantee, CDC 504 Loan Program, and 7m Microloan. Each program serves businesses with different sets of circumstances, at varying rates of interest, over various terms. Occasionally, new loans are offered by SBA on a short-term basis.

What types of SBA loans are available? SBA covers the gamut of available loans, from startups to mature businesses.

Who guarantees my loan? SBA guarantees your loan, up to a certain percentage, based on your bank, loan type, loan amount, and your ability to repay.

WHAT SHOULD I DO? Talk to your banker about all types of loans that may be available. Ask if SBA may have a loan that is a good fit for your business. If your banker can match your loan needs without benefit of SBA involvement, you may save some money. SBA loans do have a tendency to be somewhat more expensive than your standard bank loan. On the other hand, many businesses are in business, only because SBA was able to guaranty repayment in the event of default.

Additional Resources: www.sba.gov, local SBA-affiliated bank.

SMOKING POLICIES

You may want to institute a non-smoking policy at your business. Non-smokers are proven to be adversely affected by after smoke. Smoking can be a fire hazard, particularly if your business utilizes combustible chemicals. Under the Americans with Disabilities Act, you may have to provide accommodations for disabled individuals, based on their sensitivity to a smoky environment.

U.S. government anti-smoking laws apply only to employees of the General Services Administration (GSA). The government does not regulate smoking in private workplaces. However, before instituting a smoking policy, check state and local statutes. Many communities have laws that prohibit smoking in public places of business. Some local laws are more stringent than state laws.

A non-smoking policy can provide a smoke-free workplace, outside, inside, and even in company vehicles or equipment. Your policy may apply only to designated areas inside the building, or your policy may apply to the entire building but allow smoking outside the building.

If you institute a non-smoking policy, everyone who enters your business must adhere. That means that you, your family, visitors, and friends all follow the rules. Do not smoke after hours, even if you are the only one in the building. If you break the rules, expect others to do the same.

Smoking on company premises. The entire company property should be defined as company premises. Smoking areas may be defined as designated outside areas, designated inside areas, or outside the building and more than "X" number of feet from any structure. No one should be allowed to smoke near entrances and exits. Visitors and non-smoking employees should not be exposed to the site or smell of smoking upon entering or leaving your building. Smoking areas should have sufficient receptacles for smoking and non-smoking waste materials.

Smoking on breaks, lunch or company time. If an employee is on a break, he is on company time. If an employee is at lunch, he is not on company time. If you allow smoking during breaks, you are allowing smoking on company time but within the limits of your non-smoking policy. If you allow smoking, an employee on break should have the same rights as any other smoker on the premises. Smokers do not have special privileges that allow them to smoke at-will. An employee can smoke at lunch, either off the business property or at your business if he is within the limits of your smoking policy.

Smoking at customer sites. A customer site is the same as your company site. Your employees must follow the smoking rules at a customer's business site. Penalties for disobeying non-smoking rules at a customer's site are the same as the rules for disobeying your company's policies and procedures.

Does OSHA regulate smoking? OSHA has no specific laws that regulate smoking in the workplace. It does regulate exposure to a number of chemicals that are present in cigarette smoke. However, OSHA considers those chemicals to fall within standard workplace limits under normal circumstances.

Do I need a separate smoking area? You are well within your rights to provide a smoking area, just so it does not interfere with the rights of non-smokers. Smokers have rights. Non-smokers have rights. Treat both groups equally. Smokers are not the enemy. They are valuable human assets, like any other company employee.

Unions and smoking. Some states and municipalities have ordinances or statutes that require businesses to negotiate with collective bargaining units before adopting non-smoking rules. Know the rules before you install a non-smoking policy. Do not attempt to enforce a non-smoking policy that includes some employees and excludes others.

Smokeless tobacco. Most non-smoking policies only restrict tobaccos that emit smoke, such as cigarettes, cigars, and pipes. These products may be offensive and harmful to co-workers. Employees, customers, and suppliers may also find smokeless tobacco and chewing tobacco offensive, particularly when a user spits into a container or onto a floor to avoid swallowing excess tobacco juice. You may want to include smokeless tobacco in your non-smoking policy.

WHAT SHOULD I DO? No one should be exposed to the dangers of smoking, after-smoke or the unpleasant odor of smoking or after-smoke unless the individual chooses to do so. Nor should anyone be exposed to the by-products of smokeless tobacco if they find such things inappropriate or unpleasant. Be sure that smoking areas are designed to allow employees, patrons and visitors an opportunity to experience a smoke-free environment.

Additional Resources: HR specialist, www.osha.gov, collective bargaining unit (if you are a union shop), local and state statutes.

SOCIAL MEDIA MARKETING

Social Media Marketing is such a large, fast-growing, always-changing, technologically improvisational concept that it is really hard to pin it down to an acceptable definition. Users of Social Media Marketing talk about the Internet in terms of old Web and Web 2.0. The old Web is essentially an information highway that was harnessed for human participation, aimed at consumers or anyone that wanted to learn, participate and interact. The old Web was not really intended to be a communication vehicle.

Web 2.0 turned the Internet into a massive communication vehicle, enriching our abilities to relate to others across a whole new spectrum of interrelated tools such as Facebook, LinkedIn, Twitter, YouTube and MySpace, to name a few. With the advent of Social Media Marketing, we have this massive framework for interactive communication, worldwide, for the cost of an Internet connection, and a device such as a computer, smartpad or smartphone.

Social Media Marketing is a tool that an entrepreneur cannot afford "not to use." Granted, you must be active on the Web with a blog or similar tool to get the word out to your customers and business partners, but it has never been easier or less expensive than with Social Media Marketing. Suffice it to say that you *need* a valid social media presence in today's market, regardless of your product or service.

WHAT SHOULD I DO? Attend a Social Media Market workshop, seminar or webinar. Have a look at companies such as CareerTrack, SkillPath, National Seminars Training, HubSpot or Sysomos. Some are free. Others charge anywhere from $99 to upwards of $3,500, depending on whether you are happy with a webinar or feel that hands on instruction is more your speed.

The key is interaction. If you attend a course, interact with other students and businesses. Ask what they are doing to reach and get feedback from their customers. Talk to your vendors, competitors and customers to determine the best way to reach your target market, every day, consistently and effectively. In today's business environment, the entrepreneur must take every possible opportunity to find the next new customer and the next sale. Do not get left behind. Get involved.

Additional Resources: Internet, Yellow Pages, SCORE

SUPPLIERS (See VENDORS)

SWOT

The origin of SWOT is attributed to Albert Humphrey, a management consultant who conceived the analytical evaluation tool in the 1960s. Humphrey utilized data from the Fortune 500 to examine companies, based on their proposed Strengths, Weaknesses, Opportunities and Threats. Strengths refer to a company's internal attributes that give them advantages over other companies, where Weaknesses refer to those internal areas where a company is at a disadvantage to other companies. Opportunities refer to positive external elements that favor a company's efforts to profit, where Threats refer to external elements that may impede upon a company's efforts to profit.

Like many methods of analysis, SWOT compartmentalizes data into usable categories that are helpful in determining a company's ability to compete. SWOT can be useful in most businesses, whether profit or not-for-profit. SWOT has gained a great deal of popularity in recent years. Similar to any other analytical tool, SWOT simply provides a landscape to discover a set of environmental inputs that require further purification and analysis. Unfortunately, the forthcoming analysis is only as good as the person or group analyzing the data.

WHAT SHOULD I DO? SWOT is another tool in your business tool bag. SWOT is not the answer to all your problems and opportunities. It is a valuable tool if kept in perspective and should be utilized accordingly. Once you have identified your strengths, weaknesses, opportunities and threats, resist the temptation to rely solely on your findings. Put all your planning tools to work to further analyze your conclusions, thus gaining a thorough understanding of the information before moving forward. As Steven Symes of Demand Media writes, "SWOT analysis should help management begin to think about the organization and its future, instead of ending any other planning efforts."[3]

Chapter T

TARGET MARKET

Entrepreneur Magazine defines target market as, "*A specific group of consumers at which a company aims its products and services.*"[1] Here is one way to go about finding *your* target market. Draw a large target on an erasable board. Put in the circles, complete with the bull's-eye. Mark the bull's-eye "50." Mark the rings 40, 30, 20 and 10, inside to outside. Leave plenty of room to write. Now, fill in the demographics that may define your target market. Consider age, education level, gender, hobbies, home value, income level, job, location, marital status, profession, religion, sexual orientation, spending habits, travel preferences, to name a few. Enter each demographic in a ring on your target, in order of importance to the purchase of your product or service. The bullseye is reserved for the most crucial demographics and the "10" outer ring for the least crucial demographics. When you are finished, you will know where you want to concentrate your target market efforts, based on the demographics closest to the bull's-eye. For instance, if you are selling home saunas, your bullseye may contain home value, income level and profession. Your "10" ring may include gender, religion and sexual orientation. Try the exercise and refine it as you go. It's a good start to pinning down your target market.

TAXES

Most businesses that go out of business seem to have back taxes of some form that are not paid. They also lack the money to settle the debt. If you are in financial trouble, there are probably of number of people, companies, and lending institutions on your list of past-due payables. All of these debt holders have the power to sue for their share of the pie, but not quite like the power of any governmental tax unit.

If you owe a private enterprise, your debt may be forgiven via bankruptcy. Surprise! Not all taxes you owe are forgiven via bankruptcy. Not only can certain tax debt remain in force beyond the life of all other debts, it can actually grow. Penalties and interest continue to increase your tax liability, even though you are unable to pay. Due to the nature of the debt, you will not be able to borrow money to pay your tax bill because tax debt is always in first position to collect debt.

By now, you probably get the message. Always, always pay your taxes, even if you cannot pay anyone else, including yourself. Tax debt that is not discharged in bankruptcy is generally unforgiving and never goes away, even if you die. The tax people have first rights to your estate.

Business deductions—what to keep and what is deductible? Keep every receipt associated with your business. That means *everything*. When you start deciding what is deductible and what is not, you risk missing deductions. Your CPA will decide what is legally deductible.

What is lethal when dealing with taxes? Trying to do your own business income tax can be lethal. This is a recipe for disaster. Stay within the boundaries of the law. Have a CPA do your taxes, both business and personal. It is worth every penny.

Should I pay quarterly tax estimates? There are penalties for skipping estimate payments and waiting until your year-end filing to pay your taxes in one payment. Do not ignore quarterly estimates. Your CPA knows whether you should or should not pay quarterly estimates.

WHAT SHOULD I DO? This is simple. Don't mess with the IRS. Call your CPA.

Additional Resources: CPA, local IRS office, www.irs.gov.

TELECOMMUTING

Should I permit employees to work from home? If working at home were more profitable than employees working at a business location, everyone would be working at home. Control is an issue. Trust can be an issue. If you must allow an employee to work at home, pay commission or piece work rates. As long as you are paying for results only, control is not a large issue. Just make sure that quality and on-time delivery are equal to that of business-based employees.

Additional Resources: Human resources consultant.

TERMINATION / FIRING

This is an area that creates difficulties for a huge number of companies. As you grow, you may hire employees without forethought regarding longevity or the possibility that, someday, you will probably be faced with terminating someone. The termination interview starts with orientation. Company rules and regulations are spelled out in writing, and every new employee signs a statement agreeing to abide by company policies.

When termination looms, you will have had multiple opportunities to remind the offending employee of the policies he promised to obey during orientation. Thus, the termination interview becomes an extension of the hiring process.

If you are a union shop, your union contract undoubtedly states that you cannot meet with a union employee to discuss termination without specified and sufficient notification of the forthcoming meeting. Your union contract may require union representation at such a meeting or any disciplinary session.

Where shall I terminate an employee? Termination should always take place in a private environment, but never one-on-one. You never know how the employee will react. Save embarrassment for all parties involved.

How do I stay out of trouble? Know the rules and follow the rules. If you have questions, do not guess. Do not be afraid to ask questions of your attorney or Human Resources specialist before preparing for a termination meeting, which is a culmination of discipline and corrective action meetings. Termination should not be a surprise to the employee.

Do I have a right to investigate a situation that appears to be harmful to my company? You not only have the right, but you are obligated to know as much as possible about situations that may lead to termination(s). Imagine a termination meeting without the correct facts. Failure to investigate may lead to false accusations, an infuriated employee and a lawsuit. If you go to court without sufficient investigation and proper documentation, you may be liable for damages. If you are dealing with sexual harassment or a discrimination case, you should talk to an attorney or human resources specialist before moving forward. In fact, this is a good rule for any termination situation.

Should I terminate with or without a witness? Always terminate an employee with a witness present, preferably a human resources specialist. If you are a union shop, your contract will require union representation when you meet with a union employee.

At-will employment laws *(See AT-WILL EMPLOYMENT).*

Wages due at termination? If you owe it, pay it. Laws differ from state to state. If you terminate an employee, you are required to pay that employee all earned wages within a specific period of time. Fines may be imposed if you do not follow the rules. If you hire a payroll company, company officials will know the rules. If you do your own payroll, the information is readily available. Once again, ignorance is not a reasonable defense.

Wages may fall under federal or state jurisdiction. A short phone call to the proper agencies will generate an envelope full of information, some of which may require posting. Take time to read it, and stay out of serious trouble.

Documenting Termination. Everything you intend to say or do in a termination meeting should be reduced to writing prior to your meeting. This is your meeting script, and the sum total of all you plan to bring to the table. During the meeting, take notes of all that is said and also reduce that information to writing. Share this documentation with any witnesses to the termination meeting and deal with discrepancies regarding actual meeting dialogue. Dialogue should be attributed to the person(s) who actually spoke the words.

Counseling 4-step program. Many companies utilize a four-step, progressive system to deal with troubled employees. As always, check for statutes that specifically speak to employee counseling. Always counsel an employee in private.

Step 1: This is a coaching step. Meet with the employee and his immediate supervisor. Include union representation if necessary. Everything you are about to address is in your written notes. Explain that you are concerned about the employee's performance and that you have specific points to discuss. This meeting is an open forum. Keep it simple. You and the supervisor should voice your concerns first, then the employee should be given ample time to explain his side of the controversy.

When you are satisfied that all essential points have been discussed, present the employee with an action plan that you believe will put him on the right track to substantial improvement. Include a time table of reasonable length and reasonable difficulty. Spell out his duties and the company's duties. Explain that failure to adhere to the time table will result in future formal counseling. Let him know that a copy of the action plan and all meeting notes will be kept by his immediate supervisor. His signature is not required. Shake hands and wish him well. It is not necessary to place anything into the employee's file at this time.

After the meeting concludes, you and the supervisor should get your notes together and discuss anything either of you feels is germane to the situation. If things go well with the employee, the supervisor simply monitors the employee's work, coaching him toward improvement, until the employee progresses or shows cause for further counseling.

Step 2: This is a formal counseling step. A warning letter will be entered into the employee's file that provides specific consequences if his behavior does not improve within a specific period of time. This meeting should address the points that were included in the action plan from Step 1. Let the employee know what he is doing correctly and where he is failing. Explain that you have assembled an updated action plan that he is expected to complete in accordance with its time table. Explain that failure to meet the goals in the updated action plan may result in suspension or termination. Get the employee's agreement and signature. Shake hands and wish him well. Try to leave the employee with the feeling that he has a future with the company if he completes the action plan on time and adheres to policies and procedures in the future.

Step 3: This is also a formal counseling step. If you make it this far, the employee has failed to meet all, or part of the goals set forth in his action plan. You have determined that he is likely to continue to perform poorly and you are prepared to give him time off to set his mind straight. This meeting is identical to Step 2, with the exception that the action plan now includes one to three days off, with or without pay. Some companies do not believe in penalizing an employee financially for failure to follow policies and procedures. Most companies suspend employees without pay. This is your call. I personally feel that suspension with pay is the same as a vacation day. There is no lesson learned from a suspension unless is hits the employee's paycheck.

Tell the employee about your decision to suspend him. Ask him to think about his future with the company. If you think he has potential, tell him so. Give him the date and time to report back to work, or tell him you will call him when you are ready for his return. Ask him to sign a letter that lays out his suspension. If he refuses to sign, file the letter with a note, "Refused to sign." Set aside time to talk with him and his supervisor at starting time the day he returns, unless you are unsure of the date he will be invited back.

Do not be surprised if the employee does not return to work. If he feels his job is lost, he may seek other employment while he is off. If he does not return on the predetermined day, he has abandoned his job and is automatically terminated. Send his final paycheck to his home via mail, in accordance with state statutes pertaining to company property. If he wishes to return company property, pick up his check, and poses no threat to you or your company, tell him when his check will be available at the reception desk.

Step 4 (One Final Chance): If you have decided that your employee deserves a final opportunity to save his job, keep the pre-return meeting short. Keep it upbeat. Tell him what you expect. Provide an action plan with goals and dates. Put it in writing. Have him sign the action plan. Include language that lets the employee know that failure means immediate termination. Follow through accordingly.

OR

Step Four (Termination): If you have exhausted all efforts to create a viable working relationship and have decided not to retain the employee, keep the meeting to the points on your written script. Control the meeting. Remain calm, even if the employee is not. Get directly to the point. Do not vary your dialogue any more than necessary. Do not be overly negative or overly compassionate. Revisit the salient facts of past counseling sessions. Tell the truth as it happened. Cover items such as final paycheck, health insurance, severance pay, company property, outplacement possibilities, and anything else that is absolutely necessary. Do not prolong the meeting, and do not allow the employee to prolong the meeting. Leave the employee's dignity intact and wish him well. Do not offer a letter of recommendation under any circumstances *(See also Letters of Recommendation in this section)*.

Have final check ready at time of termination. If you have all the necessary information to cut the employee's final paycheck at termination, do so. Employee terminations always create positive and negative fallout. Reduce the fallout by severing the relationship immediately upon termination. If possible, do not give the former employee a reason to return to the premises.

Make separation permanent? This is your call. Some companies make all terminations permanent. Others will rehire individuals who were not terminated for cause. Many companies will not rehire former employees who were in management positions. Decide what works best for you. Many former employees carry baggage from one company to another. Why did the employee leave you to go to another company, and then decide to return to your company, where he was apparently unhappy enough to go elsewhere? You should be looking for long-term, reliable, loyal employees. If you are not completely comfortable with a re-hire, look elsewhere.

Walk a terminated employee out of the building. If the situation is tense and you expect immediate repercussions, you may want to have someone accompany the terminated employee out of the building. If not, you have already made your case for termination. Do not continue the discussion during a walkout. Do not allow a terminated employee to remain in your building alone. If it is necessary for the employee to recover personal property, he should be accompanied until he leaves the premises.

Level with remaining employees; let them hear it from you. Put out a short notice stating that Joe Smith is no longer an employee of the company, with the effective date and time. State that Mr. Smith is no longer permitted in the plant or at a customer's premises to act as an employee of the company. Let your employees know if you decide that you do not want a terminated employee on company property in the future. Do not discuss the reason for termination, now or later. Do not indicate any feelings, positive or negative, about the employee, as either may be used against you at a later date if the former employee sues for wrongful termination. If current employees question your decision, tell them that you respect their opinions but you are not permitted to share any further information. Secrets are never secret forever. Say nothing to anyone, including your family, beyond necessity to do so.

Vacation earned. All earned, unused vacation must be paid to an employee upon termination, regardless of cause.

Severance - yes or no? There are two reasons to allow a terminated employee a severance package. First, you think it is the right thing to do. The employee has been with you a number of years and has served you well, but the current situation leaves you no choice but termination. Secondly, severance provides a tool that may prevent a costly lawsuit. You offer a severance package to a terminated employee in exchange for her signature on a legal agreement that releases your company from further liability.

How much severance? This is a case-by-case decision. Severance should be fair but not extravagant. It should be consistent with terminations of other employees of equal stature with the organization. Severance packages should also be consistent with those offered by other companies in your industry. Finally, any severance package must be affordable. Many companies do not offer severance because they simply cannot afford to do so *(See also **REDUCTION IN FORCE (RIF)** for further discussions concerning severance packages)*.

Final paycheck/return of company property. Rules vary from state to state. Some states require full payment on the regular payday following termination. Others require full payment within a set number of days. Your CPA knows the rules. Company-owned property includes items such as vehicles, phones, pagers, computer equipment, tools, customer lists, uniforms, pricing information, and brochures. Some states require payment of the final check, in full, leaving the employer to file suit to recover property from a terminated employee. If your state allows you to hold final payment until you recover company property, do so. Know the laws for your state before moving forward. Play by the rules. Disgruntled former employees can be disruptive to your business and your checkbook. Expect rumors to circulate. Expect to be the *bad guy*, regardless of the situation. The truth will eventually come out.

Exit Interview *(See **EXIT INTERVIEW**)*.

Letters of Recommendation. Every Letter of Recommendation that leaves your business should be written by you or approved by you before it is promised to, given to, or sent to anyone. Never give a letter of recommendation to an employee who is terminated for cause. Never give a letter of recommendation to anyone unless you can stand behind everything you write.

An employee who quits or is laid off is terminated without fault. He is unlikely to sue for wrongful termination unless he feels as though he is a target of discrimination. He deserves a letter of recommendation if you truly feel that he was a valuable employee.

If the employee is terminated for cause, a letter of recommendation can become a very powerful tool in the hands of an attorney. You terminated the employee, and then told the world that he is suitable for employment with any other company. Bad move. You just created a potential wrongful termination lawsuit.

Reference calls. Saying something good about an ex-employee can be as harmful as saying something bad. You never know who is really on the other end of the conversation. An ex-employee who was discharged for poor performance may ask a friend to pose as a potential employer. If you say that the ex-employee did a good job with the intention of helping him find another position, you may be talking your way into a lawsuit. Consider that an ex-employee *always* wants to know what you are going to say about him because you automatically become a reference when the next potential employer requests completion of an employment application. Stick to the law and you will never get hurt.

Should I request denial of unemployment to a terminated employee? Generally speaking, it is not good practice to request denial of unemployment to a terminated employee. Denial of benefits sends a strong message to remaining employees. The message says that you do not care about the welfare of the person or his/her family. Consequently, you will probably not request that benefits be denied unless an employee quits or is terminated after being proven to have been involved in one of the following:

Embezzlement.

Thievery of company or customer property.

Employee leaves to establish his/her own company in violation of the terms of a legitimate non-compete agreement.

Employee leaves to join a competitor in violation of the terms of a legitimate non-compete agreement.

Employee fails to show up for work in accordance with company counseling procedures.

Employee walks off the job without notice or legitimate reason.

There are certainly other reasons to request denial of unemployment benefits. The foregoing are simply the most common. Any time you attempt to deny unemployment, you run the risk of having to appear before a referee or arbitrator where you and the employee will have a chance to tell your sides of the story. The employee will probably be represented by an attorney. You may also opt for representation, depending on the gravity of the situation and how much is at stake financially.

WHAT SHOULD I DO? Termination is easy to put on paper, but you will visit a completely different perspective when you are the person holding the termination meeting. You will think about it constantly in the hours leading up to the meeting. You will think about it often in the days after the termination. It is your job to give every employee every tool available to help him or her be a success. If the tools are made available and termination is the result, you have done your job. Know your boundaries and always go to a higher source if you have any question at all about the eventual outcome of a termination. A mistake here can cost you your business and a lot more.

Additional Resources: Human resources specialist, attorney.

THIEF IN THE HOUSE

Theft *is* a problem in business. There is an old axiom that states that 10 percent of employees will always steal, 10 percent will never steal, and the remaining 80 percent are a toss-up, contingent upon the state of affairs. If the axiom is true, at least 10 percent of your work force will walk off with company property, given the opportunity to do so. Depending on the source, employee theft accounts for 20 to 75 percent of all business thefts. Fifty percent is the norm. Consequently, it is prudent to take steps to prevent as much of the theft as possible.

Prevention first. Order pre-hire background checks on all new employees. Install a burglar alarm and limit users to a select few. Install cameras and record camera events 24/7. Lock inventory, vehicles, and tools at all times. Prosecute thieves if you have irrevocable evidence of guilt and an attorney's approval. Do not give a thief an opportunity to steal. Foster a company culture that is employee friendly *(See also SECURITY / SURVEILLANCE).*

If you suffer a loss, share it with your local authorities. If you involve police, the thief knows that you will go to the next level and prosecute anyone who is caught stealing. Do not involve police unless you plan to prosecute. Police are there for your convenience only if you allow them to follow through when the thief is apprehended.

Tighten up security. Put everyone on alert that a thief is in the house. Make it known among your employees that you will deal with the thief as severely as allowed by law.

Finally, you may want to create an amnesty situation. Let all employees know that the person who stole the item(s) in question may return the stolen property at a specific location, during or after working hours. This may be done without retribution and without giving up the name of the thief. No questions asked.

Can I terminate an employee without ironclad proof? This is another question for your attorney. Do not accuse anyone of theft without legal advice.

Can I suspend the employee without pay, pending investigation? If you catch the employee in the act, call your attorney and ask if you may suspend the employee.

Should I prosecute? This is your call. However, there is one caveat. Never tell anyone that you are going to prosecute unless you intend to follow through. Once again, talk to your attorney prior to proceeding.

WHAT SHOULD I DO? Many of the above questions indicate a call to your attorney. Things are not always as they appear. Know your boundaries and always go to a higher authority if you have any question at all regarding the eventual outcome of a reprimand or termination. A mistake here can be extremely costly.

Additional Resources: Attorney, human resources specialist.

TOLL - FREE NUMBERS *(See LONG-DISTANCE CALLING)*

TOOLS

Tools are broken into two categories: specialized tools and non-specialized tools. **Specialized tools** are germane to your particular product, such as diagnostic equipment, special hand tools, and electronic equipment necessary to work on your brand of products. **Non-specialized tools** are tools such as pliers, screwdrivers, hammers, wrenches, and thousands of other tools common to everyday applications.

Specialized tools and non-specialized tools are subdivided into tools purchased by the company and tools purchased by the employee. At some point, the cost of any tool, regardless of type, may become too expensive for an employee to purchase and/or maintain and may be purchased by the company.

Who buys tools? Specialized tools that are used daily by technicians are typically purchased by technicians and become part of their personal tools. Specialized tools that are utilized occasionally by technicians are typically purchased by the company and loaned to technicians when the need arises.

Who is responsible for tools? Employee-owned tools are the responsibility of the employee, period. If a tool is lost, stolen, or damaged, the employee is responsible to replace the tool.

If the tool is owned by the company, the person who borrows the tool carries full responsibility for that tool until it is returned to the tool crib in good shape. The employee receiving the tool from the user should inspect it for damage when it is returned to the tool crib. The employee signing out a tool should inspect the tool before agreeing to use it.

How do I track company-owned tools? All company-owned tools should be locked in a secure tool crib or closet. Limit access to everyone but the employee who is responsible for all company tools.

The most popular method for tracking tools is a peg board system with a place for every tool. Every space is marked with a picture, silhouette, or description of the tool. When a tool is borrowed by an employee, he signs a receipt. A copy is given to the employee and the original is hung on the board in place of the borrowed tool. The price of the tool is included on the receipt.

If you have a barcode system, put a barcode on every company-owned tool and a matching barcode on the tool peg board. Follow the same rules for checking tools in and out.

Note: A number of companies, including DIY, Durham Manufacturing, Home Depot, Lowes, and Grainger Industrial Supply, sell custom pegboard tool hangers.

What if a tool is lost, damaged, or stolen? If a tool is lost, damaged, or stolen, as a result of negligence, the cost of refurbishing or replacing the tool becomes the responsibility of the user. Value should be equal to the value of the tool at the time of the event. If a tool is lost, damaged, or stolen as a result of something other than negligence, the company's insurance should replace the tool. If someone breaks into your place of business and steals employee property, include those items on your insurance claim. They may be covered.

What tools should I purchase? Companies normally purchase all specialized tools. They also purchase non-specialized tools that are considered to be too expensive for an employee to own.

How much should I pay for tools? Purchase tools that will do the job and hold up to rugged daily use. Employees are not always careful with their own tools. They are usually less careful with company-owned tools. Tools are expensive. They become even more expensive when you lose man hours due to lost, broken, or faulty tools. Purchase quality. Most good tools have a lifetime replacement policy. Shop for price. Look for used tools. Buy only what you need. Stay within your budget.

Is the cost of lifetime replacement really necessary? Many quality tools have lifetime replacement guarantees. Buy what you need. Nothing more.

Will the manufacturer warranty the tool if it is misused? Tool warranties are similar to most other warranties. Use a screwdriver as a crowbar at your own risk.

WHAT SHOULD I DO? In a perfect world, you would purchase a tool once and replace it only if it breaks or is damaged. In the real world, most tools are lost or stolen because management gets careless, lacks organization and allows tools to be taken or lost, whether purposely or as an afterthought. Tools are usually very expensive and deserve your attention. Organize your tools and treat them as you would treat your inventory. Most businesses do a poor job of protecting their tools. Do your best to avoid loss.

Additional Resources: Internet, Yellow pages, business friends; there is a huge assortment of new and used tools in the market place.

TRAINING

Training is always necessary to some degree, if only to revisit the basics of a particular methodology and the reason for performing a task in a specific manner. Something as routine as answering the company phone requires training – and retraining. Employees deserve the best training you can afford. Training also tells your employees that you care enough about them to help them to advance their careers toward that next higher position or next higher pay grade. Proper training keeps employees safer, happier, more capable of advancing their careers, and more likely to maximize your company profit.

Types of training. Training falls into one of two categories: Formal Training and On the Job Training (OJT). Formal training may involve an individual or a group. A time, place, trainer, agenda, and curriculum are predetermined.

OJT may take place anytime or anywhere without notice, schedule, or any particular venue. OJT will involve actual tools, at a customer location, in a live situation. OJT is often more effective because the situation is live.

How much training should I provide? Training should be approached like any other expense. If training converts to profit for your company, it is good. If it does not, it is not. Here is the caveat. If a supplier requires you to comply with a training schedule in order to sell or service a particular product, you may not have any choice but to conform with that supplier's training requirements.

Training may be mandated by law, such as safety or hazmat training. Training may be necessary to ensure that employees are capable of operating machinery safely and properly. If training is mandated, bite the bullet and provide the training as specified. The company you save may be your own.

Training for whom? Newcomers should go through orientation. Orientation may involve several days, or just a cup of coffee and an understanding between a supervisor and a new employee. Training is constant. It is often planned for an individual or a group. It is sometimes spur of the moment. Training is necessary for everyone in your company.

What courses should I offer? This varies from business to business. You should assemble a training manual. Create a section for each group of employees, such as installers, technicians, sales, collections, clerks, bookkeepers, administration, and so on. Assembly will vary, depending on your business type. Subdivide each section into the types of training needed. For instance, Accounts Receivable Collections may be subdivided into tips for calling past due accounts, researching accounts, invoicing, approaching the customer, fielding objections, payment plans, and disarming hostile customers. Each section should include all information regarding appropriate training for that particular subject. Sections should be updated as needed.

Who should train my employees? Trainers may be internal or external. Internal trainers are employees whom you have chosen to train other employees. Trainers should be chosen carefully. They should be knowledgeable, entertaining, believable, and generally accepted by their audience. Many vendors and manufacturers offer *Train the Trainer* courses for their customers. You choose a trainer who is reasonably knowledgeable about a particular subject and send him to be trained as a trainer.

External trainers may present vendor products and services, certification courses, general interest seminars, or mandated training courses. Training may be held at your business, in your community, or at the office of the manufacturer or vendor that offers a particular course or certification.

When is the best time to train? Unfortunately, there is no best time to train. Example: You add a new product or service to your offerings and you are notified that training is required for three of your key people within 90 days of receipt of your first order. The timing is awful. You are forced to remove three of your best people from the work force for a week (three days of training and two days of travel) or 120 lost production hours.

If possible, try to take on new products and services during the off-season or slow months. Try to convince vendors to hold training at your site. This keeps your key people in the vicinity in the event of an emergency.

Right now you may be thinking that you cannot afford to allow anyone to take time for training. You may believe that veryone will take a few hours and acclimate to your new product and everything will go fine at that new customer's installation. Do not jeopardize your company or your product sources. If training is necessary, provide it as soon as practical.

Can I require training? You can and should require training on a number of fronts. Untrained or poorly trained employees put a drag on your operation and your profits.

Who should pay for training? Any required training is paid by your company. You are responsible for paying the employee the regular wage – straight time or overtime - for hours spent training and traveling. Put a maximum on travel time. If you feel uneasy about the mileage turned in by an attendee, utilize www.mapquest.com. Mileage should be paid only if the event is held somewhere other than your company, and the mileage for an attendee exceeds the distance normally driven from home to office.

Check out the current government mileage rate at www.gsa.com to get a benchmark rate. This would be the maximum you would pay. There is no law that governs the amount you pay for mileage. Most companies pay something less than the government rate. Employees will ask for the government rate because it is the highest rate available.

You will occasionally receive requests for employees to attend seminars and classes that are interesting to them. If you consider the training to be relevant and profitable to your business, allow the expense. If you consider the event valuable enough to allow the employee to attend on company time, pay accordingly. Otherwise, you may want to pay for the event only if it is available during non-working hours.

Overtime for training. If overtime pay for training is absolutely necessary, budget accordingly. Sometimes there is just no other way, due to time constraints or collective bargaining requirements.

What is the real cost of training? The real cost of training involves payroll for the employee attending the event and the overtime or straight time wages to replace the time lost. Mileage, event cost, and production cost round out your expenses. Opportunity cost is the loss of a sale or expertise that cannot be recovered from the loss of a day's work. Even more importantly, the cost of *not* training may exceed the cost of training.

Follow up to training? Training is valuable if two things happen. First, the employee takes valuable information from the training event. Second, the employee uses that information in a positive manner that improves your bottom line. You can never recover the time lost to training, but trained employees should be better equipped to handle every work day after the training event. Query your employees about the perceived value of their training, or about additional training they feel they need. If you find that training does not yield a profit, alter the training or the employee, or both.

Seminars for employees. One-day seminars are typically ineffective in changing behavior in the long term. However, you may want to send selected employees to a seminar to gauge individual interest in a particular subject. If interest is keen enough, you may want to further investigate the involvement of an employee(s) in an ongoing learning experience to hone skills in a particular area.

Training for me – the owner. At a minimum, you should gain a working knowledge of the products and services offered by your company. *Working knowledge* means that you can comfortably discuss your offerings with your employees, customers, and vendors at a level that allows you to guide your company through day-to-day business activities.

This does not mean that you must play engineer, accountant, and sales professional. No one can be an expert in all facets of any business concern. You should know where to find the answers to the questions and problems that you cannot comfortably address. Of course, if you are the only employee, you may need *working knowledge* in a number of areas.

You owe yourself an education. If you are going to manage a business, you should understand Income Statements, Balance Sheets, Cash Flow Statements, Accounts Receivable, Accounts Payable, and the laws and statutes that govern your particular business. Numerous business owners work all day, every day, while engaged in studies for a college degree. Not everyone is cut out for a college education, but everyone who owns or manages a business should be able to understand and dissect the above-mentioned financial spreadsheets and reports. You also must know how to convert those spreadsheets and reports to positive action that will enhance your company's profitability.

Recognition for those who train? The first recognition is a certificate that says the employee attended the training. Always frame a certificate so it gets hung on the wall. Present training certificates in a public meeting. Attendance is mandatory. Involve department supervisors in the presentation. You may want to sweeten the pot with a check, gift, or pay increase if the training is special enough to warrant such action. Checks are presented at the public meeting. Pay increases are awarded privately.

Require feedback from trainees. Whether training is performed by your staff or an outside provider, require that your employees complete feedback questionnaires with information pertinent to the quality of the training provided. The following is a sample Workshop Evaluation sheet (Figure T-1).

ABC COMPANY WORKSHOP EVALUATION

Workshop Name_____Location _____ Date _____

Your feedback is necessary to help us improve your experience.

Please rate this workshop (X): Excellent __   Very Good __   Good __   Fair __   Poor __

Please rate the speakers:

Subject Knowledge (X): Excellent __   Very Good __   Good __   Fair __   Poor __

Presentation: Excellent __   Very Good __   Good __   Fair __   Poor __

What did you like best about the workshop?

_____
_____
_____

What did you like least about the workshop?

_____
_____
_____

What's the best idea(s) you are taking away from the workshop?

_____
_____
_____

What part of the workshop had the least benefit for you?

_____
_____
_____

Would you recommend this workshop to others (X)? Yes __   No __

Why? Why not?

_____
_____
_____
_____

Thank you for your valuable input. Your comments will be taken into consideration.

WHAT SHOULD I DO? Include Training in your budget from your first day in business. Never stop training. This includes you.

TRIBAL ACCOUNTS / RESERVATION BUSINESS

If you plan to do business with Native American tribes or on Native American soil, employ an attorney to formulate the proper contracts and language to guarantee payment. Tribal business can be tricky and will require your attorney's help the first time you are involved. Tribes are sovereign entities and occasionally follow a different set of rules than nontribal businesses. You must know and respect those rules if you expect to do tribal business.

WHAT SHOULD I DO? Conducting business on Native American lands is a lot like doing business with a foreign country. Tribal lands are sovereign nations and are not always subject to the laws of the state in which they are located. If you do business on tribal land, be sure to have an agreement endorsed that states that all business between the tribal enterprise and your company is subject to the laws of the American state in which the transaction takes place. If the parties to the contract will not endorse the agreement, do not do business with them.

Additional Resources: Attorney, www.native-american-bus.org.

TURNKEY PRICE

A turnkey price is a price that is all inclusive, based on the written contract between you and the company or person providing the work. Example: The provider, such as an independent contractor, agrees to install a furnace in Building A by June 1, and provide all labor, materials, permits, inspections, green tag, warranty, etc. You walk in the building on June 2 and the building has heat throughout, at the agreed price and specifications.

The other alternative is time and materials. You pay by the hour or day and materials are at the discretion of the company installing the furnace. You do not know the price until the job is completed.

WHAT SHOULD I DO? If possible, always contract on a turnkey basis. You know the price beforehand and you are not responsible if the contractor runs into unknown or unspecified difficulties. Never agree to an open price contract under any circumstances.

Chapter U

UNIFORMS

There are advantages and disadvantages to uniforms. The disadvantage is cost. An advantage is company identification. Every uniformed employee is a walking billboard. You can demand clean, pressed clothes if you are supplying employees' uniforms. Some employees just do not have desirable clothes to wear to work. Also, employees are more apt to maintain good personal behavior at a customers' businesses if they are easily identified. Always put the employee's first name on the uniform.

Buy or rent. Consider the cost of buying uniforms. Factor in cleaning, repairs, lost, or stolen uniforms, worn-out uniforms, name changes, and logo upkeep. For example, if you have a small number of people in a clean environment, and employees are willing to wash and wear, and they need three sets of clothes each, it may cost less to buy. If the environment is less than clean, it may be less expensive to rent uniforms. When you rent uniforms, the uniform truck shows up every week with clean, pressed clothes. If your employees are supplying and cleaning their own uniforms, they should be required to be neat at all times. There is no excuse for your employees to look shoddy at work.

Should employees share the cost of uniforms? Employees have costs involved if uniforms are not provided. They must wash and press their own work clothing. Require each uniformed employee to pay half of the uniform cost, as a condition of employment. This is fair and equitable and gives the employee an opportunity to be neat, clean and presentable to your customers.

What uniform service should I utilize? Larger providers have a tendency to charge more, simply because they have a larger share of the market and can afford to choose the companies with which they care to do business. There can be huge disparities in providers' prices for producing and providing logos, name patches, and even the uniforms themselves. This is not to say that larger uniform companies will not meet the prices of smaller, regional uniform providers. Contact the three or four firms that typically service your area and secure the best price and service. If you are renting uniforms for less than 10 employees, you may have to contract with a smaller company to find an affordable price. The larger companies may not want your business.

Written agreement with employees covering loss, ruin, or failure to return uniforms. This will come into play when an employee quits or is terminated and refuses to return company property. The agreement says that failure to return uniforms in good repair will result in a deduction from the employee's final paycheck. If a severed employee pays for their uniforms, they can keep the clothing.

UNIONS

Unions are said to have been created by poor managers and substandard business practices. Unions have their good and bad points. The differences often depend on the audience. Many of the indiscretions that made unions necessary are no longer essential because of organizations and laws such as the Family and Medical Leave Act (FMLA), Occupational Safety and Health Administration (OSHA), Federal Labor Standards Act (FLSA), Americans with Disabilities Act (ADA), and Environmental Protection Agency (EPA). Certainly, we all have had discussions in support of both points of view. It is not a matter of bad or good. It is a matter of making it work. If you have a union shop, get used to the idea. Most managers find numerous faults with unions. Most union members find numerous faults with management.

The best companies have a cooperative atmosphere between management and unions. They do not always agree with each other. But they strive for a cooperative atmosphere. You can spend a lot of time and a lot of money fighting unions. In the long term, it is not productive for either side.

WHAT SHOULD I DO? If you do not have a union shop and find that there is talk of unionization in your organization, follow the rules to the nth degree and do what is best for your company in the long term.

Chapter V

VEHICLES

Most entrepreneurs drive a company car, financed by the company. Some companies provide automobiles as perks for specific employees. Make decisions concerning vehicles from a profit and loss perspective. Weigh the pros and cons and add to your fleet only when necessary and at a price you can afford.

Insurance for vehicles. There are two types of automobile insurance companies. Standard, or primary insurers include Allstate, State Farm and Nationwide, to name a few. Secondary, or nonstandard carriers, are Progressive, Geico and a number of others. In our state (Ohio) about half the automobile insurers fall into each category. Primary carriers serve companies with good credit and good driving records. Secondary carriers serve the balance. If you are insured by a secondary company and want to switch to a primary company, expect to pay higher than normal rates for two accident-free years.

Commercial automobile policies, the kind you will purchase for your business, follow more stringent guidelines than personal policies. They will be geared specifically to your industry. Generally speaking, commercial policies are driven by the number of past violations, whereas personal policies are driven more by credit worthiness.

Insurance policies are pretty dull reading. Sit down with your agent and gain a good understanding of your obligations as a policy holder. There is a policy and a type of coverage for every situation. Some coverages are standard and some are extra. Talk it through with your agent and, as always, make your decisions based on what is best and most profitable for your company.

Should I buy or lease vehicles? There really is no right answer to this question. You can buy or lease a new or used vehicle. There are advantages and disadvantages to both methods. Here are a few:

Buying your vehicles?

Advantages:

> **Company-owned** vehicles may be utilized as collateral.

> **Total cost** of the vehicle over its life is usually less expensive than leasing.

Insurance is typically less expensive than for leased vehicles.

There is no pressure to turn the vehicle in while it still has a useful life.

Payments go away once the vehicle is paid off.

If you can afford to pay cash for vehicles, your overall cost may be less than financing or leasing, depending on current interest rates.

You may be able to finance a vehicle for a time, and then pay it off if you are flush with cash.

There is no significant mileage penalty beyond the normal loss in vehicle value.

Today's vehicles are built for high mileage. As long as the vehicle is mechanically sound and attractive, there is no need to constantly reinvest in a new vehicle every two or three years because a lease has expired.

Disadvantages:

You are not forced to repair dented and marred vehicles. This can work against your company image if not addressed.

Purchase payments are usually more than lease payments, on par.

Sales tax is paid up front on the total price of the vehicle.

You never really know the trade-in or sale value of your vehicle until you attempt to sell it.

Leasing your vehicles?

Advantages:

If you contract for two or three years, you and your employees are always driving vehicles that reflect a positive company image.

Lease payments are typically a little less than purchase payments.

Leasing may afford special tax breaks.

If you dislike a vehicle, you are only obligated for the term of the lease, usually two or three years.

In most states, you pay sales tax on monthly payments only for the duration of the lease.

You always know the value of the vehicle. Buyout figures are included on your monthly lease statements.

Disadvantages:

Upfront costs can be sizeable, often thousands of dollars.

Excess mileage penalties can be significant.

A lease disposition fee of several hundred dollars may be applicable when you return the vehicle.

Insurance on a lease vehicle is spelled out contractually and is typically more than you would pay for a purchased vehicle. Lease companies will require that your insurance policy has an endorsement naming the lease company as a beneficiary.

Early termination of a vehicle lease carries heavy penalties.

Leases often require a higher credit score than an automobile loan.

You always have a lease payment, even if your business fails.

Today's vehicles are built for high mileage. Leases usually expire long before the usefulness of the vehicle.

Should I have new or used vehicles? If a used vehicle meets your specifications and forecasted costs for maintenance and upkeep, consider your overall budget, and make a decision. The vehicle should be attractive and reflect a positive company image over the long term.

How long should I keep a vehicle? If a vehicle portrays a good customer image, meets your daily demands and is cost effective, why replace it?

What is the real cost of a vehicle? In addition to the cost of the base vehicle, consider additions after purchase, such as shelving, a towing package, racking, special tires and wheels, special paint and logos, an advertising wrap, interior lighting, fuel, insurance, licensing, permits, depreciation, maintenance, and repairs.

Who should drive company vehicles? Company vehicles are not to be used by you, your family, or your employees for anything other than company business. Drivers must have a valid license with any special designations required by your business. They must also be insurable and insured. Drivers should be checked annually for loss of license, DUIs, accidents, and tickets. There is no law that says that you must allow an employee to drive a company vehicle. Drivers should endorse an agreement that requires them to notify your company if they are sited for any vehicle violation.

What about employee-owned vehicles? You have a right to require that employees who drive their vehicles on your time are properly licensed and insured and follow all the same rules and regulations that are imposed on those who drive company vehicles. Do not allow an employee to drive her vehicle for company purposes until her policy names you as an insured party and you have written proof of business vehicle coverage. You should be named as an insured party on her policy so that you will be notified if the employee cancels or loses her automobile insurance.

Maintenance on company vehicles. Everyone driving a company vehicle should be instructed to complete a daily mileage sheet that includes an area for any problems experienced with the vehicle. Problems must be reported at the end of each shift unless a particular malfunction necessitates immediate shutdown or repair. Regular maintenance should be done on time at a pre-designated maintenance facility. Failure to report a vehicle malfunction or maintain a vehicle properly should be dealt with on an individual basis.

Should non-employee family members drive company vehicles? No. If you have a weak moment and consider loaning a pickup truck to a family member to move furniture over the weekend, envision an insurance investigator sitting on your shoulder. Then say "No, my insurance does not permit it." The same goes for an employee who requests permission to perform a non-business function with a company vehicle. You should follow the same rules. If you need a moving van, rent one.

Non-smoking policy for company vehicles. Do not allow smoking in your company vehicles. Once a vehicle is exposed to smoke, it is no longer comfortable for non-smoking drivers or passengers. Smoking also reduces the vehicle's resale value. Regardless of what your automobile detailer tells you, it is nearly impossible to clean smoke residue from the interior and vent systems of an automobile. You really have no recourse with an employee who elects to smoke in a privately owned vehicle on company time.

***"How is my driving?"* sign on vehicle.** This is a great idea. Just be ready to handle the calls from those folks who are having a bad day. If your telephone number saves one accident during the life cycle of the vehicle, it is worth the trouble. Also paint a three-digit number on each vehicle. If someone has a legitimate complaint, it is much easier to remember a three-digit number than a license plate number.

Headlights on at all times. Some vehicles have running lights. Some do not. Once again, if lights save one accident in the life cycle of the vehicle, it is worth the cost to replace an occasional bulb.

Advertising on side, front, back, roof of company vehicle(s). Why not? My brother has a window tinting business. He claims that most of his business comes from calls from people who noticed the advertising on his van. His next best source is referrals.

Gas cards vs. check, cash, or service station account? First, take checks and cash out of the equation. That leaves you with credit cards or credit accounts. You may prefer gas credit cards that are accepted at stations of a particular brand, say Shell, BP, Sunoco, Mobile, or whatever suits you. You also may utilize gas credit cards that work at a number of different brand-name stations. A card and pin number are assigned to each eligible vehicle. Before pumping fuel, the employee must enter the pin number and vehicle mileage into the pin pad on the pump. Credit card bills provide vehicle number, date, time, gallons dispensed, price per gallon and sale amount. Granted, anyone with a company credit card can dispense gas into any vehicle, anywhere. But, the information provided on the bill offers enough tools that illegal purchases are going to become obvious at some point.

No system is foolproof, but with reasonable diligence you can cut your losses to a minimum. My experience says that company vehicles get the same gas mileage all the time, with minor adjustments for seasonality. Keep a running total of vehicle mileage vs. gasoline purchases by the gallon. If mileage starts creeping downward on a particular vehicle, inspect the situation. You may have a phantom vehicle that is being fueled at your expense. Or, you may have a vehicle that needs repaired or replaced.

Number of vehicles in my business. How many do you really need? How do they fit into your budget? Make the calculations and be honest with yourself. Get what you need, not what you want. Do not carry extra vehicles for down time. Your dealer may provide a free loaner when one of yours goes in for service. However, this will not help you when a specialized vehicle is out of commission.

Should I bend the rules to keep an employee with a poor driving record? Never! It may cost you your business or send your insurance rates through the roof. Most poor drivers continue to be poor drivers. Why take a chance?

Should I make a clean driving record a condition of employment? Yes, if the employee will be driving a company vehicle or a private vehicle for your business. Put it on the job application.

Should I report all accidents to my insurance company? Your insurance company does not care about fender benders that you are willing to pay to repair unless a violation is involved. All other accidents should be reported. If there is a violation, your insurance company may know before you have a chance to tell them.

Should I make my insurance company aware of an employee with traffic violations? Yes. Let your insurer knows if a violation has occurred, whether in your vehicle or in the employee's personal vehicle. A violation may affect your insurance rating, whether it happened while the employee was on or off the job. Your insurer is going to find out about the violation in good time, but your agent does not like to be blindsided. Call when a violation occurs. If you are questioning the viability of hiring a driver with violations, talk to your insurance agent before making a decision.

Additional Resources: Insurance agent, insurance carrier.

VENDORS

Some companies prefer to split vendors and suppliers into different categories. A vendor is any company or person who supplies your company with an item or service.

How should I pick my vendors? You should choose your vendors based on their ability to provide on-time delivery of a suitable product or service, at a price you want to pay, in that order. Price is the last consideration because you cannot afford to buy from a vendor who provides late or poor service, or a poor choice of products or services. Interview vendors, first at your place of business, then at the vendor's place of business.

Get three to five references and check them out. Ask about the three things they like least and the three things they like most about the prospective vendor. Keep score. Visit the references to make sure they are legitimate businesses. Do not make your choice until you have queried *all* references.

Who limits my choice of vendors? Your choice may be limited by your competition. A vendor may not want to do business with you because he is afraid of losing a competitor's business. Otherwise, vendor choice is limited by your selection criteria and the willingness of the vendor to provide reasonable products, services, on-time-delivery and payment terms that are attractive to your business.

How many vendors per inventory item? Secure three vendors per item, if possible. Give your core business to the best of the three. Alter your choice if it makes long-term sense. Play them against each other, but always remain friendly with all. Many business owners wait until a source goes away before investigating other sources. By then it may be too late. Be proactive.

Why should I have backup vendors? There is nothing quite as embarrassing as losing business to a competitor because you are unable to get materials and products for in-house orders. Always maintain friendly relationships with backup vendors for emergency orders or for products that are scarce.

Backup vendors will also keep your full-time vendors on their toes. It is a good idea to occasionally, subtly remind your full-time vendor that a backup vendor has a particular item at a lower price, or that they have quantity pricing that is not available through the full-time vendor. Do not become price or quality complacent with any of your vendors – full-time or backup.

Freight *(See also FREIGHT / SHIPPING).*

Terms with vendors. Always get the best possible payment terms from your vendors. Money is a commodity and has a cost. Always pay your vendors on time, never before. Keeping that in mind, stretch terms to vendors as much and as often as possible. The longer you keep your money, the less you need and the less it costs. Never intentionally harm your vendors. Do intentionally secure the best terms possible without creating hard feelings.

How should I handle finance charges and past-due penalties with vendors? If you are paying finance charges and penalties, you should have a long talk with your accounts payable department. Finance charges and penalties are routinely added to past-due invoices and statements. If your accounts payable department is on top of your vendor accounts, you should never have a reason to pay a finance charge or penalty.

Always try to get the next higher price break from a vendor. Always ask about the next highest quantity discount or freight-free discount when purchasing anything. If you do not train your employees to ask, they will never know if another discount is available. If you do a lot of business with a vendor, try to get the next highest discount, even though you are buying at a lower level. Always try for freight-free delivery. You will be surprised at how much you will save if you just ask.

WHAT SHOULD I DO if I order the wrong merchandise from a vendor? Suck it up. You are in error. It is not the fault of your vendor. If you are sure that you will utilize the material or product in a reasonable amount of time, ask the vendor for an extra discount. It never hurts to ask. If not, request a return shipping tag and ask the vendor to remove the restocking charge. The freight is on you. If you do not make a habit of ordering incorrectly, the vendor will likely restock without a fee. If the vendor delivers with his own vehicles, send the merchandise back on the return trip when your next load arrives.

There is one other possibility. Occasionally, your vendor rep can find a home for the errant order. You may want to call your rep before you do anything else. And, make sure it never happens again.

Warranty. Vendors have a number of methods for adopting the date of warranty origination. Here are a few examples:

Warranty may begin when the product hits your door. You can expect some perishable goods to fall under this category.

Warranty may begin the day the product is sold to the end user. This is the best case scenario, and easy for you to track.

Warranty may begin when the end user receives delivery or installation of the product. There is usually a warranty drop dead date, based on the date of purchase.

Some warranties are based on a shelf date. Warranty begins the day the product hits your warehouse shelf. If the product is not sold by a specific date, the warranty expires and you are stuck with a product that must be sold without a warranty, probably at a discount. This can happen with electronics, since some products can quickly reach obsolescence. Know the warranty limitations of your products. Check your shelves regularly.

WHAT SHOULD I DO? First, take that "No Solicitors" sign off your door. New vendors may be turned away and current vendors will get the impression that they are there for the duration because their competition is not welcome in your place of business. Most businesses work within a microcosm that is unique to their industry. In other words, everybody knows everybody. Stay close to your vendors and prospective vendors. They usually know everyone in your business. They also talk to everyone in your business – and – occasionally will tell you about everyone in your business, including competitors and other vendors. This does not mean that you should buy from every vendor, but you should take time to remember names and faces, and the products and services they offer. It never hurts to be two or three deep in vendors for a particular product or service.

Additional Resources: CPA, key vendors.

VENTURE CAPITALISTS

A venture capitalist is a professional investment fund manager. Most business people refer to venture capitalists as VCs. VCs are usually looking for a higher rate of return than other lenders. They are looking for three to five times their investment in five to seven years. VCs historically are not interested in an investment of less than $250,000. They invest somewhere between $1,500,000 and $2,000,000, on average. Much larger amounts are commonplace, depending on the VC and the industry in question.

The investment terms of VCs vary widely and dramatically. VCs will require one of their people on your board and, in some cases, as an employee of your company. It is not uncommon for a VC to pick your Controller or Chief Financial Officer (CFO). The VC wants someone in your business to protect his interests and alert him to anything that is unusual.

The VC will want stock in your company that includes preferential treatment over other shareholders, maybe even a controlling interest to get involved. He will also want preemptive rights to maintain his percentage ownership in your company by participating in future stock issues. If you get involved with a VC, you may be directed to sign away a number of controls that you, as the majority owner, may not be willing to grant to an investor. Don't forget: Once you own less than 51 percent of your company, you no longer independently call the shots. In fact, you can be fired. The VC can put you out to pasture and take over.

You may be asked to accept benchmarks for earnings over given periods of time in exchange for greater VC ownership if the benchmarks are not met. It works like this. The VC invests in your business with your agreement that you must increase profits at a specific rate each quarter for a specific period of time. If you meet the benchmarks, everything is copacetic. Each time you miss a benchmark, the VC gains a greater percentage of ownership in your business.

These are just the facts. Interpret them as you please. VCs have their place in the investment world, just like anyone else. They are generally smart, get involved in specific genres, and only look at 10 percent of the proposals that cross their desks. If a Venture Capitalist can help you grow your business, have a look at the program. There are a lot of successful companies out there that would not be where they are without the help of Venture Capitalists.

WHAT SHOULD I DO? The VC should be your last resort after exhausting all other sources. They want control, hockey-stick projections, huge returns, and possibly, eventual majority ownership of your business. VCs will demand that your company is a C Corporation before finalizing a funding agreement. Frankly, many entrepreneurs just cannot secure the funding necessary to grow their businesses without help from a venture capitalist. Like any other business investment, know where you want to go before you start looking. Do your homework and get involved if the venture matches your plans and aspirations.

Chapter W

WEBSITE *(See also INTERNET)*

Today it is hard to find a thriving business that is not represented by a website. Some business websites provide most, or all of their company's revenues. Some provide information only. Some are in multiple languages. Some allow customers to shop online. Others do not. All websites have one thing in common— they all provide a presence that can instantly reach millions of potential customers, worldwide, if presented properly.

Does a website guarantee sales? Websites do not guarantee sales. A website is just another method of contacting potential or current customers. A website is like any other business location. If you fail to attract customers, you go out of business.

You will hear a lot of talk about Search Engine Optimization (SEO). Loosely defined, SEO is a term that describes the ability to direct Internet inquiries to a specific site. SEO does not typically guaranty that anyone will come to your site. SEO can be very costly and is probably a poor investment for a new or early stage business. Attract visitors to your site via the same methods that you would normally utilize to advertise your business. Once your site becomes known and is meeting your expectations for volume and profit, you may want to investigate the advantages and disadvantages of SEO *(See also ADVERTISING).*

What is a domain name? A domain name is an Internet location. Hence, www.microsoft.com is Microsoft's Internet location. The end of the domain name may be .com, .net, .edu, .org, etc. The domain name defines the organization. In the case of Microsoft, the ending is .com, which stands for commercial. As of April 2, 2013, WHOIS Source[1] reported that among the six most popular Top Level Domains (TLDs) there are were 144,776,023 active domain names worldwide.[2] Active means that someone actually utilized the domain name to activate a website.

Do I own my domain name? No. A domain registrar maintains domain names and charges a fee that allows you to utilize a particular domain name. You contact the registrar of your choice (i.e., Godaddy.com, Register.com, NetworkSolutions.com) and pay an annual fee for the privilege of using a particular domain name. You may use that domain name as long as you pay the fee to do so. Your domain registrar will remind you that your domain will expire on a particular date.

What is .com vs. .org, .edu, etc.? These are the various Internet address endings that identify the types of businesses or institutions. Com is short for commercial and identifies a commercial business. Org is short for organizations and usually identifies not-for-profit organizations or associations. Edu is short for education and is utilized by educational institutions. These are the most common Internet address endings. There are others.

If you are a commercial business, you will probably be offered other endings, such as .net, if .com is not available in the form you request. If that is the case, you can offer to purchase the .com ending of your choice from the current owner. If .com remains unavailable, alter your name slightly until you locate an available .com.

How much does a domain name cost? Domain names start at around a dollar and may be as much as $35. Register for multiple years and get a discount. Some registrars charge a fee to transfer a domain name in or out. Some registrars offer free hosting if you register your domain name with them. Compare pricing and services before buying.

How much does a Website cost to build? Depending on your needs, websites may cost a few hundred dollars to tens of thousands of dollars to build, and just as much to maintain. It depends on the complexity of the site. Prices are truly all over the board.

How much does it cost to maintain a website? This depends on the size of your site and the economics in your area, but generally runs anywhere from $20 a month to thousands a month.

How often should I refresh my website? Constantly refresh your website. You may have noticed that the automobile dealers in your city constantly move the cars around in their showrooms. Your website is your showroom. Keep it fresh and exciting.

How will anyone find my website? How do people find your business location? Utilize business cards, e-mails, telemarketing, direct mail, Yellow Pages, newspaper advertising, word of mouth, cold calling, and anything else that comes to mind. Your website is just another business location. If you do not drive traffic to your website, your site will not make money for your company because no one will know it exists.

WHAT SHOULD I DO? It seems that everyone knows someone who builds and maintains websites. Most of them build on a part-time basis. They want to be paid in advance and deliver sporadically, if at all.

If you decide to invest in a website, get a number of references from your prospective provider, call each reference, have a look at their sites and ask the hard questions. Are you currently in business? How much did the provider charge for the website? Did she constantly try to sell add-ons? Was she receptive to change while she was building the site? Was she accurate? Did she deliver on time? Did she deliver according to contract? Does the site operate as advertised? Did she ask for more money after she began building the site?

Opt for a local supplier. Websites need constant attention and refreshment. Any time you elect to deal with an out-of-town supplier, problems multiply dynamically. You cannot afford to have your website down for a lengthy period of time. If your prospective provider is not willing to put it in writing and provide a satisfaction guarantee, find another provider.

Many website builders are computer wizards who are looking for a side job. They have little ability in site design beyond the templates they utilize. Stick with a company that builds sites for a living. You will pay more, but the product will be much better, and ongoing support will be more readily available.

Additional Resources: Internet, the company that sold you your computer(s), business friends with websites.

WOMEN OWNED SMALL BUSINESS PROGRAM (WOSB)

The Women-Owned Small Business Program was finally kicked off on February 1, 2011. According to the Small Business Administration (SBA), the program was created to allow qualifying women-owned businesses to "help agencies meet the five percent women's contracting goal and ensure a level playing field on which women-owned small businesses can compete for federal contacting opportunities."

The program "authorizes contracting officers to **set aside certain federal contracts** for eligible . . .

Women-owned small businesses (WOSBs) or

Economically disadvantaged women-owned small businesses (EDWOSBs)" [3]

The business must be controlled by one or more women who have a combined minimum ownership of at least 51 percent of the company. The owner(s) must be US citizens and must be the primary manager(s) of the business.

Furthermore, the SBA says that, "The firm must be 'small' in its primary industry in accordance with SBA's size standards for that industry. In order for a WOSB to be deemed 'economically disadvantaged,' its owners must demonstrate economic disadvantage in accordance with the requirements set forth in the final rule." [4]

Qualifications for the program. Women-owned small businesses may qualify via Self Certification or Third-Party Certification. For more on certification and eligibility requirements, *see www.sba.gov.*

This looks like a very promising program for qualified women-owned businesses. The program should open new doors to additional projects and profits. The government-wide contracting goal for WOSB has been set at five percent.

Additional Resources: Stay in touch with the SBA website at www.sba.gov. or visit the Government Contracting Classroom at (www.sba.gov/gcclassroom), or on the Women-Owned Businesses webpage at (http://www.sba.gov/content/women-owned-businesses).

WORKFORCE GUIDELINES

Number of employees. There is a simple rule in business; at least it sounds simple: Do not hire or keep anyone you don't need. Realizing the importance of this rule is the easy part. Following the rule is the hard part. The simple truth is that you may not always need everybody on your payroll. You may own a seasonal business like a lawn care company, or you may be involved in construction in an area like Alaska where outdoor operations are often at a standstill during the winter months. The question you must answer if you are doing a job in Alaska is, do you lay off your best project manager during the winter months when work is sparse, or do you continue to pay his salary? Plan for such events, in advance, long before you are forced into a corner.

Things get tough, the economy goes south and your business drops by 20 percent. Do you retain your best employee who has been with you for 20 years, even though you really cannot afford to pay her? What are your alternatives? What could you have done to avoid such a situation?

Try to keep the minimum number of employees that you require to operate efficiently and profitably. If you have a seasonal business, tell your employees the truth. If things slow down, go outside the box and try to retain your core staff. Look for alternative markets. If you sell ATV's and motorcycles in the summer, you may want to take on snowmobiles in the winter. If you sell heating and air conditioning to the residential market, you may want to break into the commercial market.

Full-time Employees. If you need and can afford full-time help, so be it. There are times when it is just not possible to afford full-time employees and you may be forced into doing a major portion of your business with part-time help. My first job out of college was management of a marine business. We were on the water in Ohio. Cold winters made us seasonal. We sold boats in the summer and snowmobiles in the winter. We repaired everything we sold. The winter revenue was just enough to keep the doors open. We rented canoes in the summer, pumped gas, repaired all types of boat motors, rigged boats, maintained rental docks, and sold anything and everything tied to the marine business.

We ran the summer business with six full-timers and six to eight part-timers, depending on the weather. We ran the winter business with three full-timers and two or three part-timers. Our part-timers were high school kids. We had a core of high school students who worked for the business all through their high school years. This made training easier when the summer season swung into full gear.

The bottom line is the bottom line. In a perfect world, you have as little labor as possible to run your business smoothly.

Part-time. UPS is heavily into the hiring of part-time people. And the company provides benefits for those part-timers as well. Part-timers can provide you with schedule flexibility and night time and weekend hours, plus save you from a host of overtime dilemmas. They will usually work for less than the full-time wage scale and typically do not expect benefits.

On the other hand, part-timers tend to be less reliable than full-time employees. They have a tendency to request schedule adjustments more often, are historically transient, are more likely to quit without notice, and seldom take the leap to full-time employment. If you have a choice, my vote still goes to full-time help.

Sources for new hires. Your best new hires will come as referrals from your best employees. No valuable employee wants to recommend a friend to you and see her fail.

Therefore, your present employee will do everything in her power to make sure the new hire, whom she recommended, becomes a valuable employee.

The second best source for new hires is the valued employee who left you on good terms. If there is no conflict of interest, a former employee can be very helpful in finding a quality new hire. The former employee will also stay in touch with your new hire. She now has a vested interest in keeping you as a friend. You may be calling her someday to invite her back to your company.

Trade associations are a great way to stay in touch with other local business people. You never know when an employee of a key competitor or vendor might approach you for a job. It is possible that a friend in the organization will tell you of an associate who is dissatisfied with her current position.

Ask your vendors about people in competitors' businesses who are dissatisfied with their jobs. You will be surprised at the names that pop up. Some may be valuable former employees who would really rather be back at their old jobs – with you. Be careful to ask about existing non-compete agreements.

Beyond these sources are search firms, newspaper ads, lead clubs, friends and customers. Most are hit and miss. Search firms are expensive, but may present more long-term, quality prospects, while saving you the expense and time to carry out your own search. Ads are poor unless they appear in a magazine, paper, or a journal that pertains specifically to your industry. Lead clubs grow stale after a few meetings. Friends, vendors, and customers occasionally come up with decent prospects.

WHAT SHOULD I DO? You may have the best customer base, plant, store, equipment, inventory, vendors and support systems available, but if you have poor employees you are doomed to have poor performance, substandard customer relations, insufficient sales and subpar profit. What is the message here? Good business is still dependent on good people to combine all parts of a business operation into a synergistic whole that functions smoothly.

Continuously check the pulse of your workforce and alter it as necessary. Most business people give attention to the workforce only when a problem occurs. Be proactive and budget the size and quality of your workforce just as you would budget sales, expenses and profits.

Additional Resources: Friends, current employees, search firms, newspaper ads, competition, state bureau of employment services, service agencies that work with the disabled community, veterans organizations. Internet. *See also* **SEARCH / STAFFING FIRMS.**

Chapter XYZ

YEAR-TO-DATE (Y-T-D)

During the course of this book, you will occasionally see the term, year-to-date. The term typically describes the period that has expired since January 1st of the current year, until the present day's date. In the event that your business year starts and ends on a date that does not coincide with a calendar year, say October 1st through September 30th, year-to-date would begin on the starting date of your business year.

ZERO-BASED BUDGETING

In the forecasting (budgeting) examples used in this book, we forecast, year-to-year, by adjusting our budgets according to the Consumer Price Index (CPI). We also suggest that each forecast expense line is revisited annually, or more often if necessary, to ensure that expenses are in line with the current economy and the financial health of your business.

In its simplest form, zero-based budgeting (forecasting) suggests that each line of expense is approached from zero rather than adding a blanket percentage to current budget figures. In a larger sense, zero-based budgeting suggests that every functional area of a business is assessed from a zero basis after every accounting period. You should utilize this approach for all your annual forecasts.

REFERENCES

Introduction

1. Noel Tichy, Noel and Charan, Ram, "Speed, simplicity, and self-confidence," Harvard Business Review. (September-October, 1989). Retrieved from http://www.blackwellpublishing.com/grant/docs/16GE.pdf

2. Franchise.about.com. (2013). Retrieved from http://franchises.about.com/od/mostpopularfranchises/a/ray-kroc-story.htm

3. Addicted2Success. 50 Famously Successful People Who Failed At First. (2013). Retrieved from http://addicted2success.com/motivation/50-famously-successful-people-who-failed-at-first/

4. Addicted2Success. 50 Famously Successful People Who Failed At First. (2013). Retrieved from http://addicted2success.com/motivation/50-famously-successful-people-who-failed-at-first/

5. Thomas Jefferson, (n.d.). Quote attributed to Mr. Jefferson, date unknown. Retrieved from http://thinkexist.com/quotation/i-m_a_great_believer_in_luck-and_i_find_the/146613.html

6. Vince Lombardi, (n.d.). Quote attributed to Mr. Lombardi, date unknown. Retrieved from http://www.changecommblog.com/2005/08/

A

1. NOLO Law for all. Cash vs. Accrual Accounting. Retrieved from http://www.nolo.com/legal-encyclopedia/cash-vs-accrual-accounting-29513.html

2. Eeoc.gov. The ADA: Your Responsibilities as an Employer. (2009). Retrieved from http://www.eeoc.gov/facts/ada17.html

3. National Conference of State Legislatures. (2013). Retrieved from http://www.ncsl.org/issues-research/labor/at-will-employment-overview.aspx

B

1. Money-Zine.com. (2007–2010). Retrieved from http://www.money zine.com/Career-Development/Finding-a-Job/Top-Employee-Benefits/

2. Board Source. How Often Should a Board Meet? (2012). Retrieved from http://www.boardsource.org/Knowledge.asp?ID=3.67

3. Stressdoc.com. The Four Stages of Burnout. (2013). Retrieved from http://www.stressdoc.com/four_stages_burnbout.htm

4. About.com. Annual Percentage Rate (APR). (2009). Retrieved from http://banking.about .com/od/loans/a/calculateapr.htm

5. Harvard Business Review, (November-December 1999). William Oncken, Jr. and Donald L. Wass. Management Time; Who's Got The Monkey?

6. New Venture Creation, Third Edition (1990) Jeffrey Timmons ISBN 0-256-07879-3.

C

1. Randal Longacher, CPA, (2011). Personal interview.

2. David Strayer, (2010, Jan 15). Dr. Strayer appeared on the Oprah Winfrey show to discuss his research on distracted driving.

3. Barron's (1987), Salary definition listed on page 508 of Barron's Business Guide, Dictionary of Business Terms.

4. Sun-tzu, (400BC). Chinese General Sun-tzu. Retrieved from http://www.quotationspage.com/quote/36994.html

5. BusinessDictionary.com: Computer Virus, (2013). Retrieved from http://www.businessdictionary.com/definition/computer-virus.html

6. CredtiorWeb.com. (n.d.) Retrieved from http://www.creditorweb.com/articles/increase-your-sales-by-accepting-credit-cards.html

E

1. U.S. Department of Labor Website, (n.d.). Retrieved from

http://www.dol.gov/dol/topic/workhours/breaks.htm

2. U.S. Department of Labor Website, (n.d.). Retrieved from

http://www.dol.gov/compliance/topics/wages-other-breaks.htm

3. U.S. Department of Labor Website, (n.d.). Retrieved from

http://www.dol.gov/dol/topic/workhours/holidays.htm

4. U.S. Department of Labor Website, (n.d.). Retrieved from

http://www.dol.gov/dol/topic/workhours/holidays.htm

5. Barron's Business Guide, Dictionary of Business Terms. (1987). page 194. Barron's Educational

Series, Inc., by Jack P. Friedman. ISBN 0-8120-3775-8

6. BusinessDictionary.com, (2013). Retrieved from

http://www.businessdictionary.com/definition/entrepreneur.html

7. Small Business Administration, Office of Advocacy. (January, 2010). Retrieved from

www.sba.gov/sites/default/files/us11_0.pdf

8. Environmental Protection Agency (EPA). (2009). Retrieved from

http://www.epa.gov/osbp/mission.htm

9. U.S. Equal Employment Opportunity Commission: The Equal Pay Act of 1963. Retrieved from

http://www.eeoc.gov/laws/statutes/epa.cfm

10. Fair Labor Standards Act (FSLA): Exempt or Nonexempt, (n.d.). Retrieved from

http://www.flsa.com/coverage.html

11. United States Department of Labor: Motor Carriers Act: Fact Sheet #19 (n.d.). Retrieved from

http://www.dol.gov/whd/regs/compliance/whdfs19.htm

12. Railway Labor Act (RLA), (1996 Edition). Retrieved from

http://www.nmb.gov/documents/rla.html

F

1. United States Department of Labor: Wage and Hour Division (WHD): Child Labor, (n.d.). Retrieved from http://www.dol.gov/whd/childlabor.htm

2. United States Department of Labor: Leave Benefits: Family & Medical Leave, (2009). Retrieved from http://www.dol.gov/dol/topic/benefits-leave/fmla.htm

3. United States Small Business Administration: Register Your Business Name: 4. What is a "Doing Business As" name? (2013). Retrieved from http://www.sba.gov/content/register-your-fictitious-or-doing-business-dba-name

5. United States Department of Labor: Work Hours: Flexible Schedules, (n.d.) retrieved from http://www.dol.gov/dol/topic/workhours/flexibleschedules.htm

6. Investopedia: Definition of 'Consumer Price Index – CPI' (n.d.). Retrieved from http://www.investopedia.com/terms/c/consumerpriceindex.asp

7. Entrepreneur.com: Franchising: Definition, (n.d.). Retrieved from http://www.entrepreneur.com/encyclopedia/franchising#

8. Access America Transport: What is LTL? (2013). Retrieved from http://www.accessamericatransport.com/ltl-shipping/

9. Small Business Administration (SBA), Facts About Government Grants, (n.d.), Retrieved from http://www.sba.gov/content/facts-about-government-grants

H

1. McClatchy Newspapers. (2013, April 3). Renee Schoof. Math is a Plus for Job Applicants. http://www.mcclatchydc.com/2013/04/03/187626/math-problems-are-a-problem-for.html

2. McClatchy Newspapers. (2013, April 3). Renee Schoof. Math is a Plus for Job Applicants. http://www.mcclatchydc.com/2013/04/03/187626/math-problems-are-a-problem-for.html

3. Harvard Business Review, (November-December 1999). William Oncken, Jr. and Donald L. Wass. Management Time; Who's Got The Monkey?

4. Run Your Business So It Doesn't Run You", by Linda Leigh Francis, ISBN 0-9657879-1-5

I

1. U.S. Citizenship and Immigration Services. Form I-9. Retrieved from http://www.uscis.gov/portal/site/uscis/menuitem.5af9bb95919f35e66f614176543f6d1a/?vgnextoid=0161831 8c9c64310VgnVCM100000082ca60aRCRD&vgnextchannel=5c1f8318c9c64310VgnVCM100000082ca60a RCRD

2. IRS.gov/. Publication 15-A. Who Are Employees? (2013). Retrieved from http://www.irs.gov/publications/p15a/ar02.html#en_US_2013_publink1000169463

3. IRS.gov/. Publication 15-A. Who Are Employees? (2013). Retrieved from http://www.irs.gov/publications/p15a/ar02.html#en_US_2013_publink1000169463

4. Jack Welch. (2005). Jack Welch former Chairman of General Electric. *Winning*. p. 63. HarperCollins Publishers, Inc., New York, NY 10022

L

1. Merriam-Webster.com. (2012). Retrieved from http://www.merriam-webster.com/dictionary/leadership

2. Jack Welch. (2005). Jack Welch former Chairman of General Electric. *Winning*. p. 359. HarperCollins Publishers, Inc., New York, NY 10022

3. The Feiner Points of Leadership. (2004). by Michael Feiner. Warner Business Books, Time Warner Book Group, New York, N.Y., U.S.A.

M

1. The Practice of Management. (1954). by Peter F. Drucker. Harper & Row, Publishers, Inc., New York, N.Y., U.S.A.

2. The Merriam-Webster Dictionary. (2014). An Encyclopaedia Britannica Company, M-W.com. Retrieved from http://www.merriam-webster.com/dictionary/manufacture

O

1. Occupational Safety and Health Administration. Small Business, Benefits and Resources, OSHA's Cooperative Programs. (n,d.). Retrieved from http://www.osha.gov/dcsp/smallbusiness/benefits.html

P

1. Small Business Administration, Office of Advocacy, Frequently Asked Questions, How many businesses open and close each year? (2011, January). Retrieved from www.sba.gov/advo

2. USA Today, Money. Bush Imposes Steel Tariffs. (2002, March 5). Retrieved from http://usatoday30.usatoday.com/money/general/2002/03/05/bush-steel.htm

R

1. Butler Consultants, Free Industry Statistics – Sorted by Highest Gross Margin. (2011, August 17) Retrieved from http://research.financial-projections.com/IndustryStats-GrossMargin

S

1. Jack Welch (2005). Jack Welch former Chairman of General Electric. *Winning*. p. 247. HarperCollins Publishers, Inc., New York, NY 10022

2. Small Business Administration (SBA) Website. Retrieved from http://www.sba.gov/content/collateral-required-these-loans

3. Chron.com. Steven Symes. Demand Media, Small Business Analysis, The Disadvantages of Using SWOT Analysis. (2013). Retrieved from http://smallbusiness.chron.com/disadvantages-using-swot-analysis-17835.html

T

1. Entrepreneur Magazine, Small Business Encyclopedia, Target Market. (2012) Retrieved from http://www.entrepreneur.com/encyclopedia/target-market#

W

1. WHOIS Source, Domain Counts and Internet Statistics. (2013 April 2). This site records daily statistics on domain names active, removed, new, expired or transferred. Retrieved from http://www.whois.sc/internet-statistics/

2. GovWin.com. (2011, March 28) Retrieved from http://www.govwin.com/knowledge/8m-and-new-womenowned-small/91266

3. SBA.com. (2010, October 7) Retrieved from http://www.sba.gov/content/contracting-opportunities-women-owned-cmall-business

4. SBA.com. (2010, October 7) Retrieved from http://www.sba.gov/content/contracting-opportunities-women-owned-cmall-business

5. SBA news release from the SBA Press Office. (2011, February 1) Retrieved from an email from James Donato of SBA.

XYZ

1. Investopedia.com. Zero-Based Budgeting (2013) Retrieved from http://www.investopedia.com/terms/z/zbb.asp

A

Absenteeism, 108
Accounting Software, 37
Accounts Payable, 30
Accounts Receivable, 28, 34
Accounts Receivable Aging Report, 35
Accrual accounting method, 17
Affairs in the office., 196
Alarm system, 127
Appraise your employees, 107

B

Balance Sheet, 26
Board Agenda, 55
Board Compensation, 55
Board meeting minutes, 55
Board Meetings, 55
Board notification, 56
Board Proxies, 56
Board quorums, 56
Bookkeeper, 102
Breach of employee contract, 163
Breaks, 116
Build to suit, 128
Business formation, 59, 66, 211
Business plan, 61, 151, 220
Business software, 102
Bylaws, 55

C

C Corporation, 60
Car Allowance, 216
Cash, 28
Cash accounting method, 17
Cash Flow, 32
Cash reserve, 68
Chargebacks on commission sales, 86
Chargebacks to credit cards, 97
Checking account fees, 74
Clean Up Time, 161
Collection agencies, 79
Collective bargaining, 104
Commission/Bonus plans, 84
Commission-only pay plan, 86
Company spokesperson, 223
Computer backup, 90
Computer repair costs, 90
Computer viruses, 89
Cost of Goods Sold, 23
Coupons, 109
Credit applications, 93
Credit card fees, 96
Credit cards for business purchases, 95
Credit Lines, 97
Credit references, 94
Credit reporting agencies, 94
Current Ratio, 29, 31, 226

D

Days Sales Outstanding (DSO), 76, 78, 226, 227
Deposits on account, 94
Disability insurance, 173
Discrimination, 41, 163
Draw, 85
Drug free workplace, 155

E

Entertainment, 124
EPA concerns, 127
Expense accounts, 216
Expense Reports, 124
Expenses, 25
External audit, 45

F

Factoring, 81
FIFO, 182
Fixtures & Equipment, 30
Flex/time, 216
Form I-9, 167
Freebies and giveaways, 109
Freight costs, 147
Freight LTL shipments, 148
Fuel surcharges, 148

G

General Partnership, 59
Grade and rank, 83
Grapevine, 160
Gross Margin, 23, 226, 227, 287
Gross Profit, 23, 134, 140, 227

H

Harassment, 164
Health club memberships, 216
Health insurance, 173
Holiday Pay, 51, 116, 117
Hourly wage, 83

I

Inbound freight charges, 148
Income Statement, 18
Independent contractors-Advantages, 171
Independent contractors-Disadvantages, 171
Infighting in the company, 195
In-House or Contract Bookkeeper, 37
Insurance, 51
Internal audit, 44
Internet Banking, 174
Internet connection, 88

Inventory, 28
Inventory – High value, 178
Inventory – No value, 178
Inventory access, 177
Inventory accountability, 178
Inventory as collateral, 182
Inventory counting, 180
Inventory distribution, 177
Inventory in company vehicles, 177
Inventory levels, 178
Inventory management, 176
Inventory management software, 181
Inventory obsolescence, 181
Inventory organization, 178
Inventory security, 176
Inventory shrinkage, 181
Inventory surveillance, 177
Inventory tracking, 179
Inventory Turnover, 179, 226

J

Joint ventures, 183

K

Key financial statements, 18
Key man insurance, 173

L

Liens, 79
Life insurance, 173
LIFO, 182
Limited Liability Company (LLC), 60
Limited Partnership, 59
Logos, 41
Long-Term Liabilities, 31
Loss leaders, 109
Lunch Hours, 116

M

Managing the day-to-day operation, 195

N

Net Profit, 25
NSF checks, 74

O

Offer letters, 155
OSHA Compliance, 205
Outbound freight charges, 149
Overdraft Protection, 75
Owner's Equity, 31
Owner's Investment, 31

P

Paid sick days, 216
Past-due accounts, 79, 80, 81, 95
Past-Due Fees, 54
Pay grades, 160
Pay raises, 84
Payment terms, 108
Payroll, 17, 45, 101, 213
Pension plans, 52
Post-dated checks, 76
Pre-Employment Testing, 157
Prepaid Expenses, 29
Production quotas, 220
Production shifts, 221
Production slowdowns, 221
Promissory Notes, 202
Proprietary software programs, 89

Q

Quick Ratio, 29, 226

R

Raw material availability, 221
Receptionist, 102
Reference checks, 156
Reimbursable expenses, 121
Retained Earnings, 31
Retaliation, 165

S

S Corporation, 60
Salary, 83
Salary range, 83
Salary-Only Pay Plan, 85
Salary-Plus-Commission pay plan, 85
Sales reversals, 87
Seed Money, 64
Seminars for employees, 263
Sexual harassment, 117, 242, 243
Sick Days/Sick Leave, 51
Signature stamp, 73
Software bootlegging, 88
Sole Proprietorship, 59
Stock options, 52
Sweetheart Rings, 67

T

Tardiness, 161
Target market, 39
Terms offered to customers, 95
Time management, 163
Time recording systems, 160
Time sheets, 161

Total Assets, 30
Total Liabilities, 31
Total Liabilities and Equity, 31
Total Owner's Equity, 31

U

Ultimatums, 195
Union pay rates, 161

V

Vacation, 50
Vehicles, 30
Voice mail, 102

W

Warranty returns, 180
Whistleblowing, 165
Working hours, 117

Y

Year-to date, 281

Z

Zero-Based budgeting, 281